THE WAR POETRY OF ANTON SCHNACK

LEGENDA

LEGENDA is the Modern Humanities Research Association's book imprint for new research in the Humanities. Founded in 1995 by Malcolm Bowie and others within the University of Oxford, Legenda has always been a collaborative publishing enterprise, directly governed by scholars. The Modern Humanities Research Association (MHRA) joined this collaboration in 1998, became half-owner in 2004, in partnership with Maney Publishing and then Routledge, and has since 2016 been sole owner. Titles range from medieval texts to contemporary cinema and form a widely comparative view of the modern humanities, including works on Arabic, Catalan, English, French, German, Greek, Italian, Portuguese, Russian, Spanish, and Yiddish literature. Editorial boards and committees of more than 60 leading academic specialists work in collaboration with bodies such as the Society for French Studies, the British Comparative Literature Association and the Association of Hispanists of Great Britain & Ireland.

The MHRA encourages and promotes advanced study and research in the field of the modern humanities, especially modern European languages and literature, including English, and also cinema. It aims to break down the barriers between scholars working in different disciplines and to maintain the unity of humanistic scholarship. The Association fulfils this purpose through the publication of journals, bibliographies, monographs, critical editions, and the MHRA Style Guide, and by making grants in support of research. Membership is open to all who work in the Humanities, whether independent or in a University post, and the participation of younger colleagues entering the field is especially welcomed.

ALSO PUBLISHED BY THE ASSOCIATION

Critical Texts
Tudor and Stuart Translations • *New Translations* • *European Translations*
MHRA Library of Medieval Welsh Literature

MHRA Bibliographies
Publications of the Modern Humanities Research Association

The Annual Bibliography of English Language & Literature
Austrian Studies
Modern Language Review
Portuguese Studies
The Slavonic and East European Review
Working Papers in the Humanities
The Yearbook of English Studies

www.mhra.org.uk
www.legendabooks.com

GERMANIC LITERATURES

Germanic Literatures includes monographs and essay collections on literature originally written not only in German, but also in Dutch and the Scandinavian languages. Within the German-speaking area, it seeks also to publish studies of other national literatures such as those of Austria and Switzerland. The chronological scope of the series extends from the early Middle Ages down to the present day.

Managing Editor
Dr Graham Nelson, 41 Wellington Square, Oxford OX1 2JF, UK
www.legendabooks.com

The War Poetry of Anton Schnack

CHRIS WALLER

LEGENDA

Germanic Literatures 35
Modern Humanities Research Association
2025

Published by Legenda
an imprint of the Modern Humanities Research Association
Salisbury House, Station Road, Cambridge CB1 2LA

ISBN 978-1-83954-316-6

First published 2025

Copy-Editor: Dr Nigel Hope

CONTENTS

FOREWORD

'The War Poetry of Anton Schnack' started life as my father's DPhil at St John's College, Oxford. This was, in fact, his second PhD: he had completed one on German Expressionist poetry at the University of London in 1977. When he died unexpectedly in January 2020, he was close to completing the edits for this book, and it has been my privilege to work with Legenda and Professor Ritchie Robertson to finish the editing process on my father's behalf.

I say my privilege because my father was a remarkable person. As well as a part-time academic, he was the consummate schoolmaster, untiring and uncompromising in his pursuit of his students' excellence — and he considered everyone to be his student — and yet empathetic and caring. From 1983 to 1990, he was Headmaster at Eltham College in Mottingham, London. However, he missed the classroom enormously and, by 1990, had gone back to school-mastering. Indeed, he was well into his seventies when he eventually retired from Clifton College in Bristol, moving to Worcester in 2017. In over fifty years of teaching, Doctor Chris Waller — 'Doc' as he was known — inspired and terrified many generations of students, helping them to develop a love of languages — he taught German and French — as well as of cricket, 1960s music and Michelle Pfeiffer. His expectations of them were always high, his academic rigour second to none, as exemplified always by the man himself.

Chris Waller was born in the small village of Wendover in Buckinghamshire in 1942. The eleven-plus took him to grammar school at RGS High Wycombe before he won an exhibition scholarship to St John's College, Cambridge to study Modern Languages. Although he went straight from there to teaching, he took time out in the early 1970s to work with Professor Peter Stern on his PhD, 'Expressionist Poetry and its Critics', first at Cambridge, then at London.[1] He also co-translated Franz Kafka's *The Trial*.[2]

My father started work on Anton Schnack's poetry in 2009. His pre-existing fascination with the First World War, especially its presentation in British war poetry, dovetailed with his knowledge of German Expressionism to make Schnack's poetry — and particularly his *Tier rang* cycle of poems — a perfect fit. Although effectively working on this part-time alongside his teaching, my father completed his DPhil in 2013. He visited Schnack's home town of Kahl am Mein twice, meeting with surviving members of the Schnack family and other acquaintances of the poet. Their memories of Anton Schnack, who died only in 1973, are woven

---

1 Christopher Waller, *Expressionist Poetry and its Critics*, Bithell Series of Dissertations, 11 (Institute of Germanic Studies: University of London, 1986).
2 Franz Kafka, *The Trial*, trans. by Douglas Scott and Christopher Waller (Picador, 1977).

into the tapestry of my father's writing on Schnack's poetry, helping the reader to understand the poet's motivations and thought processes. My father returned to Germany in 2014 to present copies of his completed DPhil to Mayor Jürgen Seitz. With the mayor, he then visited Schnack's grave at the Kahl cemetery, as well as the former garden of the Schnack family and the memorial to Schnack which had been unveiled only two years earlier; clear testament to my father's contention that there had been previous critical neglect of Schnack's poetry.

As a result, my father's work in this book represents the first full-length treatment of the poetry of Anton Schnack (1892–1973). To quote my father's own proposal for the book:

> [L]iving through two World Wars, their preludes and their aftermaths, and the twelve years of Hitler's dictatorship, Schnack in his poetry seeks to respond to, and to accommodate himself to, contemporary events. His work is not well known except within the community of the small Lower Franconian town of Kahl am Main where he spent the last twenty-eight years of his life and where, as I discovered on two visits, he is something of a celebrity. His gravestone in the cemetery there reads: 'Anton Schnack Dichter des Expressionismus und Meister der kleinen Prosa'. These words are, in fact, hardly adequate as a description of his literary career. While he was certainly a significant Expressionist poet, his short stories are mostly lightweight, playfully humorous and studiedly unengaged, especially in the context of huge social and political upheaval. There is a ludic and light-hearted quality about much of his prose work: his busy and versatile imagination, revelling in the wonders and simple joys of everyday life, often slips into dilettantism or, at worst, good-humoured triviality. In his editor's words, he presents himself as a 'leiser Aufrüttler aus Trägheit und Alltäglichkeit', and there is little in the prose that is not conveyed more succinctly and powerfully in the poetry. A post-Second World War project to create 'eine Darstellung der Angst und Furcht vor dem Kommenden' remained unrealised.
>
> The focus of this book will, therefore, be on his poetry [...] I hope to show in my book that Schnack's eight collections merit serious consideration and appraisal. They have been unjustly overlooked not only by anthologists at the time, but also by readers, literary historians and reviewers since. [...] The book begins with a general introduction to Schnack's life and work and examines his contemporary and current standing among literary historians and critics. Chapters 2 and 3 focus on the three volumes of Expressionist verse and document the cultural circles he frequented in Munich and the numerous Expressionist publications to which he contributed. The next three chapters are dedicated to *Tier rang gewaltig mit Tier* and examine it with reference to its poetic form as a cycle of sonnets and its merits and status as war poetry. The final chapter pays particular attention to Schnack's life in the Third Reich, situating the single collection he published in that era among the literary works of Inner Emigration. The book concludes with an introduction and analysis of his three post-war collections.
>
> There are, of course, numerous books and articles about, for example, Expressionism and First World War poetry, though not necessarily German: they are often broad surveys dealing in theory and generalisations. Far fewer are studies founded in detailed analysis of a single writer's individual poems and of the contexts in which those poems were produced. This is what my book seeks

to deliver. Its principal conclusions are clear: that the three early Expressionist volumes are significant documents of their time and present valuable versions of a certain kind of Expressionism; that *Tier rang* is Schnack's abiding achievement and deserves far more than the superficial attention and easy praise which it has customarily garnered; that Schnack's attitude and conduct in the 1920s and 1930s were paradigmatic examples of the phenomenon of Inner Emigration and that, while it may be tempting to relegate his later volumes to a place a long way behind their powerful predecessors and thus to overlook their considerable qualities, they still contain sufficient human insight and shrewd observation to warrant further interest.

★   ★   ★   ★   ★

My father was a born storyteller, a weaver of legends and inventor of games, stories that stay with myself, my sister, Claire, and my brother, Peter, today — the witch at the bottom of the hill, my father as a small boy being chased by a bull. For most of our childhood and before the move to London for his headmaster role, my father and mother, Rosemary, were based first in Kent and then on the south coast in Sussex. I still vividly remember building *incredibly* elaborate 'badger traps' of sticks and leaves with him when out walking in our local woods, utterly convinced that we would catch a badger or maybe a ferret this time. Peter recalls, as a small boy, playing a beach ball game with my father on his beloved Isles of Scilly that was so fiendishly involved and engrossing that a nearby buyer for Fisher Price who happened to be on the beach was so impressed that she tried to patent it. He was wonderful with the next generation as well, totally immersed in his grandchildren's company while they listened spellbound to his invented stories, complete with props that he had picked up in readiness for the occasion. And many of my earliest memories are of watching him work, bent over his desk in the sitting-room in Kent, writing incessantly, completing the first of his two doctorates on German Expressionist poetry.

All his life, my father chose only to write long-hand, eschewing first the typewriter and then the computer keyboard. He wrote prodigiously — weekly postcards to his children and then grandchildren as well as numerous letters regularly to friends, colleagues and ex-students. In fact, one of the great challenges and joys of editing this book has been getting to grips with his handwriting again. To prepare this book, my father printed out his original DPhil — and then covered it with tiny pencil amendments as well as whole added pages of new ideas. Freed from the constraints of a DPhil, he aimed to add in new depth to his original sections on the Expressionist movement and on sonnets. While he was able to finish organising his ideas on these two areas, sadly he died before his corrections could be completed; from my discussions with him just before this, he had said that he was probably about three months from completion. However, this does not detract, I feel, from the weight of scholarship in this book: it is only regrettable as we will not know what he had planned for enriching the sections on Schnack's post-First World War poetry. Indeed, for me, it has been fascinating to put together all the additions he had planned, incorporating them into what was already a rich review of Schnack's poetry.

This book was my father's final labour of love and, as I expressed at the beginning, it has been my privilege to complete the editing process on his behalf. Reading it offers one an insight into a German war poet of great power whose cycle of poems, *Tier rang*, demonstrates a deep understanding of the thoughts of a soldier — not simply a German soldier or even just a First World War soldier — as he battles the horror of warfare. The surrounding chapters aim to place this in context, both of Schnack and of Germany at the time, situating the war poems in, and simultaneously increasing one's understanding of, Schnack's earlier Expressionist writing as well as his later poetry. I am sure that you will find it interesting and I hope that you will find it useful. My father, an educator first and foremost, would be delighted to know that his ideas were still out there, helping future researchers. On behalf of my whole family and, particularly, my father, I commend this book to you and wish you well in all your future academic endeavours.

J.R.H., Worcester, June 2025

ACKNOWLEDGEMENTS

My debts are numerous and considerable. I was extremely fortunate in the supervisor of my first doctorate, the late Peter Stern, whose outstanding scholarship and teaching first inspired and challenged me as a young undergraduate and subsequently led me to Professor Ritchie Robertson, the supervisor of the doctoral thesis on which this book is based. Professor Robertson could not have been more encouraging towards me and more patient with my undisciplined first drafts. It was Professor Robertson who introduced me to Anton Schnack and who then accompanied me right through the process, from initial faltering step to finished piece. I benefited hugely from his wisdom and am deeply indebted to him. I also owe a great deal to the staff of the Taylor Institution Library (especially Helen Buchanan and Jill Hughes), to the library staff at Würzburg University and to Herr Norbert Herrmann, Chief Librarian at Würzburg's municipal library. All those I met at the Deutsches Literaturarchiv, Marbach (particularly Frau Regina Cerfontaine) and the City Archive in Würzburg were most welcoming and helpful. Special gratitude is due to Bürgermeister Jürgen Seitz, former archivist Frau Tilly Amon and other staff in the archive located in the Rathaus at Kahl am Main, Schnack's hometown. I have also benefited from long conversations held at her house in Kahl in August 2011 with Frau Ursula Stickler, Schnack's niece, and from correspondence with Prof. Dr. Hartmut Vollmer (Schnack's editor) and Ralph Roger Glöckler, Schnack's nephew. To four splendid typists — Sophie Etse, Jayne Finlay, Lydia Lantzsch and Dorothy Fouracre — fell, in succession, the responsibility for typing up my early drafts and the final version of the original thesis and coping with my complete technical incompetence.

Colleagues in the Modern Languages Department at Clifton College (especially Owen Lewis and Llew Siddons) were unfailingly supportive, and a group of young students at my school (Melissa, Mariya, Tom, Aidan, Gareth, Will and Dominic) accompanied me through the composition and seemed happy to be introduced to Schnack's verse.

I dedicate this book to my children, Jane, Claire and Peter, and my grandchildren, Jessica, Joseph, Lucas and Wren, who never questioned their father's (and grand-father's) constant absences and absorption in a necessarily selfish enterprise.

C.D.W., December 2019

CHAPTER 1

Introducing Anton Schnack

Und manches war ein geliebtes und verehrtes Buch
Und trägt noch Lavendelduft und Großmutters Kommodengeruch.

Ich liebe sie, die in den grauen Regalen steh'n,
Von niemand verlangt, durchblättert und angeseh'n.
[...]
Verschollen nun, verstaubt, vergraben in Bücherreih'n,
Werden auch unsere einst unbegehrt und vergessen sein?[1]

Unlike Georg Heym and other Expressionist poets, Anton Schnack did not, as far as can be determined, keep a diary, nor has any significant amount of early correspondence survived. Moreover, while it is true that he constantly mines the circumstances and events of his own life for much of the material which issues subsequently both into his poetry and his prose, he does so in an impressionistic and haphazard way. Since biographical information about Schnack is hard to find and since the relation between his life and his work is very close and complex, it will be useful to summarize the data of his biography. He was born on 21 July 1892 in the Lower Franconian town of Rieneck an der Sinn.[2] He was the third child of Elisabeth and Hermann Schnack, the local Gendarmeriestations-Kommandant (roughly, local police chief). His brother Friedrich, four years older, was also to become a writer. Anton had an undistinguished career in local schools in Dettelbach, Kronach and Hammelburg and in 1913 spent one year in the philosophy faculty at Munich University. Before he enlisted in the army in 1915, he had enjoyed two periods of work experience as assistant editor in Emmerich on the Dutch border and for the *Bozner Tagblatt* in Bolzano/Bozen, now in northern Italy but in 1915 still in the Austrian district of Südtirol and soon, in the final two years of the war, to be the scene of fierce fighting between the Italian and Austro-Hungarian armies. For four months from November 1915, Schnack served as an Armierungssoldat (soldier in charge of munitions) on the Somme and at Verdun before he was injured in an accident unloading ammunition. He never returned

---

1   Anton Schnack, 'Verschollene Versbücher' (1941), in *Werke*, ed. by Hartmut Vollmer, 2 vols (Elfenbein, 2003), I, pp. 393–94. Henceforth Vollmer's edition will be cited by volume and page number alone, thus I, 430.
2   For biographical details see I, 441–78. The Deutsches Literaturarchiv at Marbach holds all Schnack's published poetry and prose. Its Manuscript Department has available on request various documents relating to his life, usually reviews of his work, but frequently not dated or ordered in any way. Henceforth it will be referred to as Manuscript Department Marbach.

to the frontline. During his year in Munich he established contacts among groups of avant-garde writers frequenting the fashionable clubs, cabarets and restaurants, absorbing the atmosphere generated by the hectic cultural exchanges of the day. By the time the war ended, he was publishing poems in a variety of Expressionist magazines while working as an editor and theatre critic in Darmstadt. In 1919/20 he published four volumes of poetry, including *Tier rang gewaltig mit Tier*, a collection of sixty sonnets about the experience of military service on the Western Front.

In the 1920s Schnack worked as editor and critic for the *Neue Badische Landes-Zeitung* in Mannheim and he travelled widely to Italy, Dalmatia and southern France with his wife Maria Glöckler, whom he had married in 1924. Having given up his work as a journalist in 1929, he earned his living as a writer of poetry and, more particularly, prose, and moved to Herrsching am Ammersee (south-west of Munich), Prien am Chiemsee (between Munich and Salzburg) and, for four years between 1933 and 1937, to Berchtesgaden. He then lived in Frankfurt for six years. In 1944 he again had to enlist in the army, this time as a Landesschütze (a member of the home guard). For a short while he was held prisoner by the American forces. On his release and until his death on 26 September 1973 he lived with his wife, close to other members of his family, at Spessart 8 in Kahl am Main, north of Aschaffenburg. He is buried in the cemetery at Kahl.

His memorial stone reads: 'Anton Schnack Dichter des Expressionismus und Meister der kleinen Prosa'. In fact, he published four collections of poetry which can justifiably be called Expressionist: these are *Strophen der Gier* (1919), *Der Abenteurer* (1919), *Die tausend Gelächter* (1919) and *Tier rang gewaltig mit Tier* (1920). His other collections of verse are *Die Flaschenpost* (1936), *Der Annoncenleser* (1947), *Mittagswein* (1948) and *"Jene Dame, welche..."* (1953). He published numerous individual poems in various magazines.[3] Few of his literary reviews or letters survive in his archive at the Deutsches Literaturarchiv Marbach, but his prose works (for example, his best known novels *Zugvögel der Liebe* and *Der finstere Franz*, both written in the 1930s) and collections of his shorter prose pieces (for example, *Die bunte Hauspostille*, *Die Angel des Robinson* and *Phantastische Geographie*, all written between 1938 and 1949) can be found there. Many of the poems he collected after the Second World War had, in fact, been written in the 1920s and 1930s, whereas he continued writing and publishing prose until shortly before his death. Indeed, while the focus of this book will be directed at his poetry, frequent reference will be made to the 170 or so essays which Hartmut Vollmer, his editor, has gathered into the second volume of Schnack's *Werke*.

The trajectory of Schnack's critical reception as a poet can be simply stated: very strong initial enthusiasm (1920) was followed by virtual silence until a few years after his death when in 1985 Patrick Bridgwater championed Schnack's early poetry (more especially *Tier rang*[4]) and then some twenty years later Hartmut Vollmer

---

3   Vollmer divides these into two groups: 'verstreut veröffentlichte expressionistische Gedichte' (I, 101–46) and 'verstreut veröffentlichte Gedichte' (I, 299–419).
4   Henceforth, this abbreviation will be used *for Tier rang gewaltig mit Tier*.

began editing his complete works.[5] This pattern is not surprising because between 1920 and 1936 Schnack published no collections of his verse. From then until 1945, it was obviously very difficult, once he had decided to stay in Germany, to publish anything except party political propaganda — which he did not do. There is also no evidence that he seriously contemplated any alternative to remaining in Franconia. For twenty-five years he published only individual poems scattered over many magazines — and the single collection *Die Flaschenpost* — and his retreat from public view was matched by critical silence. The obituaries in the autumn of 1973 are predictably generous *and* very parochial and localised. Since then a few isolated voices have been raised and have succeeded in rescuing his name from complete literary oblivion. Those voices, like the voices in 1920, focus invariably on the war sonnets in *Tier rang*. Patrick Bridgwater, for example, could hardly be more generous in his praise or more painstaking in his analysis of this cycle. Having stated that 'Schnack is virtually unknown even in Germany', Bridgwater suggests that Schnack was 'one of the two unambiguously great poets of the war on the German side'[6] (the other being Stramm). More recently Ritchie Robertson wrote in similar vein describing Schnack as being 'the only German war poet, apart from Trakl, who rivals the best work of Rosenberg, Gurney and Owen'.[7] A rare pre-Bridgwater commendation is to be found in *Ohne Hass und Fahne*, an anthology of German war poetry published in 1959:

> *Tier rang* [...] ist die umfassendste lyrische Darstellung der Kriegslandschaft des ersten Weltkrieges und des Fronterlebnisses eines jungen Menschen. In sechzig Langzeilengedichten sind die Nacht und der Tod, das Leid und die Todeserwartung des Dichters die Themen, die in dynamischer Sprache gefaßt sind.[8]

Otherwise, Schnack's name has emerged sporadically, sometimes in unexpected places. Jay Winter, for example, singles out Schnack's poem 'Der Tote' from *Tier rang* and again makes a connection with the poetry of Wilfred Owen: 'Both [Owen and Schnack] understood what soldiering meant and knew that they were killers as well as victims.'[9] Winter also argues that both Owen and Schnack offer 'similar lists — a catalogue of pleasures lost, laughter not heard, courage and wisdom thrown away'.[10] In fact, Schnack, unlike Owen, was not 'a killer', nor was he 'a veteran of Verdun and the great battles of 1918'.[11] Schnack was invalided out of the frontline at the end of February 1916. This means that at most he would have experienced one

---

5   In the final paragraph of his essay 'Zu Leben und Werk Anton Schnacks', Vollmer indicates that there is more to come — novels, essays, short stories — and that they will appear in later editions (1, 469). The publishers Elfenbein in Berlin have indicated that there is no proposal to do this.

6   Patrick Bridgwater, *The German Poets of the First World War* (Croom Helm, 1985), p. 96.

7   See *The Cambridge History of German Literature*, ed. by Helen Watanabe-O'Kelly (Cambridge University Press, 1997), pp. 357–58.

8   *Ohne Hass und Fahne. Kriegsgedichte des zwanzigsten Jahrhunderts*, ed. by Wolfgang G. Deppe, Christopher Middleton and Herbert Schönherr (Rowohlt, 1959), p. 177.

9   Jay Winter, *Sites of Memory, Sites of Mourning. The Great War in European Cultural History* (Cambridge University Press, 1995), pp. 211–12.

10   Ibid., p. 212.

11   Ibid., p. 211.

week of the Battle of Verdun and nothing of the Battle of the Somme. But what is truly significant here is that Schnack is placed quite clearly in the company of an indisputably great war poet, Wilfred Owen. Ian Beckett goes into greater detail without, again, being wholly accurate. Having stated that some German poets supported the war initially, he adds that others

> became disillusioned though the German poetic tradition tended towards an idealism, abstraction and remoteness from reality which made it difficult to get to grips with the experience of war. Nonetheless, the best, like Georg Trakl and Anton Schnak [sic], are comparable to Wilfred Owen.[12]

It will become clear during later analyses of Schnack's poetry that, while it matches Owen's in quality, it is very different in kind. Owen, in the war poems for which he is celebrated, focuses principally on life and death in the trenches: Schnack offers a similar account while also conjuring a 'Gegenwelt', intimations of solace and redemption beyond, and in the face of, the horrors of frontline warfare. The poetry of Edmund Blunden or Edward Thomas might provide a closer comparison.

It is highly significant that Ernst Rowohlt published Schnack's *Tier rang* in 1920. The fact that that volume was picked up by a major avant-garde publisher like Rowohlt says a great deal for its merits and about how those merits were perceived at the time, especially when one recalls that Schnack's earlier Expressionist volumes were published by small local enterprises in what Bridgwater calls 'pamphlet collections'.[13] *Strophen der Gier*, for example, was published by the short-lived Dresdner Verlag as a fifteen-page pamphlet in 1919,[14] while the Paul Steegemann Verlag in Hanover published *Die tausend Gelächter* as a sixteen-page pamphlet in the sixteenth volume of *Die Silbergäule* — 'eine neue Bücherreihe mit bunten oft illustrierten Heften'.[15] *Der Abenteurer* came out under the imprint of Die Dachstube in an eighteen-page pamphlet called *Die kleine Republik*.[16] Although Steegemann published a large variety of texts in *Die Silbergäule* during its short life (1919–22), including literary essays, *Novellen*, political tracts and poetry (Hans Arp and Wilhelm Klemm alongside Schnack), of the three comparatively small publishing houses, Die Dachstube, based in Darmstadt, was almost certainly the most significant, partly because it metamorphosed in 1919 into *Das Tribunal: Hessische radikale Blätter*. Its motto was 'Gegen Hetze — für Gerechtigkeit. Gegen Lauheit — für Erneuerung' and it became a sanctuary for a group of radical artists and writers, the so-called Darmstädter Sezession.[17] Vollmer indicates that Schnack wrote an essay about this radical group's Expressionist exhibition in 1920,[18] but there is no record of Schnack's exhibiting any of his own work or subscribing to the journal's subversive political and social programme. However, at least two poems from *Tier*

---

12 Ian F. W. Beckett, *The Great War 1914–1918* (Longman, 2007), p. 450.
13 Bridgwater, p. 96.
14 See *Das neuste Gedicht*, H.22, May 1919.
15 Paul Raabe, *Die Zeitschriften und Sammlungen des literarischen Expressionismus 1910–1921* (Metzler, 1964), pp. 188–92.
16 Eine Flugschriftenreihe, Nr. 7.
17 Raabe, pp. 92–93.
18 I, 451.

rang ('Verdun' and 'Flucht') were first published in *Das Tribunal* before all sixty poems of that collection were taken up by the Ernst Rowohlt Verlag. It is reasonable to conjecture that in his dealings with the Ernst Rowohlt Verlag, *Das Tribunal* and other key Expressionist journals, *Der Sturm* and *Die Aktion*, Schnack found himself exposed for a short time to the rapidly developing and diversifying movement of Expressionism, if not caught up in it. The encounter with the Ernst Rowohlt Verlag in particular was thus very significant for Schnack's literary development.

Founded originally in 1908 and then effectively taken over by Kurt Wolff, the Ernst Rowohlt Verlag re-emerged as a hugely enterprising and influential concern early in 1919 on the Potsdamer Brücke in Berlin with, among others, Walter Hasenclever, Albert Ehrenstein, Oskar Kokoschka and Else Lasker-Schüler in attendance.[19] From the outset of his career Rowohlt seems to have been clear about the high ideals which he cherished for his publishing houses:

> Zwei Aufgaben hatte er sich gestellt, die an und für sich nicht zusammenhingen, aber keineswegs unvereinbar waren. Er wollte schöngedruckte Werke aller Literaturen, die bisher recht kostspielig waren, dem Publikum zu erschwinglichen Preisen zugänglich machen, und es war gleichzeitig sein Ehrgeiz und seine Absicht, der Verleger zeitgenössischer Literatur zu sein. Sein Verlag sollte der Vergangenheit und gleichzeitig der unmittelbaren Gegenwart zugewandt sein.[20]

Rowohlt immediately set about fulfilling both aims. He published the highly select Drugulin prints[21] and works by, among many others, Goethe, Shakespeare, Baudelaire and Verlaine. From his time in Bremen, where he had been born in 1887 and where he lived until 1905, and in Leipzig where he worked for Anton Kippenberg at the Insel Verlag, he ensured that he knew about the workings of other famous publishing houses such as those founded by Samuel Fischer and Eugen Diederichs. These already well-established enterprises were very different in character from what Rowohlt had in mind. Fischer, for example, published mainstream moderns such as the Mann brothers, Schnitzler and Wassermann, while Diederichs took up conservative writers such as Hermann Hesse and Hermann Löns. Rowohlt set out to rival them. He took a particular interest in contemporary German poetry from Detlev von Liliencron to Stefan George. Young, ambitious, energetic and keen to make a name for himself, he even travelled in person to Würzburg to try to persuade Max Dauthendey to let him publish a collection of the latter's poetry, in fact 'irgendein Werk'.[22] By 1912, when he was barely twenty-five, he had also published Georg Heym's collections *Der ewige Tag* and *Umbra Vitae* and

---

19   Paul Mayer, *Ernst Rowohlt in Selbstzeugnissen und Bilddokumenten* (Rowohlt, 1967), is the principal source of this information on Rowohlt's career.
20   Ibid., pp.29–30.
21   Wilhelm Eduard Drugulin (1822–1879) was a world-famous art-dealer based in Leipzig. In 1863 he sold to the newly founded Imperial Royal Austrian Museum of Art and Industry in Vienna priceless ornamental prints on single folios as well as in books, art books and sketch-books: these prints dated from the fifteenth to eighteenth centuries and originated mainly from Germany, France and England.
22   Mayer, pp. 35–37.

Kafka's *Betrachtung*, as well as winning the contract to publish Gustav Meyrink's *Der Golem*.[23] Having met Kurt Pinthus in 1909 in Leipzig, Rowohlt subsequently, in 1920, published the anthology *Menschheitsdämmerung* thus proclaiming his interest in the most avant-garde, even revolutionary poetry.[24]

His tastes remained broad and eclectic:

> Rowohlt fühlte sich keiner Doktrin, keiner Parteimeinung, keiner Richtung verpflichtet. So ist es zu erklären, daß bei ihm die Bücher des extremen Traditionalisten und Nationalisten Rudolf Borchardt erscheinen konnten, und gleichzeitig die Sammlungen *Menschheitsdämmerung* und *Die Entfaltung*, in denen die Lyrik und die Prosa der expressionistischen Zeitgenossen vereinigt waren.[25]

In the 1920s neither the number nor the variety of publications abated. Rowohlt published Balzac's complete works, Carl Ludwig Schleich's astonishingly successful best-seller *Besonnte Vergangenheit*, Robert Musil's *Der Mann ohne Eigenschaften*, Hans Fallada's first novel (*Der junge Goedeschal*), alongside non-German writers such as Ernest Hemingway and Sinclair Lewis. One contemporary critic even suggested that his name should go forward for a Nobel Prize for services to literature.[26] Schnack, whose sixty war-poems were, in every respect, unlike any other lyrical response to the experience of frontline combat, must have seemed, even in this company, a desirable acquisition.

Much early critical commentary on *Tier rang* is positive. It is, of course, predictable that the blurb on the cover of the first edition should champion the poet's cause not only by announcing 'Auf Grund seines Buches *Tier rang gewaltig mit Tier* wurde dem in Mannheim lebenden Schriftsteller Anton Schnack eine Ehrengabe von 1000 Mark aus der Amerika-Spende der deutschen Schillerstiftung verliehen',[27] but by quoting excerpts from press reviews. Hugo Bieber in the newspaper *Der Tag* writes: 'Mit Anton Schnacks Gedichten *Tier rang gewaltig mit Tier* tritt ein neues, bedeutendes lyrisches Ingenium vor die Öffentlichkeit, ein Dichter von ungewöhnlicher Breite des Erlebens, der sich eine ganz neue Ausdrucksform geschaffen hat.'[28] Hans Franck is equally effusive in the *Frankfurter Zeitung*: 'Kein Versbuch unserer Zeit kenne ich, in dem von einem, der mitten hindurchgegangen ist durch das Grauen, mit gleicher umfassender Wahrhaftigkeit das Ringen des Menschen mit dem Menschen festgehalten wird, wie in *Tier rang gewaltig mit Tier*.'[29] Schnack's name also featured in lesser-known publications. R. C. Muschler's praise in *Die Bergstadt* could hardly have been more positive:

---

23   Ibid., p.73. In the event he had sold his publishing house to Kurt Wolff before Meyrink's work came onto the market.

24   *Menschheitsdämmerung*, ed. by Kurt Pinthus (Rowohlt, 1920).

25   Mayer, p. 73.

26   Ibid., p.30. The critic in question is not named, but apparently he wrote for *Zeitschrift für Bücherfreunde*.

27   Photocopied in: Ralph Roger Glöckler, 'Die frühen Gedichtbände von Anton Schnack und ihr literarischer Standort im expressionistischen Jahrzehnt' (unpublished master's thesis, University of Tübingen, 1976), p. 70.

28   Ibid.

29   Ibid.

Dieses Buch des Krieges verdient weiteste Verbreitung [...] Wir müssen Freude haben, daß endlich einmal auch die Kriegslyrik losgelöst wird von allem tendenziösen Denken: Schnacks Eigenart und Selbständigkeit tut allen wohl, denen der Krieg ein inneres und ein Sinnenerlebnis war [...] eine Legion hat die Gefühle dieser namenlos sinnlosen Zeit festzuhalten sich bemüht, Anton Schnack aber hat das bleibende Buch über diese Jahre der Zerfleischung geschrieben.[30]

Muschler then proceeds to cast Schnack as a trailblazer in whom the greatest possible hopes of a bright future for German lyrical poetry can be safely invested: 'Anton Schnack bedeutet eine der größten Hoffnungen des jungen Deutschland. Sein bisheriges Schaffen läßt keinen Zweifel daran, daß dieser hochbegabte Dichter mitberufen ist, die seit Jahren pensionierte Lyrik neu aufleben zu lassen.'[31] In the event, Muschler's passionate endorsement was not followed up and his predictions of future glory were not realized. For the next sixteen years Schnack's literary output was limited to scattered poems in various magazines. His next collection, *Die Flaschenpost* in 1936, is a very different kind of poetry written and published at a very different time, and critical acclaim was comparatively muted.

In the context of the reception of Schnack's work, its omission from Pinthus's *Menschheitsdämmerung*, which Marie Luise Kaschnitz described as 'die poetische Bibel meiner Jugend',[32] is surely critical and rather surprising. Pinthus was one of the editors of the Rowohlt publishing house, and it is inconceivable that he did not know, or know of, Schnack's four volumes of Expressionist poetry. Nor did Pinthus take the opportunity subsequently, in the 'Nachklang' of 1922 when the twenty-thousandth copy of *Menschheitsdämmerung* was being prepared or in the essay 'Nach vierzig Jahren' in 1959, to make good, in retrospect, any omissions or indeed to suggest that there might have been significant omissions in the original version. While August Stramm, Georg Trakl, Wilhelm Klemm and Alfred Lichtenstein are generously represented, no space is found for Heinrich Lersch, Hugo Ball, Karl Bröger or Gerrit Engelke. Of the nine poets whom Bridgwater selects for analysis and characterization only four feature in Pinthus's anthology: war poetry, like lyric poetry written by women poets, is thinly represented in *Menschheitsdämmerung*.[33] Francis Sharp, in his essay '*Menschheitsdämmerung*: The Aging of a Canon', writes: 'Among the most important rediscovered younger males with roots in Expressionism are Hermann Kasack (1896–1966), Edlef Koeppen (1893–1939), Hans Schiebelhuth (1895–1944) and Anton Schnack (1892–1972).'[34] In fact, the year of Schnack's death in Sharp's list is wrong (it should be 1973), and

---

30   *Die Bergstadt*, no. 4, 4 January 1921.

31   Ibid.

32   Marie Luise Kaschnitz, *Gesammelte Werke*, ed. by Christian Büttrich and Norbert Müller, 7 vols (Insel, 1981–89), VII, p. 706.

33   By way of a response to what he sees as a shortcoming in Pinthus's anthology (Else Lasker-Schüler is, after all, the sole female representative), Vollmer has edited *In roten Schuhen tanzt die Sonne zu Tod: Lyrik expressionistischer Dichterinnen* (Arche, 1993).

34   Francis Michael Sharp, '*Menschheitsdämmerung*: The Aging of a Canon', in *A Companion to the Literature of German Expressionism*, ed. by Neil H. Donahue (Camden House, 2010), pp. 137–55 (p. 146).

the 'rediscovered' in Schnack's case raises false hopes, if only because Sharp says nothing more about him. The work and life of three of the four writers have been the subject of individual critical appraisal. Only Anton Schnack has not benefited in the same way.[35] In the same year as Pinthus's anthology appeared, Ludwig Rubiner's collection *Kameraden der Menschheit* was published. It represented the left wing of the Expressionist movement: 'Dichtungen zur Weltrevolution' was its subtitle and it was divided into sections with headings such as 'Die Internationale', 'Nieder mit dem Krieg', 'Die Empörung' and 'Die rote Schar'. Not surprisingly, bearing in mind what we shall subsequently see as Schnack's essentially apolitical stance, his poetry is not represented in the collection: Becher, Ehrenstein and Toller appear with predictable frequency, and Henri Guilbeaux's tribute to Karl Liebknecht is typical of the flavour of the anthologist's allegiances.[36] Pinthus's *Menschheitsdämmerung* and Rubiner's *Kameraden der Menschheit* occupy a central position in the history and promotion of Expressionist poetry: 'Sie [the two anthologies] spiegeln die beiden politischen Richtungen, die gleichermaßen die literarische Bewegung des Expressionismus für sich beanspruchten.'[37] Left out of both, Schnack was thus omitted from the canon and never got back in. Schnack outlived all twenty-three poets in *Menschheitsdämmerung*, with the exception of Kurt Heynicke, and it is, therefore, instructive, by considering his life and work, to be able to follow the evolution of one Expressionist poet.

It was the same story in the late 1950s, the 1960s and the 1970s when Expressionism again became the focus of literary criticism. Important books on the subject by Armin Arnold, Wolfgang Paulsen, Eva Kolinsky, Wolfgang Rothe, Roy Allen, Paul Raabe and Walter Sokel, among many other distinguished critics of Expressionism, rarely even mention Schnack's name.[38] In the account of the famous exhibition of Expressionist literature and art organized by the Deutsches Literaturarchiv at Marbach between 8 May and 31 October 1960 there is a very brief biography of Schnack and five references to Expressionist publications to which he contributed.[39]

---

35   Hans Schiebelhuth, by contrast, enjoys the benefit of Manfred Schlösser's two-volume edition of his work, in Hans Schiebelhuth, *Gedichte, Übertragungen, Prosa, Briefe, Theaterkritiken*, ed. by Manfred Schlösser, 2 vols. (Agora, 1966–67).

36   *Kameraden der Menschheit* (1919), ed. by Ludwig Rubiner (Reclam, 1971). For the Guilbeaux poem, see pp. 97–100.

37   *Deutsche Lyrik von den Anfängen bis zur Gegenwart*, ed. by Gisela Lindemann, 12 vols (Deutscher Taschenbuch Verlag, 2001), IX, p. 10. This large anthology has just two Schnack poems: 'Der Train' (p. 153) and 'An einem französischen Kamin' (p. 165).

38   The references are to: Armin Arnold, *Die Literatur des Expressionismus* (Kohlhammer, 1966); *Aspekte des Expressionismus. Periodisierung. Stil. Gedankenwelt*, ed. by Wolfgang Paulsen (Lothar Stiehm, 1968); Eva Kolinsky, *Engagierter Expressionismus* (Metzler, 1970), who has a single reference (p. 27) to Schnack's poem 'An einem französischen Kamin'; *Expressionismus als Literatur*, ed. by Wolfgang Rothe (Francke, 1969); Roy F. Allen, *German Expressionist Poetry* (Twayne, 1979); *Expressionismus: Aufzeichnungen und Erinnerungen der Zeitgenossen*, ed. by Paul Raabe (Walter, 1965); Walter H. Sokel, *The Writer in Extremis* (Stanford University Press, 1959). Martin Reso's substantial anthology *Expressionismus: Lyrik* (Aufbau, 1969) has just Schnack's 'Verdun' pp. 378–79. Becher, on the other hand, is represented by 37 poems.

39   *Expressionismus: Literatur und Kunst 1910–1923*, ed. by Bernhard Zeller, eine Ausstellung des Deutschen Literaturarchivs im Schiller-Nationalmuseum 8 May 1960–31 October 1960 (Schiller-Nationalmuseum, 1960).

Three particularly surprising, and disappointing, cases are Richard Brinkmann's very wide-ranging survey of Expressionism,[40] the anthology of First World War poetry compiled by Thomas Anz and Joseph Vogl[41] (in neither does Schnack's name appear), and Uwe Wandrey's *Das Motiv des Krieges in der expressionistischen Lyrik*.[42] Wandrey's title sounds promising, but in fact his full-length study contains only eleven fleeting references to Schnack's *Tier rang*, with no analysis or explanation of the cycle's qualities. Perhaps it is less surprising that his name should be absent from one of the best-known French accounts of Expressionism, by Maurice Godé.[43] On the other hand, and rather bizarrely, it can be found among American secret service documents. In 1943–44 Carl Zuckmayer, who emigrated to the USA in 1939, compiled for the Office of Strategic Services (the OSS, predecessors of the CIA) a report consisting of about 150 character portraits of writers, publishers, actors, directors and musicians who had held prominent positions in the Third Reich. On 28 July 1944, Werner Thormann, reader/assessor for the OSS, writes to Zuckmayer to thank him and to ask him another favour:

> Wenn es Ihre Zeit erlaubt, können Sie mir gelegentlich kurz sagen, was Sie über die folgenden Autoren wissen, deren Biographien auch auf unserem Programm stehen [Thormann lists forty names, including those of Anton and Friedrich Schnack]. Die meisten auf dieser Liste werden nicht sehr wichtig und politisch sein, aber sie erscheinen gelegentlich und man wird wahrscheinlich für eine guidance, wie sie einzuschätzen sind, sehr dankbar sein.[44]

'Not very important, not very political' was a stricture borne out by subsequent (non-)responses for the next thirty years, but after 1980, the publication date of Brinkmann's influential survey, the situation with regard to the reception of Schnack's work changed from a phase in which he was virtually absent from literary histories to one in which, as we have seen, that absence was categorized as significantly unjust critical neglect.

However, despite Hartmut Vollmer's best efforts, Schnack's lyrical poetry, even the volumes which earned so many plaudits on their publication immediately after the First World War, remains largely unknown and ignored. The appearance of Vollmer's excellent two-volume edition of Schnack's poetry and prose in 2003 certainly drew a strong commendation from a reviewer in *Germanistik* who wrote:

> Im Verlagshandel [...] sind seine [Schnacks] Texte schon seit langem nicht mehr erhältlich. Erstes, ausdrückliches Ziel der nun vorliegenden Edition ist es, diesen Mißstand zu beheben. Das Resultat ist eine umfangreiche und solide ausgearbeitete Leistung der Lyrik (Bd.I) und der Kurzprosa (Bd.II).

40   Richard Brinkmann (ed.), *Expressionismus: Internationale Forschung zu einem internationalen Phänomen* (Metzler, 1980).
41   *Die Dichter und der Krieg: Deutsche Lyrik 1914–1918*, ed. by Thomas Anz and Joseph Vogl (Hanser, 1982).
42   Uwe Wandrey, *Das Motiv des Krieges in der expressionistischen Lyrik*, Geistes- und Sozialwissenschaftliche Dissertationen 23 (Lüdke, 1972).
43   Maurice Godé, *L'Expressionnisme* (Presses Universitaires de France, 1999). This account contains fifteen references to August Stramm, none to Schnack.
44   Carl Zuckmayer, *Geheimreport*, ed. by Gunther Nickel and Johanna Schrön (Wallstein, 2002), p. 464.

> Berücksichtigt finden sich sowohl die in Buchausgaben als auch die bislang eruierten, verstreut in Zeitungen, Zeitschriften und Anthologien erschienenen Texte [...] Ein ausführliches, sehr instruktives Nachwort faßt den Forschungsstand zu Leben und Werk zusammen [...] Künftige Editionen der Romane und längeren Erzählungen, der essayistischen und literaturkritischen Arbeiten sowie von Texten aus dem Nachlaß werden angekündigt (1, 469) und wären uneingeschränkt zu begrüßen.[45]

In other quarters, however, the endorsement of the poet's stature was grudgingly half-hearted:

> Zu den ganz Großen der Literaturgeschichte zählt der expressionistische Schriftsteller Anton Schnack zwar nicht, aber zu den Anerkannten. Mit einigem Stolz blickt daher die Gemeinde Kahl [am Main] auf das Wirken des Dichters zurück, der dreißig Jahre mit seiner Frau Maria in der Gemeinde gelebt und gearbeitet hat.[46]

'Acknowledged' by whom? Ironically it is the viticulturists and oenophiles of his beloved Franconia who are now invoked to pay warmest homage to Anton Schnack, himself a connoisseur of wine and prolific writer about local wine labels. But even they might wonder who he was. A recently published tour guide of the vineyards around Alzenau features scattered lines of Schnack's verse, and at one point, under the heading 'Anton Schnack — der fränkische Weinpoet', asks the questions:

> 'Wer ist Anton Schnack' oder 'Kennen Sie Anton Schnack?' Viele Menschen, denen wir heute in Alzenau und seinen Weinorten begegnen, zucken mit den Achseln oder schütteln verneinend den Kopf, wenn sie nach diesem Namen gefragt werden. Leider ist der Mann, der die Heimat seiner Mutter und seiner Großeltern sein frühes und spätes Lebensumfeld idyllisch verklärt, schwärmerisch und doch sehr treffend beschrieben hat, heute fast in Vergessenheit geraten.[47]

On the other hand, as made clear in my own visits to Kahl in the 2010s, many local residents are quietly proud of a writer who, throughout his long life, wrote so warmly of their home town and its environs, while his surviving relatives and friends, when I visited in 2011, were pleased to share stories and anecdotes about 'Onkel Anton'.

It is possible to adduce, or speculate on, reasons for Schnack's virtual oblivion. Hartmut Vollmer, his editor, suggests two principal causes, one literary-historical, the other commercial:

> Das [the fact that Schnack has been 'forgotten'] hängt wohl zum einen mit der bekannten literarhistorischen Kanonisierung zusammen, durch die viele beachtenswerte Autorinnen und Autoren in Vergessenheit geraten. Schnacks Vergessenheit begründet sich zum anderen sicher auch mit der heute fehlenden bzw. geringen Präsenz auf dem Buchmarkt.[48]

---

45   Ralf Georg Bogner, *Germanistik* 45 (2004), p. 442.
46   Luise Glaser-Lotz, *Frankfurter Allgemeine Zeitung*, 2 August 2003, p. 60.
47   Manfred Frühwacht and Joachim Schulmerich, *Wege zum Wein: Kulturgeschichtlicher Gang durch die Stadt Alzenau und benachbarte Weinorte* (CoCon, 2011), p. 158.
48   In a letter to me dated 15 August 2011.

There is a general reluctance, Vollmer argues, to pay the inevitably large sum of money for his edition. However, he remains apparently determined not to give up, but to go ahead and produce 'eine erschwingliche Auswahlsammlung von Schnacks Werken in Taschenbuchform'. He continues to believe that Schnack's poetry, and especially *Tier rang*, deserves a wider readership: 'Ein so sprachgewaltiger Gedichtband wie *Tier rang gewaltig mit Tier* zählt sicherlich zu den großen — aber dennoch heute nicht ausreichend bekannten und gewürdigten — Leistungen des lyrischen Expressionismus.'[49] Another factor in the poet's virtual disappearance from public attention is almost certainly his steady reorientation of focus away from poetry to prose, particularly to essays and reviews. There is also a sense of scattering of resources, of a rather frivolous dilettantism. In his obituary Karl Krolow 'covers' Schnack's poetic career simply by calling him 'ein eigenwilliger Vertreter eines exotisch-bildstarken Expressionismus' and making very curt mention of the four Expressionist volumes.[50] Otherwise the obituary amounts to a generous appreciation of Schnack's prose work. This is also the pattern followed by his brother Friedrich's literary career, but whereas the latter appeared to go out of his way to seek publicity and to garner public awards,[51] Anton mounted what looks from the outside like an almost obsessive campaign of withdrawal from the public eye. A brief consideration of Friedrich's career offers an instructive and illuminating source of contrasts and similarities.

Born on 5 March 1888, four years before his brother, Friedrich died on 6 March 1977. He worked as a bank official in Würzburg, served in the army in Turkey and was interned for a brief period in 1918/19 on the island of Prinkipo. As in the case of Anton, it is unlikely that Friedrich took part in any actual fighting. He worked, like his brother, as an editor, first for the *Dresdner Neueste Nachrichten* and then for the *Neue Badische Landeszeitung* in Mannheim. In 1926 he became a freelance writer and, after much travelling, lived in Hellerau near Dresden, in Baden-Baden and finally in Munich. He was an astonishingly prolific writer, much more so than Anton. He produced collections of poetry, numerous novels, short stories, travel books, autobiographical pieces, and well-regarded studies of plants, animals and insects. If Anton was known as 'der Mädchen-Schnack' because he wrote frequently about girls and girls' names, his brother was 'der Schmetterlings-Schnack'.[52] Moreover, there seems to have been no relaxation in Friedrich's literary efforts between 1913, when he published his first collection of poetry *Herauf, uralter Tag*, and 1975, when his final prose work (entitled *Auf der Treppe der Zeit: das Jahr*

49   Ibid.
50   Karl Krolow, 'Gedenkwort für Anton Schnack', in *Deutsche Akademie für Sprache und Dichtung*, Jahrbuch 1973 (Lambert Schneider, 1974), pp. 231–33.
51   Beginning with some successful manoeuvring to get himself elected onto the committee of the Preußische Akademie der Künste in 1930, defeating Else Lasker-Schüler 14–6 in the final count. See Inge Jens, *Dichter zwischen rechts und links* (Kiepenheuer, 1994), pp. 172–73. The Stadtarchiv in Würzburg contains numerous newspaper cuttings in which Friedrich is photographed receiving honours and giving lectures, frequently on anniversaries of Max Dauthendey's birth — Dauthendey being Würzburg's favourite son.
52   See Friedrich Schnack, *Das Leben der Schmetterlinge* (Hegner, 1928), translated into English as *The Life of the Butterfly* (Allen & Unwin, 1932).

mit Estrella) appeared. His complete works were published in two volumes in 1961, he has been the subject of at least three dissertations and he was one of the 'Drei fränkische Autoren' to be honoured with an exhibition of his work in Nuremberg in 1968. He won a host of public awards, most notably the Lessing-Preis in 1929 and the Erster Kulturpreis der Stadt Würzburg in 1965. Like his brother, he evinced no interest in national politics during the 1930s but, for reasons which are unclear, his relationship with Anton moved from remote to non-existent. Perhaps the problem lay in his relentlessly prolific writing: his bibliography is three or four times longer than Anton's, but he produced nothing as striking or memorable as *Tier rang* or even Anton's three Expressionist volumes. One contemporary reviewer identified a major difference between the brothers' poetic talents:

> Wie Anton von der Malerei abhängt, so hängt Friedrich von der Musik ab. Jenem ist es um die bunten Reize der Farben, diesem um die warmen Klänge der Töne zu tun. Anton Schnack ist ein dichtender Maler, Friedrich Schnack ein dichtender Musiker.[53]

There is indeed a painterly quality about Anton's poetry and little that can be judged 'musical', but the two brothers do have something in common: they share the same fate, after their deaths, of failing to engage critical attention and interest. The entry on Friedrich Schnack in the *Deutsches Literatur-Lexikon* ends, 'geehrt, geliebt, vergessen'.[54]

Anton's campaign to safeguard his privacy was conducted with a fierce determination. This campaign, which he never felt able or willing to explain or justify, may itself have contributed to the subsequent neglect of his prose and poetry. Contemporary history, local and national, is astonishing for its virtually complete absence from his post-First World War writing. He did little to boost his public popularity or promote his own work, even refusing an invitation to read his poems to children in a local school (the Mary Ward School in Aschaffenburg).[55] He never spoke about his work, or his First World War experiences, to anyone, he did not give interviews (until his seventy-fifth birthday), he hated publicity, he played no part in the local community, he read a local paper but showed little interest in national or international affairs, and he even left it to his wife to open the door to visitors. On the other hand, he was something of a practical joker who enjoyed 'clowning around' on family occasions: Vollmer includes in his afterword old photographs of Anton playing about on bikes as 'der berädete Dichter' or trying out silly bucket-shaped hats as 'der Hutzauberer'.[56] He enjoyed performing party tricks within the confines of his secluded garden and in the company of his immediate family. However, he ventured out only rarely:

---

53   Julius Kühn, 'Die Brüder Schnack', Manuscript Department Marbach.
54   *Deutsches Literatur-Lexikon*, ed. by Heinz Rupp and Carl Ludwig Lang, 39 vols (Saur, 1993), xv, p. 532.
55   This account of Schnack's life and routines is based on two long interviews granted to me in August 2011 by his niece Frau Ursula Stickler, born 1934 in Kahl am Main.
56   I, 455, 467.

> Er hatte Hemmungen, über die Türschwelle eines lokalen Geschäfts zu gehen, um seine Zigarren zu kaufen; er lebte total zurückgezogen, er hatte Angst vor allem, vor Stufen, vor Dunklem, vor Leuten; er hielt immer seine Distanz. Von Schlechtem wollte er nicht wissen.[57]

It seems that he avoided 'problems' with his family by the simple means of never seeing them, and he engaged in a kind of silent and long-range stand-off with his brother Friedrich. The brothers, as we have seen, did not get on. Anton did not want to compete or felt that he could not compete, and perhaps he believed that, if he emerged from his sanctuary in Kahl, he would find himself in open competition. In 1973 Friedrich did not attend Anton's funeral. It was a very low-key affair, 'Anton war lautlos gestorben',[58] and his grave in the Kahl cemetery is now badly overgrown. It is tempting to regard this seemingly deliberate resolve not to keep himself and his work before the public eye as a contributory factor in the demise of his literary reputation. And so the original question remains: how is one to explain the trajectory of a poetic career which moves from being very warmly praised in 1920 and subsequently elevated to the company of Wilfred Owen and other unarguably great war poets to a point where it is left to residents of his hometown to keep his memory alive?

Richard Holmes, the military historian, comments rather ruefully on the huge impact which the poetry of Wilfred Owen has on perceptions of the First World War, especially among the young: 'Whenever I go into schools, I always find myself up against Wilfred Owen.'[59] It is extremely difficult to imagine that any German historian visiting a school in Germany would have the same experience with regard to Anton Schnack, and the huge discrepancy, Bridgwater asserts (but does not elucidate),[60] has historical roots. The remarkable resurgence of interest in the poetry of the First World War in the 1960s in England had no equivalent in Germany. George Walter, the editor of a recent anthology of (English) First World War poetry, ascribes this revival to

> a renewed fascination with the war during the 'sixties, stimulated by four years' worth of fiftieth anniversaries between 1964 and 1968, and which found expression in a variety of ways: in popular historical studies such as A. J. P. Taylor's *The First World War: An Illustrated History*, in ambitious television productions such as the BBC's *The Great War*, in plays and musicals like the Theatre Workshop's *Oh What a Lovely War* and in feature films like *For King and Country*. More importantly, it led to a rediscovery and reassessment of the literature of the war.[61]

No similar development took place in Germany. A combination of self-consciousness, shame and guilt stifled any burgeoning interest in the poetry of the two World Wars, though, in the late 1920s, there was, of course, a surge of interest

57   Frau Stickler in conversation with me.
58   Ibid.
59   Richard Holmes, quoted in Jerome Monaghan, 'A Monumental Task', *Times Educational Supplement*, 30, 15 November 2002, p. 21.
60   Bridgwater, p. 96.
61   *The Penguin Book of First World War Poetry*, ed. by George Walter (Penguin, 2004), p. xxviii.

in First World War novels, focusing on Ernst Jünger's *In Stahlgewittern*, Ludwig Renn's *Krieg*, Arnold Zweig's *Der Streit um den Sergeanten Grischa* and Remarque's *Im Westen nichts Neues*.[62] There is some substance in the rather cynical suggestion that because Schnack's poetry did not suffer the same retrospectively 'glamorous' fate of ending up, like Remarque's novel, a casualty of the book-burning atrocity of 10 May 1933, it did not earn the same degree of credibility or achieve the same level of notorious publicity. And, of course, a comparatively short novel is in any case much more accessible, and less daunting, than sixty long-lined sonnets. Moreover, Schnack, unlike Trakl and Stramm, survived the First World War, did not die (comparatively) young, lived on for another fifty years and, therefore, had ample time to (be seen to) run out of creative inspiration, even to tarnish his reputation, or, at least, not to build on it. Perhaps, despite the championing voices, Bridgwater's and Vollmer's particularly, an obvious truth, some might claim, is that Schnack's poetry has been neglected and largely forgotten because it deserves to be. In an attempt to explain and interpret what is, by any account, an intriguing literary career and a long life lived out against the admittedly distant background of a disastrous period in Germany's and the world's history, it is easy to speculate and theorize, but ultimately a fair assessment of a writer's work should veer away from speculation and issue into a close analysis of the work. In Schnack's case, that involves an examination of his eight volumes of poetry and individual poems within those volumes. Otherwise the sporadic assertions of excellence — the most recent being Peter Watson's claim that *Tier rang* is 'generally regarded as the best single collection of war poems produced by a German poet'[63] — remain tantalisingly unchallenged, neither corroborated nor repudiated, a reflex response rather than a considered conclusion.

At this point, and in light of the cursory treatment to which Schnack's work has been subjected, it is wholly appropriate to pay tribute to the pioneering work of Patrick Bridgwater and Hartmut Vollmer. In his *The German Poets of the First World War*, Bridgwater rescued the names and the reputations of a number of war poets who otherwise might have suffered complete literary neglect. His championing of such poets as Wilhelm Klemm, Alfred Lichtenstein, Karl Bröger and Heinrich Lersch (particularly of Lersch's magnificent 'Massengräber' which 'can stand beside the best of, say, Anton Schnack'[64]) is founded in meticulous and sympathetic interpretation of individual poems. In his 'authoritative critical survey of the subject', as one reviewer calls it, Bridgwater makes clear those criteria by which he is measuring his selected poets. Schnack, for example, creates 'a heightened compassionate realism', covers a wide range of war experience in poems which are 'strictly moral in the ends', employs stylization, brilliantly uses the sonnet form and,

62   See the chapter 'Remembering the War', in David Midgley, *Writing Weimar* (Oxford University Press, 2000), pp. 226–59.
63   Peter Watson, *The German Genius* (Simon and Schuster, 2010), pp. 550–52. See also p. 548 where Watson again echoes Bridgwater in linking Schnack with Stramm and Trakl as being 'outstanding'. It is as if Bridgwater's original judgement is merely being repeated.
64   Bridgwater, p. 133.

above all, displays nobility, humanity and majesty in his treatment of the subject.[65] Perhaps Bridgwater's most valuable contribution (apart from bringing a number of fine war poets to public attention and then taking them seriously through a series of scrupulous analyses) is what the same reviewer calls his 'continuous concern with teasing out the form in apparently shapeless works, showing how form illustrates meaning'. By seeking to establish the source and date of every single poem and essay, scattered over a considerable number of sometimes ephemeral publications, and by painstakingly compiling the known facts of Schnack's life, Vollmer rendered an even more valuable service for anyone interested in following and understanding Schnack's development as a writer. It is not at all surprising that in his Acknowledgements he has so many individuals and archives to thank for their support, including a full page on the Tutepastell branch of Schnack's family in Mexico. Between them, Bridgwater and Vollmer have done a great service to Schnack and his admirers.

★　★　★　★　★

In 1910, the same year as Anton Schnack was coming to the end of his undistinguished secondary school career in Hammelburg in Lower Franconia and the presence of a new cultural movement in explicit revolt against (what its proponents saw as) the tired conventions of Naturalism and Impressionism was beginning to make itself felt in cities throughout Europe, the poet and critic Margarete Susman published her highly influential book, *Das Wesen der modernen deutschen Lyrik*.[66] By 1918, she had published four collections of poetry, and having in the 1890s studied in Munich, she had moved from Switzerland to study in Berlin and later to live in southern Germany. It would have been difficult for her as a very active writer and journalist not to be aware of the new, exciting cultural phenomenon whose strands have traditionally been gathered under the name of Expressionism. She certainly had views about the movement which she marshalled in a full-length study, *Der Expressionismus*.[67] Susman is best known today, though, for her literary-historical commentary and observation, more particularly for her insistence on the non-biographical, autonomous 'Ich' of the lyric voice. In the process she argued that the self of the poems is part of the fiction of the poem and does not establish biographical identity. The significance and implication of that insight are huge and have particular relevance for Expressionist poetry, in which the lyrical I in its multiple manifestations is constantly confirmed and asserted.

On several occasions in his afterword to Schnack's *Werke*, Vollmer refers to the biographical nature of Schnack's work:

> Es [the 'harmlessness' of Schnack's work] resultiert besonders aus seiner ausge-prägten Verbundenheit mit der Natur und der fränkischen Heimat und der unentwegten Zuwendung zur eigenen Biographie, vor allem in Form von (oft

65   Edward A. McCobb, reviewing Bridgwater's book in *Modern Language Review*, 81 (1986), pp. 1044–45. McCobb himself quotes from Bridgwater, pp. 97–99.
66   Margarete Susman, *Das Wesen der modernen deutschen Lyrik* (Strecker & Schröder, 1910).
67   Margarete Susman, *Expressionismus* (Städtische Kunstgewerbeschule, 1925).

melancholisch, aber auch humorvoll-ironisch getönten) Erinnerungen an die Kindheit und Jugend.[68]

Vollmer proceeds to underline the point by consistently relating the facts and chronology of Schnack's life and inserting them into an account of Schnack's work which is then thus placed in a firm biographical framework. For Vollmer, Schnack is deeply implicated in his work, the protagonist within it, a felt presence no matter how many imaginative games he plays, dreams he pursues or fanciful flights he makes (and, as we shall see, he prides himself on the fertility of his imagination), no matter how many alter egos he creates for himself. From first poem[69] to last,[70] from first prose essay[71] to (posthumous) last,[72] 'das empirische Ich' is either actually present or strongly suspected of being present. Throughout his life, Schnack's poetry is thus based unashamedly on his own experiences, a life sepia-tinted with nostalgia and one which he dreams up and invents and embellishes. This should not surprise us, because at various points in his short prose works he explains his methods. On one occasion, for example, he casts himself as a pining lover at his desk and he relates how the fictional title-figure Elena has sent him some flowers and letters:

> Nun stehen sie [the marguerites] unter der Hut meine Lampe, die mich Nacht für Nacht bescheint, wenn ich dasitze und die Geschichten niederschreibe, die ich erlebt habe oder erleben möchte, oder die mir zwischen Traum und Wachen in die Vorstellung und in das erregte Spiel meiner Phantasie kommen.[73]

He has his dreams, he sets his imagination loose, he engages in wishful thinking, he inhabits various roles, and at times, for example in his brief Expressionist phase, a tendency towards self-mythologizing, even self-aggrandizing, emerges. A kind of fictionalized autobiography or documentary fiction results. He clearly does not feel confined within one single personality and grants himself free access to a range of different identities (wanderer, adventurer, sybarite, explorer) between which he slips effortlessly. It is a straightforward and seamless process because the lyrical I has created for himself the space where he wants to be and the selves he has always dreamed of assuming. Susman writes of 'das lyrische Ich' as 'eine Form, die der Dichter aus seinem gegebenen Ich erschafft'.[74] Moreover, it is not difficult to find examples, way beyond the period of German Expressionism, where her argument still resonates. Almost one hundred years later, in 'Parenthesis' in his collection *A History of the World in 10½ Chapters*, Julian Barnes, musing on the art of the novelist, writes:

> Poets seem to write more easily about love than prose writers. For a start, they own that flexible 'I' (when I say 'I' you will want to know within a paragraph

68   I, 441.
69   'Einer Italienerin', *Die Aktion*, 5.31/32, 7 August 1915, cols.399ff.
70   'Blanchefleur, die Weiße Blüte', *Spektrum des Geistes*, 21.5 (1970), pp. 80f.
71   'Ma', *Die Sichel*, 1, August 1919, pp. 19–21.
72   'Hymne an eine Landschaft', in *Der Spessart*, H.11, November 1976, S. 20.
73   Schnack, 'Elina', in *Werke*, II, 387–91 (pp. 387–88).
74   Susman, p. 16.

or two whether I mean Julian Barnes or someone invented; a poet can shimmy between the two, getting credit for deep feeling and objectivity).[75]

Writing both poetry and prose, Schnack shares none of Barnes's discomfort and 'shimmies' with apparent ease between the empirical and the lyrical I: indeed he welcomes the interchange between the two. Barnes's American contemporary, Philip Roth, offers a different retrospective, less compromising slant on his own career: 'Making false biography, false history, concocting a half-imaginary existence out of the actual drama of my life is my life.'[76]

Schnack was at pains not 'to make a drama of his life', but there is no doubt that his life in good measure was made up of selves and events he created for himself. The habit of casting himself as an adventurer, wanderer, an intrepid explorer, as Don Juan, Casanova and Robinson Crusoe, is never broken. The empirical self, though, passes through various phases — a short-lived flirtation with Expressionism, then the violent shock of service in the frontline in northern France, a decade of travel in the 1920s, a long period of 'inner emigration' and finally, after a short brush with the American military at the end of the Second World War, almost three decades of retreat to his hometown in the familiar Franconian countryside. Schnack's poetry and prose amount to a faithful and accurate chronicle of his life, but at the same time his imagination rarely flags, his dreams remain vivid, and the lyrical self never tires of 'creating' fictional selves. The lyrical self, under the banner of Expressionism, vulnerability and virtual extinction, soon ensues, before a kind of balance and reconciliation are achieved in the long phase of studied withdrawal. However, in the aftermath of the self-indulgent hedonism of his gap year, the febrile, social atmosphere in Munich, and the grim realities of his time on the frontline, it is as a full-fledged Expressionist poet that he casts himself and first introduces himself to us.

75   Julian Barnes, 'Parenthesis', in *A History of the World in 10½ Chapters* (Jonathan Cape, 1989), p. 227.
76   Philip Roth, 'The Art of Fiction', interview with Hermione Lee, *Paris Review*, 93 (1984) [accessed 8 March 2025].

CHAPTER 2

Positioning Schnack — Expressionism

Der Expressionismus ist also, wie jeder Gott
dieser Art, nicht zu photographieren und nicht
zu definieren. Er war ein Sammelsurium
von Tendenzen, Namen und Compagnons.[1]

Anton Schnack's name, as we have seen, appears rarely in literary histories and anthologies: where it does, the narrative of his career follows an apparently simple pattern. He began that literary career as an Expressionist poet, produced a cycle of First World War poetry of remarkable power and originality and then, settling in Franconia, dedicated himself to composing lighter verse and prose in a bucolic, almost Georgian vein. Of course, no literary career, especially one which lasted more than fifty years — as Schnack's did — is without its idiosyncrasies and ambiguities, its detours and distractions, occasions when a writer, perhaps reacting to particular historical events or a dramatic change in personal circumstances, makes a sudden unexpected break away from what had previously seemed a straightforward trajectory. In Schnack's case, such an occasion — or rather series of occasions — clearly occurred not only in 1914, but also in the 1930s and 1940s, where the picture of his life and career (and thus any account of them) does indeed become more blurred and problematic. About one aspect of that career at least there can, however, be little dispute: his debut as an Expressionist poet and a prolific contributor to various Expressionist magazines and publications, including all of the most influential and substantial.[2]

In the section 'Zu Leben und Werk Anton Schnacks', in the first volume of the poet's published works, Hartmut Vollmer simply takes it as read that Schnack was caught up in the artistic movement which Paul Raabe characterized as a 'Stimmengewirr und Gesinnungsbabel [...] ein Sammelbecken aller wirren und unentwirrbaren Strömungen'.[3] Vollmer refers to Schnack as an original 'Lyriker des Expressionismus', as a writer who published 'keine spektakulären Bücher abgesehen

---

1   Ludwig Marcuse, *Mein zwanzigstes Jahrhundert* (List, 1960), p. 74.

2   The term 'Expressionism' has been capitalized to indicate the specific historical phenomenon of that movement between the years 1905 and 1925, as opposed to any sort of general expressionistic tendency in the arts before or after that period.

3   Paul Raabe, 'Eine historische Skizze', preface to *Die Zeitschriften und Sammlungen des literarischen Expressionismus 1910–1921* (Metzler, 1964), pp. 16–17.

von seinen ersten expressionistischen Gedichtbänden' and who expressed himself in the 'in atemlosen gereimten Langzeilen entströmende, von sinnlichen Eindrücken bestimmte Diktion, die zum lyrischen Charakteristikum des Expressionisten Anton Schnack wurde' (I, 448). The label 'Expressionist poet' is thus attached without further elaboration, and Schnack's credentials as a bona fide member of the proliferating Expressionist groupings in southern Germany are asserted, without a gloss or qualification. Vollmer includes Schnack's volume of war poetry, *Tier rang gewaltig mit Tier*, in the writer's portfolio of characteristically Expressionist work. This seems right and justified. After all, what Vollmer defines as the 'wesentliche Stilmerkmale des expressionistischen Dichters Anton Schnack' — 'die sprachliche Dynamik und Impulsivität, die "überquellende" Bilderflut, der wortgewaltige Ausdruck inneren Erlebens, die Dominanz sinnlicher Wahrnehmungen, die den Versen "Wahrhaftigkeit", Authentizität verleihen' (I, 450) — can be applied, without amendment, to the war poetry, although a special case needs to be made for that poetry. 'Dionysisch' and 'schäumend' are two further epithets which Vollmer quotes to restate the Expressionist character of Schnack's early work (I, 445).

There is no record of Anton Schnack's ever applying the term 'Expressionist' to himself or to his work, nor does the word 'Expressionism' appear in any of his published prose or poetry,[4] but this is not unusual. Neither Heym nor Stramm nor Trakl, for example, three of the most typically Expressionist poets in Pinthus's *Menschheitsdämmerung*, used this term, which emerged for the first time in 1911, with reference to Georges Braque and Pablo Picasso.

It was used, for example, in the catalogue for the twenty-second exhibition of the Berlin Sezession, but it was only as a result of Kasimir Edschmid's influential lecture 'Expressionismus in der Dichtung', held in December 1917 and printed in *Die Neue Rundschau* in March 1918, that 'Expressionism' entered common currency.[5] Corroboration of Vollmer's confident ascription of Schnack's name to the movement can be found in contemporary literature — in a footnote to the written version of a speech delivered in 1920 by Kasimir Edschmid, Schnack is described as someone who published 'Expressionistische Lyrikbände'.[6] And subsequently, in 2003, on the thirtieth anniversary of the poet's death, a contributor (unnamed) to a local newspaper writes:

> Es scheint, als ob der expressionistische Dichter das Inferno, das er an der Front des Ersten Weltkriegs in Frankreich erlebt hat, nur schwer in Worte oder Sätze fassen kann.[7]

The heading of an article in another contemporary paper reads:

> Expressionistischer Dichter der Heimat und der Stille. Kahl begeht dreißigsten Todestag von Anton Schnack.'[8]

4   The nearest he gets is a fleeting reference, almost an aside, to Futurism in a short essay 'Donnersammlung anlegen' in the collection 'Flirt mit dem Alltag' (1956), II, 334.
5   See Peter Sprengel, *Geschichte der deutschsprachigen Literatur 1900–1918* (Beck, 2004), pp. 107–10.
6   Kasimir Edschmid, *Frühe Schriften* (Luchterhand, 1970), p. 307.
7   Anon., 'Das Inferno "Verdun" und "Brevier der Zärtlichkeit"', *Main-Echo*, 6 December 2003.
8   L. G-L, 'Expressionistischer Dichter der Heimat und der Stille', *Rhein-Main*, 2 August 2003, no.

These ascriptions, far apart in time, are, of course, brought together on the simply worded memorial stone in Kahl cemetery: 'Anton Schnack Dichter des Expressionismus [...]'.

It is hardly surprising that Schnack should have earned this label, for this new exciting artistic movement appeared to open its doors to anyone who wished to enter. In his personal account of the development of the movement, Kasimir Edschmid argued that the huge range of writers who could be guaranteed to appear in what he called 'die neue Menge' — from, predictably, René Schickele, Ernst Stadler, Franz Werfel and Frank Wedekind to more marginal 'Expressionists' like Hans Carossa, Richard Dehmel, Johannes Schlaf and Ernst Lissauer — pointed to just one conclusion: 'Daß die literarische Bewegung dieser Tage nicht ausschließlich geschlossene Gesellschaft war *huis clos*, wie Sartre später sagte, sondern eher ein nach allzuviel Seiten hin offener Club.'[9]

The wholly inclusive nature of this literary phenomenon and hence the ubiquity of Expressionist writers led to a surfeit which appalled both Kurt Pinthus, the editor of *Menschheitsdämmerung*, and those initiates granted entry to that anthology's sacred pages: 'Es gab [at the time of its publication] in Deutschland plötzlich offenbar nur noch Expressionisten, und es grauste den Kenner und die Eingeweihten vor dieser Heuschreckenplage des Geistes.'[10] Another idiosyncratic metaphor underlines the diverse nature of the poets whom Pinthus *did* include: 'Zweihundertfünfundsiebzig Gedichte und dreiundzwanzig Autoren von explosiver Spannkraft und intensiver Gläubigkeit — sie kommen nicht aus einer wohl assortierten Handschuhschachtel, und sie brauchen keine katilinarische Existenz-Platzanweisung, so gut es auch der Zoowärter des Rowohltschen Etablissements meinte.'[11] It is not unusual, however, for modern critics and commentators to call the iconic status of Pinthus's anthology into question. Peter Sprengel, for example, draws attention to what he calls Pinthus's rather dubious account of the 'Entwicklungsgeschichte des Expressionismus', to the disproportionate amount of space allocated to his 'friends', Hasenclever and Werfel, represented by nineteen and twenty-seven poems respectively, and to the anthologist's over-emphasis on the significance of 'Menschheitspathos' in the literary movement.[12] While Schnack was not selected by Pinthus, he was one of innumerable writers swept along by a movement which descended, like a 'plague of locusts' in Edschmid's phrase, on many German cities — in his case particularly Munich. Edschmid's series of negatives rather ironically captures the essence of this glimpse into a promised land: 'Kein Programm und kolossales Durcheinander. Weder Schule noch Zenakel noch Rezept.'[13] Schnack's three early Expressionist volumes will in their turn be paeans to this suddenly burgeoning freedom which manifested itself in all kinds of different ways, not just artistically and editorially, but also in the spheres of sexuality and morality.

177.

9   Kasimir Edschmid, *Lebendiger Expressionismus* (Desch, 1961), p. 199.
10   Ibid., p. 200.
11   Ibid., p. 208.
12   Sprengel, pp. 586–87.
13   Edschmid, *Lebendiger Expressionismus*, p. 200.

*   *   *   *   *

Despite the 'heterogeneity of the Expressionist rebellions' (sic)[14] and multiplicity of personalities who for a brief while aligned themselves with those rebellions, it is possible to see the movement as a single dynamic, if hugely disparate, artistic enterprise. Expressionism's recorded life-span was short: cultural historians tend to restrict it to fifteen years between 1910 and 1925. In his memoirs Max Krell (1887–1962), writer, critic and editor of the Ullstein publishing house, describes the movement's astonishing impact:

> Es [Der Expressionismus] wurde an keinem Ort und überall geboren; sein Kommen lag in der Luft. Er hatte viele Väter. Man begegnete ihm zuerst in den jungen kämpferischen Zeitschriften Berlins (Der Sturm, Die Aktion, Die Weißen Blätter, Darmstadts (Das Tribunal), Innsbrucks (Der Bremer) in den Kabaretts von Zürich, in den Vortragssälen Wiens und Frankfurts, auf den Theatern von Hamburg und Prag. Er drang überall durch, wo Deutsch gesprochen wurde, und seine Bücher erschienen zuerst in unbekannten Verlagen und eroberten schnell die grossen.[15]

Krell's depiction demonstrates how it is quite easy to lapse into quasi-expressionistic hyperbole when it comes to any attempt to assess Expressionism's character and impact.[16] Nevertheless, there is no doubt that for a short while, even though overshadowed by a catastrophic war and that war's aftermath, Expressionism was a remarkable, widespread European phenomenon. It was a movement of explicit protest, of rage against the establishment, reacting against the prevailing aesthetic prejudices — the limited outlook of Naturalism with its subjection of the artist's/poet's voice to external reality and its emphasis on social determinism and mimetic reality, the implacable rigidity of Stefan George-style 'art pour l'art' programme — and against what it saw as the superficiality and frivolous sensibility of Impressionism. The principal object of Expressionist scorn and revolt was the stultifying values of middle-class morality and materialism: a 'Bürgerschreck-Atmosphäre' prevailed.[17] If 'Epatez le bourgeois' was a typical Expressionist slogan, the conviction on which the whole movement rested was contained in Kasimir Edschmid's assertion that 'Seit der Romantik war Stagnation.'[18] A consequence was that there was a powerful urge to favour extremes, of feeling and attitude, and to prize unreason[19] and emotional and physical intensity for their own sakes. 'Aufbruch' was another popular mantra, encapsulating the determination to make

14   Stephen Eric Bronner and Douglas Kellner (eds), *Passion and Rebellion: The Expressionist Heritage* (Croom Helm, 1983), p. 6.
15   Max Krell, 'Expressionismus — Glück und Ende', in *Expressionismus: Aufzeichnungen und Erinnerungen der Zeitgenossen*, ed. by Paul Raabe (Walter, 1965), pp. 306–08 (p. 306).
16   Donahue (ed.), p. ix.
17   Franz Jung, *Der Weg nach unten* (Luchterhand, 1961), p. 69.
18   Kasimir Edschmid, 'Expressionismus in der Dichtung', *Die Neue Rundschau*, 1.29 (1918), pp. 359–74, repr. in Thomas Anz and Michael Stark, *Expressionismus: Manifeste und Dokumente zur deutschen Literatur* (Metzler, 1982), pp. 42–55 (p. 43).
19   See Oswald Pander, 'Revolution der Sprache', *Das junge Deutschland* 1.5 (1918), pp. 147–48, repr. in Anz and Stark, *Manifeste*, pp. 612–13.

a new start, at whatever cost, a sense that an era was coming to an end, and needed to come to an end. Revolution and a feverishly 'subversive excitement', borne along by an ultimately destabilizing and unfocused enthusiasm and by promise of a better future, hung in the air. For some that revolution was not a matter of bringing down the government or deposing the emperor, but a massive ethical mission, a kind of humanitarian epiphany. For others revolution meant revolution in the traditional street-fighting sense. All tendencies and preferences seemed accommodated.

At the same time, Expressionist poets and dramatists, in particular, were driven by a compulsion to aggrandize the cause and to apostrophize the means, frequently with the noblest intentions, in order to realize, before a sometimes bewildered and sceptical public, its often eloquently, but sometimes unclearly articulated aims and projects. Not for nothing were the Café des Westens in Berlin and the Café Stefanie in Munich known colloquially as 'Café Größenwahn'. With religion no longer the centre of contemporary culture, a grandiose humanitarianism with a kind of all-pervasive religiosity and a secularized messianic fervour took over. Nietzsche's glorification of life on earth amounting to a fervent vitalism lay at the core of the Expressionist writer's credo with the result that Expressionist programmes and manifestos were founded in the conviction that no holds (moral, political) were barred, nothing was out of bounds or beyond the pale. The whole world (no less) was available for necessary redemption and accessible to Expressionist zeal. Between 1911, when Schnack left school in Hammelburg, and 1925, when he began to travel outside Germany, he experienced their febrile atmosphere at first hand, initially as a student and young bachelor about town (principally Munich and Darmstadt), then as a features editor and theatre critic on the *Darmstädter Zeitung* and then on the *Neue Badische Landeszeitung* in Mannheim. Moving in these cultural circles, in and out of clubs and cafés, to and from magazine editors' offices, Schnack could not have failed to notice and absorb the revolutionary and openly subversive spirit. He could have rejected it as the latest fashion, or he could have resolved to make his own contribution. He chose the latter course.

The call, implicit and explicit in Expressionist poetry and drama, to defy parental and state authority and to challenge an increasingly industrialized, dehumanized society, overseen by a stale culture establishment wedded to the past, had a considerable appeal for whole swathes of diverse writers, while the threat, and the reality, of war only served to intensify a sense of emergency. The appeal was urgent, often strident and extreme, presenting itself in imperatives, proclamations, lectures and manifestos:

> Die Tatsache dieser Bewegung, die man ruhig Expressionismus nennen kann, ist nicht zu bezweifeln [...]. Eine Bewegung ist keine Mache oder das Arrangement einer Gruppe Interessenten. Vielmehr, aus zahlreichen zunächst dunklen Ursachen sozialer politischer menschlicher Art wächst sie, hier flammt es, dort flammt es bei Feinfühligen, Scharfhörigen, Hellsichtigen auf, durch sie kommt die Maschine zu ihren ersten Kolbenstößen und Umdrehungen.[20]

---

20   Alfred Döblin, 'Von der Freiheit eines Dichtermenschen', in *Aufsätze zur Literatur* (Walter, 1963), pp. 23–32 (pp. 23–25).

It was difficult to ignore. Even some of the most distinguished writers of the day — Thomas Mann, Rainer Maria Rilke, Stefan George and Robert Musil — who were without exception out of sympathy with all that Expressionism stood for and seemed to represent — found time and space to pass judgement on it. Rilke's repudiation of the movement, for example, is contained in a letter to the actress Anni Mewes in September 1919 and is helpful and instructive in enabling us to situate Anton Schnack within the movement. Dismissing (what he sees as) those Expressionist writers who advocate love for all mankind, Rilke uses the image of a train leaping off the rails to voice his principal concern that Expressionism is formally and emotionally undisciplined and virtually out of control. For Rilke, it mistakes an appearance of intensity for the actual quality of intensity and is a premature manifestation of inner dynamism. It is, in short, a clear example of the 'image-less act' ('Tun ohne Bild') as defined in his Ninth Elegy, activity without necessary intellectual and artistic shaping. In a striking visual image, he deplores the way in which the Expressionist poet's inspiration and good intentions (which Rilke does not deny him) inevitably degenerate into arbitrariness and adventitiousness:

> Der Expressionist, dieser explosiv gewordene Innenmensch, der die Lava seines kochenden Gemüts über alle Dinge gießt, um darauf zu bestehen, daß die zufällige Form, in der die Krusten erstarren, der neue, der künftige, der gültige Umriß des Daseins sei, ist eben ein Verzweifelter.[21]

Rilke is by no means alone in attaching images of volcanic eruption and seismic explosions to his depiction of a movement which regularly invites metaphors. Thomas Mann writes of the Expressionists' 'souveränen, explosiven rücksichtslos schöpferischen Erlaß des Geistes'[22] while Gottfried Benn, retrospectively, describes Expressionism as 'ein Aufstand mit Eruptionen, Ekstasierung, Hass, neuer Menschheitssehnsucht'.[23] In similar vein, in his résumé of the movement, Alfred Döblin, writing in 1918, has recourse to the image of chemical reactions:

> Es war und ist eine Bewegung, eine atmosphärische Welle, wie ein wanderndes barometrisches Maximum und Minimum. Keine Richtung im Gegenteil: Gärung ohne Richtung: etwa Zeitströmung im Sinne von Brandes,[24] nicht einmal so bestimmt und gezielt wie etwa ganz allgemein 'Romantik'.[25]

Friedrich Gundolf, speaking for Stefan George, and, like Rilke, focusing on what he sees as Expressionism's formlessness and atomization of language, draws on an analogy with physics:

21   Letter to Anni Mewes, 12 September 1919 in: Rainer Maria Rilke, *Briefe in zwei Bänden*, II: *1919 bis 1926*, ed. Horst Nalewski (Insel, 1991), pp. 30–31.

22   Thomas Mann, *Betrachtungen einer Unpolitischen* (Fischer, 1918), pp. 563–83, repr. in Anz and Stark, *Manifeste*, pp. 90–92 (p. 90).

23   Gottfried Benn, 'Einleitung zu *Lyrik des expressionistischen Jahrzehnts*', in *Sämtliche Werke*, VI: *Prosa 4*, ed. by Holger Hof (Klett-Cotta, 2001), pp. 208–20 (p. 218).

24   Georg Brandes (1842–1927): best known for his *Die Hauptströmungen der Literatur des 19. Jahrhunderts*, lectures given at Copenhagen University and published from 1872.

25   Alfred Döblin, 'Von der Freiheit eines Dichtermenschen', *Die Neue Rundschau*, 29.2 (1918), pp. 843–50, repr. in Anz and Stark, *Manifeste*, pp. 69–74 (p. 69).

> Man zerschlägt die Sprache in ihre alogischen, augenlosen Kleinteile, in ihr vorgeistiges Kinderlallen, weil dies Zerschlagen selbst schon etwas 'ausdrückt.' Was auf bloßem Zweck oder Trieb beruht, wird mit irgendeinem Selbstzweck oder Selbsttrieb enden, d.h. in der Atomisierung [...] jede Zielerei [sic] endet im Tanz der Atome durcheinander oder im Kreisen der Atome um sich selbst. Der Expressionismus schafft keine Keimzellen des neuen Lebens, sondern zeigt die Keimzellen des alten.[26]

The essence of Döblin's and George's (and others') critiques is that Expressionism is emotionally incontinent as it cuts a swathe through traditional syntax without producing anything new and is ultimately direction-less and literally point-less. By this token, language, as used by Expressionist poets, 'explodes', exposed as it is to consistently high emotional temperature, and the shards come down where they will. In fact, it is possible to discern two principal directions or wings, even if the profiles of both are blurred, volatile and flabby. On the one hand, there is a 'pure' aesthetic wing, empty of the social and political and driven by the cult of a self, imposed on the external world and stretching to a glorification of primitivism and to a vitalistic unleashing of all instincts and atavistic tendencies. On the other, there is an overriding ambition to liberate humanity from all constraints and to release the essential good in Man and to launch a moral and political campaign in the name of a philanthropic, altruistic enterprise founded in a longing for a cosmic brotherhood, and borne along on a wave of heroic emotionalism that transcends the individual to embrace all mankind. It was, put simply, 'ich' versus 'wir' as made manifest above all in the two best-known Expressionist journals, *Der Sturm*, whose editor, Herwath Walden, insisted on keeping it 'above the conflict', not so much apolitical as metapolitical, preoccupied with aesthetic and artistic matters such as Lothar Schreyer's Wortkunstwerk theories,[27] and Franz Pfemfert's *Die Aktion*, a radical political journal intent on looking outside and beyond itself and compelled by an (at times) nebulous humanitarianism, fiercely antiwar and, by the time of the Revolution in November 1918, the official organ of the Antinationale Sozialisten-Partei.[28] The two magazines were only ten minutes apart geographically — *Sturm* in Potsdamer Straße, *Aktion* in Nassauische Straße — and equally passionate in their commitments, but their ideologies and ambitions were totally at variance. Anton Schnack wrote for both journals, but there was, as we shall see, nothing ambiguous about his actual allegiances.

★   ★   ★   ★   ★

---

26   Friedrich Gundolf, 'Stefan George und der Expressionismus', *Die Flöte*, 3 (1920/21), pp. 217–23, repr. in Anz and Stark, *Manifeste*, pp. 92–97 (pp. 93–94).
27   Lothar Schreyer, 'Expressionistische Dichtung',*Sturm-Bühne*, Folge 4/5 (1918/19), pp. 19–20, Folge 6 (1918/19), pp. [1–3], repr. in Anz and Stark, *Manifeste*, pp. 623–29.
28   It should be added that Herworth Walden's politicization, as evidenced in his so-called 'Bolshevik writings', dated only from 1927 and subsequently he fled the Nazis and went to Moscow where his sympathies for the avant-garde aroused the interest of the Stalinist Soviet authorities. He died in Saratov prison in October 1941.

At the time Germany possessed a rich cultural infrastructure of cafés, theatres, cabarets, music halls and art galleries, all supported by an array of small, private publishing houses and of larger national enterprises. Literary and political journals, emerging in response to demand and interest, were a vital part of the cultural scene and were quick to promote Expressionist and other avant-garde developments in the arts. The variety of artistic activity and creativity in such German cities as Munich, Berlin, Dresden and Leipzig, repeated in Vienna, Zürich and Prague, rivalled that of London and Paris. Darmstadt was another smaller area of intense activity, and it was in Munich and Darmstadt that Schnack apparently found inspiration for the three Expressionist volumes which launched his literary career. Munich especially was a glamorous and exciting place for a young writer to try to find his way and to further his artistic ambitions and education: what Peter Sprengel calls the 'Gemeinschaftsgeist der Boheme'[29] of the Schwabing district of the city was a special lure for famous and not so famous names alike. It was also a city where the playing of parts, the adopting of different personae and the donning of masks were regular features of cultural life in café, theatre and shadow-plays: 'Nach Paris war München die zweite Stadt der Bohème [...] Seine heitere, lebensfrohe, aber der Mystik keineswegs bare Atmosphäre zog die Ritter der Windmühlen magisch an.'[30] Schnack in his Expressionist poetry presented his voice in a variety of different guises, and if he never actually cast himself, or the lyrical I in his poems, as Cervantes's famous knight-errant, he did not scruple to assume the masks and the personae of other literary or historical characters — Don Juan or Casanova, for example. In 1913 Schnack attended the Philosophy Faculty at Munich University. Margarete Susman, progenitor, as we have seen, of the concept of the lyrical I, had studied philosophy and art history at the university some years earlier. At the time, and for the next few years, it seemed as if everyone with literary and cultural interests felt bound to come to Munich. In 1919, for example, when Schnack published his first collections of poetry, Kurt Wolff, the leading publisher of Expressionist literature and colleague of Ernst Rowohlt, who was to publish Schnack's *Tier rang*, moved there from Leipzig. The most notorious visitor of all was Adolf Hitler, who came to Munich in 1914 to paint and sell postcards and, subsequently, to join up with the List regiment. A recently published history of Hitler's First World War experiences makes clear the special nature of what the author calls 'the German Mecca for artists':

> Munich's art scene made it possibly the most liberal and cosmopolitan of Germany's cities. Lenin, who had lived in Munich a few years before Hitler, had been attracted by its left-wing political subculture. Under the aegis of a benevolent and — compared to existing alternatives — progressive royal house, the Munich of fin-de-siècle artists and of Lenin peacefully coexisted with traditional, conservative ways of life and with a growing number of industrial workers.[31]

---

29   Sprengel, p. 121.
30   Richard Seewald, 'Im Café Stefanie', in *Expressionismus*, ed. by Raabe, p. 85.
31   Thomas Weber, *Hitler's First War* (Oxford University Press, 2010), p. 11 and p. 23.

The vibrancy and artistic vitality of the city are caught in the opening pages of Thomas Mann's short story *Gladius Dei*, written in 1902. In what amounts to a paean to Munich and to the city's artistic life, its first sentence is simply 'München leuchtete' and the long introduction ends:

> Die Kunst blüht, die Kunst ist an der Herrschaft, die Kunst streckt ihr rosenum-wundenes Zepter über die Stadt hin und lächelt. Eine allseitige respektvolle Anteilnahme an ihrem Gedeihen, eine allseitige, fleißige und hingebungsvolle Übung und Propaganda in ihrem Dienste, ein treuherziger Kultus der Linie, des Schmuckes, der Form, der Sinne, der Schönheit obwaltet. — München leuchtete.[32]

In response to this cultural prosperity, cafés and cabarets became central to the way of life of Munich's artists and writers and one of the two principal agencies or intermediaries for the promotion of Expressionism in all its guises — the other being journals and magazines. The Elf Scharfrichter (with Frank Wedekind as one of the Scharfrichter), Germany's first political cabaret, opened in Türkenstraße 28 in April 1901. It was superseded two years later by *Simplicissimus*, a café much frequented by artists at Turkenstraße 87, named after the satirical magazine, *Simplicissimus*. Café Stefanie, destroyed in the Second World War, was located at what is now Amalienstraße 25 at the intersection with Theresienstraße. Established artists (for example Der Blaue Reiter group) met in the Café Bauer or in the Café Luitpold, which is still to be found in the Brienner quarter of Munich.[33] Hitler's favourite café in the city was the Carlton Tea Rooms across the road from the Luitpold.

Many historical accounts and memoirs, perhaps tinged at times with a glowing nostalgia, testify to the significance and proliferation of such venues. They provided a congenial space for an astonishing host of talented, often eccentric and uninhibited writers and artists, mavericks and trailblazers, prophets and armageddonists, reminiscent in some cases of Robert Tressell's 'ragged-trousered philanthropists' (1910). The link between Bohemianism and Expressionism was always close, and became ever closer, through inter-personal contacts and ideo-logical accords. Poets, dramatists, scientists, politicians and actors mingled together to discuss, debate and share. Everyone seemed to know, or to be intent on meeting, everyone else, and an amazingly knowledgeable clientèle often held the floor in some of the cafés where the names of poets such as Goethe, Schiller, Hölderlin (among numerous others) and philosophers (especially Nietzsche) would be casually and freely invoked. All cultural genres — from literature to painting, from dance to music and film and drama, from lithography and wood carving to architecture — were represented, with the result that an unprecedented, if short-lived, cultural cross-pollination and interpenetration took place with Oskar Kokoschka appearing alongside Marinetti (reading from his Futurist manifesto), and Dr Gottfried Benn, prominent Expressionist poet, with Carlo Mierendorff, politician and social

---

32   Thomas Mann, 'Gladius Dei', in *Frühe Erzählungen 1893–1912*, ed. by Terence J. Reed and Malte Herwig (Fischer, 2004), pp. 222–42 (p. 225).
33   The Luitpold is the only Munich café to feature in Noël Riley Fitch's *The Grand Literary Cafés of Europe* (New Holland, 2006).

scientist, eventually fiercely opposed to Nazism and sentenced to long spells in a series of concentration camps. The atmosphere was unashamedly cosmopolitan and internationalist, and, by all accounts, stimulating and deliberately controversial. The cafés and restaurants, like the writers and polemicists, fell in and out of fashion but were constantly refreshed by regular visits by writers and painters from Austria, Switzerland, and Russia who would drop in unbidden as well as being invited to deliver readings or lectures. Students would gravitate to them rather than to university halls: a gloriously haphazard randomness of mood, style and appearance prevailed. In a retrospective autobiographical essay, Schnack relates how he and his friends enjoyed doing the rounds of the diverse establishments on offer:

> Ich war in der Faschingszeit des München von 1914 in eine Schar von Studenten geraten [...] Wir waren eine übermütige und fröhliche Gesellschaft, der die Münchener Faschingsluft Blut und Glieder lockerte, das Geld floß aus den Händen, von Redoute ging es zu Redoute, von Bal paré zu Bal paré, von Bierkeller zu Bierkeller und von Atelier zu Atelier. ('Ohne Geld ein Faschingsheld', II, 454–58)

An exemplar of the kind of cosmopolitanism, internationalism and diversity which characterized the early heady days of Expressionism was the figure of Ernst Stadler. Born in Alsace, he was a member of the radical coterie of writers known as the Stürmer-Kreis. After a period as a Rhodes Scholar at Oxford, he taught German and comparative literature in Strasbourg and Brussels, and was appointed to a professorship at Toronto University. He was killed in battle at Zandvoorde near Ypres on 30 October 1914. Within a few years of preparing a thesis for his tutors at Magdalen College, Oxford, on Wieland's translations of Shakespeare (living 'das vorgeschriebene Collegeleben junger vornehmer Gentlemen'[34]), he became a major contributor to *Menschheitsdämmerung* and produced two of Expressionism's most significant collections of poetry, *Praeludien* (1905) and *Der Aufbruch* (1914). One wonders what his Oxford tutors, had they received *Praeludien* and *Der Aufbruch*, would have made of the blatantly Expressionist entreaty, directed at a mythical 'Raubtier', embedded in a series of imperatives in the poem, 'Leoncita':

> Brich aus, Raubtier,
> Stürme an ihren erstarrten Reihen,
> Aufgerissenen Mäulern, schreckerstickten Schreien,
> Vorbei
> In deine Welt!
> Brich aus, Raubtier!
> Brich aus![35]

and of the Expressionist battle-cry in one of Expressionist poetry's best-known poems, 'Das Wort': 'Mensch, werde wesentlich!'[36]

---

34   See Otto Flake, 'Halbfertiges Leben', in *Expressionismus*, ed. by Raabe, p. 157.
35   Ernst Stadler, *Dichtungen, Schriften, Briefe: Kritische Ausgabe*, ed. by Klaus Hurlebusch and Karl Ludwig Schneider (Beck, 1983), pp. 112–13.
36   Ibid., p. 120.

Ernst Stadler's influence on Schnack's early poetry, particularly on its form, will become clear. Of even greater significance in Schnack's development as an Expressionist poet is Frank Wedekind, whose impact on the contemporary literary, political and social scene in pre-war Munich was huge. He lived in the city off and on from 1889 until his death in 1918 and was a regular visitor to Café Stefanie and the 'Künstlerkneipe' Simplicissimus — Sprengel's 'Brennpunkte' of the city's Bohemian subculture.[37] It is reasonable to conjecture that Schnack's Bohemian way of life and appetite for adventures would have taken him at times to both cafés and into the ambience of Wedekind and his followers. Wedekind's so-called Lulu plays (*Erdgeist*, 1895, and *Die Büchse der Pandora*, 1904) pushed the boundaries of what was deemed acceptable at the time: their unabashed depiction of sexuality and violence provoked public outrage and scandal, and offered audiences unsettling visions of the fragility of school, family and church institutions. Characters in the plays, revelling or wallowing in deeds or words of unabashed transgressiveness, play diverse roles within their community, but the metaphor of role-playing in no way precludes individual autonomy: it conveys a sense of social beings whose personalities are culturally shaped and modified by interaction with others. A sense of an exhilarating repudiation of all constraints, expressed in the pursuit of intense sexual gratification, ensues. The Lulu plays, of all Wedekind's work, and their depiction of a society torn and undermined by lust and greed, provide the best example of exploring the potential freedom of multiple roles and feed directly into a society where people have begun seemingly to question conventional morality and standards of sexual behaviour. Brecht's 1918 play, *Baal*, written when he was studying at Munich University, is comparable and reveals Brecht's indebtedness to Wedekind of whom he was a great admirer: Baal, the anti-hero, addicted to sexual excess and alcohol, rejects all middle-class conventions and traditional values. He ends up driving Johanna, whom he has seduced, to suicide, spurning his pregnant mistress, Sophie, and murdering his friend, Eckart, all in a relentless atmosphere of transgression and carnal debauchery. And yet Brecht mainly sidestepped any temptation to write the kind of Expressionist poetry which fills the pages of *Menschheitsdämmerung*, presumably on the basis that it had, in his view, little to say about concrete social and political realities. An unnamed reviewer in the *Frankfurter Zeitung* (30 January 1910) of a so-called 'sexualreformerische Schrift' had drawn attention to the proliferating writing on sex: 'Die Literatur über die verschiedenen Erscheinungen des Sexuallebens vermehrt sich in einer unheimlichen Geschwindigkeit' and elicited, a year later, a commentary on the phenomenon entitled 'Der Sexualbazillus' in *the Münchener Allgemeine Zeitung* (21 January 1911).[38] The Expressionist cult of the self and of passion for its own sake led to a call among many writers for the unchaining of Eros, for the total liberation of sexuality. For Gottfried Benn, for instance, the goal of instinctual liberation often took the form of an unleashing of all atavistic instincts and desires. By this time Freud's *Drei Abhandlungen zur Sexualtheorie* (1905)

---

37 Sprengel, p. 121.
38 For a more general survey of eroticism and sexuality in Expressionist literature, see Arnim Arnold, *Die Prosa des Expressionismus* (Kohlhammer, 1972), pp. 136–65.

and 'Die "kulturelle" Sexualmoral und die modern Nervosität' had been published to considerable public interest. His focus on human sexuality — on the status of the sexual component in any understanding of the human psyche — and his emphasis on the importance of repressed desires and, above all, his proposition that people can be cured of their problems by making conscious unconscious thoughts and motivations and thus gaining valuable insight into the human psyche — all this, and much more of his teaching, was bound to appeal to writers like the Expressionists keen to concentrate on self-analysis and self-exploration. His *Totem und Tabu: Einige Übereinstimmungen im Seelenleben der Wilden und der Neurotiker* (1913) resonated even more deeply. Perhaps acknowledging Freud's title, J. M. Ritchie, in his account of the Expressionist movement, refers to its 'taboo-breaking obsession with sex and sadism' and, in citing as a paradigmatic example Karl Otten's edition of '*Ego und Eros*': *Meistererzählungen des Expressionismus*, Ritchie quotes Otten's reference to 'the fervour whipped up by Freud' and his claim that he intended his anthology to be 'ein tolles Buch [...] bis zu den Ellenbogen in Blut und bis zu den Hüften in Weib wütend'.[39] The unapologetic and extreme carnality of such imagery is not limited to Expressionist prose narratives: it permeates much Expressionist poetry, including Anton Schnack's first Expressionist collection, *Strophen der Gier*, containing a poem entitled 'Ode an Lulu', which is presumably intended to conjure up images of Wedekind's Lulu, symbol, at the time, of sexual licence (I, 13–14). Moreover, Erna and Lulu, both in titles, are the only female names to appear in *Strophen der Gier*, and, according to his niece,[40] Schnack liked to sign himself Lulu.

If Schnack did not actually meet Wedekind in Munich (or Freud, based in Vienna), he could hardly have escaped the cultural climate which was at least partly shaped by Wedekind's iconoclastic plays. We know too from an autobiographical essay which he published in 1932 that Schnack and his friends enjoyed doing the rounds of the kinds of establishments where no doubt the latest theatrical scandal would be aired. Here, Vollmer relates, 'in der bayrischen Metropole kam Schnack mit der avantgardistischen Literatur in Kontakt, mit Autoren wie Hugo Ball, Klabund und Erich Mühsam' (I, 446). Ball (1886–1927), like Schnack, studied at Munich University. He was producer at the Munich Kammerspiele playhouse, well informed about developments in abstract art, remained a pacifist throughout the First World War and then in 1916 founded, with Tristan Tzara and Richard Huelsenbeck, the Dadaist movement in Zürich. Erich Mühsam (1878–1934), chess-playing customer at the Café Stefanie, became one of the leading agitators for a federated Bavarian Soviet republic in 1918. In 1911 he founded the newspaper *Kain* as a forum for communist-anarchist ideologies: he used *Kain* to ridicule what he perceived as excesses and abuses of authority and he was a fierce opponent of any kind of censorship. Klabund (pseudonym for Alfred Henschke, 1890–1928) was also a student at Munich University at the same time as Schnack: a great friend of Frank Wedekind, he subscribed wholeheartedly to the Bohemian way of life. He was a prolific writer of plays (best known for *Der Kreidekreis*, 1925, which Brecht took as a source for his *Der kaukasische Kreidekreis*) and of poetry (best known for *Dragoner*

39   J. M. Ritchie, 'The Expressionist Revival', *Seminar*, 2 (1966), pp. 37–49 (p. 40).
40   In conversation with me.

und Husaren, *Die Soldatenlieder* of 1916 and *Totenklage* (1928). A fierce opponent of the war, he wrote an open letter in 1917 to Wilhelm II calling upon him to abdicate. He was subsequently charged with high treason and lèse-majesté. Ball, Klabund and Mühsam were plainly far from reluctant to enter the public arena and to convert fiercely held beliefs into radical political action. It is impossible to know how or if they had influence on Schnack, but the least that can be said is that Klabund, for example, published poetry in some of the same magazines as Schnack — *Jugend*, *Simplicissimus* and *Die Schaubühne* (subsequently *Die Weltbühne*). The thirty war sonnets which constitute his *Totenklage* collection will provide a useful point of comparison with the sixty sonnets of Schnack's *Tier rang*.

★　★　★　★　★

The second important phase of Schnack's cultural experience and education took place in Darmstadt where he lived from October 1918 to October 1920. At this time Darmstadt was a microcosmic version of Munich in 1913/1914: Wedekind had also stayed and worked there in 1910. Except for a few months in 1914 when he was working in Bolzano and in late 1915 and early 1916 when he was stationed in northern France, Schnack was always within easy travelling range both of Munich and Darmstadt between 1914 and 1918. The Darmstadt publishing house Die Dachstube (which issued a magazine with the same name) published his second volume of Expressionist poetry, *Der Abenteurer*, in 1919, and the two years he spent in Darmstadt working as an editor and theatre-critic for the *Darmstädter Zeitung* were fruitful in terms of social and professional contacts:

> Bis zum Herbst 1920 arbeitete Schnack in Darmstadt, lernte hier u.a. Kasimir Edschmid, Hans Schiebelhuth, Fritz Usinger und Carlo Mierendorff kennen und schloß sich den kunstrevolutionären Kreisen der 'Dachstube' und der 'Darmstädter Sezession' an. Ebenso wurde er Mitglied der im Herbst 1919 von Alexander Abusch in Nürnberg gegründeten Vereinigung 'Das Junge Franken', die sich zum Ziel setzte, "durch Vorlesungen, Ausstellungen, Vorträge Förderung und Verbreitung seelengeborener und ethischer neuer Kunst'[41] zu erreichen. (I, 448)

Three of the five names listed in this excerpt are particularly important in the context of demonstrating the diversity of the company which Schnack was keeping at the time. Kasimir Edschmid (1890–1966) studied in Munich and Paris, Giessen and Strasbourg, and frequented Bohemian circles in each of those cities. He began as a champion of Expressionism before converting to a more realistic style, and, for over fifty years between 1911 and 1966, produced volumes of poetry, numerous Novellen and novels, short stories and treatises. He also provided valuable historical accounts of the development of Expressionism in Germany and of Expressionist writers. Records indicate that he knew everyone who featured in cultural circles and had a voluminous knowledge of their routines and haunts. He was, therefore, a useful point of contact for any aspiring young writer like Schnack. Hans Schiebelhuth (1895–1944) studied, like Schnack, in Munich in 1913/14 before working on *Das*

41　*Die Bücherkiste*, 8–10 (1919), p. 125. See I, 448.

Tribunal in Darmstadt. Schnack also published poems in this journal. He wrote poetry (the 1921 volume *Wegstern* contains his best work),[42] but he was, and still is, best known for his translations of the American novelist Thomas Wolfe's *Look Homeward, Angel* (1929) and *From Death to Morning* (1935). His influence on Schnack, particularly on the sonnets of *Tier rang*, is, I believe, considerable. Unlike both Edschmid and Schiebelhuth, Alexander Abusch (1902–82) was essentially a political writer and journalist who, by the age of fourteen, was a member of the Freie Sozialistische Jugend and two years later had joined the Communist party: his influence on Schnack was more political in nature. This means that Schnack's decision to join Abusch's organisation *Das Junge Franken*[43] looked like a significant political statement. In the event, Schnack must soon have parted company with Abusch. The latter went on to take part in the revolutionary skirmishes in central Germany, to be arrested twice for high treason in 1920 and 1922, then to become Chief Editor of *Rote Fahne*, the journal founded by Karl Liebknecht and Rosa Luxemburg in November 1918 as the principal organ of the left-wing revolutionary Spartakusbund. Schnack's name does not appear in this context in any contemporary account or in his own biographical sketches. By the time Abusch, after holding many high-ranking positions in the Communist Party hierarchy, had become a leading member of the Central Committee of the Sozialistische Einheitspartei Deutschlands (SED)[44] and of the Deutsche Wirtschaftskommission in the Soviet-occupied zone in post-Second World War Germany, Schnack was already living in quiet seclusion in Kahl am Main.

Anton Schnack may well have come into contact with such leading activists as Alexander Abusch and Erich Mühsam, the latter a frequenter of the café scene, anarchist, agitator, and may indeed have known them personally, but the extent of his own political engagement between, say, 1912 and 1920 is far from clear. A clue (but no details) can be found in a radio broadcast recorded on 9 June 1992 in the Regionalstudio Mainfranken in Würzburg and transmitted on 19 July. Three speakers address the topic 'Mir ist in Franken vieles wert und teuer. Zum 100. Geburtstag des Dichters Anton Schnack'. The speakers (unnamed) take us through Schnack's life:

> Er fand in Darmstadt für sein lyrisches, expressionistisches Werk Beifall und Resonanz, gründete gemeinsam mit dem Dichter Kasimir Edschmid eine literarische Vereinigung, gab die Zeitschrift 'Die Dachstube' heraus und beteiligte sich an Protesten der Jugend, die nach Krieg und Chaos eine Welt des Friedens, ohne Haß und Grenzen gründen wollte [...] Aber auch Darmstadt schenkte auf Dauer dem Dichter nicht die erhoffte Erfüllung. Ferne Ziele lockten immer noch. Er besuchte Italien und Frankreich [...][45]

---

42   His complete works — poems, translations, prose, letters and theatre reviews — were published in two volumes in 1966, edited by Manfred Schlösser.

43   This was presumably based on *Junges Deutschland*: those writers such as Karl Gutzkow, Theodor Mundt, and Heinrich Laube who in the mid-nineteenth century sought to maintain the principles of democracy and liberalism in the face of a spirit of absolutism in politics and obscurantism in religion.

44   The governing Communist Party of the GDR from 1949 to 1990.

45   The three-way discussion can be found on CD and in transcript in the Stadtarchiv of Gemeinde Kahl am Main dated 12 November 1992: Author — Franz Schaub: Editor — Rainer Lindenmann: Director — Ralf Sarrazin. For this quotation see p. 7 of the transcript. Henceforth I shall refer to

There is no corroborative evidence that Schnack 'founded a literary organisation' or that he edited *Die Dachstube*, nor are there any details available of 'the youthful protests in which he took part', either in the numerous contemporary articles and subsequent memoirs or in his own autobiographical sketches, both prose and poetry. Already, it seems, he was showing signs in Darmstadt of being happier living to one side of the main action, 'abseits der großen Durchgangsstraßen', as the Erster Sprecher in the radio programme explains. Having travelled widely in the 1920s, attracted by 'ferne Ziele', he was content to withdraw almost completely from public life, eventually preferring the tranquillity of Kahl am Main to the hectic pace of life in Munich or Darmstadt, or even Würzburg and Aschaffenburg. The Erster Sprecher adds: 'Anton Schnack war ein Grandseigneur in seiner gelben, efeuumrankten Ritterklause, wie er sein Haus gerne nannte — ein Weinschenk in der Gartenlaube, ein Märchenerzähler in seinem holzgetäfelten Arbeitszimmer.' There is something almost Stifteresque about his yearning for an uncluttered and unpretentious life, a yearning which pervades both his poetry and prose throughout his literary career:

> Wer ihn ('Regen [...] von einer Dachtraufe') vernimmt, vernimmt noch mancherlei: die Knistergeräusche alter Häuser, die langsam aus den Fugen geraten, das blecherne Drehen eines Turmhahnes, das dumpfe Kartenklopfen aus einem Wirtshaus, das peinigende Widerschlagen eines Fensterladens, knisterndes Fichtenholzfeuer: Geräusche, die nur das abseitige Leben bietet.
> (II, 463)

His actual participation in public or political life during those key years of 1913 to 1920 was minimal. Just two occasions are recorded: the first when he added his signature (alongside those of Döblin, Schickele, Schiebelhuth, Wolfenstein, among others) to a document defending Kasimir Edschmid against an attack by the writer Harry Kahn in *Die Weltbühne* on 14 October 1920;[46] the second, much more significant, when he joined in an 'Aufruf an die revolutionäre französische geistige Jugend' penned by Kasimir Edschmid and published in the first edition of *Das Tribunal* in July 1919. Schnack's name can be found among almost forty others, including those of Rubiner, Toller, Goll, Kaiser, Däubler and Schiebelhuth. The tone of the appeal is clear from the outset:

> Geehrte Herren, meine Kameraden! Die Grenzen fallen, es ist Zeit, sich zu vereinigen. Es gibt gegen den Haß nur einen Kampf, er ist uns gemeinsam. Es gibt nur eine Gesinnung: gerecht zu sein. Es gibt nur eine Taktik: unsere Absicht deutlich zu machen. Wir senden Ihnen den Gruß, wir wissen, er wird nicht ohne Echo sein. In dem Sumpf der Haßwürfe offizieller Institute, Zeitungen, Persönlichkeiten wird unsere Stimme, neben der einiger Pazifisten und Sozialisten, die einzige sein, die, sich vereinigend, hinüber und herüber Kameradschaft und Willen bezeigen wird, uns, die Welt, die Menschen weiterzubringen.[47]

This is an extremely rare example of Schnack's approaching the activist, left-

this material simply as the Regionalstudio Mainfranken transcript.
46   Edschmid, *Lebendiger Expressionismus*, pp. 221–22.
47   Edschmid, *Frühe Schriften*, p. 162.

leaning wing of the Expressionist movement, thus aligning himself with such ardently committed political figures as Rubiner, Toller and Kaiser. Edschmid's rhetorical language was certainly not Schnack's, and the public stance which Edschmid adopted, interventionist, humanitarian and cosmopolitan, typical of the left wing of Expressionism, found no echo in Schnack's writing, either at the time or afterwards. And even though he contributed to Moritz Lederer's Mannheim-based *Der Revolutionär* — 'politisch-literarische Zeitschrift nach den Vorbildern von Franz Pfemfert in der revolutionären Einstellung and von Karl Kraus in der Polemik'[48] — he apparently made no attempt to incite or encourage rebellion or to engage in polemical discourse. This does not, of course, undermine his credentials as an Expressionist writer: it simply means that he belonged to the non-political, non-activist branch of the Expressionist movement. His allegiance to 'literary' Expressionism, the so-called 'pure' aesthetic wing, can be gauged by considering the number and kind of magazines and journals to which he contributed numerous poems between 1915 and 1925.

The significance and the sheer number of these contemporary Expressionist magazines cannot be overstated: literary magazines after all are frequently international instruments of cultural politics and innovation. They are also important as informative and nostalgic markets, indispensable to any reader who wishes to be enlightened about the roller-coaster contemporary social and political landscape and, in turn, to any writer who wants their critical and creative writing to be showcased. The number and diversity of the magazines were eye-catching, and Alfred Döblin, for one, was deeply impressed by their quality and their proliferation.

> Der Fortschritt über das neunzehnte Jahrhundert hinaus ist unerkenntlich. Man denke, zu Goethes Zeiten: gerade wenn Gedanken fehlen, stellt ein Wort zum rechten Zeit sich ein. Jetzt ein Wort? Eine Zeitschrift, zwei Zeitschriften, ein ganzes Dutzend Zeitschriften. Rededelirien. Alle Menschen haben Ansichten...[49]

Judging by Thomas Mann's depiction of the local population and visitors milling through Munich's streets, young university students in particular were enthu-siastic subscribers: 'Junge Leute, die das Nothung-Motiv pfeifen und abends die Hintergründe des modernen Schauspielhauses füllen, wandern, literarische Zeit-schriften in den Seitentaschen ihrer Jacketts, in der Universität und der Staats-bibliothek aus und ein.'[50]

In his introduction to *Die Zeitschriften und Sammlungen des literarischen Expressio-nismus 1910–1921*, Paul Raabe declares:

> Das literarische Leben [zwischen 1910 und 1925] spielte sich im Häusermeer der Großstädte ab, im Trubel eines hektischen Alltags, in dem Lärm der Automobile,

---

48   Paul Raabe, *Die Zeitschriften und Sammlungen des literarischen Expressionismus: Repertorium der Zeitschriften, Jahrbücher, Anthologien, Sammelwerke, Schriftenreihen und Almanache 1910–1921* (Metzler, 1964), p. 65.
49   Alfred Döblin, 'Neue Zeitschriften',*Die Neue Rundschau*, 30 (1919), pp. 621–32 (pp. 622–23).
50   Thomas Mann, *Gladius Dei*, p. 197.

im Zauber der Lichtreklame. Die jungen Autoren bildeten ein Kollektiv, eine Gruppierung von Individualitäten und Gesinnungen [...] man begrüßte den Futurismus als das gemäße Lebensgefühl [...] man schrieb keine Romane mehr [...] Diese Wenigen waren eine kleine Schar, eine 'Dichter-Sezession' in den Jahren bis zum Kriege. Aber sie demonstrierten ihr gemeinsames Wollen, und kein Mittel war dafür besser geeignet als die Zeitschriften, deren große Zahl und bunte Folge ein Charakteristikum expressionistischer Literatur ist.[51]

Schnack contributed to over thirty of such publications, not least to the three most famous: *Die Aktion, Der Sturm* and *Die Weißen Blätter*, all of which championed Expressionism and promoted Expressionist writers and artists. As 'Ausdruck gemeinsamen Wollens' their intention was clear — 'durch Worte zu wirken'.[52] Franz Pfemfert and Herwarth Walden, as we have seen, were wholly committed to, and resolute in, their aims, which they cherished for their respective publications. Each individual editor had complete control over the content, the style, the format and any political or cultural slant. Pfemfert, for example, editor of *Die Aktion*, was a thoroughgoing opponent of any form of capitalism, nationalism or imperialism. He was passionately anti-war and, in the name of an undefined community spirit, was hostile to the concept of the rights of the individual to a private existence. He was all for revolutionary transformation and radical syndicalism, a political programme which did not exclude anarchistic sabotage or industrial boycotting. He ensured that his magazine aligned itself with the kind of activism which Ludwig Rubiner practised and preached, particularly in his famous essay/manifesto, 'Der Dichter greift in die Politik' (1912). Walden, editor of *Der Sturm*, certainly began as a fierce critic of the bourgeois, of 'der alte Mensch', but then very quickly became a champion of abstract art: the painters of *Die Brücke* and *Der Blaue Reiter* were warmly welcomed to the magazine's pages. Paul Klee, Wassily Kandinsky, Franz Marc and Pablo Picasso, and many others, found sanctuary in some of its early editions. René Schickele, editor of *Die Weißen Blätter*, encouraged a more open-minded approach founded in a strong pacifist stance. He wanted his magazine to be 'nicht nur der künstlerische Ausdruck der neuen Generation, sondern auch ihr sittlicher und politischer'.[53]

It seems as though Schnack, who wrote for all three of these magazines, very different though they were from each other in aim and execution, selected them indiscriminately and was pleased merely to be published. Schnack's first published poem, 'Einer Italienerin', for example, appeared in *Die Aktion* on 7 August 1915. However, he also contributed poems to *Die Schöne Rarität* which, motivated by a 'zeitübliche reformatorische Absicht',[54] strove for a higher standard than some of its rivals and accepted graphics and woodcarvings alongside lyric poetry. In fact, if any pattern is to be discerned, it could be argued that Schnack often chose the 'better-class' magazines untainted by politics and polemics. The pen-portrait of the magazine *Die Sichel*, based in Regensburg and Munich, read: 'Es handelt sich

---

51 Raabe, *Zeitschriften und Sammlungen des literarischen Expressionismus 1910–1921*, p. 5.
52 Ibid., p. 9.
53 Ibid., p. 48.
54 Fritz Schlawe, *Literarische Zeitschriften 1910–1933* (Metzler, 1962), pp. 43–44.

um eine vom Expressionismus beeinflußte, die moderne Kunst ohne Polemik und unverkrampft vertretende Zeitschrift von Niveau.'[55] The magazines *Neue Blätter für Kunst und Dichtung*, *Die Rote Erde* (with a strong religious strain) and *Der Orkan*, to all of which Schnack contributed, came into a similar category. A particularly interesting example is the Dresden-based *Menschen* in which three of the poems in *Strophen der Gier*, his first Expressionist volume, appeared. Founded in 1918 by Felix Stiemer, *Menschen* promoted the ideas of the Expressionist Working Group, an amalgam of pacifism, radical politics, and a belief in the potential of the new art to transform humankind. Its editors were careful to distinguish their efforts politically from *Der Sturm* and *Die Aktion*:

> Fern aller Verliebtheit in ekstatischer Verzückung wird der Kampf gegen Selbstbeharrung aufgenommen; keine Flucht mehr in ein anderes Land, das phantastisch-poetische Spiegelungen kultiviert, kein Sturm von Aktionen, die in giftiger Ressentimentspolemik versanden, sondern gemeinsamer Angriff, Forderung und Verheißung.[56]

Under a new editor, Walter Rheiner, *Menschen* moved cautiously and steadily to the left from 1918 onwards. With the murder in Berlin of the communist leaders Karl Liebknecht and Rosa Luxemburg, who had both written for *Die Aktion*, Rheiner took an outright leftist stance and for a time abandoned art for politics. The first issue in January 1919 carried the statement:

> Karl Liebknecht und Rosa Luxemburg hielten als Einzige dieser vier Jahre die Fahne der Revolution hoch. Sie wurden heute durch die Maßnahmen der 'revolutionären' Regierung ermordet. Die Bestie triumphiert über den Geist des Sozialismus! Die feile Journaille jubelt über 480 Leichen und 1000 Verwundete überzeugungstreuer Ideenkämpfer. MENSCHEN! Die Regierung ist des vielfachen Mordes schuldig! Die Menschenschlächter des Militarismus sind ihre gedungenen Schergen. Ehre und Ruhm ihren toten Gegnern! Wir neigen uns vor ihnen zur Erde. Klärt auf! Sprecht! Redet! Schreit![57]

More Georg Büchner (and more Georg Heym for that matter) than Anton Schnack, whose political allegiance (if any) or socialist sympathies cannot be deduced from his writing, these sentiments and this language are typical of a journal to which Schnack was apparently happy to contribute examples of his poetry. The fact that he contributed to it did not, however, mean that he endorsed the precepts and imperatives which, after a more sedate art-based launching, it proclaimed and developed.[58] On the contrary, as with his support for other Expressionist publications, Schnack simply dipped into the movement, writing *his* kind of poetry, following a path which rarely took him directly into the public arena or linked him to the political and social concerns of the day.

Various conclusions can be drawn from the life which Schnack led in the

---

55   Ibid., pp. 19–20.
56   *Menschen*, 1.1 (15 January 1918), p. 4.
57   *Menschen*, 2.2 (15 January 1919), p. 1.
58   For a description of the way in which *Menschen* subsequently evolved, see Joan Weinstein, *The End of Expressionism* (University of Chicago Press, 1990), pp. 140–60.

momentous years immediately before, during and after the First World War. First, it becomes clear that his busy social life in Munich's and Darmstadt's cafés and restaurants and his numerous contributions to a variety of Expressionist magazines meant not only that he inevitably came into contact with many Expressionist writers of different political persuasions, but also that he would not have looked out of place in the company of those writers who found themselves in such classic anthologies of Expressionist poetry as Pinthus's *Menschheitsdämmerung*. Second, on the evidence of his poetry, Schnack seems to have been completely untouched by the political activities and convictions of such activists as Abusch and Mühsam. He was in an ideal position, both in Munich and in Darmstadt, to observe, and to participate in, the significant political activity going on around him. Apparently he did not participate or did not participate much, and none of his observations found their way into his poetry or into his autobiographical prose sketches. Astonishingly, in the three volumes of Expressionist poems he wrote between 1915 and 1919 and in all of his subsequent autobiographical essays, there is no reference to the outbreak of war, to the progress of the war, to those returning (or not returning) from the war, or to the November 1918 Revolution, even though it was in Munich that a 'Workers' and Soldiers' Council' forced the last King of Bavaria, Ludwig III, to abdicate. For that matter, there is, in Schnack's work, no trace of a literary credo, no theorizing, no interpretation of his own work or anyone else's. His choice of magazines was, at least in one sense, indiscriminate because, in making the choice, he was not intent on lending support to the editor's particular point of view or to the publication's mission statement — whether it be Pfemfert's fierce anti-war stance, Walden's esoteric views on art and poetry and subsequent turning to communism, Schickele's pacifism or Rheiner's radical revolutionary claims for Expressionist art. Third, the logical implication of this is that Schnack's literary response to the new movement should place him *not* on its ethical, philanthropic, humanitarian and altruistic wing, but rather in the company of those for whom writing poetry was essentially a personal, politically unengaged literary exercise.

CHAPTER 3

Anton Schnack —
Expressionist Poet

Schnack's first published poem was, as already noted, 'Einer Italienerin', which appeared in *Die Aktion* in August 1915. He then published nothing for two years, but, according to Vollmer (I, 448), spent the intervening time working on new poems and on 'Verse vom Schlachtfeld' after three months' service on the frontline in 1915 and early 1916. A flurry of single poems then emerged in such journals as *Die Schaubühne* and *Die Schöne Rarität*, and his first poem ('Im Gebirge') for *Der Sturm* appeared in January 1918. By the autumn of 1919 he had produced his three Expressionist collections and, a year later, *Tier rang*, for which he was awarded a prize by the Deutsche Schillerstiftung. The four collections were for the most part drafted and re-drafted at his mother's house in Alzenau in the north of the Aschaffenburg district of Lower Franconia, but they issued from the particular first-hand cultural experience which he had had in Munich and, subsequently, in Darmstadt. The Expressionist poet Ernst Blass, in his essay 'Das alte Café des Westens', sought to describe that experience and the intellectual climate of his generation:

> In der Luft lag vor allem van Gogh, Nietzsche, auch Freud, Wedekind. Gesucht wurde ein postrationaler Dionysos. Van Gogh: Das war der Ausdruck und das Erlebnis, dem Impressionismus und Naturalismus entgegengesetzt als flammende Konzentration, als Jünglingseichtheit, Unmittelbarkeit, Subjektstiefe, als Exhibition und Halluzination [...] der Mut zum eigenen Ausdruck; Nietzsche: Der Mut zum eigenen Selbst und eigenen Erlebnis; Freud: die Tiefe und Problematik des eigenen Selbst; Wedekind: Die zwischenmenschliche Problematik und Explosion.[1]

The concept of self in the phrases 'Der Mut zum eigenen Selbst und eigenen Erlebnis' and, in connection with Freud, 'die Tiefe und Problematik des eigenen Selbst', is a very useful marker in any attempt to characterize Expressionist poetry in general and Schnack's poetry in particular.[2] After all, it is customary to see the Expressionist movement as affirming 'the primacy of a passionate subjectivity against traditional

---

[1]   Quoted in Raabe, *Expressionismus*, p. 38.

[2]   See Ritchie Robertson, 'Modernism and the Self 1890–1924', in *Philosophy and German Literature 1700–1990*, ed. by Nicholas Saul (Cambridge University Press, 2002), pp. 150–96. Robertson's terms 'the minimal self' and 'the embattled self' are particularly relevant to my argument. See ibid., pp. 162–66 and 166–74.

social norms and artistic forms',[3] as 'the expression of inner feelings rather than any verisimilitude to nature',[4] its subjective orientation inherited from the Romantics. Moreover, the strong autobiographical nature of Schnack's work, of the 'lyric I' in his poetry, has already been underlined. Early in a discussion of 'das Apollinische' and 'das Dionysische' in *Die Geburt der Tragödie* Nietzsche borrows an image from Schopenhauer's *Die Welt als Wille und Vorstellung* to indicate the vulnerability of the individual self:

> Wie auf dem tobenden Meere, das, nach allen Seiten unbegränzt, heulend Wellenberge erhebt und senkt, auf einem Kahn ein Schiffer sitzt, dem schwachen Fahrzeug vertrauend; so sitzt, mitten in einer Welt von Qualen, ruhig der einzelne Mensch, gestützt und vertrauend auf das *principium individuationis.*[5]

It is clear that Apollo represents most notably that trust in the *principium individuationis*, but when, in his diagnosis of his own age, Nietzsche predicts how the Apollonian consciousness of self will be invaded and fused with the Dionysian, all trust, all calmness will inevitably be undermined. Vulnerability became crisis, a crisis of subjectivity, and the succeeding generation of Expressionist poets (more Dionysian than Apollonian)[6] took it upon themselves to seek ways of articulating a series of new experiences concerning the fragmentation and alienation of the individual self, combined at times with attempts at reintegration of the self into the world outside. Faced by this crisis of identity, the individual writer has a number of recourses — he can lament his loss and accept it passively; he can slip into an attitude of self-contempt and self-loathing; he can reassert his identity, perhaps in moderate tones, more likely in extravagantly hyperbolic language; he can seek refuge in new self-imposed personae or behind a series of masks. The situation for the Expressionist poet was compounded by the fact that the disintegration of individual identity was mirrored by the demonic anonymity of the city, which became the predominant symbol of the malaise of the time, and, of course, by a catastrophic war. That disintegration was often accompanied by despair as in Gottfried Benn's poem 'O, Nacht':

> O, Nacht! Ich will ja nicht so viel.
> Ein kleines Stück Zusammenballung,
> Ein Abendnebel, eine Wallung
> Von Raumverdrang, von Ichgefühl.[7]

The lyrical I in Expressionist poetry appears in many guises and with many qualifications; with Gottfried Benn as 'das späte Ich' washed up on the shores of

---

3   Bronner and Kellner, p. 1.
4   Weinstein, p. 3.
5   In Nietzsche, *Werke Kritische Gesamtausgabe*, ed. by Giorgio Colli and Mazzino Montinari, III: *Die Geburt der Tragödie. Unzeitgemäße Betrachtungen I–III* (De Gruyter, 1972), p. 24.
6   Compare Gottfried Benn, 'Dionysos kam in das nüchterne Volk der Hirten', in Gottfried Benn, 'Expressionismus', in *Gesammelte Werke*, ed. by Dieter Wellershoff, 4 vols (Limes, 1959), I, pp. 240–56 (p. 245).
7   Gottfried Benn, 'O, Nacht', III, p. 53.

time in a poem of that name written in 1921–22; with Georg Heym, whose diaries and poetry are full of expressions of almost Kafkaesque self-contempt,[8] as one of his heroes (Nietzsche, Hölderlin, Grabbe, Büchner, Kleist, Byron' and, above all, Keats) or, if not one of them, as Danton, a terrorist, a sculptor, a cuirassier lieutenant, almost anyone. Heym is a wearer of masks ('Ich bin zerblasen wie ein taubes Ei [...] was Sie sehen, ist nur die Maske, die ich mit soviel Geschick trage'),[9] with so much skill, in fact, that of the 246 poems Heym wrote in 1911, the last full year of his life, only twenty-six contain the pronoun 'ich'. Similarly, the lyrical I in the poetry of August Stramm, who is intent above all on sonic and verbal experimentation, apart from occasional outbursts of desperate self-assertion, virtually disappears altogether in the thirty-one poems of the *Tropfblut* cycle of war poems. In fact, the Ich appears only in one poem ('Angststurm'). In Albert Ehrenstein's two collections, *Die weiße Zeit* (1914) and *Der Mensch schreit* (1916), the lyrical I is 'embattled', under threat from all angles:

> Ich kenne die Zähne der Hunde,
> in der Wind-ins-Gesicht-Gasse wohne ich,
> ein Sieb-Dach ist über meinem Haupte,
> Schimmel freut sich an den Wänden,
> gute Ritzen sind für den Regen da.[10]

It then undergoes a crisis of identity before enjoining Death to claim it, in a ghastly parody of the last couplet of Goethe's 'Wandrers Nachtlied' ('süßer Friede, | Komm, ach komm in meine Brust!'):

> Ich? Wer bin ich?
> Ich bin ein Zeitblock,
> der bröckelt ab und fällt zurück ins Meer.
> [...]
> Ich bin ein Häuflein Erde.
> O komme bald und menge mich,
> Erde in die Erde.[11]

Franz Werfel, in a poem from his early collection *Der Weltfreund*, articulates most emphatically this sense of utter disorientation and dislocation, amounting almost to atomisation:

> Mein Mittelpunkt hat keine Kraft.
> Nichts reißt er mehr in mich herein.
> Von allem bin ich hingerafft
> Zu tausendfach zerstäubtem Sein.

---

8   See such lines as: 'Und wieder krieche ich in mich hinein | Und schrumpfe in mich wieder wie ein Wurm | Und senke mich in meiner Leiden, | Sturm | , Ein Taucher in der Meere Totenschrein' in the poem 'Liebe'. Heym thus, unwittingly presumably, picks up Nietzsche's maritime metaphor with regard to the vulnerable individual. Georg Heym, *Dichtungen und Schriften*, ed. by Karl Ludwig Schneider, 4 vols (Ellermann, 1964), I, p. 326.
9   Heym, III, entry for 6 July 1910, p. 138.
10   Albert Ehrenstein, 'Wanderers Lied', *Werke*, ed. by Hanni Mittelmann, IV/I: *Gedichte* (Boer, 1997), p. 63.
11   'Der ewige Schlaf', ibid., pp. 64–65.

> [...]
> Ein windiges Gerüste ist mein Wesen,
> Dadurch das räuberische Leben fährt.
> Wo ist, wo ist der Besen,
> Der mich zusammenkehrt?[12]

Ironically Werfel answers his own rhetorical question: the self 'hingerafft | zu tausendfach zerstäubtem Sein' can be turned to advantage. Not only Werfel, but also other Expressionist poets such as Stadler, Becher and Rubiner sought to benefit reality by overwhelming and reshaping it with the irresistible power of their selves. They were eager to engage in the dramatic act of 'sich ausschenken', 'sich fortschenken' and of 'Sichverschenken' (all Stadler).[13] Intense optimism prevails as the poet revels in a vitalistic fervour:

> Dann hat ein Sommertag die Augen aufgeschlagen
> [...]
> O Himmel, der sich neigte. Über alles Glück und Gnade —
> Erfüllung, Segen, tiefste Spende, lächelndes Sich-Geben —
> Der Sommer blüht. Mein ward die Erde. Über glanzumströmte Pfade
> Reißt mich ein Wunderwort hinaus ins Licht: Das Leben.[14]

So confident now is the Expressionist poet in the health and nobility of his individual self that, before emerging into the light, he wishes to disperse that self over the whole world. The lyrical I dominates the scene again: the revolution he initiates is beneficent, unlike the one which Heym's 'terrorist' almost certainly has in mind.[15] It is a question not only of placing the lyrical I in the centre of the universe, but of situating the centre of the universe in each I.[16] The influence of Walt Whitman's poetry comes sharply into focus at this point. His *Leaves of Grass* (1855) had first been translated into German by Johannes Schlaf in 1907 and then by Franz Blei as *Hymnen an die Erde* seven years later. This cycle was certainly known to Franz Werfel, who paid homage to Whitman in his poem 'Der Patriarch'. The all-powerful first-person narration, the sublime confidence of a lyrical I who is not to be limited to or confused with the person of the historical Walt Whitman and, bypassing birth and death, has transcended the boundaries of self, the premise that the narrator of, for example, 'A Song of Myself' in the cycle does not represent a single individual but a host of identities and possibilities ('I am large, I contain multitudes', 51) and not least the long rolling lines of verse — all of this prefigures and ultimately shapes the poetry of Werfel, Becher and Stadler. On the evidence of Schnack's three collections of Expressionist verse, and of *Tier rang*, it has a pervasive influence there, too, both thematically and formally. The drama of identity which in Whitman's case is rooted in the political and social drama of a nation in crisis

---

12   Franz Werfel, 'Mein Mittelpunkt hat keine Kraft', in *Das lyrische Werk*, ed. by Adolf D. Klarmann (Fischer, 1967), p. 54.
13   Ernst Stadler, *Dichtungen, Schriften, Briefe*, ed. by Klaus Hurlebusch and Karl Ludwig Schneider (Beck, 1983), see the poems 'Tage IV' (p. 124), 'In dir' (p. 146) and 'Form ist Wollust' (p. 138).
14   Ibid., 'Traum und Morgen', II, p. 246.
15   See the diary entry for 9 October 1911, Heym, III, p. 168.
16   Theodor Däubler, *Die neue Rundschau* (1916), pp. 51–63.

(over issues of slavery, women's rights, religious revival and free love) is repeated in Germany, some fifty years later, against a background of huge cultural and social upheaval, of moral and political revolution, of a strong sense of the old world coming to an end and, of course, of a catastrophic world war.

There is indeed something dramatic, even melodramatic, about the way in which the lyrical I, sometimes shadowy in the background, often dominant in the forefront of the action, is depicted in the poems of *Strophen der Gier*, *Der Abenteurer* and *Die tausend Gelächter*. The last poem in *Menschheitsdämmerung*, Franz Werfel's 'Lebens-Lied', provides a helpful way into an examination of the particular character of those poems. Its final couplet reads:

> Das über allen Worten
> Verkünd' ich, Mensch, wir sind!!!!¹⁷[17]

'Wir sind' is no less than a proclamation of faith and a characteristically Expressionist battle-cry intended for fellow activists: it is also a confirmatory paean to the glorious fact of being alive (hence the title 'Lebens-Lied') and thus of being ready to confront all of life's vagaries. For Schnack, the 'wir' becomes an 'ich' set upon hedonistic self-indulgence which will erase or mitigate any vagaries and the 'life-song' is dedicated to unbridled sexuality embedded in a kind of self-dramatising libertinism. The lyrical I in *Strophen der Gier* (no longer a song, but strophes of lust) remains from the outset locked into himself, hardly capable of taking into account the female lovers drawn into his orbit, let alone of taking up Werfel's implicit challenge and investing in a grand humanitarian project. In 'Ma', an early autobiographical prose piece which Schnack also published in 1919, he writes in almost confessional mood: 'Ich war verbohrt in mich, vergraben, ich lebte, lautlos, kreisend in einer Sphäre, deren Periphäre und deren Zentrale Feuer war, Furioso, Vermaledeiung, Brandmal' (II, 7–9), simmeringly alive, but fated to live under a curse, a stigma, condemned to a cycle of sexual repression. Schnack's first short collection is an account of a release from that cycle of eruption of 'Feuer und Furioso'.

The image of womankind which emerges in the process is of a piece with the general stereotypical view perpetuated in a *Männerbewegung* which is in turn founded in what Barbara Wright calls 'an aggressively masculine stance'. In her essay 'Intimate Strangers: Women in German Expressionism', she argues that women in Expressionist poetry tend to 'appear as scenery, part of stage setting for the poem's message', rarely 'a focus more a prop',[18] in the same way as they had often appeared as 'mere' companions and appendages in Munich's and Darmstadt's cafés and restaurants (though Else Lasker-Schüler for one was more than an appendage!)[19]. They can also be victims of 'casual brutality' in Expressionist writings where *das Weibliche* is acknowledged as a source of primal power, which men in a show

---

17   Pinthus, p. 329.
18   Barbara D. Wright, 'Intimate Strangers: Women in German Expressionism', in *A Companion to the Literature of German Expressionism*, ed. by Donahue, pp. 287–320.
19   It is worth noting that over 300 women contributed to the magazines of the movement (see Paul Raabe's Index to *Expressionismus*, p. 289).

of instinctual masculine self-assertion are bound to challenge and overcome in
a perverse cycle of vicious repulsion and irresistible attraction. The dismissive
comment on chance encounters in Gottfried Benn's poem 'D-Zug' — 'Eine Frau
ist etwas für eine Nacht | Und wenn es schön war, nach für die nächste'[20] — is as
disconcerting in its way as scenes in Oskar Kokoschka's provocatively entitled play,
Mörder, Hoffnung der Frauen (first performed in 1909 when it sparked riots in Vienna),
in which the Warriors and the Maidens are shown locked in a primitive sexual
antagonism which ends in mass murder. Such examples lie at the extreme ends of
the spectrum of Expressionist attitudes towards women, but they are not rare. Paul
Hatvani (1892–1975), Austrian author, critic and journalist, called Expressionism
a 'Revolution für das Elementare' which can be fulfilled only in an 'Idee der
Weiblichkeit'. By his account, woman is *the* elemental force in the universe — 'das
Weib ist das Element. [...] dieser weibliche Stoff des expressionistischen Künstlers
[wird] ein Urquell seiner erhöhten Männlichkeit'. He concludes that, enjoying 'eine
sinnliche Bezüglichkeit zum Geschlecht', Expressionism represents masculinity to
the highest power.[21]

There is no doubt who is in control in the collection *Strophen der Gier*, but a
strident self-obsessiveness sets the tone and shapes the action. The pronoun 'wir'
does (rarely) appear, and the thrill of union in sexual ecstasy is not denied:

> Langsamer Wuchs in die Nacht, überregnete von den Gebeten Deiner Geilheit,
> bewußtseinlos, Tier an Tier,
> Blut dunkle Zeichen brennend, nicht Ich, nicht Du, nur Zweiheit-Einheit,
> Ineinanderfließen,
> *Ein* Reif, geglüht, gereift. Oh sel'ger Schmerz im Hirn, da ich Dein Silber sah
> und jungen Purpur, daß ich 'Ich' war und 'Wir' ... ('Ode an Lulu', I, 13–14)

Certain linguistic and grammatical tics typical of Schnack emerge here and serve to
imply the man's dominance over the woman despite the sexual consummation and
the compliments he pays her at various points: the use of the accusative case in the
phrase 'Langsamer Wuchs in *die* Nacht' to underline the intensely dynamic nature
of the love-making; the transitive use of a usually intransitive verb ('brennen') and
simultaneously the use of a present participle with a direct object ('Blut dunkle
Zeichen brennend'); the capitalizing of Du/Dein (and Ich) as if the 'loved' one is
being abstracted and invested with a kind of divine status. This is a paradoxical
development because the emphasis in the poem is on the physical, animal nature of
the passion ('Tier an Tier'), on the animal heat which is generated by the passion and
which then melts physical coldness ('*Ein* Reif, geglüht, gereift'). Indeed, Schnack
does not scruple to employ the substantive 'Brunst' in this context, to describe
womankind as 'Bestie der Perversität' ('Weib', I, 9) and to refer to the smells and
aromas of sexual couplings. A perfect unity, a glorious physical amalgamation of Ich
and Du, has been achieved, underlined by the tightly-knit assonance of 'Zweiheit-

20   Benn, *Gesammelte Werke in vier Bänden*, III, p. 27.
21   Paul Hatvani, 'Versuch über den Expressionismus', *Die Aktion*, 7 (1917), cols. 146–50, repr. in
Manifeste und Dokumente zur deutschen Literatur 1910–1920, ed. by Thomas Anz and Michael Stark
(Metzler, 1982), pp. 38–42 (quotations from Section II, p. 39).

Einheit', but in the next seven lines (following the quotation above) the lyrical I immediately reasserts itself, making demand after demand on the Du, focusing solely on its own needs and desires. And then in the last line the 'wir' (no longer capitalized) reappears:

> [...] über Deinen köstlichen Thron
> Stieg mein Blut, oh wir sind (Beide) Blühende nun, ein Gobelin, nicht schöner
> in den Schlössern, verwachsen sind wir, seltsame Verwandtschaften ...

'Steigen' and 'blühen' in Expressionist poetry always indicate physical passion and fulfilment: the present participle as adjectival noun ('Blühende') draws attention to the immediacy and representative nature of the couple's union. 'Gobelin', the name of a French family of dyers who in the seventeenth century began to manufacture high-class tapestry, accentuates the closeness, the almost interwoven character of that union, more beautiful than anything that could be found in the grandest of surroundings, but the use of 'verwachsen' carries a double-edged undertow. The verb 'verwachsen' certainly can mean 'grown together', but it also means 'deformed' and 'misshapen'. Something of the negative implication of 'verwachsen' spills over into the normally neutral 'ver-' of 'Verwandtschaften'. The fact that the relationship is then described as 'seltsam' does nothing to make us believe that this is a pure, long-lasting union. The erratic alternating use of du/dein and Du/Dein suggests that he is sometimes generalizing and idealizing, sometimes holding the memory of a particular female form and body in his mind. Moreover, this poem does not end: the absence of a full stop intimates a mysterious, enigmatic future. Its very title 'Ode an Lulu' is presumably intended to conjure up images of Wedekind's Lulu. And so the wir/Wir does not represent a perfectly balanced and equal blend of desires and needs, but a physical arrangement in which the lyrical I soon resumes and retains complete control. A great deal of posing and posturing goes on here alongside a habit of self-observation, if not self-admiration. In this particular setting the lyrical I remains firmly centre-stage, and Hermann Korte's phrase 'Megalomanien und Allmachtsphantasien', which he regards as characteristic of early Expressionist writing, seems wholly appropriate here.[22]

★   ★   ★   ★   ★

Strophen der Gier can reasonably be described as a lyric cycle only in a very general interpretation of the word, for it is what Helen Mustard, in her study of lyric cycles, calls 'a small collection of lyrics held together by the uniform character of a single mood'. It certainly cannot be counted among what she describes as 'those superior cycles which are united by a fundamental concept, not merely a mood, and whose members are interlinked in the subtlest and most intricate ways'.[23] Indeed, there is little that is subtle or intricate about Schnack's first cycle. It is a small group of poems thrown together in a random configuration, based on memories of the

---

22   Hermann Korte, 'Lyriker des Expressionismus', in *Deutschsprachige Lyriker des 20. Jahrhunderts*, ed. by Ursula Heukenkamp and Peter Geist (Erich Schmidt, 2007), p. 329.
23   Helen Meredith Mustard, *The Lyric Cycle in German Literature* (King's Crown Press, 1946), p. 3.

author's wild days spent in Bolzano just before the outbreak of war in 1914 when
he was barely twenty-one years old. Five years on, those memories are still steeped
in a kind of careless sensuality. All parts of the female body and particularly what
Freud called 'erotogenic zones' (see his 1905 publication, *Three Essays on the Theory
of Sexuality*) are celebrated and, in the very act of writing and recording, the lyrical
I seems to be repeating and rehearsing all the aspects of the physical pleasure
experienced at the time. Indeed, one of his early loves, Erna Biëlka, is reduced to a
series of sexually charged present participles:

> Lang aufgeschossen, Gerte, Weidenzweig, sich Biegende, anmutig Beugende
> der Hüften schlankes Schloß,
> Libelle Wiegende auf Trottoirs, Tänzerin, schwebend [...]
> Kleine Knospen Aufblühende, Kühlung für heiße Stirnen; Leib, schäumender
> [...] ('Erna Biëlka', 1, 8–9)

These present participles ('sich Biegende [...] Beugende [...] Wiegende ...Aufblühende',
and there are others — 'Atmende [...] Hinhorchende ...' — all with feminine-looking
endings, all used as adjectival nouns, and outnumbered by fourteen more present
participles used as adjectives) create an effect of immediate experiencing and yet, at
the same time, make the female figure somehow ethereal and merely representative
of her gender, robbing her of any individuality. There are examples of the past
tense in the cycle, but the fondness for present participles lends an eternalizing
quality to the woman's actions. Schnack achieves the same effect by reducing the
usually anonymous women to bizarre neologisms such as 'Wüterin' and 'Wühlerin'
(though 'Jägerin' in the same poem, 'Erna Biëlka', is less odd): the feminine gender
is clearly highlighted, but there is something disparaging about such confections.
In fact, the 'Kühlung für heiße Stirnen' turns out to be not very effective because
the atmosphere pervading the cycle remains relentlessly hedonistic and sybaritic:
every female form is compliant and mysteriously empowered to bring out the
animal in the lyrical I who is constantly passing through what Korte calls 'ein
Selbstdarstellungsritual', constantly yielding to 'eine Neigung zur Theatralisierung
der eigenen Autorschaft'.[24]

> Kaum daß ich rein saß, zart und verzagt, zählend die süßen Sterne, nun Stier,
> nun Tier.
> Oh, böse Grausamkeit, Sturm in den Adern, säend viel Fieber, blauverglasend
> alle Glieder [...] ('Abendlied', 1, 8)

The sound-patterns in the consonants and the long and short vowels in that first
line — 'daß', 'saß', 'zart', 'verzagt', 'zählend', 'süßen Sterne', 'Stier', 'Tier' —
seem to underscore and accentuate the abiding sense of physical satiety. If every
woman unhesitatingly offers him sexual satisfaction and refuge in the midst of
his accesses of existential angst ('Seltsam greifen mich Dinge an'), the places he
describes become scenes of unlicensed pleasure, seraglios created apparently for his
pleasure alone, uninterrupted and uninvaded by other human beings. In the same
poem the lyrical I ('ein buntes Bild') confidently wanders the streets, but there are

---

24   Korte, pp. 319–20.

hints of discomfort (the 'lachende Mäuse in alten Decken' are perhaps mocking spectators) and even of menace in the 'Falterflug, vergrauter, um den Ruß der Lampenzwiebel', in the image 'schwärzer bluten meine Gebete über den Rand der Hände', even in the eye-catching use of the accusative case again in the line 'Weiß wachse ich ins Tuch des Bettes' (1, 7–8). However, the final two words of the poem, 'Brut' and 'Gier', reassert the scene's strong undertow of sexuality. Earth becomes a pimp, and the natural world becomes an accomplice, mobilized in support of the lyrical I's erotic longings.

> Erde, der starke, wilde Zuhälter
> Duftet seltsam und hüllt alles in braune Süßigkeit [...]
> Kleine Falter im Ried und das schwankende Licht der Leuchtkäfer,
> Junge Sehnsucht ist roter Mohn geworden;
> Alle Lilien sind Fleisch und flüstern mit heißen Liebesworten
> Den schönen Sternen zu, die einsam sind ... ('Abend', 1, 7).

Brown fields and evening (superficial echoes of Trakl), the South and green swamps (one thinks of Benn), poppies, stars, brows, red clover, velvet, fire, blood, all usually in the context of torrid sexual encounters — these are the typical paraphernalia of the poems in *Strophen der Gier*, and many of them will re-emerge in later cycles.

The most interesting aspect of this early collection is that it enables us to have a preview of how later, more substantial volumes will develop. Amounting as it does to a short series of lustful paeans to the female form, it is also a showcase for some of the skills and techniques which characterize Schnack's best work. If not from the first poem ('Abend') then certainly from the second ('Abendlied'), the verse is demonstrably Schnack's. The lines are long and irregular ('Erna Biëlka' has one line of 36 syllables), the sound patterns and the alliteration are striking ('Oh satte Seltsamkeit, oh See, so südlich! Oh selige Verneinung!', 1, 9) and a habit of seeking idiosyncratic rhymings is established. There are typical examples in almost every poem: in 'Träumerei im Café', for instance, we find 'Bogenlampennacht'/'entgegen-lacht', 'Toren'/'Muschelohren', 'rufen'/'Sandsteinstufen' (1, 11), characteristic pairs where the very length of the rhyming words or, conversely, the linking of long and short words, becomes Schnack's trademark. The only poet I can think of who composes rhymes in a similar way is Hans Schiebelhuth. Sometimes the massive compound nouns used by Schnack (as with 'Bogenlampennacht' or, in 'Abendlied', 'Lampenzwiebel') look simply clumsy, or overwhelm their smaller partner; sometimes, too, the rhyming is lazy and does not work — 'Wiese'/'Ineinanderfließen' (in 'Ode an Lulu'), 'Dunkel'/'Dschungel' (in 'Liebesstrophe'), 'Mohnwiesen'/'hinzufließen' (in 'Sehnsucht nach der Stadt'). As in *Tier rang*, the attention paid to rhyming has a further purpose beyond the playful or merely aesthetic — this time to contain, and thus somehow to shape, not the horrors of war but the memories of a joyfully youthful time. Indeed, *Strophen der Gier*, and particularly the poem 'Träumerei im Café', introduces us to some of the women and places and incidents which will be so regularly invoked and recalled in his volume of war poetry as a consolatory bulwark against the nightmarish visions of trench warfare. There is even a sonnet ('Sonett der Gier', 1, 12–13) rhyming abba

/ cddc / efg / efg, pointing the way to its successors in the later collection. The presence of some formal control means that the language of Schnack's poems is not quite as radically subversive and destructive as the work of some of the poets whom Pinthus must have had in mind when he speaks of 'Sprachzertrümmerung' in his survey of Expressionist verse in the introduction to *Menschheitsdämmerung*,[25] but that does not diminish or dilute the Expressionist character of Schnack's poetry.

Strophen der Gier is a volume, after all, which is founded in, and virtually dedicated to, emotion — feeling, in this case, lust at all cost, in all circumstances. Walt Whitman's *Song of Myself* again comes to mind:

> Through me forbidden voices,
> Voices of sexes and lust, veil'd and I remove the veil
> [...]
> I believe in the flesh and the appetites
> (Section 24, *Song of Myself*, 1892 version)

There is no one to represent reason and reasonableness which are nowhere to be encountered or, rather, are always compelled to withdraw. In the poem 'Weib', the female partner is once again reduced to a present participle ('Schürzende', the very first word of the poem): this is woman generalized, little more than a sex object in thrall to a lyrical I who will not be denied (I, 9–10). Moreover, the strong implication is that 'der reine Geist', 'das Großhirn', retreats before 'das Tier' in us,[26] while in 'An eine Gespielin', the brain appears to have few answers to the puzzles which preoccupy the poet (such as 'wer weißte die Wolken?'), and by the end of that poem the lyrical I is once more succumbing to its fever 'nach deinen Brüsten [...] nach deinem Haar, nach deinem feuerroten Mund' (I, 10–11). Two totally unexpected and unusual dative cases ('tiefe Rätsel dem Hirn' and 'dem flachen Mädchenkinderleib') catch the eye in this poem: the strain thus placed on the dative case seems to underline the message of this cycle: that woman is there to *give* herself, to *be given*, *to* man. The 'du'/'Du' of the poems is invariably simply womankind, invested presumably with memories of specific women who brightened the days of the young assistant editor Anton Schnack in Bolzano in 1914. In one poem ('Sehnsucht nach der Stadt'), the slim girls metamorphose into 'Frauen', as if the lyrical I is growing up in the telling of the story (I, 12). In another poem 'Erna Biëlka' (I, 8–9), the act of love-making seems to amount literally to physical entanglement: natural landscape is replaced by female bodyscape full of 'Schlingpflanze [...] Liane [...] Binse [...] Klette und Klammer'. The language of the poems, too, is replete with Expressionist features: abstraction, exclamations, imprecations, invocations, stop-start sentences interspersed with long extended lines, unusual syntax, a general sense of escalating tension and of hectic pace, an insistent tone, questions introduced by 'wer' left unanswered hanging in the air, the

25   Pinthus, p. 13.
26   'Großhirn' (cerebrum) is a technical medical/scientific term, reminiscent of the language favoured by Gottfried Benn. It must be said that 'der reine Geist' and 'das Großhirn' are very strangely juxtaposed, because, with the verb in the singular, it looks as if they are intended to be synonyms, or at least complementary.

accumulation of substantives and powerful verbs, then substantives standing alone. The endeavour to re-enact scenes of past physical delight is so urgent and intense that a momentum is achieved which passes beyond rational control and sweeps the reader along. Occasionally, though, the action is brought to an abrupt halt, not so much by a striking image — though there are examples of these — but by a memorable line: in the poem 'Abendlied', 'Wieder rauchend vor der Nacht die große Not, die dumpfe und zerstückelnde wieder und wieder' (I, 8) takes us beyond more commonplace Expressionist confections towards the consistently striking imagery of *Tier rang*. Perhaps it also takes us back towards Trakl again — Schnack's 'große Not' (if admittedly less powerful) puts us in mind of the 'gewaltiger Schmerz' of 'Grodek', one of the greatest of all German First World War poems.

The figure of the lyrical I in the poems of *Strophen der Gier* clearly draws on autobiographical experience or wishful thinking: at this stage of his poetic development the lyrical I casts Schnack as the archetypal Expressionist poet — a masterful lover, a free-wheeling student in search of new experiences and yet (implicitly) claiming to be already experienced, a libertine (in the style of Joris-Karl Huysmans's neurasthenic aristocrat Des Esseintes whom Schnack admired),[27] the one who feels everything more deeply than anyone else and who is entitled (because passion on its own justifies and endorses all actions) to project his self through the world. The lyrical I thus enables the poet to experiment with other identities, to explore his own identity and sexuality, to cultivate particular self-images and to create exciting alter egos. A modern example of the same poetic process is the volume *Jilted City*, published in 2010 by the Oxford-based poet Patrick McGuinness. Its final section, 'City of Lost Walks', was written, we are told, by the Romanian poet Liviu Campanu and translated by McGuinness. In fact, Campanu is a fiction, a fully imagined other person, a late middle-aged writer. The guise of Campanu gives McGuinness 'new ways to be myself. It was never done as a hoax,' he explains in a recent interview, 'it was done as an experiment in a voice [...] as a poet, I spent quite a lot of time trying to be the kind of person I wasn't.'[28] A similar process seems to be happening in the poetry of Anton Schnack. In his case, in this very early phase of his career, the principal 'voice' is that of a lyrical I which will not be shifted from the path of intense self-indulgence.

Other conclusions should be drawn from this early cycle in order to prepare the way for subsequent collections and to confirm Schnack's status as an Expressionist poet. The individual poems in *Strophen der Gier* constitute a series of one-to-one, but inherently one-sided, physical encounters in which the lyrical I asserts a presumptuous masculinity and allows for little response from his partner. There is a strong aura of adolescent sexual exploration and experimentation about these encounters, after the manner of the main characters in Wedekind's *Frühlings Erwachen*; the experience of lying with a woman is all that matters, and it is unarguably *his* experience, bereft of moral considerations and thoughts about possible consequences. It becomes immediately clear that these are not love poems

---

27   See Schnack's 1924 essay 'Zimmer in der Dämmerung', II, pp. 354–56, particularly p. 355.
28   Patrick McGuinness, 'Altered States', *Daily Telegraph*, 31 December 2011.

in the traditional Romantic/romantic sense because the nature and status of the du/Du are blurred and there is no emotional equilibrium or equality founded in mutual thoughtfulness between the couple, but then there are very few love poems of this kind in the Expressionist oeuvre. Moreover, there is a deliberate rejection of the Romantic trope of the lyric poet's infinitely grateful retreat to Nature for peace and consolation:

> Zuviel der schweren Krähen, der Frühlinge, singend in Birkenhainen,
> Süß waren zwar die Lager im Gras und die dunklen Flöten der Knaben,
> Doch die Sicheln singen zu oft.
>
> ('Sehnsucht nach der Stadt', 1, 12)

The countryside is rejected in favour of the city, and the lyrical I disdains lying in the grass with his partner's body for the opportunity of fulfilling the desire 'steilzüngelnd über Stadt und tausend Frauen trinken hinzufließen...', ibid.) in the cities. Women, as well as being reduced to a series of present participles and weird confections ('Gespielen', 'Wühlern', etc.), appear variously as 'Weib', 'Frau' and 'Mädchen'. Barbara Wright shows that 'Weib', always used in a derogatory sense in Expressionist poetry, is the term most frequently employed in, for example, *Menschheitsdämmerung*, followed by 'Mädchen', then 'Frau' as a distant third,[29] and certainly the curt bluntness of the monosyllabic 'Weib', beginning and ending with a harsh consonant, even sounds bleak. This use of 'Weib' is of a piece with the Expressionist writers' tendency to identify with those marginalized in society — prostitutes, criminals, prisoners, the sick, lunatics — and the lure of prostitutes in particular for the male partner makes city life attractive in *Strophen der Gier* ('Trunken aber mach mich die weißen Schenkel der Kokotten'; 'Sehnsucht nach der Stadt', 1, 12). The word 'Tier', like 'Weib', carries special significance in the cycle: it rhymes with 'Gier' (as in the last quatrain of the poem, 'Abendlied', 1, 8) in the same way that 'Weib' rhymes with 'Leib' and is used in *Strophen der Gier* to denote the ferocity of animal coupling ('Nur manchmal das Tier schreit in uns, bäumt sich, will springen [...]'; 'Weib', 1, 10), whereas in *Tier rang* it connotes a desperately instinctual and primitive fighting-for-life. The frank eroticism of the poems and their obsession with the female body conjure images of Egon Schiele's paintings, his sitting and resting female nudes, for instance, an exhibition of which Schnack may well have visited in Munich in 1911 and even subsequently reviewed for the *Bozner Tagblatt*. The form of the poems prepares us for *Tier rang*: the long lines of verse, reflecting the slim contours of his partner's long body, and the consistent rhyming are wholly characteristic of the later cycle where the writer's determination to miss nothing out in his descriptions of frontline conditions threatens to burst the bounds of individual lines. In the same way, in *Strophen der Gier*, he is set upon making the most of his carnal exploration and we are spared no detail of his liaisons, real or imaginary, even if it leads to a fifty-five-syllable line as in 'Sehnsucht nach der Stadt'. While there are many evocative and striking visual images ('Müd an der Stiege das Spinnenspiel, das silberne, zappelnd die blauen Mücken. | Und dies gelbe Blume im Topf. Kinderhände. Kindermund, Echo über die Hügel, so matt verhallt';

---

29   Wright, p. 301.

'An eine Gespielin', I, 10), there are an equal number of rather embarrassing images, the embarrassment arising from clumsy conflations of references to the natural landscape and anatomical details of the female form. At such points *Strophen der Gier* confirms Hellmut Thomke's judgement on Expressionism's neurotic relationship to sexuality:

> Die oft peinliche Haltung des Sexuellen im Gefolge Whitmans, Schlafs, Bölsches... gehörte zu den Erscheinungsformen des Vitalismus vor und nach der Jahrhundertwende und trat im Expressionismus schließlich in besonders krasser Form zutage ...[30]

★   ★   ★   ★   ★

Schnack's second volume of Expressionist verse is entitled *Der Abenteurer*. Certain words in the Expressionist poet's vocabulary acquired an almost mystical aura — 'Pathos', 'Aufbruch', 'Leben', 'Erlebnis', etc. 'Abenteuer' belongs in this company. It has various connotations and layers of meaning. It certainly promises excitement, raises hopes of travel, new encounters and new experiences, possibly in distant lands, but, much more than all that, it symbolizes blessed release from the stultifying and self-diminishing bourgeois way of life and way of thinking, proof that one is actually alive and living. Above all, it holds out the hope that the individual adventurer/wanderer (the words are interchangeable), seeking 'Abenteuer', shaking off the constraints of bourgeois morality, will finally be able to be themselves. There was, of course, nothing new or original in this ambition: Heinrich Drendorf in Stifter's *Der Nachsommer* was a recent example of a young man setting off on a journey of self-discovery and thus following a routine which was taken for granted in the nineteenth century and long before. It just happened that in their determination to break free and start again whatever the cost and with little thought of the future, Expressionist poets came at the end of a long line of such 'adventurers' and took the phenomenon to another level. After his two years of travelling, Drendorf was always coming back, expecting to find his parents, his fiancée, Natalie, and his home in good order and his old world waiting for him, untroubled and intact.

The lyrical I is frequently the person who Schnack wishes to be or, retrospectively, the person he wishes he had been. In a poem written in 1931, 'Von der Reise zurück', the (fictional) lawyer Dr Alfred Schönwiese places an advertisement in a newspaper in which he enthuses about the people encountered and the places visited on his travels and then ruefully wonders what would have happened if ...

> Aber wenn ihn ein Abenteuer hätte weiter und weiter getrieben
> In ein verwegenes Dasein, gärend von Leidenschaften, Weibern und Trieben?
> Was dann, wenn er verkommen wäre in den Kneipen von Neapel, Marseille, Antwerpen
> Und er hätte gepfiffen auf Gattin, Beruf, Freunde und Erben ...? (I, 289)

The 'Abenteuer', the 'verwegenes Dasein, gärend von Leidenschaften, Weibern und Trieben' could be a summary of one of the encounters so vigorously depicted in

30   Hellmut Thomke, *Hymnische Dichtung im Expressionismus* (Francke, 1972), p. 21.

Strophen der Gier and *Der Abenteurer*. Then Schönwiese endeavours to persuade his readers that all is well, all is back to normal again:

> Doch mit dem 'Zurück von der Reise' versichert er allen Leuten:
> 'So sehr mich auch Meere, Berge und fremde Frauen freuten,
> Die Verführung ging doch nicht so weit. (I, 289)

It is impossible to know the extent to which Schnack regarded the adventurer/ wanderer as an ideal or compensating persona, but, particularly in his later prose-pieces, he returns again and again to the magical, almost mystical, figure of the wanderer:

> [...] ich lobpreise den Wanderer, der betörend durch die Dichtung aller Weltvölker streift. Er macht Märchen, Sagen, Epen und Balladen unheimlich und gespenstisch. Immer wieder reißt der Wanderer die Fesseln von sich und schreitet in die tiefe Nacht hinaus, an die brausenden Flüsse und in die rauschenden Wälder. Die Sehnsucht nach der Ferne, nach dem Unerforschten and Unerlebten verzehrt ihn. Auch ich bin ein Wanderer und habe meine Träume. (II, 541–42)

When the lyrical I, this time in the guise of a piano teacher, describes the wanderer as someone 'der betörend durch die Dichtung aller Weltvölker streift', one needs to look no further than German literature for examples. It is a rich pedigree — from Goethe's two 'Wandrers Nachtlieder', Wilhelm Müller's 'Winterreise', Heine's *Die Harzreise*, but also including Nietzsche's 'Der Wanderer und sein Schatten' and, in Schnack's own time, Walter Flex's First World War bestseller *Der Wanderer zwischen beiden Welten*. Moreover, Wagner's Wanderer (Wotan in disguise) in *Siegfried*, the third of the four operas of *Der Ring des Nibelungen*, and Goebbels's verse-play *Der Wanderer* belong in this sequence. The best contemporary example is Wedekind's play *Der Marquis von Keith* (1901) which

> handelt [...] von einer Existenzform, mit der sich Wedekind nicht gerade identifizierte, in der er aber doch ein Gleichnis seiner eigenen riskanten Position als außenseiterhafter Künstler erkannte: der Existenz des Abenteurers. Mit der Figur des hochstaplerischen Abenteurers Keith greift Wedekind einen Gestalttyp auf, der für die Entwicklung der Wiener Moderne höchste Aktualität besaß.[31]

Schnack's adventurer/wanderer looks familiar to us from Romantic poetry (Byron and Wordsworth in particular), from Eichendorff (whose name is frequently invoked by Schnack)[32] and Heine, from Lamartine and Leconte de Lisle, and, above all, from a contemporary of Schnack, Alain-Fournier, whose *Le Grand Meaulnes* (1913) is sometimes translated as *The Wanderer*.[33] Birgit Dahlke, in her study *Jünglinge der Moderne: Jugendkult und Männlichkeit in der Literatur um 1900*, shows not only how the Wandervögel movement was prospering at the time along with magazines written for young people looking for open-air adventures away from domestic routines but

---

31   Sprengel, p. 542.
32   See, for example, II, 50, 337 and 407.
33   Ironically, Alain-Fournier was killed at Epargue near Verdun on 22 September 1914, very near where Schnack was to be posted fourteen months later.

also that adventure books also were very popular among the young.[34] *Die Abenteuer des Robinson Crusoe von 1719* was a special favourite not least with Anton Schnack, who often adopts Defoe's character as alter ego and even, subsequently, makes his own contribution to the genre with the story, *Die Angel des Robinson* (1946). There is, however, a key difference between the figure of the carefree nature lover or the Romantic wanderer/adventurer (say, Alain-Fournier's Augustin Meaulnes and François Seurel or Eichendorff's Taugenichts) and the Expressionist version. Very little sense of the glorious abundance of Nature and of Nature's power to offer solace and peace to man survives in Expressionist poetry. Instead, the lyrical I appears as a restless, homeless nomad, self-pitying, driven and for ever on the move. Kurt Heynicke, Schnack's almost exact contemporary, writes for example: 'Ich bin ein Wanderer auf der Straße, | aus meiner Dornenkrone tropfen Steine auf die Brust' and 'Ich bin ein Wanderer | und darf nicht verweilen.'[35] It is true that in *Tier rang* there are frequently references to the beauty of the Franconian countryside, but these serve principally as a compensation for the stark realities of the battlefield and it is only with *Die Flaschenpost* (1936) that Schnack retreats to more traditional, and more traditionally Romantic, attitudes and themes. Perhaps a better comparison is with the road-trip adventurers of the later Beat Generation, writers like Jack Kerouac, who, in the 1950s and 1960s, went 'on the road' looking for excitement principally in terms of sexual experimentation and substance abuse. If there is none of the latter in *Der Abenteurer*, there is certainly plenty of the former.

Much in *Der Abenteurer* is familiar to us from the earlier *Strophen der Gier*. Once again the lyrical I as some kind of Lord of Misrule presides while numerous and diverse women emerge in a kind of highly charged, intensely sexual and sensual nostalgic haze. They are exotic (one comes from Brazil, the biblical character Abishag who tended King David is invoked, another poem is dedicated 'to an Italian woman'[36]), they participate in the lyrical I's more or less perverse and grotesque games, they are courtesans, they meet him in 'Bordelle' and 'Lasterhöhlen', they are dancers, they have glamorously seductive names (Paola, Gina Enthregi), they help to conjure up memories of blissful times in Bolzano:

> Ein Abend auch, (in Südtirol) in Laubengängen Musik der Kaiserjäger, ich war dabei, ich ging vorüber,
> Ich warf mit Rosen ins Gewühl, ich lachte laut, ich schwenkte meinen Seidenhut, [...] ('Die Begegnung mit Paola', 1, 20)

This is the typical pattern of events: a scene is set (a dance, a ball, an orgy), pandemonium and licentiousness prevail, everything threatens to collapse into total chaos, and the lyrical I appears not to restore order, but to act as hat-waving centre of attention. Franz Werfel saw the theatre as a crucial venue for everyone

34   Birgit Dahlke, *Jünglinge der Moderne: Jugendkult und Männlichkeit in der Literatur um 1900* (Böhlau, 2006), pp. 197–210 and particularly the chapter 'Das Männlichkeitsnarrative des Abenteurers', pp. 220–28.

35   Kurt Heynicke, 'Erhebung' and 'Gedicht' (respectively), *Jeder Tag: Das lyrische Gesamtwerk* (Scheffler, 2000), pp. 59 and 193.

36   See the poems 'Im Hotelgarten', 'Der Abenteurer' and 'Einer Italienerin' (1, 18, 17 and 26). For Abishag see 1 Kings 1. 15.

and everything to come together, and so the stage, cabaret, cinema, variety theatre became the preferred places for a sort of synaesthetic realization of a kind of Gesamtkunstwerk in which all cultural genres and artists could participate.[37] Poetry, for example, was to be performed, as most famously in the Neopathetisches Cabaret in Berlin and the Cabaret Voltaire in Zürich. Under this aspect, the artist assumes the role of a director. There is certainly something very theatrical about the master of ceremony's role in *Strophen der Gier*. Indeed, the lyrical I shifts more and more into centre stage, appearing in only four of the ten poems of *Strophen der Gier* but in ten of the twelve which make up *Der Abenteurer*. Silvia Schlenstedt, in her *Nachwort* to Martin Reso's anthology of Expressionist poetry, shows how the Expressionist poet, for example Werfel in her account, is prone to 'Überschätzung der eigenen Möglichkeiten' and to a habit of 'Selbstüberschätzung', an overestimation which takes him all the way to being a monomaniacal ruler of his self-created world: 'Durch ein leidenschaftliches Zureden soll der einzelne aufgerufen werden, sich zur Wehr zu setzen, er wird durch den Dichter zum Alleinherrscher seiner Welt gemacht.'[38] The lyrical I as musketeer-adventurer-libertine observes the orgy in almost voyeuristic fashion:

> Helden, Ritter und das Antlitz böser Dirnen. Tänzer schwebten in der Luft, spielend mit braunem Speer,
> Der Madonnen Sehnen. Courtisanenworte. Weiße Nacht aus tausend weißen Lenden.
> Lieder der Bambuspfeifer. Triller auf kecken Flöten. Staub gestreut über dunkle Haare [...]
> Reiter auf Eseln. Kugeln fliegen rot in die Luft. Affen zupfen an einer alten Gitarre. ('Groteske Nacht', I, 21)

It is no longer 'Weiber', let alone 'Frauen' or 'Mädchen', but 'Dirnen' and 'Courtisanen'. The noise is deafening, it is a vision of corybantic debauchery, seedy and sordid in its potential for violence, and while there are all kinds of participating women (whores, dancers, queens, madonnas) and animals (donkeys and apes), the poem ends on a self-mythologizing note as it so often does in the three Expressionist volumes:

> Ich: Säbelglanz, Geheimnis, Antlitz. Dirnen erheben sich, um mich an sich zu pressen.
> Ich bin unendlich schön. Die Seile hängen leer, die Tänzerinnen kommen zu Exzessen.
> Über dem Mond hängt eine Wolke. Ich muß ergriffen sein, denn ich bin plötzlich auf dem Seil zu schauen. ('Groteske Nacht', I, 22)

It seems as if an entire Dada-esque wardrobe has been ransacked to adorn this hybrid spectacle which amounts to something between a catwalk extravaganza, a faux-military performance art *évènement* and a cheap circus tournament. This poem, typical of those in *Der Abenteurer*, may well be an example of what Hermann Korte calls a 'Selbstverständigungsgedicht' in which the ritualistic and the theatrical

---

37   See Thomas Anz, *Literatur des Expressionismus* (Metzler, 2002), pp. 149–52.
38   *Expressionismus: Lyrik*, ed. by Martin Reso (Aufbau, 1969), pp. 647 and 654.

predominate: 'Zelebration und Ritual waren [in Expressionist poetry] Formen poetischer Selbstinszenierung, in denen die hochbedeutende Exklusivität der eigenen Dichtung und des eigenen Künstlertums sakrosankt war.'[39]

In *Der Abenteurer,* the lyrical I is no longer a voyeur: he is caught up in the military glamour ('Säbelglanz') of the imperial officers who are present, he is interestingly enigmatic and invested with mystery ('Geheimnis'), he is blessed, in a gesture of self-aggrandisement, with a 'countenance', not a mere face. Everything is in excess and to excess. The moon is hidden by a cloud which temporarily blocks out the orgiastic revelries. Overwhelmed by the maenadic atmosphere and 'seized' by the uncontrolled and apparently uncontrollable emotions on display, the lyrical I then finds itself walking the tightrope which the bacchic dancers have left empty. This is lyrical I as master of ceremonies, as ringmaster, as compère of some shady cabaret show, a puckish agent of chaos and defiance in the face of what Expressionists regarded as grossly hypocritical morality. The louche cavorting and riotous exhibitionism throw down a challenge to the contemporary censor. The circus atmosphere, the sexual explicitness, the gender interchangeability and femininity seen as animal, all served to create the kind of exuberant sensationalism which prevails in *Der Abenteurer* and even more so, as we shall see, in *Die tausend Gelächter.* Once again, in this context, it is difficult *not* to think of Franz Wedekind's plays. In the prologue to *Erdgeist,* for example, the Animal Tamer opens the scene by speaking to the audience as though they were in a circus and he proceeds to show off Lulu as a rare animal. His first words are:

> Hereinspaziert in die Menagerie,
> Ihr stolzen Herrn, ihr lebenslust'gen Frauen,
> Mit heißer Wollust und mit kaltem Grauen
> Die unbeseelte Kreatur zu schauen.[40]

This is Lulu's world, but the words have come straight from *Strophen der Gier, Der Abenteurer* and *Die tausend Gelächter.* The fact that the penultimate poem of Schnack's first cycle is entitled 'Ode an Lulu' merely reinforces the connection. 'Decadent' is an obvious word to describe the atmosphere which permeates all three cycles until one remembers that, in a highly ironic reversal and with a predictable homage to Nietzsche, this is to be turned against despised bourgeois attitudes and conventions by, for example, Erwin Loewenson, champion of Expressionist poets, George Heym's literary executor and co-founder of Der Neue Club:

> Dekadent ist alles, was dem Diesseits, dem Leben, dem Bravourstück solitärer Kraft, dem Abenteuer, dem heidnisch-unschuldigen Lachen aufatmender Körperlichkeit und den Sensationen Esprit trunkener Nerven abhold ist [...]; daß wir es wissen und uns dagegen wehren, verdanken wir zum größten Teil Nietzsche.[41]

---

39   Hermann Korte, 'Energie der Brüche: Ein diachroner Blick auf die Lyrik des 20. Jahrhunderts und ihre Zäsuren', in *Lyrik des 20. Jahrhunderts,* ed. by Heinz Ludwig Arnold (Text + Kritik, 1999), pp. 63–106 (pp. 68–69).

40   Frank Wedekind, *Werke,* ed. by Elke Austermühl, Rolf Kieser and Hartmut Vinçon, 8 vols (Häusser, 1996), III/I, p. 315.

41   Erwin Loewenson, 'Zur Schopenhauer-Psychologie: Der Masochismus des Unterbewußtseins'.

'Bravourstück solitärer Kraft' is no doubt how the ringmaster would like to regard his performance.

What is also familiar in this collection is the form of many of the poems. Although only one poem in *Strophen der Gier* is a sonnet, half of the poems in *Der Abenteurer* are written in sonnet form, or at least in the sonnet form which Schnack was to perfect in *Tier rang gewaltig mit Tier*, where virtually all of the sixty poems are sonnets. As in that latter volume, the lines of verse vary hugely in length — the opening poem, for example ('Der Abenteurer' — a sonnet), has lines of almost fifty syllables, while another sonnet ('Sexus') has fourteen- and fifteen-syllable lines. The classic sonnet form is shattered here, although now and again (as in 'Wunsch vor dem Schlaf' and 'Sexus') an ostensible attempt is made to maintain the traditional sonnet shape of two quatrains and two tercets (or one sestet). Schnack's escalating recourse to the sonnet form can possibly be explained as a last-gasp compromise. By all accounts (for example, from his surviving family), a good solid member of the middle class himself, from an evidently upright and law-abiding Franconian family, Schnack was not able to 'go the whole way' in matching riotous content with equally undisciplined poetic form. Like Dr. Alfred Schönwiese, he might claim that 'Die Verführung ging nicht so weit'. The sonnet form thus acts as containment and discipline: it performs a similar function, it will be suggested in *Tier rang*, but there, of course, what is being 'contained' is very different. The rhyming in *Der Abenteurer* is once again eye-catching. The poem 'Im Hotelgarten' (I, 18) contains 'Purpurrachen' and 'Lachen', 'überpudert' and 'verludert', 'Sensationen' and 'thronen' — such combinations are wholly typical. These end-rhymes, both original and ingenious, in no way dilute or diminish the Dionysian urgency of the atmosphere, and they barely contain it. In typical Expressionist fashion everything is either 'fiebernd' or 'fieberhaft'. The lyrical I does not speak its words but screams them:

> Oh, ich schrie Worte aus von dem, von allem, von dem Purpurprunk,
> Von knisternder Verseidigung, von Land, dem leiblichen, [...] ('Sexus', I, 19)

The delight experienced in observing and describing the female body is unmistakable:

> Ewiges Elfenbein, gemeißelt; oh die Brust, gefüllt, verprallend, rötlich,
> rund; gemacht,
> Um zu durchstrahlen Samtverschnürung. ('Sexus', I, 19)

Nobody is at rest, eight of the twelve poems end, or rather do not end, with ...,
the physical urgency is relentless, movement is all. Schnack conveys this even in his characteristic use of prepositions and their cases. Where logically we would expect a dative case, we are startled by his use of the much more dynamic accusative. In the same poem, for example, Schnack describes visions of 'Raufereien her in Spelunken, von einer Trunkenheit, wo über <u>den</u> Mund hing der Rauch von Schaum' (I, 17), an apparently conscious conceit because in 'Groteske Nacht' he writes 'Über <u>dem</u> Mond hängt eine Wolke' (I, 22) and by the last poem of the cycle we have 'über

Lecture in Der Neue Club, 23 November 1910, unpublished. Quoted in Gunter Martens, *Vitalismus und Expressionismus* (Kohlhammer, 1971), p. 192.

meiner Stirne' twice in quick succession, one again with the verb 'hängt'. Another ploy which has an unsettling, disorientating effect is to use intransitive verbs transitively, as in the lines 'Alles glänzt ihr Auge' in the poem 'Einer Italienerin' (26), or to confuse subject and object as in 'Unendlichkeit ergreift das Volk' in 'Groteske Nacht' (I, 21) and 'sie lullt kein Wiegenlied' ('Müdigkeit, I, 24) — what is the subject, what is the direct object here? Such grammatical and semantic dislocation is, as Hellmut Thomke has pointed out, typical of Expressionist poetry.[42] And yet there is, since *Strophen der Gier*, a clear development which is perhaps best encapsulated in Schnack's increasing use of verbs prefixed by 'ver-', indicating, as that prefix often does, a sense of fading and decaying, dying and disappearing, subsiding and waning — 'verludert', 'verwölkt', 'verwebt', 'verprallend', 'verleuchtet', 'verquollen', 'verwühlt', 'verlebt' (contrasting with 'verliebt' in the same poem), 'verwesend', 'verfinstert', 'verwahrlost', 'verlodert', 'verkniffen'. This is not an exhaustive list: some of these past and present participles are neologisms. A striking example occurs in the poem 'Abenteuerliche Silhouette' (I, 19–20), where the lyrical I is portrayed as being 'verseidigt von der Frau', suggesting both the corruptly soft ways of the woman and her elemental power and Schnack's frequent creation of them contrasts with the methods employed by another Expressionist poet who experimented with language and who, like Schnack, wrote for *Der Sturm*. August Stramm customarily removed prefixes in order to draw out the essential, substantial quality of a verb and thus avoid the merely descriptive, interpretative and adventitious. Schnack, on the other hand, insists on retaining the 'ver-' and on devising as many verbs with that prefix as he can in order to underline the inevitably fading, diminishing nature of the Expressionist ecstasy. They seem to imply doubt and distance inherent in that ecstasy alongside the usual connotation of an element of corruption — a 'corrupted love' ('verliebt'), a life battered by sexual excess ('verlebt'). Even 'veredelt' (in the poem, 'Im Hotelgarten' (I, 23)), invariably used in a positive sense, bears a hint of corruption. Such poetic techniques will appear, transmuted, in *Tier rang*. Even occasions when the lyrical I seems most confident, almost imperious, can be jeopardized by the sudden injection of one such neologism:

> Nun erscheine ich, ein Lächeln der Dunkelheit... verquollen, leicht befressen
> Von den wilden Krankheiten [...] ('Groteske Nacht', I, 22)

The fading, the diminishing of Expressionism, accompanied by a strong sense of disillusionment, all emerge in *Der Abenteurer*. The lyrical I tires of the role of trail-blazing physical 'vagabond'.[43] There is now a mixture of moods and plunges in emotional temperature. The same array of diverse women and pleasures is evident, but so is the impression that the women are growing older and the pleasures a little stale. They appear in all kinds of guises and disguises, few of them flattering: as 'Huren', 'Frauen', 'Weiber', 'Kokotten', 'Dirnen der Häfen', but also as 'Trikottänzerinnen' and 'Hirtinnentöchter', even once as 'Göttin'. The stranger concoctions seem merely to compound the disparagement of womankind. Indeed,

---

42   See Thomke, especially pp. 146–48 and 172–75.
43   The word is Schnack's. See 'Das fränkische Jahr' in *Eine Kalender-Kantate (1934)* (Pattloch, 1952), p. 92. This essay is not in Vollmer.

the 'Trikottänzerinnen', we read in 'Groteske Nacht', 'wuchern', a verb which invariably has an impersonal subject (usually plants, particularly weeds) and means 'run out of control' or 'proliferate in a malign way', with, as a secondary meaning, heavy financial implications. The word 'Mädchen' appears just once (in 'Groteske Nacht'), only then to be qualified there as 'krank und arm' (1, 22). Intimacy, too, has been eroded: a 'du' had appeared frequently in *Strophen der Gier*, but now appears only once, and then in capitalized form, in *Der Abenteurer* (in 'Sexus'). Moreover, the fact that in some poems, Schnack begins to omit question-marks as he lies there trying to remember what he actually knew about his partners somehow indicates a less-than-serious nature of the self-interrogation *and* of the original relationship. Women become more elusive, at least in the memory: they elude his remembering ('Ich weiß nichts mehr von ihr: war sie wie warmes Wasser, blau, blühte köstlich die Schale | Im Marmor ihres Leibes?' ('Ekstase', 1, 24). Nor can he recall details of their trysts — 'irgendwo' appears four times in his reminiscences about Gina Enthregi. He seems slightly baffled and disconcerted by his poor remembering, but then he never really presented himself as committed to any of his companions. Any 'ecstatic encounter' was devoid of emotional engagement. While his body may have been fully occupied, his heart and mind were not. And where he does seek details, the direct questions emerge in a desperate torrent: the earlier certainty, embedded in hedonistic self-gratification, is now hedged by conditional tenses and verbs in the subjunctive mood, as he describes himself:

> [...] ganz mit dem beschäftigt: wie läge unterm Tuch die Haut [...] wie wölbe
> sich das Knie? Hellrosig-rot? wie glühe Flaum der Achsel? goldbronzen,
> kupferiggeflammt?
>   Wie böge sich Leib dicht bei Leib [...] ('Die Begegnung mit Paola', 1, 21)

The poet is tired, and if he is still pleased and prepared to be heedless and cavalier, 'hineinzufallen ins Gelächter einer Nacht, zu Schmausereien, Trinkgelagen, brüllend, schäumend, wild, | In Tänze, sinnlich, in Bordells [...]' ('Wunsch vor dem Schlaf', 1, 25) that pleasure and preparedness are overwhelmed by the black mood which is the central and abiding feature of the last poem in the collection, appropriately entitled 'Umnachtung'. Its first line sets the tone: 'Über meiner Stirne ist es dunkel geworden, über meiner Stirne hängt alles hernieder' (1, 27). That darkness issues by the end into images of death, destruction and decay. The combination of Eros (sexual impulses and their ensuing amorous desires) and Thanatos (destructive, aggressive eschatological urges) is evident here. In the very last line of the cycle, the lyrical 'I' uses the kind of self-denigrating language and the kind of images familiar to us from the poetry of Benn, Heym and Ehrenstein:

> [...] nun verfaule ich unter der Haut, hänge hinab zum Tod
> Mit Brand im Antlitz, leise bin ich, ein Lied, ein herbstliches, Erde werde ich
> werden und auf den Straßen liegen, alt, wie Kot ... (1, 27)

Those lines not only point to scenes which dominate *Tier rang*, but, in the final analysis, they remind us that the human body has a purely functional purpose as well as being the object of male lust. It is a subdued and chastening demise instinct with disillusionment, there is a strong sense of an era coming to an end, and the disillusionment stems at least in part from the fact that the lyrical I feels that he has left behind, been made to leave behind, the countryside and is now condemned to live in the city, a reverse of the process noted in *Strophen der Gier* where he had wanted to make the move. He feels ill at ease there: 'Die Stadt ist groß. Ich kenne mich in ihren gleichen Straßen nicht mehr aus' ('Müdigkeit', I, 24). In a low-key reminder of a favourite Expressionist topos and a concept propagated in Freud's 1899 study, *Die Traumdeutung*, Schnack blames his father for compelling him to go there, to the city with its meretricious laughter and wild songs, thus abandoning meadows and silent country summers and shepherds' fires: 'Was ließt du mich in die Städte gehn, Vater [...]' (ibid., I, 24). At this juncture one is reminded of some of Brecht's poems, especially 'Vom armen B.B' and 'An die Nachgeborenen' ('In die Städte kam ich zur Zeit der Unordnung').[44] The wild songs are not the peaceful lullabies which the lyrical I now craves: 'Die Stadt ist groß, sie lullt kein Wiegenlied'. And the worst thing of all is that he does not know what the countryside now means to him: 'Was ist das Land mir noch, da mir schon alles Blut über die Städteabende sprang' (ibid., I, 25). This whole opposition of city versus countryside is, once again, an Expressionist (and Romantic) topos, and Schnack is rehearsing that opposition by depicting the extravagant pleasures of city-dwellers, and at least implying the corrupting forces of the modern industrialized world. Where Schnack differs from fellow Expressionist writers (for example, Georg Heym), who are typically urban poets, is in his habit, even more evident in *Tier rang* than here, of casting a nostalgic glance backwards to the countryside, as he remembers it from his youth. For Schnack, nature (in *Der Abenteurer*) becomes by the end of the cycle a source of consolation not only for the volatile Expressionist poet, but also, as we shall see in *Tier rang*, for the First World War soldier. But the last word of the cycle, as already indicated, is 'Kot...', a shocking conclusion after all the joy in the earlier paeans to sex and sexual pleasure. The word 'Sexus', title of the third poem, cannot fail to evoke images of Roman orgies, but 'Kot' is a reminder of the reverse side of Expressionist 'Selbstüberschätzung'. The same word and the same image reappear in all their harshness, not softened by the addition of the dative -e, in the self-disparaging, self-pitying tone of Walter Hasenclever's lines:

> Ich selbst hier im dumpfen Kote
> Ich letztes erbärmliches Tier,
> Ich Hund vor einem Stück Brote,
> Ich rufe und schreie zu Dir.[45]

'Das Tierische' of the first poem in the *Der Abenteurer* cycle, the fiercely sexual 'Tier' of the poems in the first cycle, *Strophen der Gier*, has shrunk to a rather subdued and passive spectator, tired, prey to dark moods and dark thoughts. For the first time the lyrical I is seen to be vulnerable, slightly enfeebled and querulous: the wanderer/adventurer has reached not a goal or a haven, among discomforting memories, but an uncomfortable no-man's-land between countryside and city, between domestic stability and alien uncertainty.

---

44   Bertolt Brecht, *Gedichte IV: Gedichte 1934–1941* (Suhrkamp, 1961), p. 144.
45   Walter Hasenclever, 'Tod 14', quoted in Uwe Wandrey, *Das Motiv des Krieges in der expressionistischen Lyrik*, Geistes- und Sozialwissenschaftliche Dissertationen 23 (Lüdke, 1972), p. 173.

★   ★   ★   ★   ★

Die tausend Gelächter (1919), the third of the three volumes of Schnack's Expressionist verse, takes its title, in fact, from the poem 'Der Abenteurer' in the previous collection. The brain falls sick, we read, 'zerstört von den Nadeln der Abenteuer, von den tausend Gelächtern der Nächte'. The lyrical I, appearing in all but one of the poems, begins by resuming control and presiding over events. The loose cycle of fourteen poems is dedicated to 'Ma aus Franken', Maria Glöckler from Kahl am Main, Schnack's future wife. The fact that it is dedicated to her does not mean that Schnack feels obliged to soften the voice of the lyrical I in the poems or to spare Ma any of the more exuberant outbursts which are already familiar from earlier collections. Nor is there any question of traditional love poetry in the Romantic mode. The title of the first poem, 'Fremde', is ambiguous and revealing: 'foreign land' or 'strange woman'? And the ambiguity is not clarified when, later in the poem, we read 'Da stand ich gläubig und versunken | In tausend Wunder dieser Fremde eingegraben, [...]' (I, 31). The tone is set from the first line of this poem: 'Da stand ich mitten im Gedränge', typically claiming the central position and thus a superior view of events, but by the final poem, 'Unrast', there are spells of regret and remorse during which considerable reservations are voiced about the value of the life that has been led, and an inventory of sins is drawn up in the aptly titled 'Sündenregister':

> Ich zeichnete an meines Leibes jungen schlanken Linien Nacht für Nacht,
> Zerstörte ihn, verheerte ihn, zerschlug sein Fleisch mit scharfen Wollustruten
> Und warf ihn in die Bäder, in die Thermen rauchverblauter Gluten
> Und grub Gesundheit ab in seinen Adern, Schacht für Schacht. (I, 39)

The body of the lyrical I may have been 'destroyed' during all those nights of sexual indulgence so that it has aged before its time, but the nocturnal debauchery is depicted with such barely concealed erotic fervour in the by now well-established kind of simmeringly lustful language of *Der Abenteurer* and *Strophen der Gier* that we begin to doubt the sincerity of the confession. The omnipresent rhyming and the ingenuity of that rhyming just about contain the sexual fervour without beginning to diminish it and the ploy of having a long rhyming word ('Wollustruten') overwhelming a much shorter one will become a feature of *Tier rang*. The first line of the final tercet of 'Sündenregister' certainly sounds a warning in an image which, not for the first time, is reminiscent of Georg Trakl's verse (though the jokiness of the second line is not):

> Der weiße Ton des Wahnsinns schwebt aufsteigend hinter seiner [his body's]
> Stirne Mauern,
> Mein schlanker von den Nächten abgeklärter Leib nicht Jahre wird es dauern,
> Bis die Erstarrung steigt mit hartem Glanz in Wimpern und in jedes Glied!
> (I, 40)

The odd word-order in the second line of the tercet ('Mein schlanker [...]') has a disconcerting effect and is again a favoured characteristic of the poet. There are other poems in the cycle which are freighted with the same degree and with the same kind of carnal satyrism without necessarily carrying any kind of remorse for past 'sins' — see, for example, 'Ode der Liebe' and 'Nacht-Juli'. In 'Großes Gefühl', typically Expressionist bravado bursts forth: 'Ich will mich über alles versprengen, über alles ruf' ich mein Blut hinaus, über Lärm und Lied'. This mission to project his internal vision into the external world, repeated in the line 'Dies wird ein süßer Abend sein, wenn ich über allem blühe'[46] in the same poem, can perhaps be best understood by contrasting it with the method of Rainer Maria Rilke, whose creative movement works in the opposite direction. Unlike the Expressionist poet who seeks to benefit reality by overwhelming and reshaping it with the irresistibly transforming power of his self, Rilke's whole endeavour, at least at the time of *Neue Gedichte*, is to take time (ravages of which the lyrical I in Schnack's poem 'Tagebuchblatt' is all too aware) and against the deformations and devaluations of the modern world: 'Soweit man das absehen kann, ist aber meine lyrische Arbeit [...] ein persönliches Besitzergreifen, eine Bewältigung der Außenwelt.'[47] Where Rilke writes of a 'persönliches Besitzergreifen', the Expressionist poet is ever eager to engage in the dramatic act of 'sich ausschenken,' 'sich fortschenken' and of 'Sich verschenken'[48] and now, in Schnack, of 'sich versprengen'. The concern that it is not easy to imagine how either Rilke's or the Expressionist poet's declaration of intent might look or work in practice, beyond the page, beyond the saying of it, in no way diminishes the ardour of their respective personal commitments. Nor, in either process, is there any suggestion of a dilution of power in the poet (in Rilke's project) or in the lyrical I (in the Expressionist poet's mission). As far as the latter is concerned, there is an interesting tension at work: on the one hand, the Expressionist poet feels almost jealously proprietorial about his self (Hermann Korte uses the words 'Exklusivität' and 'sakrosankt' in this context[49]), but on the other hand he is driven by an intense ambition to dispense and to disperse that self in a grand externalizing gesture for the good of mankind. Yet, despite that grand gesture, as on other occasions in the two earlier volumes, loneliness intervenes in Schnack's *Die tausend Gelächter* and a powerful sense of existential alienation and dislocation makes itself suddenly felt. The lyrical I feels cut off from the past, and the only recourse is to refuse to inquire after 'den Dingen der Heimat' and to plunge into the pleasures available in foreign places:

> Da stand ich mitten im Gedränge:
> Abschied und Abfahrt, Flug durch Dunkel, Flug durch Tag,
> Verfetzte Wiesen, Wälder, Hänge, Hag,
> [...]
> Alles war ausgelöscht mit einem jähen Schlag [...]
> Da stand ich gläubig und versunken
> In tausend Wunder dieser Fremde eingegraben, [...] ('Fremde', 1, 31).

---

46   One would have expected 'über alles' (Acc), especially as in the poem 'Ekstase im Tanz' (i, 34–35) Schnack writes: 'Reichtum blüht groß über den schmalen Arm.' Moreover, in the line quoted immediately before, Schnack is intent on retaining the (more) dynamic accusative case with the verbs 'sich versprengen' and 'hinausrufen'. In both instances the verbs are followed by 'über alles'.

47   Rainer Maria Rilke, *Briefe*, ed. by Horst Nalewski, 2 vols (Insel, 1991), 1, pp. 293–94.

48   All Stadler. See p. 44 for sources of these infinitives.

49   Korte, 'Energie der Brüche'. See n. 39 for the full quotation.

The 'Da stand ich [...]' exemplifies the dramatic or theatrical nature of the lyrical I's posturing which goes from 'Da stand ich [...]' to 'Da kam ich her [...]' to 'Ich ging von ihr, von wem?' because all that matters to him in his narrative are his arrivals and departures, his origins and destinations. In fact, it is not quite the only recourse: there are always women to tempt him — 'Aus schnellem Drange neuen Blutes wagend | Schritt ich den Frauen nach gelockt von ihrem Stolz' ('Fremde', I, 31). The temperature of the sexual encounters with women who, unlike in *Der Abenteurer*, are never named runs no less high in this volume than in the earlier ones and it is surprising in some ways that the official censor (as far as we know) did not intervene, as happened with Wedekind's plays and poems:

> Ich zeichnete an meinem Leib und viele heiße Hände zeichneten mit mir
> Und gruben oft und langbedächtig in der Nacht und schlürften
> Mit reifem Mund an seinem Quellenschacht in niegestillter Gier
> Und blauten Ringe um die Augen [...] ('Sündenregister', I, 39)

Sexual innuendo and double entendres and dubious metaphors proliferate:

> Dunkles liegt über ihrem Knie, Reichtum blüht groß über den schmalen
> Arm. ('Ekstase im Tanz', I, 35)
> Klein und schmal spähte ihr Portal in mich, offen und groß brach es ins Licht
> unter der Glut meiner silbernen Scheiter [...] ('Ode der Liebe', I, 32)
> In vielen süßen Frauenleibern liegt verschwendet seiner [lyrical I's body]
> Kräfte Gold
> Und wuchert dort, umrauscht von fremdem Blut, [...] ('Sündenregister', I, 39).

'Tier' appears regularly in this context once again — the female partner as animal, the relationship as animalistic, the lyrical I as animal — he even wonders on one occasion, 'Wer hatte mich gemacht zum Tier, zum tollen [...]' (I, 40). It is almost as if the lyrical I is now playing a semi-detached observing role and is reviewing its own sexual performance. The influence of Hans Schiebelhuth is perhaps discernible here: like Schnack, he was at Munich University in 1913, like Schnack he was part of the Darmstädter Sezession in 1919, and Schnack, in a rare surviving document, wrote an admiring review of a selection of Schiebelhuth's poetry in 1919.[50] In 'Hymne des Maropampa', in long irregular lines, not dissimilar to Schnack, he offers a paean to the thrills of exotic adventure and travel — and to Eros. The poems of Richard Dehmel, particularly of those collected under the headings *Weib und Welt* (1896), which the courts deemed obscene and blasphemous, and *Die Verwandlungen der Venus* (1907, subtitled 'Erotische Rhapsodie mit einer moralischen Ouvertüre'), were hugely influential in the pre-First World War era for their provocative challenge to middle-class values and attitudes and should also be referenced in this context. The form of his poems (but not the content or the sentiments) are very different from Schnack's:

> Gieß aus in mich die Schale deiner Glut!
> Befrei mich von der Sünde: von dem Grauen
> vor dieses Feuerregens wilder Brut,

---

50   Schnack, 'Der Lyriker Hans Schiebelhuth', in *Feuer* 1919/1920, pp. 829–31.

von diesen Wehn, die wühlend in mir brauen!
[...]

Es schießt die Saat aus ihrem dunklen Schooß,
die lange schmachtend lag in spröder Hülle;
ich will mich lauter blühn, lauter und los
aus dieser Brünstigkeit zu Frucht und Fülle.[51]

The image of the maturing fruit with all its sexual connotations (accentuated by 'Brünstigkeit'), the starkly visual immediacy of the fifth and sixth lines, and Dehmel's introduction of dynamic verbs such as 'gießen', 'befreien', 'wühlen', 'schießen', 'schmachten' and, above all, 'blühen' prefigure Expressionist poetry in general and Schnack's *Die tausend Gelächter* in particular.

Nevertheless, the feeling of estrangement persists, despite all the physical fervour. The promise of permanent unity encapsulated in the 'nur Zweiheit-Einheit' in the early 'Ode an Lulu' seems to be in jeopardy. The lyrical I is detached, he thinks, from his own body, as we saw in 'Sündenregister' — a poem in which he appears to give his body, at least the younger version of it, a personality and a will of its own, separate from him, and then to review it from a distance. Certainly, by the final poem in the cycle the detachment from his past is complete. The Du of 'Unrast' is not a Maria Glöckler figure, as might have been expected, but the lyrical I. In by far the most moving poem in the three collections, the lyrical I draws up an inventory of everything associated with his past, from which he has now, apparently deliberately and wilfully, become separated — everything from 'weißen Blumen und dem Hirt der Ziegen' to 'Muttertränen und den ersten roten Erdbeerfunden' ('Unrast', I, 41–42). His motives for tearing himself away may be unclear to him — 'Von diesem allem löst Du Dich leicht, warum? Aus Not, aus Sehnsucht, aus Begierde?' (I, 41) — but what is painfully evident is that at the present time, as he looks back and remembers (or perhaps on an experimental return home), he feels not a tinge of regret ('Nicht eine Träne hängt an Deiner Wimpern dunklem Lid', I, 41). It is as if he had never been there, as if he had never realized at the time how fortunate he was. Alienation is, of course, a very common trope in contemporary literature, and the lyrical I's own sense of estrangement is demonstrated when he regrets that he has allowed himself to be tempted away. Again there are echoes of Eichendorff:

Du sahst nur auf den Flüssen das Eilende von flachen Fischerkähnen
Und hörtest nur Posthörner, die im Tale klangen ... (I, 41)

He now finds himself unanchored in life, 'Fremd alledem, was Sippe, Sitz und Sitte heißt' (I, 41; once more the alliteration underlines the point) and intent on devising another life for himself. The lyrical I's attention is again focused upon himself and his self. In true Expressionist fashion the lyrical I is central, the 'Alleinherrscher'.[52] Not one of the poems in *Die tausend Gelächter* reorientates that focus: it is *his* soul, *his* body, *his* heart, *his* forehead, *his* brain, the imperious insistencies of his needs.

---

51   Richard Dehmel, 'Venus Primitiva', in *Gesammelte Werke*, 3 vols (Fischer, 1913), I, pp. 276–78.
52   Reso, p. 654.

It is true that there are more descriptions of nature (for example, 'Unter alten Bäumen', I, 36), but the lyrical I always intervenes, and echoes of his favourite Romantic poet, Joseph von Eichendorff, soon fade. A rhyme such as 'Lilienfluren' and 'Huren' (in 'Aus Dunkelheit herausgewandert', I, 37–38) makes the link more dubious. The lyrical I is not interested in the intricacies of human relationships: rather, he is preoccupied with personal epiphanies, the sense of enlargement suddenly granted, say, by the silhouettes of certain trees in certain lights (see the poem 'Unter alten Bäumen') or by the appearance of stars above him (see 'Nacht-Juli'). Feeling, *his* feeling, is all that counts and is counted, an obsession which is further emphasized in this collection by the reiterated retreat from any moderating thought or thinking. If 'Stirn', as a word, is precious to him by virtue of being close to 'Stern', it ceases to be benign as the home of 'Hirn' and 'Gehirn', of man's rationalizing faculties. Where Gottfried Benn laments that 'Ein armer Hirnhund, schwer mit Gott behangen. | Ich bin der Stirn so satt [...]'[53] Schnack writes: 'Ich aber war mit meiner Stirn, die eckig war, verbrannt, zerdacht, zernagt, gebleicht, gequält, ein ungeheures, rätselhaftes Buch' ('Sie und Ich', I, 32–33). 'Zerdenken' (a neologism) and 'Zernagen', not to mention 'verbrennen' and 'quälen', are sonically and visually powerful enough verbs to highlight the debilitating impact of those rationalizing faculties. The lyrical I, already rendered vulnerable by distance from the steadying influence of home, is further disorientated by this stand-off between feeling and thinking.

The Expressionist poet's uncritical, undiscriminating homage to feeling, to *his* feeling, is paralleled by an equally passionate anti-intellectualism and anti-rationalism. There is no time or space or wish for psychological insights. There is instead a crude immediacy and aggressive directness about all the physical engagements: 'Die Kunst [Expressionist], die das Eigentliche nur will, scheidet die Nebensache aus. Es gibt keine Entremets mehr, keine Hors d'oeuvres.'[54] It is then not a huge step to render women as mere slaves to man's feelings, first as prostitutes and then as little more than animals. Here again the poem 'Aus Dunkelheit herausgewandert', already pinpointed as the key poem in the cycle, takes us back to familiar territory:

> Aus Dunkelheit herausgewandert, aus dem Gewölbe Nacht [...]
> Sah eine Frau in Rot, verführerisch, kokett. Sah Dunkel, Abend ohne Glanz.
> Sah Häuser ohne Süßigkeit, gekauert, alt, mit schrecklichen Fassaden.
> Und hörte Lärm, gewaltig. Läufe rauschender Klaviere, die dunklen Türen
> hin und wieder, dumpf ein Tor. Da hinging Weib, ein Tier,
> Fürstlich, dämonisch, krank, perversen Zug am Mund. [...] (I, 37–38)

The eccentric and stark construction 'Da hinging Weib, ein Tier' underlines the remoteness and anonymity of the female presence, and the close alignment ('Weib, ein Tier') draws attention to the carnal nature of any sexual relationship. The adjectives 'dämonisch' and 'pervers' are reminders of Expressionist writers' view of women as 'elementar', a threat to man, but also a way to self-fulfilment for

---

53 'Untergrundbahn', Benn, III, p. 31.
54 Kasimir Edschmid, 'Über den dichterischen Expressionismus' (1917), in *Frühe Manifeste: Epochen des Expressionismus* (Wegner, 1957), pp. 36–37.

him. Nothing and nobody is allowed to share, let alone overshadow, the lyrical I's dominion, and so all the female 'partners' remain anonymous — 'eine Frau in Rot', 'eine träumende Frau', 'eine Geliebte', 'matte Somnambule, Ermüdete', 'sie', even merely 'Weib' and a spectral present participle, 'eine Gehende'. It seems at times as if the female body and anatomy are reduced to a kind of ersatz-landscape through which and over which the lyrical I roams like a wild animal — 'und darum [her body] lag ich Tier, ich Dunkelheit [...]' ('Nackt in der Landschaft,' I, 40–41):

> Da ich gewaltig war, war sie auch groß, war sie auch Landschaft, Tier.
> ('Gewaltige Nacht', I, 33–34)

Now he is also 'Tier': we recall 'Tur an Tur' in 'Ode an Lulu' (I, 13–14) and at the same time we look forward, literally, to *Tier rang gewaltig mit Tier*.

The lyrical I continues to be cast as a violent/powerful figure, virtually irresistible, almost out of control at times. But, as is usual with Schnack, a certain formal restraint is sustained. Eight of the fourteen poems in the cycle are sonnets, following the usual pattern of abba / cddc / efg / efg, and the rhyming is as ingenious as ever. The long, and never disappointed, wait for the rhyming partner at the end of teeming main and relative clauses also imposes a kind of order. The restlessness engendered by the waiting is anaesthetized by the cleverness of the rhyming. The poem 'Sie und Ich', for example, has 'Es'/'Noblesse', 'Zinnober'/'Jobber', 'überflogen'/'Wipfelbogen'. 'Geflirre' and 'Geschirre', 'Tor' and 'umgor' and 'Nabel' and 'Babel' also catch the eye and the ear. Tension is ratcheted up, an escalating sense of emergency and physical or emotional crisis is generated, the reader is unsettled, by typical Schnack (and Expressionist) ploys. The main verb may be tantalizingly delayed (for ten lines in 'Nacht-Juli'). Poems are frequently launched into a stream of consciousness with no preamble and no verb ('Gewaltige Nacht' starts 'In Franken. Mai. Der Silberfluß' (I, 33)). Furthermore, there is an arrhythmic mixture of one- or two-word 'sentences' and long sprawling lines of more than forty syllables. Main clauses are lost sight of under a welter of relative clauses and sentences begin with verbs leaving us looking for a subject. There are stray pronouns which confuse rather than elucidate (see the poem 'Nackt in der Landschaft'), interrogatives hang unanswered in the air and memories slip into incomprehensibility. The meaning of certain lines is sometimes impenetrable or at least the syntax is tortuous and looks startlingly 'wrong' ('Ich weiß Dich südlich' (I, 39) in the poem 'Erinnerung' and 'und an den Tagen stolz, | Die südlich unterm Kleid, der Gärten wuchsen, königliche, purpurne, verwucherte, am Baum' in 'Gewaltige Nacht' (I, 33)). Of the fourteen poems in the cycle, 'Aus Dunkelheit herausgewandert' offers the best illustration of Schnack's methods and style. It is a huge sonnet with irregular line-lengths (sometimes over forty syllables, others in the mid-twenties), it rhymes relentlessly (except for 'Fassaden' and 'Santen') and we have to wait until line 8 for a main verb. The customary stream of consciousness (or of remembering) is constantly interrupted by subordinate clauses and further 'explanations' reflecting the haphazard nature of remembering, and all kinds of Romantic paraphernalia (rustling forests, crossed by wanderers, lights at windows, starlit nights, birds in flight) are deployed before human intervention

('Weib'/'Tür') takes over. In other poems, an intransitive verb is used transitively[55] and there is a frequent accumulation of hard-consonanted past participles — 'bezuckt', 'bezittert', 'zerfetzt', 'geätzt', 'heraufgewittert', 'unenträtselt' and the Benn-like 'urahnererbt' — and of 'ver-' prefixed verbs — 'vergeilt', 'verroht', 'verblaßt' (all in the poem 'Tagebuchblatt'). 'Bezucken' and 'bezittern' are striking neologisms. Perhaps these multiple 'ver-' prefixed verbs are intended if not as harbingers of doom, then at least of eroding passion and failure. In the last poem of the cycle, 'Unrast', the lyrical I, once again cast in the role of adventurer/traveller/pioneer, sets out from home looking for a new life:

> Das steil und riesenhaft sich aufstellt, dunkel, finster, groß,
> Und wie aus Gärten wächst, verwildert ohne Ruhe, abenteuerlich und
> hoffnungslos. (I, 42)

Do the adjectives 'dunkel, finster, groß' refer to the war? Is the juxtaposition 'abenteuerlich' and 'hoffnungslos' significant? From Vollmer's account of Schnack's life (I, 474–77) it seems that Schnack was preoccupied with the preparation of the poems of *Tier rang* at the same time as he was working on the three Expressionist collections. It is highly likely, therefore, that a sense of imminent upheaval should impinge on the last poems of *Die tausend Gelächter*, and with that sense comes the conclusion that the days of excess and self-indulgence are over. The lyrical I, master of those days, his credibility rooted in that mastery, cannot but begin to feel undermined.

Vollmer appends a number of uncollected poems ('verstreut veröffentlichte expressionistische Gedichte') to the three collections. For whatever reason, they were not deemed worthy by Schnack of inclusion. Indeed, they contain few variations in Schnack's traditional imagery and content. Three do stand out, however, as being different. The fierce social criticism of 'Sturz der Reichen' catches us by surprise with its reference to 'die Erhabenen' pouring forth 'aus den Goldabenden der Konzerte [...] aus der erhabenen Ruhe ihrer Gemäche [...] aus den knarrenden Fauteuils der Klubs' (I, 116–17). Equally unusual is the degree of sensitivity and compassion evident in the poem 'An eine Jüdin' where, before we move into a familiar description of the I's intensely physical relationship with a Jewish woman (still addressed as an abstract physical pronoun), we read:

> Zwischen Dir und mir brennt der Gram
> Deines Volkes, das die Verfluchung bekam,
> Der Ghettos Leid grub sich Dir tief am Munde [...] (I, 114–15)

And the huge sonnet 'Lied an Frankreich' is even more astonishing (I, 113–14). Having listed favourite French cities and favourite French writers, the lyrical I vows that Germany will never again inflict war on France. An unapologetically anti-war protest poem, it is unlike anything else Schnack has written. It was published in *Das Tribunal* after the 1918 November Revolution 'als Gruß an Frankreich'. It was then recalled by Schnack because, one day on the Rhine Bridge at Mannheim-

---

55   For example, the verb 'sinnen' which in normal use is almost always intransitive except, occasionally, when it means, or amounts to, 'planen'. See the penultimate line of Schnack's poem 'Tagebuchblatt' (I, 37). 'Sinnen' is also used transitively by Trakl in his poem 'Abendländisches Lied'.

Ludwigshafen, he had apparently seen a French soldier kick an aged invalid down the steps. In another isolated and wholly uncharacteristic gesture, almost thirty years later, Schnack dedicated 'Lied an Frankreich' to Charles de Gaulle and Konrad Adenauer as creators of Franco-German friendship after the Second World War (I, 427). Such human compassion ('Die Jüdin'), such social conscience ('Sturz der Reichen'), and such broad political and historical awareness ('Lied an Frankreich') find no place in Schnack's collected Expressionist poetry. Their inclusion would certainly have diminished the uncompromising sexual frenzy of those three published volumes. Presumably it was not Schnack's purpose to dilute 'pure' Expressionism even by straying for a very short while into the activist camp, but it was 'pure' Expressionism only in the sense that it was bereft of the social and political.

★   ★   ★   ★   ★

So far we have seen how the lyrical I has remained strong and vigorous, seeking and finding a sense of renewal and freedom by experimenting with fictional selves like the wanderer and the adventurer and by playing a series of roles on ground and in circumstances of his choosing. There have been, it is true, intimations of self-doubt and vulnerability, but the constant pursuit of intense physical pleasure has usually warded off all anxieties. However, the final poems ('Umnachtung' and 'Unrast') of *Der Abenteurer* and *Die tausend Gelächter* suggest that a development and a decline have been taking place. The lyrical I moves from being relentlessly self-assertive, determined to take up and hold a position in the centre of events, to an awareness of instability and insecurity, of not being quite sure of any countervailing sanctuary as home is abandoned and alien city life has to be embraced, and, worst of all, of outgrowing a hedonistic lifestyle. The (Expressionist) phase of solipsistic over-indulgence will provide numerous happy and fortifying memories which may help to shore up morale in times of peril (as does indeed happen in *Tier rang*), but that is probably the best that he can say of it because the lyrical I now feels guilty about the past ('Sündenregister') and nervous about the future ('Umnachtung'). Moreover, war is much too serious for any continuation of play-acting. War will impose only one role upon Schnack and other poets in the frontline, that of being a serving soldier, and on a daily basis, under the threat of death, war will confront him, in the starkest possible outline, with himself, and with his self. The over-wrought dramatics, characteristic of much Expressionist poetry, will now become literally a life-and-death drama, in the so-called 'theatre of war'.[56] War will take away freedom, not only the freedom to be *who* he wants to be, but the freedom to be *where* he wants to be. In the final poem of the three collections, 'Unrast', he reproaches himself for failing to acknowledge the luxury of the freedom he used to enjoy at home and realizes that he is condemned to 'ein fremdes Leben [...] unbekannt und ganz verwaist' (I, 41). But, claimed by an event way beyond his control and imagining, the wanderer now has a specific destination: the adventurer

56   It seems that the term 'theatrum belli' was used for the first time in 1737 in connection with the Crimea in the Russian–Turkish war of 1735, but it is wholly appropriate in this context.

is now being offered the greatest adventure of all, but neither the destination nor the adventure turns out to be part of any Expressionist poet's grand design.

After 'Unrast', Schnack did not publish another poem which could be remotely described as Expressionist: the nearest he came was the single poem 'Aschaffenburg' (1929, I, 314–15), which for a short time landed him in trouble with the local authorities in Kahl, but was, in fact, 'merely' suggestive and sleazy with none of the unalloyed carnality and sensuality of the three Expressionist collections. For a while he had followed the fashion of the day. This abrupt break with the past applied to virtually the entire Expressionist generation, not least because many of the poets had already been killed in the war. While Schnack never again referred in his writings to this phase of his life or to the poetry which he composed during those years, Gottfried Benn, on the other hand, who survived both world wars, always retained and regularly recorded fond memories of the movement of which he had been a leading member. In a letter to Erna Pinner (18 January), he relates how he has just written the introduction to the collection, *Lyrik des expressionistischen Jahrzehnts* (1955):

> Da bin ich in Germany [sic] der einzig noch Lebende von der Generation [...] Dabei [while writing the introduction] habe ich noch mal jene Jahre 1910–1914 an mir vorüberziehen lassen, diese herrlichen, großartigen Jahre — war es nur die Jugend, die das so strahlend heute sehn läßt oder war es doch eine wirklich glänzende bewegte geniale Zeit mit so viel Möglichkeiten, die dann kaputtgingen? Diese Jahre und dann 1918 bis 1933 waren wohl Deutschlands und Berlins wunderbarste, ich möchte sagen: Pariser Jahre, so voll Talenten und so voll Kunst. Wird nie wiederkommen.[57]

Benn's continued enthusiasm for the movement's aspirations and achievements is plainly evident here even if he skirts around his own notorious opportunism *after* 1933 and he is wrong about being the only survivor (for example, Kurt Heynicke and Wilhelm Klemm, both well represented in Pinthus's *Menschheitsdämmerung*, and, of course, Anton Schnack survived well beyond 1955).

Expressionism's demise in the early 1920s was indeed swift: a useful barometer of that demise is the fact that the forty-four Expressionist magazines that were being published at the end of 1919 had dwindled to eight by the end of 1922.[58] In the 1930s it was generally disparaged and dismissed as 'entartet' and many of its survivors were harassed by the authorities. After the Second World War it was again poorly received and reviewed by cultural historians, but in recent years its reputation as a trail-blazing avant-garde force has been much restored and the achievements and diverse contributions, across the arts, of individual writers and artists has been acknowledged. It is easy to downplay those achievements. Thomas Anz's reappraisal, therefore, seems sober and balanced:

---

57   *Dichter über ihre Dichtungen: Gottfried Benn*, ed. Edgar Lohner (Heimeran, 1969), p. 223.
58   Francis Michael Sharp, '*Menschheitsdämmerung*: The Aging of a Canon', in *A Companion to the Literature of German Expressionism*, ed. by Neil H. Donahue (Rochester, NY: Camden House, 2005), pp. 137–56 (p. 146).

Bei aller Kritik am Expressionismus sollte man sich bewußt sein: Die expressionistische Moderne stand mit ihren dominant anarchisch-libertären und mit ihren skeptischen Tendenzen beiden großen totalitären Bewegungen des 20. Jahrhunderts politisch wie ästhetisch fern. Und beide Bewegungen hielten ihrerseits den Expressionismus von such fern, verbal und mit physischer Gewalt.[59]

If Benn, Arnolt Bronnen, Hanns Johst and Kurt Heynicke (among very few others of the Expressionist writers 'gingen dem Nazismus ins Garn'[60] and Walden and Becher joined the Communist Party, Schnack, having left his Expressionist past behind, steered well clear of political controversy in the 1930s, apart from one or two skirmishes with the local authorities and one apparently serious lapse of judgement.

That criticism of Expressionism to which Thomas Anz refers is undoubtedly founded in the Expressionist poets' conviction of the primacy of the self which led, particularly in Schnack's case, to a huge reliance on autobiographical material and left, in theory and practice, little room in their work for anything else:

Der stark subjektive Zug und die autobiographische Selbstreflexivität, die der expressionistischen Literatur eigen sind, nährten vielfach den Zweifel in der 'allgemein-menschlichen' Bedeutung der Kunstbewegung überhaupt. 'Sie, weltfremder als alle Dichter vor ihnen, warfen ihr eigenes Ich in alle ihre Gestalten, waren unfähig etwas zu erfassen, was nicht sie selbst waren?'[61]

A world war was manifestly too large to set aside and the lyrical I had to make way, its former dominance inevitably submerged, if there was going to be any attempt at a serious literary engagement with, and response to, that war, and posing as 'weltfremd' would no longer be an option on the battlefield. Indeed, while a characteristic Expressionist mantra had been 'kein Außen mehr', a frontline combatant soon realized that battles are fought 'outside', and 'draußen' became a standard translation for 'on the battlefield'. Franz Marc (1880–1916), a major Expressionist painter and founding member of the 'Der Blaue Reiter', for example, writes in his tragically affecting essay, 'Im Fegefeuer des Krieges', written in the autumn of 1914 and published posthumously:

Was wir Krieger in diesen Monaten draußen erleben, überragt in weiten Bogen unsere Denkkraft [...] wer ihn [diesen entsetzlichen Krieg] draußen miterlebt und das neue Leben ahnt, das wir uns mit ihm erobern, der denkt wohl, daß man den neuen Wein nicht in alte Schläuche faßt.[62]

Killed instantly by a shell at the Battle of Verdun in March 1916, Marc did not have the opportunity to enjoy, let alone portray or help to shape, 'das neue Leben'.

---

59   Anz, p. 202.

60   Krell, p. 308.

61   *Manifeste*, ed. by Anz and Stark, p. 358, quoting Gerhard Reinboth, 'Die Betonung der schaffenden Persönlichkeit bei der "Jüngsten", *Das literarische Echo*, 23.16 (1920/21), 15 May 1921, cols. 966–68 (quoted from col. 967).

62   Franz Marc, 'Im Fegefeuer des Krieges', *Der Sturm*, 1 (1916), , p. 2, repr. in Anz and Stark, *Manifeste*, pp. 303–05 (p. 303–04).

However, Expressionist poets, to their great credit, came closest of all German writers to responding convincingly to the challenge of depicting the experience of war. Most were anti-war, many were ardent pacifists. Initially, for a few months, they may have welcomed the war, in the spirit of the English war-poet Julian Grenfell:

> I adore war. It is like a big picnic without the objectlessness of a picnic. I've never been so well or so happy. No one grumbles at one for being dirty. I've only had my boots off once in the last ten days, and only washed twice.[63]

But war was not a picnic, nor was it 'objectless', nor was it a kind of Boys' Own adventure. Schnack's bitter sense of disillusionment is evident in his own 'Aufbruch', 'Fahrt nach dem Westen', at the very beginning of *Tier rang*. As he sets out, the 'Abenteurer' of the three Expressionist volumes is immediately described as being 'voll Tod, voll Graun, voll Schwermut' and 'voll Angst' (I, 45–46). By the end of the war, the beginning of the end of Expressionism and all of the hopes (personal and political, social and moral) invested in it was clearly discernible. Kurt Tucholsky's poem 'Dantons Tod' (1920) signals that end. Tucholsky was probably not aware of Georg Heym's habit of casting himself in the role of one of the French Revolution's leading figures, but the very title of his poem allows the conclusion that the time for all role-playing was over:

> Und ernüchtert seh ich den grauen Tag.
> Wo ist der November geblieben?
> Wo ist das Volk, das einst unten lag,
> von Sehnsucht nach oben getrieben?
> Stille. Vorbei. Es war nicht viel.
> Ein Spiel. Ein Spiel.[64]

It was all 'Ein Spiel. Ein Spiel', and the I, never averse to games and masquerades, who dominated *Der Abenteurer* and Schnack's two other Expressionist volumes, is now totally exposed, 'ein Ding, wertlos wie diese Dinge: Sand, windverweht; Bergblume, abgemäht; Glas, hundertfach zerbrochen [...] ein Tier, hineingestoßen in die Feuerhölle: Front ...' (I, 46). In fact, the I, making his way to the frontline, in 'Fahrt nach dem Westen', the first poem in *Tier rang*, a cycle which purports to be a first-hand, close-up account of frontline experiences, does not appear until the last couplet of the sonnet. This in itself is an intriguing development, a considerable narrative survey, after the central role of the lyrical I, the self who speaks and chronicles his life in the earlier volumes. As a way though of introducing *Tier rang* and in order to appreciate its originality, it will be helpful not only to pursue and describe the development, but also, first, to examine the poetic form for which Schnack has shown a clear predilection in the Expressionist collections — that of the sonnet cycle.

---

63   Julian Grenfell in a letter to Ethel Grenfell dated 24 October 1914. Quoted in Martin Löschnigg, *Der Erste Weltkrieg in deutscher und englischer Dichtung* (Winter, 1994), p. 27.
64   Kurt Tucholsky, *Gedichte*, ed. by Mary Gerold-Tucholsky (Rowohlt, 1983), p. 291.

CHAPTER 4

The Cyclical Structure of
Anton Schnack's *Tier rang*

Das Verhältnis von Strophe zu Gedicht
wiederholt sich [...] in größerem Umfang als
das Verhältnis von Gedicht zum ganzen Zyklus.[1]

The term 'poetic cycle' implies centre, link and movement. The centre of a poetic cycle promises unity and is its motivating force, its basic impulse, its essential theme to which each individual unit or poem relates: the relationship between whole cycle and individual poem can thus mirror the relationship between poem and strophe. Link in this context suggests coherence and refers not only to the connection between one poem and another (adjacent or distant), but also between poem and thematic centre or between one part of a cycle and another and even between one cycle and its predecessors. Movement signifies development and refers to the way in which a cycle's principal theme is elaborated and its creative impulse works itself out: that movement can, for example, be linear and continuous with a destination intimated or prefigured, or it can be circular when the writer wants to take us back to his starting point, as with the *Sonette* cycle which his friendship with Bettina Brentano and Minna Herzlieb inspired Goethe to write. This chapter will demonstrate that Anton Schnack's *Tier rang* is situated in a long tradition of lyrical cycles and that it derives many benefits from being cast in that form and, with reference to Cordula Gerhard's excellent study of cycles in Expressionist poetry,[2] more specific and concrete terms for the typical components of a poetic cycle will be suggested.

The advantages which accrue to the writer of poetic cycles are numerous. Coherence and stability, a uniformity of style and tone and atmosphere, a reinforcement through repetition and identification of message and viewpoint, the lacing of visual and phonic patterns which are pleasing to the reader's ear and eye, a certain contentment that goes with familiarity, the freedom to develop an argument or a plot line or to trace a journey in the fashion of a play or a novel, the opportunity to offer full scope to the uncertain field of subjective memory and the intricate

---

1   Wolfgang Kayser, *Das sprachliche Kunstwerk: Eine Einführung in die Literaturwissenschaft* (Francke, 1976), pp. 168–69.
2   Cordula Gerhard, *Das Erbe der 'Großen Form': Untersuchungen zur Zyklus-Bildung in der expressionistischen Lyrik* (Peter Lang, 1986), p. 254.

web of subjective meditation — all become available. Moreover, there is also the challenge of seeking to achieve a compromise or balance between the rights of individual poems and the inherent necessities of the cyclical form so that individual poems thus remain autonomous and valid while being bound into the whole. Stefan George, for example, maintained that a poetic feature has merit only as part of a larger whole. As a prolific writer of lyrical cycles himself, he may well have had cycles in mind when he proposed that:

> Der wert einer dichtung ist auch nicht bestimmt durch einen einzelnen wenn auch noch so glücklichen fund in zeile strofe oder grösserem abschnitt. die zusammenstellung das verhältnis der einzelnen teile zueinander die notwendige folge des einen aus dem andern kennzeichnet die hohe dichtung.[3]

The successful integration of an individual poem in a cycle thus becomes a necessary precondition of 'high poetry': the members of a cycle are then not regarded as distinct entities, because their meaning and importance are comprehensible only in their relationship to the other members. George's point is extreme because it is certainly possible to imagine a wholly effective cycle of independent, isolated poems which are valid and valuable in themselves: his point is, however, a good one and can be applied to another, but similar, context. For example, few would deny that Georg Heym is a fine poet, but his poetry is enriched, as is our understanding of him, by being situated in the larger framework of *Menschheitsdämmerung*, more specifically in the 'Sturz und Schrei' section of Pinthus's anthology and then, when his poetry begins to change in content and form, in 'Erweckung des Herzens'. Something extra is earned in the process, a kind of bonus: 'Durch die Zusammenordnung zu einem Ganzen entsteht ein Mehr gegenüber einer bloßen Addition.'[4]

In a rare autobiographical sketch Schnack recounts how *Tier rang* came into being: 'In meinem Gepäck brachte ich ein Bündel von Gedichten mit, "Tier rang gewaltig mit Tier", an die achtzig langzeiligen Gedichte, ein klagendes, empörtes und in den Farben verwirrendes Panorama von Leuchtraketen, explodierenden Granaten [...].'[5] He was sent home from the frontline in spring 1916, spent four years refining and, presumably, redrafting and editing the (approximately) eighty poems before selecting sixty for publication in *Tier rang* in early 1920. Twenty-three of the final sixty appeared in periodicals such as *Die Sichel*, an Expressionist magazine for literature and art, between July 1917 and September 1919. At the same time Schnack was compiling the three Expressionist volumes, *Strophen der Gier*, *Der Abenteurer* and *Die tausend Gelächter*, which appeared in that order in 1919. It must have been a complex enterprise to be creating four separate volumes at the same time, making appropriate choices for each, while also selecting poems for public consumption in periodicals. Given this time-frame and the lengthy period of gestation which certainly provided space and scope for careful deliberation, it would be very surprising if the four volumes did not share common features and forms, even

---

3   Stefan George, 'Über Dichtung', in *Sämtliche Werke in 18 Bänden* (Klett-Cotta, 1982–2013), XVII, p. 69.
4   Kayser, p. 169.
5   Glöckler, p. 14.

common themes. Indeed it is possible to see the three earlier volumes individually as cycles, collectively as one cycle and then as linking with, or feeding into, *Tier rang*. There are all kinds of idiomatic and lexical links across the four volumes, eight of the fourteen poems in *Die tausend Gelächter* are sonnets and clearly prepare the way for the fifty-five sonnets of *Tier rang*, and the lyrical I, encountered as a dominant force in the three earlier volumes, re-emerges in 'Fahrt nach dem Westen', the first poem of the *Tier rang* cycle. In the final poem of *Die tausend Gelächter*, aptly entitled 'Unrast', the lyrical I is flagging, his power is waning, his morale is low and his disillusionment with his life of self-centred adventure is growing. At least twice in *Tier rang* he appears to bid grateful farewell to that life. The last line of 'Nacht des 21. Februar' reads:

> Ich sah mich sein: ein Ding, verloren dem Gesetz der Unerbittlichkeit, dem
> Ruf des Todes, bös geworfen an die Fenster; ich sah mich überdrüssig, steif und
> aller Abenteuer satt (I, 65).

The idiosyncratic, but wholly characteristic, use of the dative case ('verloren dem Gesetz') somehow underscores the completeness and helplessness of the physical surrender to 'Gesetz der Unerbittlichkeit'. And a little later in the cycle, in the poem 'Vor dem Sturm', fearing the worst and expecting to die in the imminent attack, the lyrical I launches into a series of desperately nostalgic vocatives:

> Oh Weib, oh buntes Abenteuer, Tand, oh Rausch; und dann vorbei,
> verlöscht, vernichtet; wer kümmert sich um meine junge Lende,
> Um meine Augen, träumerisch und dunkel, wer weiß, daß ich die
> Flöte blies und daß ich war in mancher blauen Ferne! (I, 82)

Moreover, if the three earlier Expressionist volumes depict the lyrical I as animal in thrall to sexual instinct and imagination, the lyrical I of *Tier rang* is condemned and reduced to being another kind of animal, cold and murderous: 'Nacht war lebendig von grausigem Schall. Tier rang gewaltig mit Tier' ('Der Angriff') (I, 86).

   Tier rang is, however, far more than just a sequel to its three predecessors. Though, frustratingly, there is no written record of how he set about choosing and organizing its sixty poems, Schnack clearly intended it to be a cycle in its own right and had the space to take a great deal of trouble composing it, sifting through the material brought back from Verdun, deliberately selecting and rejecting, initially trying out some of the poems in various magazines before finally settling on the present version. The distinction which Helen Mustard makes between 'arranging' and 'composing' is relevant here. In the introduction to her study of lyric cycles in German literature she writes:

> I distinguish, first of all, between cycles that are *arranged* and those that are
> *composed*. Cycles always originate in one of these two ways: they are either ex
> post facto arrangements of poems not intended previously as a group or they
> are conceived from the very beginning as a group form.[6]

By her definition we can already say that *Tier rang* is 'composed'. Carl Spitteler characterizes the lyric cycle by drawing attention to, and making a stark contrast

---

6   Mustard, p. 5.

with, the very different qualities of a 'collection': 'Ein Sammelbuch ist nicht organisch gegliedert, nicht übersichtlich proportioniert, hat keinen Mittelpunkt und keinen Gesamtbeobachtungspunkt.'[7] As will be seen, *Tier rang* is not simply a 'Sammelbuch': it is 'organisch gegliedert [...] übersichtlich proportioniert' and it does have both 'Mittelpunkt und Gesamtbeobachtungspunkt'. The cyclic form enables Schnack to create a whole system of meaning rather than a mere collection of meaningful pieces. In fact he achieves a very subtle balance. Unlike, say, Rilke's *Stundenbuch* cycle where (for example, in the third book) if it were not for the large capitals indicating the beginning of a new poem we would not know where one poem ends and another begins, and unlike the *Peregrina* cycle where Mörike deliberately dropped the titles of individual poems before publication in *Gedichte* (1838),[8] Schnack devised and retained titles for all sixty of the poems in *Tier rang* and thus ensured their individual identity and autonomy. Yet, at the same time, it is as if he acknowledged that war was too big a subject to be encompassed in an individual poem or even a collection of isolated lyric poems, a 'Sammelbuch'. Out of a desire to embrace the experience of living and dying in the frontline and realizing that it was impossible to compress a theme of such scope and complexity within the bounds of a single lyric, he chose the cycle as the best poetic form available to him.

In doing so, Schnack was inserting himself into a long tradition. Helen Mustard begins her survey in the nineteenth century by suggesting that until then, particularly in the seventeenth and eighteenth centuries, cycles were just loose clusters of poems whose connection was superficial and external — in her terms, 'arrangements' — because pre-nineteenth-century poets were principally interested in the form of individual poems, in odes or sonnets, for example. It was only with Goethe and the Romantics that cycles began to be seen as 'compositions', coherent and integrated because they were conceived from the beginning as a higher, interconnected unit. Moreover, themes or narratives became as important as form. Novalis's *Hymnen an die Nacht* are probably the best example of a Romantic cycle. The central, closely related themes are clear — the insufficiency of the material world, the need for transcendence, the night interpreted as the threshold between life and death, the quest for experiences that point beyond the limitations of the here and now — and, as with Schnack's *Tier rang*, we follow the fortunes of a lyrical I, sometimes in relation to a Du, as he sets out on that quest. The six members of the cycle are so tightly and skilfully interwoven that their full significance and depth emerge only if they are read successively and as a whole. The movement of the cycle is shaped by a series of urgent questions ('Muß immer der Morgen wiederkommen? | Endet nie des Irrdischen Gewalt? | Unselige Geschäftigkeit verzehrt | Den himmlischen Anflug der Nacht?', II)[9] to which the lyrical I seeks answers, and

---

7   Carl Spitteler, 'Über den Wert zyklischer Sammlungen', in *Kritische Schriften* (Artemis, 1965), p. 120.

8   In the novel *Maler Nolten* the *Peregrina* poems do indeed have titles, but for the second and final version of the cycle Mörike omitted the titles, perhaps, Mustard adds, 'feeling that titles tend to isolate the members of a cycle too much' (Mustard, p. 136).

9   *Hymnen an die Nacht*, in Novalis, *Schriften*, I: *Das dichterische Werk*, ed. by Paul Kluckhohn and Richard Samuel, 2nd edn (Kohlhammer, 1960), pp. 130–57 (p. 132).

thematic, sonic and formal patterns link the individual members together. Ludwig Tieck's two cycles, *Reisegedichte eines Kranken* and *Rückkehr des Genesenden*, are very different: they trace Tieck's trip to Italy in 1805–06 and are little more than diary entries in blank verse, an account of the events of the journey and descriptions of cities and countryside. The individual poems are arranged chronologically, but they are totally independent of each other. They could be interchanged almost at will without distorting the character of the cycles. This kind of cycle, where the poems are arranged in a loose narrative outline, became popular with other Romantic poets such as Heine, Eichendorff and Wilhelm Müller, but the Naturalist poets, especially Hermann Conradi and Arno Holz, appeared to favour a loose amalgamation of Novalis's and Tieck's variations of the genre.

Conradi, for example, can be regarded as an intermediate point between Novalis and Schnack. His *Lieder eines Sünders* (1887), like Tieck's *Reisegedichte*, takes us on a journey, the journey of the lyrical I's soul from the depth of 'Trauer' (the opening poem in *Inferno*, the first book of the cycle) to triumphant redemption in *Gipfelgesänge* (the seventh and concluding book), but there is, as in Novalis's *Hymnen*, a coherence, a unity and a logic about the development of the events described. The journey presents itself, like Schnack's *Tier rang*, as a series of relay stations. In Conradi's cycle the soul pauses to reflect on past sins, on present mourning and on hope not only for redemption, but also for reconciliation and integration with the whole of God's creation. It wrestles with seemingly insurmountable obstacles and set-backs and stressful questions: Schnack's volume depicts a lyrical I wrestling with the animal in man as it emerges on the battlefield. In an overwrought tone not very different from that of Werfel, Rubiner and Becher, Conradi's Expressionist successors some thirty years later, the lyrical I in *Lieder eines Sünders* pleads for cosmic unity and casts himself, again like later Expressionist writers, as an agent for that seismic change, a role which, given the particular circumstances of the First World War and Schnack's own non-activist nature, the lyrical I in *Tier rang* is unlikely to assume:

> Oh! Daß mir noch ein Etwas — Schicksal — Gott —
> Nennt, wie Ihr's wollt! — die Kraft, die riesengroße,
> Weltbändigende, gäbe, daß ich alles,
> Was sich entringt in Farben und Gestalten
> Dem ewig unerschöpften Schoße,
> Erfassen und behalten könnte!
> [...]
> In eins — in eins möcht' alles ich verballen —
> In eins — in eins möcht' alles ich verkitten —
> Und was ich je voll Götterlust durchfühlt —
> Was mich durchwühlt [...][10]

The couplets beginning 'In eins...' are significant here. They are confronting what the lyrical I intimates is a disintegrating reality, what Cordula Gerhard describes as 'den im Zuge des Abbaus aller transzendentalen religiösen Beziehungen sich bedrohlich ankündigenden konsequenten Zerfall der Wirklichkeit in unverbundene

---

10   Hermann Conradi, 'Schwarze Blätter', XI, in *Gesammelte Schriften*, 3 vols (Müller, 1911), I, p. 75.

Einzelteile'.[11] Within a few years, of course, that sense of a disintegrating reality had become a crisis, most famously in Hugo von Hofmannsthal's *Chandos-Brief* ('Es zerfiel mir alles in Teile, die Teile wieder in Teile und nichts mehr ließ sich mit einem Begriff umspannen. Die einzelnen Worte schwammen um mich'[12]) and, subsequently, in the quest for a foothold in a crumbling world, a quest for what George called 'den fussbreit festen grund'[13] and Rilke expanded into 'ein reines, verhaltenes, schmales Menschliches, einen unseren Streifen Fruchtlands zwischen Strom und Gestein'.[14] Schnack's own quest was much less metaphorical: it invariably took him back, especially during his most reflective moments on the frontline, to the towns and villages, the rivers and the forests, of Lower Franconia. Poetic cycles coincidentally, perhaps as a response to this sense of human isolation and disorientation, resumed a popularity which had lapsed for a while after the Romantic era; notable examples were George's *Der Teppich des Lebens* (among many others) and Rilke's *Stundenbuch*, *Sonette an Orpheus* and *Duineser Elegien*. Moreover, in the preceding generation, a trend for long cycles had been set. Conradi's *Lieder eines Sünders*, Ferdinand Avenarius's *Lebe!* (1893) and especially Arno Holz's astonishing *Phantasus* (1898/9), consisting of no fewer than 1,000 poems and intending to offer a kind of world-view in a format where all the lines of verse on the page are centred on an axis giving both a right and left jagged edge,[15] took on this compulsion for long cycles. And so Naturalist poets, and Rilke and George after them, hugely expanded the possibilities of lyric expression and thus enlarged the cyclic form into something complex and versatile. Poets ceased to be 'mere' interpreters of personal experiences and became interpreters of the world in which they lived. Many Expressionist poets followed suit. After all, Pinthus's *Menschheitsdämmerung* is far more than a 'Sammelbuch': critics and reviewers at the time, Pinthus explains in his 1959 retrospective, may have called it 'Die erste und einzige Sammlung dieses Kreises', but his subtitle was 'Symphonie jüngster Dichtung'.[16] Composed of four sections, the 'symphony' reads just like a cycle. It bears testimony to Gerhard's claim, at the conclusion of her survey of literary trends in the Nietzsche-dominated eras of Symbolism and Jugendstil, that the cyclic form reigned supreme: 'In diesem geistigen Zusammenhang ist auch der Griff zur zusammenzwingenden Zyklusform quer durch alle literarischen Stömungen um die Jahrhundertwende bis hinein in den Expressionismus zu sehen.'[17]

Helen Mustard devotes considerable space to analysis of George's and Rilke's poetry, but she has little to say about Expressionist cycles. Stadler, Zech and Heynicke

---

11   Gerhard, p. 223.

12   Hugo von Hofmannsthal, 'Ein Brief', in *Sämtliche Werke*, XXXI: *Erfundene Gespräche und Briefe*, ed. by Ellen Ritter (Fischer, 1991), p. 49.

13   Stefan George, *Sämtliche Werke*, VIII, p. 104.

14   Rainer Maria Rilke, 'Die zweite Elegie', in *Werke: Kommentierte Ausgabe in vier Bänden*, II: *Duineser Elegien: Gedichte 1910 bis 1926*, ed. by Manfred Engel and Ulrich Fülleborn (Insel, 1996), p. 207.

15   In fact, Holz worked on *Phantasus* until 1924/25. It appeared originally (1898/99) as two booklets of fifty poems each, then on 336 pages in 1916 and on 1,345 in 1924/25. By 1961/62, it had swollen to 1,584 pages!

16   Pinthus, p. 7.

17   Gerhard, p. 97.

receive a brief mention as does, rather bizarrely, Friedrich Schnack.[18] However, Cordula Gerhard, while deferring to Mustard's pioneering research by using many of the same sources, focuses on Expressionist poetry. Neither she nor Mustard refers to Anton Schnack. In seeking to show that Expressionist poets habitually reached for a cyclical structure to confront and control what Wolfdietrich Rasch calls 'die Aufspaltung der Realität in zweckbestimmte Einzeldinge und zusammenhanglose Fakten [in] einer Welt der Maschinen und maschinell hergestellten Gegenstände',[19] an existential malaise magnificently identified and diagnosed in Rilke's Ninth *Duineser Elegie*, Gerhard analyses Stadler's *Der Aufbruch*, Werfel's *Wir sind*, Heym's *Der ewige Tag* and Stramm's *Du. Liebesgedichte*.[20] Basing her conclusions on these analyses, she offers a working definition of what she calls 'einen "echten" Zyklus, also ein nicht nur in sich zusammenhängendes sondern auch in seinen Teilen sich bedingendes, "gerundetes" großes Ganzes'.[21] She stipulates that individual poems should be clearly bound together, that they should relate to each other and exert a decipherable influence on each other. These individual poems will thus, by creating what she calls 'ein Mehrwert', a bonus feature, build the cycle up into 'ein echtes Gemeinsames'. 'Motifs', which, she argues, are crucial in underpinning all cyclical structures and weaving their components together, became a regular characteristic of poetry at the turn of the century and beyond into the Expressionist era. As an alternative to, or companion of, the term 'motif', Gerhard offers 'Bildkreis', 'Bezugsgegenstand', 'Moment der Deutung' and 'geistiges Erlebnis'. If this key feature appears in many varied guises, there is no doubt that the single paramount element of a lyrical cycle is its core idea, the fundamental viewpoint from which the poet starts, the cycle's basic motivation. Gerhard settles finally for its 'motivisches Apriori', a term which she borrows directly from Kayser.[22] If there is such a centre, Kayser argues, such a definite theme within a cycle, it can then be debated and illuminated from the most varied angles: 'Dann sind die Gedichte des Zyklus gleichsam das buntfarbige Spektrum, das als Abglanz die einheitliche Lichtquelle ahnen läßt.'[23]

A second ingredient for Gerhard will be the cycle's form, its 'lyrischer Ablauf'. A narrative aspect will inevitably be ingrained in the cycle. It will move forward under the impact of its cluster of motifs according to a linear or spiral, circular or zigzag or staccato pattern. However it moves, there will be an ultimate sense

---

18   Mustard, pp. 245–48.

19   Wolfdietrich Rasch, 'Fläche, Welle, Ornament', in *Zur deutschen Literatur seit der Jahrhundertwende* (Metzler, 1967), p. 219.

20   Gerhard is at pains to justify her choice of *Du* rather than *Tropfblut*, the in some respects more obvious example of a lyrical cycle. She gives as her reason the fact that Herwarth Walden, and not Stramm, selected and ordered the war-poems of *Tropfblut*. In the event Stramm was delighted with Walden's selection. Gerhard, p. 187.

21   Ibid., p. 22.

22   See ibid., pp. 22–28 for all these terms, including 'motivisches Apriori'. Kayser writes (p. 169): 'Es kann sich auch um ein letztlich unsagbares geheimes Zentrum, ein motivisches Apriori handeln.' Joachim Müller, some sixteen years before the first edition of Kayser's study, employs the term 'motivische Mittelpunktsbezogenheit'. See his 'Das zyklische Prinzip in der Lyrik', *Germanisch-Romanische Monatsschrift*, 20 (1932), pp. 1–20 (p. 12).

23   Kayser, p. 169.

of completion and fulfilment: 'Das "thematische Apriori" kommt am Ende eines Zyklus auf einer höheren Stufe zu sich selbst zurück, es hat sich in den Gedichten ausgesungen und — mehr oder minder — vollständig [...] seine lyrische Form gefunden.'[24] Then there is the question of interdependence, the relationship of the individual poem to the whole cycle. The individual poem has its own autonomy and validity, but these are enhanced and enriched by its relationship with the whole. Finally, but still under the heading of interdependence, Gerhard lists the connection between, and among, single poems — is there an indirect link (of motif or symbol or image) or a more direct interlocking of one poem with another in a continuous line? Gerhard also seeks to demonstrate that these characteristic features can be identified within the framework of two principal kinds of poetic cycle: the first works on the surface and has a clearly discernible forward movement (invariably, linear, spiral or circular) which guarantees a certain logic and coherence. The second has a 'Tiefenstruktur', is 'dislinear-kreisend' in that each individual poem, circling as it were on a thematic axis, takes issue with the cycle's 'Grundmotiv' and, by repetition and identification, is more likely than the purely linear approach to unlock 'das richtige, weil tiefere Verständnis des Inhalts'.[25] A good example of the first kind, the 'Oberflächenstruktur', where the poem follows a linear progression from a starting point to a loftier conclusion is, as we have seen, Conradi's *Lieder eines Sünders*. George's *Der Teppich des Lebens* is, on the other hand, a 'Tiefenstrukturzyklus', in which we find an endlessly circling movement round the cycle's core idea with no sense of linearity or progress towards some kind of elevated final synthesis. George is not so much interested in tracing the path to a goal, but in illuminating and interpreting that path. It is poet as exegete, not as chronicler. In examining Schnack's *Tier rang* in greater detail, it is useful to refer to these two kinds of cyclical structure and to Gerhard's four criteria.[26] However, the three general terms — unity, development and coherence — with which we began will be replaced, instead, by the more specific terms — core idea, narrative aspect and interdependence.

If one argues, as Walther Brecht does in relation to the poetic cycles of Conrad Ferdinand Meyer,[27] that the cyclical form is an expression of a writer's ambition to bring order to chaos in what is perceived as a disintegrating world, it is possible to understand why a poet might want to encapsulate the unprecedented horrors of the First World War in a cycle and, furthermore, as we shall see in Chapter 5, compound the effect by then choosing the sonnet form, itself a symbol of order and reconciliation, for the individual members of the cycle. The cyclical form thus becomes a kind of protective caul, in which the sixty individual poems in *Tier rang*, all but five of which are sonnets, take shelter. Each poem in *Tier rang* has its own title, but twenty-seven of the sixty do not come (literally) to a full stop,

---

24 Müller, p. 8.
25 Gerhard, p. 59.
26 It is probably more accurate to talk in terms of three criteria because Gerhard's third and fourth criteria simply represent two different kinds of interdependence.
27 Kayser singles out, and praises, Brecht's *C. F. Meyer und das Kunstwerk seiner Gedichtsammlung* (1918). Kayser, p. 169.

they seem to run into, or meld with, the next: the appropriateness of the category 'lyrischer Ablauf' comes into focus here. These sequences of unstopped poems arrive in flurries, often at significant moments in the narrative of the campaign: for example, the first three 'unfinished' poems of the cycle describe the soldier-poet's 'Aufbruch'.[28] Later, a cluster of six poems (from 'Maas' to 'Dorf Ivoiry')[29] offer a depiction of the villages and sights before and around Verdun. Later still, a small group ('Im Gebirge', 'Im Paß', 'Bei Woltschach' and 'In der Ebene')[30] captures the essence of the flight into southern Italy. A sense of the speed, the confusion and the fluidity of events which must surely have marked that flight is thus communicated, highlighting at the same time one of the benefits of the cyclical form. While these individual poems, focusing, for example, on a shattered home or church, or the corpse of an unnamed soldier lying by the roadside or the encampment around the town of Montmédy, are extremely powerful in themselves, self-sufficient and evocative of a countryside under annihilating pressure, they are also landmarks on a continuing journey, and Schnack succeeds both in integrating them into the whole and granting them their own identity and integrity. The achieved effect is very similar to that noted by Robert Musil in Rilke's poetry:

> Bei ihm [Rilke] sind die Dinge wie in einem Teppich verwoben; wenn man *sie* betrachtet, sind sie getrennt, aber wenn man auf den Untergrund achtet, sind sie durch ihn verbunden. Dann verändert sich ihr Aussehen, und es entstehen sonderbare Beziehungen zwischen ihnen.[31]

Schnack's own success is achieved on two different levels, first the general and the abstract, then the particular and concrete, with the result that a real coherence and uniformity are generated across the whole cycle. This sense of abiding and general coherence is reinforced by Schnack's insistent repetition of the particular and the specific. Once again patterns emerge, most sharply with reference to what has already been signalled as a poetic cycle's most important feature. The core idea upon which *Tier rang* is founded is the conviction that war not only destroys and kills, it 'desecrates' ('entheiligt', 'Im Granatloch', I, 70), it contaminates the beauty and the purity of the natural world:

> Blut war entfallen einer Stirne, Blut war
> entronnen einem Herzen, einem Munde entblühte es schmal und leis,
> Ein Blut durchglühte die Mitternacht des Schnees stärker als alle Flutungen
> der Scheinwerfer, stärker als ein Schwarm von leuchtenden Kugeln, oh,
> wer es entsühnen dürfe? ...
> Mitleidig färbte es Schnee [...] ('Schnee', I, 75)

However 'sympathetic' the blood's contact with snow may be, there is no hiding the fact that it comes from 'Sterbende [...] mit Stimmen, wimmernden, bebenden,

28   I, 45–47.
29   I, 51–56.
30   I, 88–92.
31   Robert Musil, 'Rede zur Rilke-Feier in Berlin am 16. Januar 1927', in *Gesammelte Werke*, ed. by Adolf Frisé, VIII: *Essays and Reden* (Rowohlt, 1978), pp. 1238–39.

wühlenden, ungeheuern'. War bestializes ('vertiert') and distorts ('verzerrt')[32], it coarsens ('verroht',[33] and we remember how 'verrohen' is the key word in Paul Bäumer's lament about the impact of war on his young friends in Remarque's novel[34]), and strips all participants of their innocence and of their very soul.[35] It guarantees that beautiful memories remain just memories, never to be revisited or re-enacted because inevitable death will soon kill them too:

> Ich werde eingehn in den Tod [...]
> ich werde nie mehr wiederkommen
> Zu bunten Schmetterlingen, Blumen, zu den Frauen, zu einem Tanz
> und einem Geigenspiel,
> Ich werde irgendwo zu Steinen niedersinken mit einem Schuß im Herzen [...]
> ('In Bereitschaft', I, 81)

War marks man eternally with the sign of the fratricidal murderer Cain and it brings shame and disgrace upon him: the words 'schändlich' and 'Schandbarkeiten' and 'Schmach' alternate across three poems.[36] War diminishes ('Wir sind Verlorene [...] wir sind so dunkel und alt, | Klein wie Zwerge'[37]) and, above all, worst of all, war corrupts. A powerful moral dimension is introduced by Schnack's recourse to the verb 'verderben' in its various forms. An unnamed village is described not as destroyed but as 'verdorben' in the last line of the poem 'Nächtliche Landschaft':

> Über die Unzahl der Feuer, über Gelächter und Irrsinn, über Kreuze auf
> Wiesen, über Qual und Verzweiflung, über Trümmer und Asche, über Fluß
> und verdorbenes Dorf ... (I, 55)

The brain of the lyrical I is rendered 'ganz verderbt von Gram' ('Abend im Argonnerwald', I, 54), the rarer form of the past participle underlining the crude corruption and depravity wrought by constant exposure to battle; the experience of standing guard throughout the night reduces a sentry to being 'blind und blöd, wahnsinnig, elend, dumpf und dumm, inmitten der Verderbnis', the alliteration in 'blind und blöd [...] dumpf und dumm', a typical conceit with Schnack, introducing a note of irony to the victim's desperate state;[38] the village of Cierges is depicted as emerging 'aus diesem scheußlichen Verderb' ('Dorf Cierges', I, 59), the 'Gestank von angesengten Dielen [...] von Fäulnis, Schutt, Verwesung' ('Dorf Cierges', I, 58) now compounded by a kind of moral degradation. The cyclical structure of *Tier rang* enables Schnack to repeat and highlight his abiding conviction that war brings moral delinquency as well as physical decay and destruction. Instead of the stark and usual 'töten' which never appears, various 'dysphemisms', all implying a

---

32   'Dorf Montfaucon', I, 59.
33   'Im Graben', I, 68.
34   Early in chapter II of *Im Westen nichts Neues* we read 'Was wir [young generation of German soldiers] wissen, ist vorläufig nur, daß wir auf eine sonderbare und schwermütige Weise verroht sind.' Erich Maria Remarque, *Im Westen nichts Neues* (Propyläen, 1929), p. 26.
35   'Im Graben', I, 68.
36   See the poems 'Die Batterien', I, 66, 'Abend im Argonnerwald' I, 54, and 'Schlaf in Ivoiry', I, 57 respectively.
37   'Im Graben', I, 68.
38   'Abend im Argonnerwald', I, 54.

deeply personal engagement in the moral shaming, are used — 'den Tod werfen', 'Tod geben', 'ein Schlachten' and the substantive 'Mord',[39] which appears more frequently as the cycle progresses. This is the cycle's core idea, the axis upon which it revolves and to which it constantly returns, in both a centripetal and centrifugal movement. In the end, in the penultimate poem, the lyrical I suddenly becomes complicit in the murderous action, deriving sadistic joy, even aesthetic pleasure, from a skilful launching of hand grenades at the enemy, thus adding yet another corpse to the final apocalyptic scene portrayed in 'Am Tor des Todes':

> ... Daß ich den Tod warf, lächelnd, boshaft, in das Gewühl,
> anbrausend unter Rauch und Staub, anbrüllend nach dem Gas,
> Das weit schon war; schon nördlich; daß ich ihn bogig warf,
> gewandt, zehnmal, noch öfter, schneller
> In ihre blaue Müdigkeit ... (I, 96)

Indeed, the final two poems of *Tier rang* are an illuminating example of what Gerhard in her description of the characteristics of a lyrical cycle calls 'Interdependenz' and 'Verknüpfung der Gedichte untereinander' in that they serve directly as mediators of the core idea. The words 'Toten', 'Himmel' and, particularly, 'unbegraben' in the last line of 'Handgranatenwerfer' are picked up in 'Am Tor des Todes'. The usual ... at the end of 'Handgranatenwerfer' invites the reader to make the connection:

> Oh, daß ich Tod warf
> lächelnd boshaft und schuld bin an Verwesung, an einem Toten, der
> unbegraben, bleichend, unter den Sternen eines ewgen Himmels ruht! ...
> (I, 96)

This line weaves almost seamlessly into 'Seltsam: hinabzusteigen in die weißen Knochen der Toten, die schon jahrelang unter dem Himmel sind, frei und unbegraben, bläßlich dämmernd' (I, 97). The lyrical I has killed the man whose memories we then find in 'Am Tor des Todes'. The link is not as close as Josef Weinheber achieves in his sonnet sequence 'An die Nacht' in which, as a variation of the 'sonnet redoublé',[40] the last line of one sonnet becomes the first line of the next and the final sonnet of the sequence (XV) consists of the first lines of the preceding fourteen sonnets.[41] But Schnack's sonnets point the way to what Weinheber, twenty years later, creates in *Adel und Untergang*, and particularly in *Späte Krone*. The lyrical I, absent from the last poem of *Tier rang*, has progressively diminished during the course of the campaign under the impact of the horrors witnessed, and his final act of hurling grenades brings shame and guilt and, ironically, signals his own extinction. This core idea of the corrupting influence of war is perfectly shaped within the cycle — the first poem ('Fahrt nach dem Westen',

---

39   See, respectively, as examples, the poems 'Handgranatenwerfer', I, 96 for 'dealing death', 'Dorf Montfaucon', I, 60 for the verbal noun 'Schlachten', and such poems as 'Der Horchposten' I, 72 and 'Die Sprengung', I, 73 for 'Mord'.

40   In the traditional version of this form each of the fourteen lines of the first sonnet in a sequence of fifteen sonnets becomes, in order, the final line in each of the succeeding sonnets. See *The Penguin Book of the Sonnet*, ed. by Phillis Levin (Penguin, 2001), p.345.

41   Josef Weinheber, *Sämtliche Werke*, ed. Josef Nadler and Hedwig Weinheber, 5 vols (Otto Müller, 1954), II, pp. 251–59.

I, 45–46) points us towards hell ('Feuerhölle: Front'), the cycle takes us through the stages of the journey, and the final poem lands us in hell, or, rather, at its door.

The grimness of that fateful journey is reinforced by all kinds of detailed lexical and semantic interdependence ensuring at the same time that we never lose sight of war's fatal malevolence. The negative and dominating effect achieved by the repeated use of the verb 'verderben' is just one example: that effect is compounded by Schnack's familiar ploy of using 'ver-' prefixed verbs with an essentially neutral or even positive meaning and, by situating them in a wholly bleak environment, casting doubt on their neutrality or positivity. In the poem 'Morgen bei Brieulles' (I, 57–58) we find the trio 'versilbert' (of the town of Brieulles), 'verschönt' (of the grass growing there) and 'verlächelt' (not 'verlacht', but a neologism, clearly used here as a positive reference to the castles in the town). But the end of the poem ensures that we do not forget that the frontline is not far away ('Die Front flucht donnernd wieder. Die Sonne steigt gewaltig, übermächtig, groß') and that the 'ver-' prefix will soon, therefore, be resuming its usual connotation of evanescence: silver, grass and smile will then lose their fresh lustre. Indeed, the past participle 'verloren' immediately follows. In other poems in the cycle there are whole clusters of such verbs, often neologisms, invariably carrying manifestly dark connotations: 'Gefangene Franzosen' has 'vertiert', 'vererzt', 'verenden', 'verdämmernd', 'verzerrt', 'verging', 'verteufelt' and 'verbrannt'.[42] 'Im Schacht' has 'verglänzten', 'verflort', 'verkrustet' and 'vergast'.[43] There are numerous other examples which, along with verbs prefixed with 'zer-' and 'ent-' (as in 'entfallen', 'entronnen', 'entblühen' and 'entsühnen'[44]), accumulate to create an impression and atmosphere of irreversible decay and decline. The cyclical form, with its network of interlacing and interlocking verbs, its repetitions and cross-references, guarantees that the decline will move inevitably to death and apocalyptic annihilation.

It is not just verbs and other lexical iterations which serve the core idea and exemplify the interdependence of the individual components of the cycle. Particular images (or motifs) recur. The fragility of human life is encapsulated in references to damaged hands and hair: 'Handstumpf' becomes 'zerrissen', then 'zerstückt', while the 'süße Hand' in the first line of the first poem bridges the whole cycle and metamorphoses into 'wunderliche Hand, klein und ohne Fleisch' in the last poem among the detritus of battle where a girl's hair slips through the same 'wunderliche Hand'.[45] In contrast, images of 'Samt' and 'Seide' offer gentle consolation, especially when they are recalled amidst the lyrical I's desperate remembering of times past: the 'real' battle between men and machines can then be replaced, with characteristic sibilant alliteration, by 'die seidne Schlacht der Schmetterlinge'.[46] If silk and velvet and butterflies conjure up repeated images of threatened beauty, 'Sterne' (fifty-two appearances) and 'Gestirn(e)' (eighteen) represent the solace of permanence. Stars,

42   I, 76–77.
43   I, 68–69.
44   'Schnee', I, 75.
45   See respectively 'Im Graben', I, 68; 'Rauch', I, 74; 'Sturm', I, 83; 'Fahrt nach dem Westen', I, 45; 'Am Tor des Todes', I, 97.
46   'Auf Beobachtung', I, 71.

after all, are probably the last natural phenomenon upon which a dying soldier's eye falls: they are also out of reach of man's guns and neutral, shorn of nationalism and prejudice. Schnack rarely uses the word 'Kopf': he prefers 'Stirn(e)' (mentioned forty-seven times) as in 'Gebrüll aus Kaminen: es jubelt ein Tod des Absturzes, Stirnen fallen ins Bodenlose.'[47] In fact, 'Stern' and 'Stirn' are listed so frequently in such proximity that the compound noun 'Gestirne' could equally well be regarded as serving both: 'Dörfer [...] wo Sehnsüchtige gegen die Sterne weinten und manche Stirne gezeichnet war von klaffender Einsamkeit'.[48] And the poem 'Sterne' begins disconcertingly with 'Saht ihr meine Stirne voll Lärm [...]?'[49] In contrast, the futility and sordidness of war are expressed in the recurring and always disparaging use Schnack makes of the resonances implicit in the substantives 'Tand' and 'Zeug'. In the poem 'Der Rückzug', 'Tand' is just one more token of destruction left in the countryside on the fictional flight into Italy ('[...] ganz gewaltige Zerstörung und Schnur der Fuhren | Voll Drähten, Decken, Heu, voll alten Dingen, Mist und Tand').[50] In a rare access of bitterness it has become 'göttlicher Tand' by the last poem. Similarly, the 'seltenes Zeug' filling the new recruit's imagination and dreams in 'Fahrt nach dem Westen' is 'verworrenes Zeug' at the end.

The suffering wrought by war is graphically captured by repeated images of dying or dead horses. It is particularly interesting to note how Schnack moves from 'Rosse' to 'Pferde' to 'Gaul'. 'Rosse' carries a resonance of ancient battles (as in the last line of the poem 'Zerstörte Kirche' which also incidentally contains 'verdarb' twice in close proximity).[51] 'Pferd' is used for dying and dead horses in current battles where they are often twisted into grotesque configurations. 'Gaul' is usually saved for a description of a horse's particularly gruesome death as in 'Der Rückzug' where under wheels 'im klirrenden Geschirr brach endend hin ein Gaul'.[52] In the course of the cycle horses suffer a similar fate to that of the lyrical I: they are diminished or, rather, de-individualized by, for example, being referred to as 'hundertfacher Huf'.[53] The noblest of war animals is humiliated: either crushed beneath wheels or left dead with its legs 'zum Himmel gestreckt'.[54] Man too is degraded, robbed of dignity and moral decency, by war. These are the 'Grunderlebnisse' of *Tier rang* which, taken together, amount to its core idea.

The narrative aspect of the cycle can be briefly demonstrated. There are interruptions and pauses for reflection, but essentially the progression is linear and logical. To a certain point it appears to trace precisely the journey which Schnack himself made between November 1915 and the end of February 1916. The Germans did indeed launch the Battle of Verdun on 21 February 1916 ('Nacht des 21. Februar'), but from that point onwards the cycle is the fictional creation of

---

47   'Im Paß', I, 90.
48   'Nächte', I, 63.
49   'Sterne', I, 74.
50   'Der Rückzug', I, 87.
51   'Zerstörte Kirche', I, 48.
52   'Der Rückzug', I, 86.
53   'Im Süden', I, 96.
54   'Flucht', I, 88.

Schnack's imagination. As the German army attacks, then retreats, then flees, the cycle follows its movements with strict logical and chronological linearity. Ralph Glöckler suggests that the cycle describes seven clear-cut phases: the 'Aufbruch', the journey to Verdun, typical nights on the frontline, natural phenomena, anonymous people, the route into battle, the flight into Italy and onto a corpse-filled battlefield.[55] It is equally possible to view the cycle as a three-part structure: the first twenty-three poems (up to and including 'Nacht des 21. Februar') outline the preparation for the attack, the next twenty-three describe the attack itself, while the final fourteen cover the flight, a rest, the incursion into Italy and apocalypse. It makes little difference to the perception of a distinct linear progression whichever division is preferred. An accurate geographical and historical development is evident, a sense of completion is achieved and the mood of the lyrical I is also seen to develop from an initial position where he is assailed by doubt and fear, through increasingly mounting dread, to a conviction that he is fated to die very soon. Waging war may be a wholly irrational, illogical human activity, but Schnack is as interested in conveying and ensuring sequentiality as he is in exploiting the poetic technique of accumulation. Brief reference to Heym's methods should serve to highlight the nature of Schnack's achievement in *Tier rang*, for in one respect at least Heym's separate volumes can be regarded as cycles.[56] *Der ewige Tag*, for example, conjures up an unrelievedly bleak picture of a dark and dangerous world, a dictatorial imagination is clearly at work, but there is such a remarkable pattern of formal organization, and such a cumulative, consistent negation and negativity, that each poem can be seen as just another component of the depiction of the realm of death and dead people. However, whereas Heym can identify no coherent sequence or chronological, rational development in the events of human life ('Ich glaube, daß meine Größe darin liegt, daß ich erkannt habe, es gibt wenig Nacheinander. Das meiste liegt in einer Ebene. Es ist alles ein Nebeneinander'[57]) and merely piles up simultaneous, equivalent image on image in clusters of association in typical Expressionist fashion, Schnack both follows that trend of steady, almost tortuous accumulation (a 'Nebeneinander') and, at the same time, ensures that *Tier rang* advances in a logical, linear progression (a 'Nacheinander'). For Schnack sequentiality is as important as accumulation. The cyclical form of *Tier rang* allows Schnack to trace two journeys: a new recruit's journey to northern France which ends in death on a battlefield there, alongside an equally convincing depiction of a mind and a human spirit progressively and incrementally threatened to extinction. He tries to obviate, or at least postpone, that extinction by retreating to memories of happier times and happier places where the lyrical I appears strong and vigorous again, and literally comes into his own. This insistent polarity, present horror versus past bliss, is just one of many 'binary visions'[58] which shape the structure

---

55   Glöckler, pp. 70–97.
56   The fact that Georg Heym wrote no fewer than ten letters to his publisher, Rowohlt, insisting on particular titles, layout and ordering of poems for *Der ewige Tag* suggests that he had something like a cycle in mind.
57   Heym, entry for 21 July 1910, III, p. 140.
58   Paul Fussell, *The Great War and Modern Memory* (Oxford University Press, 1975/2000), pp. 79–80.

and the content of the cycle and are invigorated by being situated within a cycle. Other polarities include the shattered fields of Verdun and the peaceful landscapes of Franconia, the unremitting bleakness of life now and the untrammelled joy of life then, the cramped world of the trenches and the vast open heavens, the ephemerality of human life and the eternity of the stars, noise and silence, night and day. These polarities which help to move the narrative of the two journeys along are aspects of the quality of a multi-faceted interdependence which is characteristic of *Tier rang* and which, as we have seen already, reinforces the mediation of the cycle's core idea. That interdependence shows itself principally by three means — the way each individual poem is presented, the voice and stance adopted by the lyrical I, and Schnack's choice of images and vocabulary.

A sense of close-textured interdependence issues most obviously from the appearance of the poems on the page: monumental blocks of fourteen consecutive long lines, whose ponderous geometry offers no stanzaic relief. Moreover, many sections of *Tier rang* are in a voice which, although not to be identified with the poet's empirical self, is decidedly the poet's own voice, depersonalized not by masks any more (as in the three earlier Expressionist volumes) but by the studied, self-distancing reticence which seems to have been characteristic of Schnack's public and private persona. Indeed, the lyrical I becomes increasingly distant, before disappearing completely. The tone of that voice is infused with compassion, implicit and yet powerful, with no trace of patriotic or nationalistic prejudice or fervour. A sense of interdependence is also ironically achieved by the complete absence of 'Big' words,[59] of flag-waving exhortations, even of the traditional vocabulary of war: a list of the words which do *not* appear in the cycle and which one might reasonably have expected makes interesting reading — 'Deutsch', 'Deutschland', 'Vaterland', 'Frankreich', 'Kaiser', 'Land' (meaning individual country, rather than countryside) and 'Soldat'. Moreover, 'Krieg', 'Friede', 'Feind', 'Volk' (but then only as 'Volk der Vögel')[60] and 'Opfer' (but then only as a religious sacrifice)[61] appear just once each. The void left by the absence of these patriotic words of orientation is filled by neutral vocabulary such as 'Stirn', 'Sterne', 'Brunnen', 'Samt', 'Fenster', 'fern', 'Reiter', an anonymous 'einer' and a querulous 'wer?'. Any kind of jingoistic or bellicose militancy is muted into virtual silence. Weapons tend to be left over from old battles,[62] 'Heimat' invariably refers to Franconia and is invoked with a painful nostalgia,[63] flags turn out to belong to a sailing boat,[64] 'Heer' usually refers to armies of birds or mysterious riders, nationality and destination unknown.[65] In the case of 'the deserter' we do not know whose side he is deserting from or fleeing

---

59   The term is Robert Graves's. See his essay 'Big Words', in *Over the Brazier* (The Poetry Workshop, 1916), p. 11. For Graves the 'Big Words' were such pre-war concepts as Valour, Honour and Glory. Their German equivalents do not feature in *Tier rang*.
60   'Schreckliche Vision', I, 94.
61   Ibid.
62   'Zerstörte Kirche', I, 48.
63   For example 'Im Graben', I, 68.
64   'Morgen bei Brieulles', I, 57.
65   'Zerstörte Kirche, I, 48.

to.[66] A particular kind of ambience is created where Man is reduced to animal and the individual self is placed under escalating threat. The uniformity of tone founded in a resolute non-partisanship and non-participation (until the fateful intervention in the penultimate poem of the cycle) is reinforced by the stance which the lyrical I adopts almost until the very end, that of the physically unengaged observer. The word 'Fenster' appears not just in the context of windows blown out by shell-fire in wrecks of houses, but as a reference to the favoured vantage point for the lyrical I who ruefully invokes peacetime experiences, observations and longings:

> Stirnen [...] voll Sehnsucht nach Spielen,
> Nach einem Tanzabend, nach der Feierlichkeit einer Gewitternacht vom
> Fenster aus gesehen, nach großer Städte nächtlichem Laternenbrand![67]

The figure standing at a casement window is familiar to us from Romantic poetry, but where, for example, in Eichendorff's 'Sehnsucht' the lyrical I enjoys all the sounds 'der prächtigen Sommernacht', wondering at 'ein Posthorn im stillen Land', the lyrical I in Schnack's *Tier rang* is left with a scene of utter devastation.[68]

Form, tone and viewpoint are uniform throughout the cycle, and a louring mood of alienation, interwoven with a general sense of human extinction, hangs over each poem in turn. Questions remain unanswered, perhaps unanswerable, and there is no apparent questioner or interlocutor. Despair mounts when no one responds:

> Wem gehört dies: ein Knabenarm? [...] Wem gehört ein anderes: weiße Stirn?
> [...] Wer ist hinter uns? [...] Wer ist der Schauerliche?[69]

Smoke and gas blur outlines of human figures and natural features; 'einer', 'eine', 'man', 'wir', 'wer', 'sie' and other pronouns, all undefined, replace named subjects, except in memories and dreams where real figures like Jeane (sic), Antoinette, Margarethe, Eugenie and Nina are invoked; the fourteen very long lines of 'Die Sprengung' have just one 'einer' and one 'wer' as a subject while the dreadful sounds of war hold sway:

> Dann brach Gewitter los, wild, groß und offen. Dann böses Brüllen
> Bestieg die Luft; ein Donnern dunkel [...]
> Als stampfe Lärm von Millionen Füßen.[70]

Frequent recourse to the conditional tense and the subjunctive mood compounds this abiding sense of unreality and anonymity:

> Wie? riefe wer, gewaltig, brüllend, und wer in Schächten grabend
> Vernähme dies erschreckten Angesichts? [...]
> Wie würd ich meine Stirne in Vergessenheit tief niedertauchen [...]

---

66   'Der Überläufer, I, 77–78.
67   'Sterne', I, 75.
68   For example the opening lines of Eichendorff's poem: 'Es schienen so golden die Sterne, | Am Fenster ich einsam stand | Und hörte aus weiter Ferne | Ein Posthorn im stillen Land.' Joseph von Eichendorff, *Sämtliche Werke*, ed. by Harry Fröhlich and Ursula Regener, 18 vols (Kohlhammer, 1993), I/I, pp. 33–34. Schnack was a great admirer of Eichendorff's poetry.
69   'Flucht', I, 88.
70   'Die Sprengung', I, 73.

Wie würd ich steinern sein [...]
Wie würd ich rätselhaft vor diesem Tode bangen [...][71]

And all the time battlefield action is kept consistently at arm's length in such observations as 'da fern ein Schlachten tobte'[72] where the idiosyncratic word-order and the use of the verbal noun instead of the more usual 'Schlacht' seem to connote lack of human engagement, until the shocking consequences and the aftermath of that action are made abundantly clear in such poems as 'Am Tor der Todes' and 'Flucht'. The descriptions, for example, of the journey to the front, of the terrified wait for action, of the battlefield itself and of the consequent flight are graphic and intensely moving, but a distance is always maintained. Protest (for instance, about the behaviour of the enemy or the callous stupidity of the generals) and cynicism (for instance about the purpose of it all) do not intervene: a relentless consistency of form, tone and attitude both permeates the cycle and is strengthened by it.

This consistency, or rather interdependence, founded in a wealth of detailed lexical ingenuity and of interlacing images which are more or less directly linked to the central crisis of the cycle, demonstrates that *Tier rang* is more than merely a linear 'Oberflächenzyklus', progressive, mimetic in a naturalistic way. It is also what Gerhard calls 'ein in sich kreisender (pendelnder) Tiefenstrukturzyklus, symbolistisch orientiert'.[73] Such a combination is very rare in Expressionist poetry: the poetic cycles of, for example, Stadler, Heym, Werfel and Stramm are all 'symbolistisch bestimmt in ihrem Verzicht auf eine oberflächliche, lineare Progression zugunsten einer tiefenstrukturellen Pendel/Kreisbewegung um ein motivisches Apriori'.[74] Schnack, as it were, takes the cycle on a stage further by successfully merging linearity and core idea. The only other cycle that springs to mind which resembles *Tier rang* in this respect is that of another sadly neglected Expressionist poet. Paul Zech's *Die eiserne Brücke* (1914), consisting of seventy-two sonnets, is divided into three clearly delineated sections (*Das grüne Ufer*, *Zwischenspiel* and *Das gebirgichte Ufer*) of thirty, twelve and thirty poems respectively.[75] It traces the journey from paternal home to demonic city: this theme has a strong Expressionist flavour and forms the basic polarity, the critical experience which is the essence of the volume. Publishing *Tier rang* six years later, during which time the First World War has run its catastrophic course, Schnack moves beyond a characteristic Expressionist topos, one which he has already addressed in *Die tausend Gelächter*, and seeks to render justice, as we have seen, to the unprecedented horrors of that war. Like Zech, he chooses sonnets as his favoured form. The choice of a cycle of sonnets offers him the double promise of literary protection and reconciliation. In the next chapter *Tier rang* will be examined in the light of that choice.

---

71 'Ein Tag', I, 62.
72 'Dorf Montfaucon', I, 60.
73 Gerhard, p. 208.
74 Ibid., p. 218.
75 Paul Zech, *Die eiserne Brücke* (Verlag der Weißen Blätter, 1914).

CHAPTER 5

The Sonneteer Anton Schnack

Wenn einer Dichtung droht Zusammenbruch
Und sich die Bilder nicht mehr ordnen lassen,
[...]
Alsdann erscheint, in seiner schweren Strenge
Und wie das Sinnbild einer Ordnungsmacht,
Als Rettung vor dem Chaos — das Sonett.[1]

The status and importance of the sonnet are beyond dispute. Barbara Herrnstein Smith, in her *Poetic Closure: A Study of How Poems End*, asserts that 'the sonnet is one of the most highly determined formal structures in Western poetry and is probably the most familiar single form in the history of literature',[2] a judgement supported by H. W. Belmore in his study of Rilke's poetry: 'The sonnet is perhaps the most sharply defined form in European poetry, with a record of ever-recurring popularity unparalleled by any other definite form.'[3] Anton Schnack's *Tier rang* is a sonnet sequence of an unusual kind. Its originality is best appreciated if it is placed within the history and tradition of the sonnet form. The German sonnet in particular has a long history and a very rich tradition. There are several recurring features in this highly determined formal structure to which Schnack gives a distinctive individual twist: for example, its often astonishing formal variety and versatility and its frequent preoccupation with conflict and, sometimes, reconciliation. In this chapter, some of the key features of its traditions and development will be documented and the kinds of sonnets Schnack composed specifically for his volume of war poetry will be outlined.

In her invaluable introduction to a recent anthology of sonnets, Phillis Levin is at pains to stress that any serious assessment of the sonnet form (or of a particular sonneteer) should attend to its past and its traditions:

> It may help to conceptualize the sonnet as a room (or stage) that can be divided in a number of different ways to serve many functions. Since its overall dimensions and circumference do not change, whatever occurs within that space will always be determined to some degree by its size and haunted by the presence of its former occupants. Even if we rearrange, replace or remove some

---

1   Johannes R. Becher, 'Philosophie des Sonetts oder Kleine Sonettlehre: Ein Versuch', in *Bemühungen II* (Aufbau, 1972), pp. 603–32 (p. 603).
2   Barbara Herrnstein Smith, *Poetic Closure: A Study of How Poems End* (University of Chicago Press, 1968), p. 50.
3   H. W. Belmore, *Rilke's Craftsmanship* (Blackwell, 1954), p. 8.

of the furniture, the marks will still be there to remind us of how things were positioned in the past.[4]

Over the centuries German writers have proved to be enthusiastic 'occupants' of the space presented by the sonnet, not always without ruction or schism. It is possible to identify three golden ages for this form in German literary history — in the seventeenth century, in the first half of the nineteenth century and among Expressionist poets in the first two decades of the twentieth century. It has prospered particularly at times of social turmoil and national conflict. In the 1930s and 1940s, for example, it again came into its own in the works of Reinhold Schneider, Rudolf Hagelstange and many others, though, with the exceptions of Gerhard Schumann and Heinrich Anacker, it was not taken up by openly National Socialist poets. Its journey from the Sicilian court of Frederick II, where Giacomo da Lentino created it in the thirteenth century, to the prisons and camps where opponents of Hitler sought refuge in it could hardly have been more tortuous:

> Für viele Autoren war bereits die 'undeutsche' Form des Sonetts ein Akt der Opposition. Während die meisten Nazi-Barden die Sonett-Form zugunsten des Marschlieds verschmähten, entstanden in der Opposition Sonette und Sonettsammlungen von Reinhold Schneider, Rudolf Hagelstange (*Venezianisches Credo*), Georg Britting (*Die Begegnung*), Albrecht Haushofer (*Moabiter Sonette*) [...] Marie Luise Kaschnitz, Wolf von Niebelschütz [...]. Sie drangen in die Gefängnisse und Lager ein, man fand sie bei der letzten Habe Gefallener, man reichte sie in den Bombenkellern der Großstädte von Hand zu Hand.[5]

From acting as a mediator of love and praise for an idealized lady at an elegant Italian court to being a vehicle of political and humanitarian protest and a paradigm of contained stability under a modern dictatorship the 'Sonnet's scanty plot of ground'[6] has been called upon to serve and fulfil numerous purposes down the centuries in European literature. The spectrum of the sonnet's diversity and versatility is huge. The first three lines of Edmund Spenser's (1552–99) sonnet, 'What guyle is this [...]',

> What guyle is this, that those golden tresses,
> She doth attyre under a net of gold
> And with sly skill so cunningly them dresses,
> That which is gold or heare may scarse be told?[7]

have given way 400 years later to the grim horror of J. R. Becher's poem (1956) 'Der Lagerraum Auschwitz', a perfectly configured sonnet:

> Die Kinderschuhe staun sich bis zur Decke,
> Und Frauenhaar ballt sich im Lagerraum,
> Ein Ballen liegt verpackt in einer Ecke — [8]

---

4   *The Penguin Book of the Sonnet*, ed. by Phillis Levin (Penguin, 2001), p. xxxviii.
5   Ingo Zimmermann, *Reinhold Schneider: Weg eines Schriftstellers* (Union, 1982), p. 136.
6   See the final sestet of the sonnet 'Nuns fret not at their convent's narrow room', in William Wordsworth, *Poetical Works*, ed. by Ernest de Sélincourt and Helen Darbishire (Clarendon, 1946), p. 1.
7   Quoted in *The Penguin Book of the Sonnet*, ed. by Levin, p. 13.
8   Johannes R. Becher, *Gesammelte Werke*, VI: *Gedichte 1949–1958*, ed. by Johannes-R.-Becher-Archiv der Akademie der Künste der Deutschen Demokratischen Republik (Aufbau, 1972), p. 406.

It is indeed difficult to think of a major German poet, with the exceptions of Hölderlin, Schiller, Klopstock and Benn, who has not tried his hand, more or less enthusiastically, at the form. The list of German sonneteers, of writers revealing an interest in the form or expressing views about it, is not limited to poets: Hegel, Fichte, Schopenhauer and Marx, for example, all entered into the debate which in the nineteenth century swirled around what was seen to be an alien (non-German) form.[9] Its obituary has been written more than once, sometimes in a tone of good riddance, at other times with a sense of nostalgic regret, but it has never faded completely from the literary landscape. Walter Mönch in his seminal study of the sonnet suggests that sonnets also prospered immediately *after* periods of social turmoil: 'Es ist auffällig, daß in Zeiten, die großen Erschütterungen folgen, das Sonett zu wuchern beginnt.'[10] With *Tier rang* published two years after the end of the First World War, and certainly at a time of 'great upheavals', Schnack inserts himself firmly into the tradition of the German sonnet although, frustratingly for reader and researcher, he is not on record with any comment about his own view of the sonnet or of his approach to it.

An account of the development of that tradition by documenting the variations in form and content which the sonnet accommodated from the early nineteenth century onwards may be viewed as an intriguing narrative in itself. Such an account should be the best means of indicating the extent and nature of Schnack's divergences from the traditional genre and help to substantiate the initial claim that his negotiations with the sonnet form were strikingly innovative. Long enough to invite personal self-expression, too short for lyrical effusion, the sonnet has proved to be astonishingly versatile in its subject matter and more surprisingly, at least in the twentieth century, in its form. The earliest sonnets record the conflict between the law of reason and the law of love, but then over the succeeding centuries the sonnet has been called upon to be a haven for complex emotions and memories, 'an innate holding pattern, a guarantee that however dangerous or overwhelming the subject, the duration of the encounter will be brief'.[11] It has also accommodated satire, wit, invective, grotesqueries, sublime scorn, wary tenderness, passion, potted literary biographies, ecclesiastical history and encomiastic epitaphs. This inventory, far from all-inclusive, is a summary of John Fuller's study of the versatility of the English sonnet,[12] but it could apply no less to German poetry. War, it is noted, does *not* feature as one of the likelier subjects, though many outstanding exponents of the form seemed to engage in a private war of frustration and impatience of their own. Robert Frost, for example, who composed as many as thirty-seven sonnets, was very uncomfortable with its restraints as he makes clear in *The Constant Symbol*, the essay he wrote to introduce the 1946 edition of his poetry:

> Any worry is as to whether he [the poet] will outlast or last out the fourteen
> lines [of the conventional sonnet] — have to cramp or stretch to come out even

---

9   See, for example, Georg Wilhelm Friedrich Hegel, *Ästhetik* (Aufbau, 1966), II, pp. 501–02 and p. 528.
10   Walter Mönch, *Das Sonett: Gestalt und Geschichte* (Kerle, 1955), p. 257.
11   *The Penguin Book of the Sonnet*, ed. by Levin, p. lxxiv.
12   John Fuller, *The Sonnet* (Methuen, 1972).

— have enough bread for the butter or butter for the bread. As a matter of fact, he gets through in twelve lines and doesn't know quite what to do with the last two. Things like that and worse are the reason the sonnet is so suspect a form and has driven so many to free verse and even to the novel.[13]

Frost's conclusion that the poet's almost inevitable impatience with the constraints will eventually issue in the compromise of having to settle for blank verse or prose will come into focus in any discussion of Schnack's sonnets, and many German poets harboured not so much suspicion as bitter resentment of the sonnet's intimidating discipline.

An abiding feature of all audits of the sonnet's purposes is an acceptance that the form of the sonnet is suitable to express reconciliation. It is, therefore, somewhat ironic that at particular points of its development it has provoked considerable heated debate. A clear line stretches — with a hiatus in the first half of the eighteenth century and the final decades of the nineteenth — between the early sonnets of Weckherlin, Opitz, von Zesen and Fleming (in the sixteenth and seventeenth centuries) and those of Becher, Weinheber and Schneider (among many others) in the 1930s, 1940s and 1950s. And along that line there have been bewilderingly contrasting phases of belligerent contentiousness and comparatively cooperative tranquillity. Indeed, particularly at the beginning of the nineteenth century, the tone struck by some German writers and literary commentators was anything but conciliatory. The terms bandied around at the time — 'Sonnettenüberschwemmung', 'Sonettenwut', 'Parteienstreit', 'Sonettenschlacht', 'eine literarische Fehde' (between its champions and denigrators) which distended into a full-scale 'Sonettenkrieg' — reinforce the surprising association between sonnets and violent emotions.[14] This emerges from the principle that a sonnet is, or should be, based on a dialectical shaping which involves the concise statement of a problem or conflict and then its proposed resolution, on a protasis (proposition) and on an apodosis (conclusion). Ever since Wordsworth's canonical sonnet ('Nuns fret not at their convent's narrow room; | And hermits are contented with their cells [...]') illustrated the dialectic of freedom and imprisonment in form, claiming that the confinement of form itself can come to mean freedom and offer 'brief solace', the flexibility of the sonnet form has been more widely accepted, whether within the structure of a single sonnet or through the shifting narrative perspectives of the sonnet sequence, such as *Tier rang*. Josef Weinheber successfully exploited its flexibility, but by his account the outcome of any conflict was always peaceful. The final tercet of his poem 'Das Sonett' reads:

> Die Zeit entscheidet viel. Der Streit vergeht.
> Versöhnt mit sich, hat nun die Welt sich gerne
> Und gibt sich hin: mit Traum und mit Gebet.[15]

---

13   Quoted in H. A. Maxson, *On the Sonnets of Robert Frost: A Critical Examination of the 37 Poems* (McFarland, 2005), p. 6.

14   For a further discussion of these terms and of the various phases of the 'sonnet war' see W. E. Yates, *Tradition in the German Sonnet* (Peter Lang, 1981), pp. 19–20 and Hans-Jürgen Schlütter, *Sonett* (Metzler, 1979), pp. 15–18.

15   Weinheber, II, p. 493.

What precisely was the substance of the 'Streit' which dominated the literary scene in Germany between 1800 and 1820? First, quite simply, there were, in some writers' view, too many sonnets being written — hence the neologism 'Sonettenwut', which presumably means an obsession with writing sonnets. It was Goethe who first used the term in his poem 'Nemesis' (a perfectly shaped traditional sonnet!), whose final tercet reads:

> Ich höre wohl der Genien Gelächter;
> Doch trennet mich von jeglichem Besinnen
> Sonettenwut und Raserei der Liebe.[16]

The fact that '-wut' rather than, say, the less dramatic 'Zorn' forms part of the compound indicates the intensity of the temperature at which the feud was conducted. In the sonnet 'B. und K.', one of his unpublished 'Invektiven-Sonette mit Coda', Goethe takes sides in the literary feud between the Schlegel brothers and their opponents, in this case, Böttiger and Kotzebue. The Leipzig public, who had championed Kotzebue, Goethe called 'Parterrekloake'.[17] Moreover, the sonnet was often criticized in Germany for its foreign, Romance origins. Concerns were expressed in some quarters (Jean Paul called the sonnet 'ein ausländisches Qualgedicht'[18]) that the purity of the bloodstock of German prosody was being fatally tainted by pernicious Southern (that is, Italian) influences — 'Versüdlichung des Nordens',[19] the name given to the contagion, was almost certainly the reason for the National Socialists' almost wholesale rejection of the form. The critic and essayist Karl Reinhardt had in his sights both the superabundance and miscegenation of the German sonnet when he wrote in 1803:

> Der Sonette giebt es im Deutschen eine so ungeheure Menge, daß man das große Bedlam, Erde, über und über damit tapezieren könnte; allenfalls blieben noch genug übrig zu einem Futteral von papier maché für den Mond. Außerdem welcher Reichthum, welcher Segen an Trioletten, Madrigalen, Terzinen, achtzeiligen Stanzen, Assonanzen, Variationen und was der Italiänisch-Spanisch-Französischen Siebensächelchen mehr sind! Warum doch unsre poetischen Spielmätzchen immer nur mit ausländischen Formen tändeln?[20]

'Reichthum' and 'Segen' beat a heavy ironic resonance because another of the charges levelled against the sonnet form was its inherent difficulty, which was seen not so much as a blessing or even a challenge, but as an intimidating and ultimately pointless burden. Christoph Martin Wieland, for instance, described it as 'das schwerste aller poetischen Spielwerke',[21] and Gottfried August Bürger declared: 'Die undankbare Schwierigkeit des Sonnettes [sic] wurde beinahe, und

---

16   'Nemesis', in Johann Wolfgang Goethe, *Sämtliche Werke: Briefe, Tagebücher und Gespräche*, ed. by Friedmar Apel and others, Deutsche Klassiker-Ausgabe, 40 vols. (Deutscher Klassiker Verlag, 1986–2000), II: *Gedichte 1800–1832*, ed. by Karl Eibl (1988), p. 256.

17   Ibid., p. 753.

18   Schlütter, p.17.

19   The term is Karl Reinhardt's. See his essay 'Der deutsche Sonettismus', in Jörg-Ulrich Fechner, *Das deutsche Sonett* (Fink, 1969), pp. 340–41.

20   Reinhardt, 'Das poetische Joujou', in Fechner, pp. 338–39 (p. 338).

21   Quoted in Fechner, p. 336.

zwar in Sonnetten selbst, zum Sprichworte.'[22] Other critics dismissed it as nugatory and meretricious (note Reinhardt's verb 'tändeln' in the above quotation), a trivial exercise in mere ingenuity, with a resulting lack of conceptual depth. It is no surprise that, alongside 'Klinggedicht' and 'Klingklang in Schellen und Reimen',[23] substantives ending in '-elei' recurred in the repudiations of the sonnet form. 'Empfindelei', 'Reimkünstelei', 'kalte Künstelei', 'die Sclaverey mit den Reimen'[24] were the most frequent and underscore how the sonnet was perceived as somehow artificial and spurious, the plaything of the clever and nimble dilettante. In such hands the sonnet became not so much an imposing work of art as a self-conscious artifice, and this was indeed the criticism levelled against the form by a much later reviewer (and distinguished poet), Wilhelm Lehmann: 'Gleicht das Sonett nicht einer verrosteten Kanne mit verstopftem Mund? Ist es nicht das Instrument preziöser Empfindelei, die sich anstrengt, einem Strophen- und Reimschema zu willfahren?'[25]

In contrast to this charge of lightweight frivolity, there frequently emerged the criticism that the sonnet was too tightly structured and constraining, for it has been cast, from its inception, in a framework of firm prosodic rules, and its denigrators were quick to argue that a compulsion to obey those rules led inevitably to a narrowing of the poet's vision and a stifling of his spontaneity: Johann Christoph Gottsched, for example, compared the sonneteer to someone 'der mit geschlossnen Beinen tanzet'.[26] In a sonnet entitled 'Aus Helgoland (II)' the political polemicist Anastasius Grün (1806–76) employed the images of an 'enge[r] Fähre' and 'ein Sarg' to make the same point. A sonnet by its very nature characteristically asks the questions: how to balance reflective subjectivity and regulatory rigour, how to reconcile brilliant license and a commitment to rules, how, in such a small field of play, to move from contradiction and opposition to resolution or revelation with no significant diminution of spontaneity?

Not all poets, of course, felt constrained or handicapped by the sonnet's inherent limitations, but it took a poet of Goethe's stature, and then only after setting aside initial scruples about the sonnet's 'Regelzwang',[27] both to identify the contentious elements and then to transform them into a masterly sonnet. The second tercet of his poem 'Das Sonett', published in 1806, is:

> Nur weiß ich hier mich nicht bequem zu betten,
> Ich schneide sonst so gern aus ganzem Holze
> Und müßte nun doch auch mitunter leimen.[28]

22   Quoted ibid., p. 319.
23   The phrase is Friedrich Hebbel's. See *Deutsche Sonette*, ed. by Hartmut Kircher (Reclam, 1979), p. 430.
24   These neologisms are the creation of, respectively, Johann Haug, Johann Voss, Friedrich Bouterwek and Christian Weise. Haug and Bouterwek can be found in Fechner, pp. 354 and 368. Voss and Weise are quoted in *Deutsche Sonette*, ed. by Kircher, pp. 430 and 436.
25   *Deutsche Sonette*, ed. by Kircher, p. 449.
26   Johann Christoph Gottsched, *Versuch einer Critischen Dichtkunst: Ausgewählte Werke*, ed. by Joachim and Brigitte Birke, 12 vols (De Gruyter, 1971), VI/2, p. 223.
27   Kircher refers to Goethe's 'Abneigung gegenüber dem Regelzwang'. *Deutsche Sonette*, ed. by Kircher, p. 434.
28   Goethe, *Sämtliche Werke*, II, p. 408.

And two years later he writes in 'Natur und Kunst':

> Wer Großes will, muß sich zusammenraffen:
> In der Beschränkung zeigt sich erst der Meister,
> Und das Gesetz nur kann uns Freiheit geben.[29]

Goethe thus made a virtue of obeying traditional prosodic rules. He quickly came to see that the sonnet, like so much else in a writer's life, attracts contradictory artistic impulses: in choosing and succumbing to the form, the poet is consciously agreeing to follow the rules, but that willing surrender, he believes, will release creative energy. Goethe's seal of approval, reinforced by the magnificent cycle of seventeen sonnets inspired by his feelings for Minna Herzlieb, no doubt helped to ensure the survival, perhaps even the longevity, of the sonnet. A century and a half later Johannes Becher, an Expressionist poet whose literary agenda could hardly be more different from Goethe's, was preoccupied over a lifetime with the form and was prepared to accord huge prestige to it: 'Das Sonett erscheint uns als die Grundform der Dichtung [...] Unter einer poetischen Grundform verstehen wir die Form einer Dichtung, welche ihre wesentlichsten Bestandteile am konzentriertesten, am "reinsten" enthält.'[30] What then were the rules imposed by the classical Petrarchan sonnet with such 'schwere[r] Strenge' and so often chafed against by many of Goethe's contemporaries? First it should be indicated that, although some poets and commentators complained about the restrictions of the sonnet, it is in fact a varied form. The Italian or Petrarchan sonnet, the version most favoured by German poets, consists of fourteen lines, two quatrains and two tercets, with a volta after the second quatrain, rhyming abba abba (rima baciata) cde cde (rima incatenata) with possible variations in the sestet and with lines of ten to twelve syllables. The French sonnet is also founded in the Petrarchan form or consists of two quatrains and a rhyming couplet and a final quatrain, with a volta after the second quatrain, rhyming abba abba (rima baciata) cc dede (rima alternata) with variations possible in the final quatrain and lines of equal length (no more than twelve syllables). The English or Shakespearean sonnet consists of three quatrains and an heroic couplet, rhyming abab cdcd efef (so-called Sicilian stanzas) gg, with a shift after the second quatrain and a turn before the heroic couplet with lines of regular length (between ten and twelve syllables).[31] By this account the two sonnets quoted in this chapter can be described as follows: Goethe's sonnets are Petrarchan, while Becher's 'Das Sonett' is a mixture of Petrarchan and English in its quatrains and back to Petrarchan in its tercets. Even this very small sample shows that variations on classical forms are possible, perhaps inevitable, but the following features are mandatory — a sonnet should consist of fourteen lines, it should rhyme, it should have lines of regular length (no more than twelve syllables) and it should have a volta, a change in tone or mood or voice or tempo or perspective, a shift in focus, a swerve in logic, a change of heart during its course.

Gottsched, in the mid-eighteenth century in his *Versuch einer Critischen Dichtkunst*,

---

29   Ibid., p. 838.
30   Becher, 'Kleine Sonettlehre', p. 603.
31   *The Penguin Book of the Sonnet*, ed. by Levin, pp. 337–45.

was the first to seek to codify these rules for his German readers.[32] He insisted on fourteen lines and stipulated that these lines must be of equal length, that they must be alexandrines, that there should be two quatrains and two tercets, that the rhyming of the quatrains should be abba abba and that the two tercets should rhyme cde cde — this is very close to the Petrarchan pattern, indeed very close to Goethe's 'Das Sonett' and 'Natur und Kunst' except that the two Goethe poems have lines of eleven syllables. But it was A. W. Schlegel who, some fifty years later in a lecture on the sonnet given in Berlin in the winter of 1803–04, endeavoured, in his own words, 'das Sonett so viel als möglich mathematisch zu restauriren'. In the lecture he, like Gottsched but applying much greater detail and with fierce logic, laid down the rules:

> Das Sonett besteht in vierzehn Zeilen, welche durch Abschnitte des Sinnes in vier Glieder, zwey von vier Zeilen, die vorangehen, und zwey von drey, die nachfolgen (Quartetts und Terzetts). Die Verse werden von gleicher Länge genommen [...] und zwar wählt man die umfassendste und allgemeinste der gereimten Versarten, welche in der Sprache üblich ist, z. B. bey den Franzosen den Alexandriner und ehedem leider auch bey uns.[33]

For the rhyme pattern he stipulated two rhymes reappearing four times in the quatrains, and in the tercets two rhymes reappearing three times or three rhymes twice. For Schlegel the sonnet offered 'in seiner Concentration einen Gipfel der Reim- und Verskunst'. As far as he was concerned, the rhyming is all important. Resorting to geometrical metaphors, he argued that the rhyming literally shapes the sonnet with the two quatrains looking like squares, the octave resembling a cube and each tercet a triangle. He did not use the word volta (or 'Wendung'), but it is clear that he expected a threefold 'dramatic' development — 'Exposition, Fortgang und Katastrophe' — with antitheses leading perhaps to 'eine enigmatische Sentenz am Schluß'. Schlegel's attempt at a stringent definition of the sonnet form assumed almost canonical status. Even in the twentieth century, Becher's 'Philosophie des Sonetts oder Kleine Sonettlehre' repeats and reinforces much of the substance of Schlegel's famous lecture: both Becher's essay and Schlegel's lecture are borne by the same patrician, almost magisterial, tone and both served to keep the sonnet in the forefront of literary attention at very different points of German history. Schlegel's scrupulously, almost pedantically, enunciated rules reiterate the familiar features — fourteen lines, each of the same length, each no more than twelve syllables long — but what is particularly interesting about his lecture is that he pays an inordinate amount of attention to rhyming (masculine and feminine rhymes, patterns and permutations of rhyming), but has little to say about the Petrarchan volta or about appropriate (or inappropriate) subject matter or about metre. As far as metre was concerned, he was probably seeking to counter the charge that sonnets were little more than self-important 'Kling-Gedichte', thin on content, vehicles for amateurish verbal acrobatics — 'der magere Zirkusgaul des Dilettanten', as a much

---

32   Gottsched, vi/2, pp. 220–31.
33   August Wilhelm Schlegel, *Kritische Schriften und Briefe*, ed. by Edgar Lohner, 7 vols (Kohlhammer, 1965), iv, pp. 185–94.

later critic called them.[34] Cautious adherence to strict metrical patterns might well give rise to the kind of soft-centred mellifluence noted by many of the sonnet's fiercest critics.

Schlegel's prescriptive taxonomy of the sonnet was hugely influential in the first half of the nineteenth century, simultaneously restoring the sonnet's reputation and credibility, creating powerful expectations and re-establishing a tradition. That tradition weighed heavy on his successors:

> Wohl kaum eine Lyrikform ist so untrennbar an ein Gewicht von Traditionen und Assoziationen gekettet wie die Sonettform. Ein Dichter, der beschließt, sich ihrer zu bedienen, muß deshalb nicht nur in der Lage sein, seine Gedanken in dieser kurzen, durch vorgeschriebenes Reimschema und Metrum streng gefaßten Gedichtform zu konzentrieren oder eine Abweichung von diesen Normen allenfalls vor sich zu rechtfertigen, sondern er muß auch mit dem erwähnten Gewicht der Traditionen rechnen, sie gewissermaßen im Leser vorausprogrammieren.[35]

And it was not until the beginning of the next century that that weight was at least partially lifted and there occurred a supple flexing of the sonnet's rigid verse. Under the influence of Baudelaire and the French Symbolists Verlaine, Rimbaud and Mallarmé the form was loosened and subsequently found itself in something of 'a paradoxical position, as much to be worked against, even overcome, as it is to be recalled and cultivated'.[36] French influence superseded Italian, in the work, for example, of Rainer Maria Rilke, whose sonnets offer a particularly instructive example, not least because he negotiated with the form throughout his career and, according to one reviewer, 'wrote sonnets at decisive stages' in that career.[37] In his *Sonette an Orpheus* the development was more of a considerable prosodic shake-up than a mere relaxation. Indeed, Hartmut Kircher maintains that Rilke's sonnets can be justifiably described as 'unsonettisch' because they are 'durch Auflösung von innen her bedroht'[38] while Helmut Heißenbüttel takes that stricture one stage further and implies that threat has become a kind of literary sacrifice with the sonnet as victim: in Rilke's sonnets, he suggests, 'die spezifische Form [ist] zur in sich zerbröckelnden Mumie geworden'.[39] Despite many differences, Rilke resembles Schnack in the freedom with which he treated the sonnet form.

Rilke's own account of the genesis of the *Sonette an Orpheus* makes Heißenbüttel's image of the traditional sonnet's fate appear slightly less dramatic. The fifty-five sonnets which make up the cycle came to him in a hectic rush in the two weeks after his ecstatic revelation by which he had completed the *Duineser Elegien* in

---

34 Ernst Robert Curtius in 1948, quoted in Kircher, p. 449.
35 Andrea Hugelshofer, 'Rückerts Sonettzyklus *Amaryllis*: Zwischen petrarkistischer Liebeserklärung und moderner Uneigentlichkeit', in *Rückert-Studien VI. Jahrbuch der Rückert-Gesellschaft 1991–2* (Ergon, 1992), pp. 38–68 (p. 39).
36 Sandra L. Berman, *The Sonnet over Time* (University of North Carolina Press, 1988), p. 149.
37 Ernest L. Stahl, 'Rilke's Sonnets to Orpheus: Composition and Thematic Structure', *Oxford German Studies*, 9 (1978), 119–38 (p. 120).
38 Kircher, p. 441.
39 Helmut Heißenbüttel, *Über Literatur* (Walter, 1966), pp. 224–27 (p. 226).

February 1922, several of them emerging in one day, almost simultaneously, 'so daß mein Bleistift Mühe hatte, mit ihrem Auftreten Schritt zu halten'.[40] While Rilke retained the Petrarchan shape of two quatrains and two tercets and only a slightly variegated rhyme scheme (either abab/cddc or abba/cddc, then either efg/gfe or efe/gfg with modifications occurring not only between different sonnets, but also *within* individual sonnets), he breaks with orthodoxy and tradition by varying the lengths of the lines considerably — sometimes as short as four or five syllables (I, ix) or even three (II, i), sometimes as long as fifteen syllables (I, xxiv) or even nineteen (II, xvii). The first three *Sonette* are written in the traditional structure of fourteen lines in iambic pentameters: of the remaining fifty-two, only five are composed in that manner, and trochaic and dactylic metres predominate. Having, as it were, rehearsed the genre fifteen years earlier in the *Neue Gedichte* (of the 189 poems in the two parts, forty-seven are sonnets, but already here we find many examples of enjambement overrunning the division between octave and sestet), Rilke wanted a more relaxing, less disciplined form for his principal message: 'Gesang ist Dasein. Für den Gott ein Leichtes', and he did not scruple at any irregularity. Indeed, he brought the sonnet closer to the hymn or the ode, manifestly still poetry, nowhere near the rhythmic prose produced by some of his Expressionist contemporaries. Intent on not destroying the form, he wondered nevertheless whether he had ended up with sonnets at all:

> Ich sage immerzu Sonette. Ob es gleich das Freieste, sozusagen Abgewandeltste wäre, was sich unter dieser, sonst so stillen und stabilen Form begreifen ließe. Aber gerade dies: das Sonett abzuwandeln, es zu heben, ja gewissermaßen es im Laufen zu tragen, ohne es zu stören, war mir, in diesem Fall, eine eigentümliche Probe und Aufgabe: zu der ich mich, nebenbei, kaum zu entscheiden hatte.[41]

In the event, while the lines of the fifty-five sonnets are irregular in length and frequent variations in metre occur (with dactyls and trochees preferred to the recommended iambs), and while the strict line of the sonnet is frequently dissolved through the medium of long striding enjambements (firmly rejected by Schlegel) and syntactic breaks, the whole cycle is founded in the classic dialectical structure which is familiar from the seventeenth century onwards. Through the medium of song, Rilke proclaims, there should be unity and unification among all potentially conflicting orders of being — between the visible and the invisible, between 'being' and 'been', between life and death, between 'Diesseits' and 'Jenseits', between the poet's inner world and external reality. The *Sonette* are a diversified and yet coordinated poetic work, an authentic cycle, unlike the *Neue Gedichte*, which are essentially largely disjointed pieces despite Rilke's later efforts to shape them formally and thematically into some kind of cyclical order. It seems wholly appropriate that a cycle of poetry issuing from the conviction that poetry should be a place of metamorphosis is itself accommodated within a poetic genre whose traditional restraints are then relaxed and readjusted to suit new purposes. The changes do not, it is true, amount to a formal metamorphosis. Rilke, who,

40   Letter to Katharina Kippenberg, 23 February 1922, in Rilke, *Briefe*, II, pp. 224–25.
41   Ibid., p. 225.

according to Judith Ryan, was both 'elegiac and restorative [...] avoiding the avant-garde gesture of making a break with the past, received elements from tradition and combined them according to his own catalytic methods'.[42] His experimentations with form were, as it turned out, not exactly radical, not as radical as Schnack's, for example. Two impulses are at work here, but not in conflict — to modify the traditional sonnet form *and* to retain the basic sonnet structure, all in the name of imposing upon the sonnet the huge new responsibility of resolving in Rilke's case the existential crises which he identified in the first decades of the twentieth century. For this purpose he crafted a freer, looser and more independent form which, however, never looked likely to bring him close, or closer, to Expressionism or Expressionist poets. There was none among English poets who rendered a similar service. Edward Thomas, Rilke's close contemporary, remained convinced of the sonnet's intimidating rigidity:

> I have a dread of the sonnet [...] It must contain fourteen lines and a man must be a tremendous poet or a cold mathematician if he can accommodate his thoughts to such a condition. The result is [...] that many of the best sonnets are rhetoric only.[43]

Rilke's almost complete repudiation of Expressionism was founded, above all, in his concerns with poetic form and in his perception of that movement's inherently arbitrary and undisciplined nature. The Expressionist poet behaves, according to Rilke, in a wilfully unpredictable and uncontrolled way, and thus produces poetry notable only for chaotic formlessness.[44] Rilke never modified his view, although he had read Georg Heym's poetry,[45] which certainly does not fit this stereotype of the Expressionist poet. For Rilke poetic form and formal restraint, epitomized to particular effect in the sonnet, offered a bulwark not so much against political turmoil (as it did twenty years later for Schneider and Haushofer), but against personal disintegration and the spiritual and moral impoverishment of the age. A similar assertion could be made about Heym's poetry, or indeed Georg Trakl's. Rilke may not have thought of Heym or Trakl as Expressionist poets, but that is how they are traditionally regarded and thus they disturb his stereotypical view of the movement. In a warm appreciation of Trakl's 'Helian', Rilke does not resort to the metaphor of a bulwark against chaos, but chooses to praise the poem, with references to 'fences' and 'enclosures', for its powers of containment.[46] If Heym and Trakl can be said to belie the stereotype of the Expressionist poet which Rilke promotes, it can be reasonably argued that all those Expressionist writers

42   Judith Ryan, *Rilke, Modernism and Poetic Tradition* (Cambridge University Press, 1999), pp. 221 and 227.
43   Letter to Jesse Berridge, 7 November 1902, in Edward Thomas, *Letters of Edward Thomas to Jesse Berridge,* ed. by Anthony Berridge (Enitharmon, 1983), p. 36.
44   See his letter to Anni Mewes, 12 September 1919, Rilke, *Briefe,* II, pp. 30–31.
45   Karen Leeder and Robert Vilain (eds), *The Cambridge Companion to Rilke* (Cambridge University Press, 2010), p. xv.
46   Rilke's actual words are: 'Es ['Helian'] ist gleichsam auf seine Pausen aufgebaut, ein paar Einfriedungen um das grenzenlos Wortlose: so stehen die Zeilen da. Wie Zäune in einem flachen Land, über die hin das Eingezäunte fortwährend zu einer unbesitzbaren großen Ebene zusammenschlägt.' Letter to Ludwig von Ficker, 8 February 1915, *Briefe,* I, p. 563.

(like Schnack) who joined the long line of German sonneteers were also breaking free from that stereotype. And it was a considerable number. Richard Sheppard describes the phenomenon in the following terms:

> It is an odd paradox that the sonnet form enjoyed an extraordinary popularity among Expressionist poets: Blass, Boldt, Becher, Goll, Heym, Klemm, Trakl, Werfel and Zech *inter al.* were all particularly attached to 'this old-fashioned' form, as though to a pre-structured system, and a large number of poetic publications by Expressionists took the form of sonnet sequences [...][47]

Sheppard adduces various reasons for this popularity: that sonnets offered a 'taming, conserving element', that the classical form dignified frequently unattractive subject-matter, that its strict configuration 'emphasised the contrast between a conventional and an advanced mode of consciousness', and that the Expressionists' ambiguous relationship to the sonnet form was 'the literary equivalent of their ambiguous relationship with the Wilhelmine "system"'. Perhaps there is no need for such ingenious explanations of what Peter Rühmkorf, in the introduction to his anthology of Expressionist poems, calls 'dieser scheinbar ungebrochene Respekt vor der herkömmlichen Vierzeilerstrophe'.[48] Experimental writing in response to the war was not common, for the majority of war poets adhered to conventional rhyme, metre and poetic syntax simply because they were amateurs and, therefore, not familiar with experimental techniques. Moreover, in times of national crisis and an overwhelming sense of personal vulnerability, a withdrawal into conservatism seems a natural psychological and emotional reaction. The literary equivalent of such an 'old-fashioned' (to use Sheppard's word) response was the sonnet, which at the same time offered any Expressionist poet with iconoclastic tendencies ample opportunity to rebel against its time-honoured restrictions. Robert Newton, in his study of Expressionist poetic form, maintains that it was precisely because he was seeking to create 'dramatic tension' and intensity that the Expressionist poet reached for the sonnet.[49] A proliferation of interjections and exclamations, dislocated word-order and syntax, irregular line lengths and metrical patterns, eccentric rhyming and hectic but staccato pace, all straining to be contained within the traditional form, became common phenomena among Expressionist sonneteers, and particularly for those very few who, like Schnack, sought to reflect the reality of the battlefield, that is the content of their poems, in the formal structure. Newton also makes a helpful distinction between 'Formauflösung' (abandonment of form), 'dis-formation' ('variation of or change from a form which is initially established in the poem') and 'trans-formation' (a change 'from one well-observed form to another equally well-observed but different one').[50]

★   ★   ★   ★   ★

47   Richard Sheppard (ed.), *Expressionism in Focus* (Goethe Institute, 1986), pp. 37–39.
48   Peter Rühmkorf (ed.), *131 expressionistische Gedichte* (Wagenbach, 1976), p. 12.
49   Robert P. Newton, 'Some Aspects of Expressionist Form in the *Menschheitsdämmerung*' (unpublished doctoral dissertation, Johns Hopkins University, 1964). See in particular the section headed 'The Sonnet', pp. 141–54. This quotation is from p. 152.
50   Ibid., p. 211 (footnotes).

The German sonnet, as we have seen, can boast a rich pedigree of diverse practitioners and theorists and, in writing *Tier rang* between 1916 and 1920, Schnack was not only inserting himself into that long tradition of sonnet-writing, but also helping to sustain the genre's considerable contemporary popularity. Reference to many of the sonnets of *Tier rang* and a close analysis of two particularly striking examples should help to establish precisely what kind of sonnets Schnack composed for his cycle of war poems.

As a cataclysmic event in European history, the First World War is an extreme example of the kind of national and global upheaval in which sonnets demonstrably flourished. Yet it is remarkable that Schnack should reach for the sonnet genre to relay his own war experiences, for in all the audits of the sonnet's traditional purposes, war, or rather frontline combat, seldom figures, though Peter Sprengel, having just characterized the sonnet as a 'Passepartout für vielfältige Inhalte', does list, as rare examples, Walter Ferl's *Hinter der Front* (1914), Hans Ehrenbaum-Degele's *Das tausendste Regiment* (1917, posthumous) and Richard Schaukal's *Eherne Sonette* (1914) as sonnet cycles from the First World War.[51] He could also have included Siegfried Schlösser's *Sonette* (1916), as Patrick Bridgwater does in the Epilogue of his study on German First World War poets.[52] Friedrich Rückert's *Geharnischte Sonette* (1814) are the only substantial collection of war poems I can think of which approach, but remain far removed from, Schnack's *Tier rang*. The seventy-four sonnets of Rückert's collection turn out, on examination, to be simply stirring exhortations to the Prussian people to join in the Wars of Liberation against Napoleonic domination and make no attempt to portray the battles in which, in fact, Rückert himself did not take part. The hectoring patriotic urgency is kept under tight control (these are, after all, 'geharnischte Sonette'), and the form matches, and merges precisely with, the sonnets' content. Traditionally shaped with two quatrains followed by two tercets, regular line-lengths each of eleven syllables, iambic metre, consistently rhyming abba abba cdc dcd, Rückert's sonnets are relentlessly upbeat in tone as imperatives, vocatives and exclamation marks abound and rhetorical flourishes are enlisted to reinforce the call to arms. The two tercets of the first poem (after seven 'Vorklänge'), for example, read:

> Auf denn, die ihr aus meines Busens Ader
> Aufquellt, wie Riesen aus des Stromes Bette,
> Stellt euch in eure rauschenden Geschwader!
>
> Schließt eure Glieder zu vereinter Kette,
> Und ruft, mithadernd in den großen Hader,
> Erst: Waffen! Waffen! und dann: Rette! Rette![53]

These multiple exclamation marks, reverberating with irresistible fervour, are replaced in *Tier rang* by the querulous interrogatives heavy with self-doubt which the landscape of the frontline unleashes on the poet's consciousness. Rückert's highly traditional *Geharnischte Sonette* had a considerable influence on the patriotic

51   Sprengel, p. 603.
52   Bridgwater, p. 160.
53   Friedrich Rückert, *Gesammelte poetische Werke*, 12 vols (Sauerländer, 1882), I, p. 7.

verse of Adelbert von Chamisso, Georg Herwegh and Ferdinand Freiligrath: it was only with early twentieth-century poets such as Rilke that that influence waned. Schnack's 'dis-formations' (to use Newton's word) of the sonnet genre continued that process of change.

There is no record of Schnack's ever using the word 'sonnet'. Returning from the frontline in February 1916, he relates retrospectively how he brought with him 'ein Bündel von Gedichten [...] an die achtzig langzeiligen Gedichte'.[54] Moreover, unlike Rilke (with his *Sonette an Orpheus*) and Rückert (with his *Geharnischte Sonette*),[55] Schnack eschews the word 'sonnets' in his title, though that title, *Tier rang gewaltig mit Tier*, draws attention to the traditional dialectical and often confrontational nature of the genre. Nor does 'sonnets' appear on the flyer produced by the Ernst Rowohlt Verlag in April 1921 publicizing the volume: one reviewer quoted on it states that Schnack has created 'eine ganz neue Ausdrucksform',[56] but no reviewer describes that form as 'sonnet'. Again unlike Rilke and Rückert and the great majority of other German sonneteers, Schnack gives each of the sixty poems of *Tier rang* a title, thereby placing a heavier accent on visual form and indicating that this is a poetics of inscription rather than speech. Each individual sonnet's chiselled shape, separated out on the page under titles, isolates and highlights its particular theme. After all, the sonnet's capacity to depict the lyric self and to capture the mutability and mobility of an inner self is widely acknowledged with the result that the lyrical I can be presented as a persona in thrall to process, changefulness and perennial self-questioning. Given that the tradition of sonnet-writing in German literary history is so rich, it seems only natural, to us now and to reviewers at the time, that Schnack should join that tradition within which another tradition, already noted by Walter Mönch and continuing, according to Hartmut Kircher, into the period after the Second World War, is embedded: 'Wie oft während und nach Kriegen bzw. in Zeiten besonderer politischer Bedrängnis, so war auch vor und nach 1945 eine Phase reicher Sonettproduktion zu verzeichnen, die quantitiv die Sonettflut der Romantik wohl noch übertrifft.'[57] The sonnets of Reinhold Schneider, Rudolf Hagelstange, Josef Weinheber and Albrecht Haushofer are obvious examples of this trend, which emerged, it has already been suggested, because of a need felt for a withdrawal into conservatism in such catastrophic times.[58] Kircher's prepositions are very significant here — sonnets 'during' and 'after' wars, but not necessarily *about* wars. There is an important difference, and it is in that difference, that the

---

54   Glöckler, p. 14.
55   Patrick Bridgwater also mentions Josef Winkler (*Eiserne Sonette*) and Richard Schaukal (*Eherne Sonette*) in this context. There are numerous other examples. Bridgwater explains Schnack's diffidence by saying that Schnack was not 'flamboyant', nor was he writing 'patriotic poems, let alone swashbuckling ones'. Bridgwater, pp. 96–97.
56   Glöckler, p. 102. The reviewer in question was Dr. Hugo Bieber writing for *Der Tag*.
57   Kircher, p. 446.
58   Writing about his own cycle of sonnets, *Venezianisches Credo* (1946), Hagelstange puts it differently: 'Ihr [the sonnets of *VC*] Thema war die Überwindung des zeitlichen Chaos durch Besinnung auf über- und außerzeitliche Kräfte des Menschen, und die Sonette boten sich an wie Quader, mit denen man bauen konnte.' See Hans Bender (ed.), *Mein Gedicht ist mein Messer: Lyriker zu ihren Gedichten* (List, 1961), p. 38.

originality, the innovativeness and even the uniqueness of Schnack's *Tier rang* will be shown to lie. Schnack turns to the ordered sonnet form in a time of crisis both during and after the war to write about that war.

It has already been noted that *Tier rang* is a *cycle* of sonnets. A particular danger attaches to such a continuum. The alarm is raised most articulately by Weinheber, himself a prolific composer of sonnets at a time of national upheaval, but writing to a totally different agenda from Schneider and Hagelstange. Having rejected the notion that somehow the sonnet form does not suit the German character, Weinheber adds:

> Wenn nun das deutsche Sonett, das schon an und für sich weniger durch Melos als durch metrische Präzision ausgezeichnet ist, gleich neunundzwanzig weitere Sonette nach sich zieht, damit der Zyklus sich runde, so kann es schon wohl zum Schlaftrunk werden, und etwas Leierhaftes und Ödes eignet ja auch wirklich den meisten Sonettzyklen, und das in dem Maß mehr, je korrekter die Sonette gebaut sind. Das Gefühl hiefür hat wohl unsere modernen Dichter bestimmt, den überlieferten Jambenraster und die strenge Reimordnung aufzugeben, die Starrheit des Verses durch Enjambement aufzulockern und so das ganze Gebild unruhig zu machen und ihm neues Blut und neuen Ton zuzuführen.[59]

As Weinheber's authoritative voice is invoked so frequently in this context, it should be interposed at this point that a connection can be reasonably made between his unambivalent support for the National Socialist regime (who, in turn, promoted his work) and his equally clear advocacy, in theory and in practice, of Schlegel's and Gottsched's rules for the sonnet: 'Am Werk Weinhabers, der von den Nationalsozialisten sehr gefördert wurde, lassen sich aber auch exemplarisch mögliche ideologische Wechselbezüge zwischen unbedingter Unterwerfung des künstlerischen Subjekts unter ein Gesetz und dem realen historisch-politischen Hintergrund beobachten.'[60] Uwe-K. Ketelsen argues the case in his essay, 'National-sozialismus und Drittes Reich'.[61] What might be true of Weinheber's 'neunund-zwanzig weitere Sonette' could presumably be even truer, in Schnack's case, of fifty-nine 'further sonnets'. In all sonnets, patterns of rhyme, syntax, sound and meaning both reinforce one another and exist in dynamic tension with each other. In the sonnet cycle, the choices available to the sonneteer expand exponentially, and so does the pressure on the poet to introduce variation. All composers of lyric cycles, including even Shakespeare with his collection of 154 sonnets, have to negotiate a way round this inherent danger of inducing monotony or even narcolepsy, an ailment to which Germans with their predilection for sonnet cycles, according to Weinheber, are especially vulnerable.[62] The seventy-four sonnets of Rückert's cycle fall into this category and end up having a numbing effect on the reader from whom considerable patience and stamina are implicitly required. Weinheber recommends the renunciation of a strict iambic metre and rhyming pattern, as well

---

59   Lecture given on 27 June 1944, Weinheber, IV, Prosa I, p. 271.
60   Kircher, p. 444.
61   Uwe-K. Ketelsen, 'Nationalsozialismus und Drittes Reich', in *Geschichte der politischen Lyrik in Deutschland*, ed. by Walter Hinderer (Reclam, 1978,), pp. 291–314 (p. 306).
62   In the same lecture Weinheber speaks of the German 'Vorliebe für die zyklische Reihe'.

as a recourse to enjambement, as a way of loosening the traditional sonnet's bonds, of (in an odd phrase which has National Socialist resonances) making the whole configuration 'restless' and introducing 'neues Blut und neuen Ton'. Certainly it is only by generating interesting metaphors, paradoxes, eye-catching rhymes, new permutations in rhythm and sound, texture and syntax, that the composer of a long sequence like *Tier rang* will stand any chance of averting the danger which Weinheber identifies. The challenge confronting Schnack is compounded by the fact that the poet's focus in *Tier rang* is relentlessly directed at the imagined and actual horrors of the battlefield: such unbroken grimness in poems which look the same on the page and, when read aloud, sound the same, could easily issue into sterility and tedium. It was, however, more likely that these reactions would be provoked by a faithful reproduction of the traditional sonnet as the modern poet strove to come to terms with the accelerating pace of twentieth-century life or, in Schnack's case, the unprecedented circumstances of a twentieth-century war. Schnack's fellow Expressionist poet Paul Zech for one was keen to distance himself from outmoded and redundant versions of the genre. With reference to his own volume of sonnets *Das schwarze Revier* (1912) he writes:

> Man wird nun einwenden können, eine ganz moderne explosive Stoffmasse in die antike, geruhige Form eines Sonetts zu zwängen, ist ein Mangel an Gestaltungskraft. Das starre metrische Schema hemmt die grandiose Wucht des Gegenwartrhythmusses [...]. Nun muß ich sagen, daß diese vierzehnzeiligen Gedichte garnichts, auch garnichts mit einem Petrarca'schen Sonett gemein haben.[63]

The image of 'squeezing modern material into an antique form' has powerful resonance in any assessment of Schnack's 'noble sonnets memorably mutilated'.[64]

All sixty sonnets in *Tier rang* are fourteen lines long, with five exceptions: 'Der Tote' (I, 49–50) and 'Der Kanal' (I, 52–53), which have only thirteen lines; 'Schweres Geschütz' (I, 67) and 'Ich trug Geheimnisse in die Schlacht' (I, 84–85), which both have fifteen lines; and 'In Bereitschaft' (I, 81), which has only twelve lines. By the time *Tier rang* was published, Schnack had already rehearsed the form not only in his three Expressionist collections, but also in *Das Tribunal* and *Die Junge Kunst*: poems such as 'Lied an Frankreich' (I, 113–14), 'Aufwachende Erinnerung' (I, 119–20) and 'Der Geheimnisvolle' (I, 120–21) prefigure what is to become the norm in *Tier rang*. By the time of his next substantial volume, *Die Flaschenpost* (1936), Schnack had abandoned the form almost completely: in the 'great upheavals' of the 1930s and 1940s he did not, unlike, for example, Reinhold Schneider, resort again to the sonnet genre. A random glance at any of Schnack's sonnets is enough to tell us that we are not looking at anything resembling the attenuated shapes of Stramm's war poems in *Tropfblut*, or the regular architectonic structures of Rückert's *Geharnischte Sonette*, or the classically graceful lines of a Weinheber sonnet — not even the looser forms of Rilke's *Sonette an Orpheus*. There is certainly something heavy, even ponderously majestic, about Schnack's lines, but Becher's fundamental

---

63   Quoted in Wolfgang Paulsen, *Expressionismus und Aktivismus* (Gotthelf, 1935), p. 136.
64   Bridgwater, p. 110.

criterion of 'schwere Strenge'[65] implies the kind of austere discipline not evident in the sonnets in *Tier rang* which, from the outset, liberate themselves from A. W. Schlegel's detailed prescriptions.

Other contemporary poets experimented with varying lengths of line in their verse. Long, rolling lines are an occasional feature of Stadler's work (for example, the programmatic 'Fahrt über die Kölner Rheinbrücke bei Nacht', a rhyming sonnet with lines of irregular length of more or less thirty syllables, or his 'Pans Trauer': fourteen lines in one bloc, striking rhymes, lines of twenty-two syllables).[66] Anthologies offer examples of sonnets by Johannes R. Becher, Rudolf Leonhard, Ludwig Rubiner and Jesse Thor, all of whom at times favoured long, teeming lines of twenty-five syllables mingled with other lines of just four. The shortest line in Becher's 'Gedichte für ein Volk' has five syllables, the longest thirty-five.[67] Another poet whose name is often invoked in this context is Franz Werfel. However, his sonnets (such as 'Große Oper' and 'Katharina', from the *Weltfreund* collection)[68] tend to be regular, usually decasyllabic versions of the classical form, a far remove in content and structure from the poems in *Tier rang*. Max Dauthendey wrote few sonnets, but the innovative vocabulary and rhythms and irregular line lengths in the poetry of Würzburg's favourite son, with a primary school and street named after him, were in all probability known to Schnack, who retained a life-long allegiance to one of Franconia's most beautiful cities. None of these poets is as insistent and persistent in the use of the long line as Schnack. However, the most frequently cited point of comparison is Walt Whitman, who served briefly in the Civil War. He wrote only three sonnets ('Patroling Barnegat', 'On Journeys through the States' and 'Poet'). These contain no rhyming (Whitman rejected it from the outset), no discernible metrical pattern, no voltas, and few lines consistently approaching Schnack's in length. Whitman's lines progress in vast sweeps or 'movements' to the beat of onrushing waves, whereas Schnack's press inexorably but jerkily onwards to the irregular rhythm of an agitating pulse towards a striking end-rhyme. Moreover, none of Whitman's sonnets reads or 'feels' like a sonnet, and while his influence on German poetry and poets was considerable in terms of promoting long lines and certain existential attitudes, it was negligible in relation to the formal development of the German sonnet, and there is, in fact, no evidence in Schnack's poetry or prose that he knew Whitman's work.[69] Interestingly, though, Ferdinand Freiligrath, who translated some of Whitman's poems for the *Augsburger Allgemeine Zeitung* (24 April 1868), evaluates the poet's work in terms which could almost be applied to *Tier rang*: 'Sind das Verse? Die Zeilen sind wie Verse abgesetzt, allerdings, aber Verse sind es nicht. Kein Metrum, keine Strophen. Rhythmische Prosa. Streckverse. Auf den ersten Blick rauh, ungefüg, formlos, aber dennoch für ein feineres Ohr des

---

65   Becher, 'Kleine Sonettlehre', p. 603.

66   Stadler, pp. 169 and 108–09.

67   Johannes Becher, *Becher und die Insel: Briefe und Dichtungen 1916–1954*, ed. by Rolf Harder and Ilse Siebert (Insel, 1981), pp. 70–72.

68   Franz Werfel, *Das lyrische Werk*, pp. 38–39.

69   The influence of Whitman's poetry on the Expressionist generation has already been mentioned in Chapter 3.

Wohllauts nicht ermangelnd.'[70] The reference to 'rhythmic prose' is particularly apposite.

★   ★   ★   ★   ★

'Abendlicher Marsch' (I, 80–81) is probably the most personal poem in Schnack's collection, and the person in the poem feels under huge threat. Since 'Am Feuer' (I, 49), the poet has been an observer — of frontline features and incidents, the listening-post, explosion, smoke, stars, snow, captured French soldiers, a deserter, horsemen — but then in the poem 'Der Flieger' (I, 79–80) an overwhelming sense of imminent death prevails: 'Tod liegt auf mir, würgend, riesenhaft und wie ein schauriges Gewicht'. The dead bodies which were (safely) 'fern' in 'Am Feuer' he can now see in all their horror, on the battlefield towards which he will soon be marching. Observer is going to become participant, is going to attack and be attacked, the mood and the tone are correspondingly bleak, the earlier sense of vulnerability has now intensified into despair, and urgent hopes ('Ich möchte [...] ich möchte [...] wir wollen') which in the earlier poem were not yet extinguished are now bankrupted and corrupted by cynicism and bitter irony. The lyrical I relates his worst fears, describes the scene, depicts death, tantalises himself with possibilities, gives voice to the near-certainty of his own obliteration:

Mein Gesicht ganz im Staub, mein Name in dem Munde irgendeines. Dunkel umkreist sich das Land mit Dunst.
Ich möchte Mutter rufen, innig, zärtlich, ich möchte Geliebte sagen, schön und mit Wohllaut... Umsonst! Reiter machen sich auf zum Traben
Gegen nahenden Mondschein, gegen westliche Wälder voller Unzeug, roten Insekten, brütenden Raben;
Ich möchte mitreiten, ich möchte silbern werden im Nachtschein der Ferne, nahe sein der gewaltigen Feuersbrunst
Die ins Gesicht blendet, die entsetzlich ist; unirdisch, mit Rauchgewölk...
Aber wir verlassen alle Süßigkeit, wir gehen dumpf
Gegen die Schlacht an, die in Gräben trommelt, die irrsinnig ist schon sieben Tage, die Tote häuft
Immer höher, die schwer atmet, grollend, bös. Wer wüßte dies, daß er zur Nacht im Blut ersäuft
So wie im warmen Wein? Vielleicht spiel ich im Morgengraun mit einem kostbar schönen, abgerissnen Rumpf?
Oder unterzugehn im Rauch der Greuel wie müder Sternfall in Wäldern, wie im Meere ein Schiff, weiß und voll Duft aus Südland;
Oder von ewigem Schlaf überkommen sich hinzulegen bei Negern, tot, noch dunkler als sonst, noch abenteuerlicher im Umriß,
Noch fabelhafter. Oder auch dies: herauszutreten wieder, mit Blei im Gesicht, zerschossen, Hände verloren wie etwas Überflüssiges, Gas im Schlund,
Scharf geätzt. Süß ist die verdunkelte Zukunft, herrlich das Nichtwissen.
Nächtlich wird es überall, selbst im Hirn, Tand

70   Ferdinand Freiligrath, *Freiligraths Werke in einem Band*, ed. by Werner Ilberg (Volksverlag, 1962), p. 256.

Ist Erinnerung, die Leben dahinten, weit in Ost oder Süd rote und weiße
Städte, Weiber, Gelächter an Tischen, nur Tod ist gewiß,
Tatsächlich und nahe, nur Eiter im Stirnbein, Verschüttung und Angst
und das stete Denken: Seltsam geh ich im Abend zugrund. (I, 80–81)

From first line to last, with interjections of immediately stifled longings, a dreadful
foreboding informs every word. As often with Schnack, physical elements are
stressed from the outset: the lyrical I's face is covered with dust from the roads.
Someone says his name — a casual word from a fellow-soldier, or an order from an
officer. '[I]rgendeines' implies that it does not matter who says his name and that,
therefore, his own identity no longer matters. He seeks to re-establish it by calling
his mother and his beloved: the conditional, and repeated, 'ich möchte' suggests
that something prevents that from happening. Opposition is latent in the double
use of the preposition 'gegen', which Schnack regularly mines for its ambiguity: it
carries the meaning of 'towards' and 'against'. Both are appropriate in this context.
Horsemen soon put a stop to his ruminations, to his quest for kindness and
euphony, as they set off westwards towards forests of 'red insects', 'brooding ravens'
and other 'unthings' all heavy with menace. 'Unzeug' is a striking, unexpected
inclusion, conjuring up not so much an impalpable force, but something material
(as in 'Zeughaus'). For a moment he would like to ride along, he feels tempted to
join the nocturnal horsemen as they move towards the mighty conflagration, and
once again he gets no further than expressing the wish. Anything is better than
the dull darkness into which he and his fellow infantrymen are setting out ('wir
gehen dumpf | Gegen die Schlacht an'). Horsemen in these poems always have
something mysterious, almost superior and remote, about them: they ride in and out
of and across the poems, they are (literally) not earthbound and they always seem
to survive. The 'crazy' ('irrsinnig') battle is, we learn, seven days old, and ironically
that battle seems to have a life and character of its own. It is piling dead bodies up,
it is panting with the effort, rumbling sullenly, evil, alive with dead bodies and
growing taller on those bodies. Two unanswered questions serve to increase the
sense of helplessness and escalating horror. The 'roten Insekten' have already made
us think of spilt blood, and he wonders out loud if anyone could possibly know that
the soldiers would be drowning by nightfall in blood. The linking of blood and
wine ('[...] im Blut ersäuft | So wie im warmen Wein') is something of a cliché, but it
conjures up in our minds visions of the South (to which he refers in the penultimate
line of the poem) and the vineyards of Franconia. And if not drowning in blood,
then perhaps by dawn he will be toying with a torso rent from its body and (with
bitter irony) 'kostbar schönen', though clearly not valuable or beautiful enough to
be spared. Two questions are then followed by three possibilities, all ghastly, and
all incrementally ratcheting up the horror and violence to an extreme pitch, to a
nightmarish vision of himself emerging from the battle with his face shot to pieces,
his hands gone, his throat burnt by gas ('Munde' in the first line has been replaced
by 'Schlund' and dehumanized and bestialized in the process). The first stage on
the way to the final nightmare had seemed bad enough — 'unterzugehn im Rauch
der Greuel', but at least the similes which reinforce the image contain stars and a

ship, white and full of scent from the South. And the second stage in the rhetorical cataloguing of possibilities (or ... or ... or) sees him 'von ewigem Schlaf überkommen sich hinzulegen bei Negern',[71] dead, darker than usual, 'abenteuerlicher im Umriß', 'fabelhafter' — taking us back to the mysterious night-riders whom he felt tempted to join earlier, because with them he might ride away from, or even rise above, the beckoning horrors of the battlefield. 'Abenteuerlicher im Umriß'? In comparison with the earlier 'submerging in smoke' and by dint of killing the enemy and thus being able to lie with them, he creates a self-aggrandizing myth, more than a myth, of his own ('fabelhafter'). The idiosyncratic use of infinitives with 'zu' and no main verb/subject ('hinzulegen [...] unterzugehn'), so typical of Schnack's technique in *Tier rang*, draws attention to the anonymity and the inhumanity of much that is happening here.

However, in accordance with the 1919 Expressionist collection, the lyrical I once again casts himself as an 'adventurer'. Now in 'Abendlicher Marsch' his blood will be spilt not in some self-assertively expansive gesture but in another cause. The Expressionist fervour and delirium of the earlier collections have subsided and ended up here on the Somme amid, in the last line, 'Eiter im Stirnbein, Verschüttung und Angst'. If that vision echoes Gottfried Benn's *Morgue*, the very last line ('Seltsam geh ich im Abend zugrund') with its sense of disorientation and alienation ('<u>Seltsam</u> geh ich'), with the evening setting, with the choice of the verb 'zugrundgehen' and not 'sterben', with the image of 'going down', foundering, in the evening ('im Abend' and not 'am Abend'), merging with the dark — all conspires to make us think of the poetry of Georg Trakl. The two penultimate lines have prepared us for that shocking combination of stark realism ('Eiter...') and the mellow, elegiac, mysterious and elusive 'Seltsam geh ich...'. 'Seltsam' is another of Schnack's favourite adjectives: it suggests that the lyrical I never feels wholly at home in the world, particularly in the world of the battlefield where events are beyond rational explanation and comprehension. He is mystified, ill at ease, thoroughly disorientated.[72] It is wonderful *not* knowing, the poet claims, what will happen, and the future plunged into darkness is 'sweet'. Yielding to that darkness, he finds that night has swamped even his brain — future hopes are thus extinguished. And as for memory and remembering — so often redeeming and consoling — they are summarily dismissed by the lead-word 'Tand', first in a new sentence, last in the line, brutal in its abruptness: 'Tand | Ist Erinnerung'. Life behind the memories is gone, no matter if those memories (of 'rote und weiße Städte, Weiber, Gelächter an Tischen', reminding us again of his Expressionist collections) are of the distant East and South (prefiguring some of Gottfried Benn's post-*Morgue* poems) and therefore ostensibly safe, well away from the battlefield. This dependence on memory, or on the ability to conjure memories, has a fragile aspect: the very nature of memory, voluntary and involuntary, both frightening, is that it simultaneously controls us

---

71   Probably from one of the five battalions of Senegalese Tirailleurs sent to the Western Front early in the First World War. See Marc Michel, *Les Africains et la Grande Guerre: l'appel à l'Afrique* (Karthala, 2003).

72   For example, the first line of 'Am Tor des Todes': 'Seltsam: hinabzusteigen in die weißen Knochen der Toten [...]'. I, 97.

and indulges the dangerous fantasy that we have a degree of creative control over our lives. 'Tand' stands close to 'Tod' in the line and sounds and looks very like it, and if 'nur Tod ist gewiß | Tatsächlich und nahe', then the implication must be that 'Tand' (or 'Erinnerung') is also doomed. The memories, the possible better future, the heroism and adventure are 'Tand', so much ephemeral frippery. For Schnack, 'Tand' is always used — and used more and more frequently — to carry this sense: in the poem 'In Bereitschaft' (I, 81) much-loved 'Tanz' has decayed into much-derided 'Tand', and in the final, majestic 'Am Tor des Todes' (I, 97) the carnage and the detritus of the battlefield are summarized as so much 'göttlicher Tand', the frippery of a God who is 'unbekannt, der Rätsel größtes' (I, 95).

'Abendlicher Marsch' is a wholly typical Schnack sonnet: it has fourteen lines; it rhymes abba/cddc/efg/efg (forty-three out of sixty poems in *Tier rang* follow this pattern); line length varies between forty-one syllables (line 11) and twenty-three syllables (line 7); there is no question of clearly defined quatrains and tercets or of scannable lines, nor of an easily identifiable volta, but there is a chronologically organized sequence of events, broken, by interrogation and speculation. Present time, filled with desperate cravings ('Ich möchte [...] ich möchte [...]') and general observations about the nocturnal scene, gives way after the first four lines to an acknowledgement that the quest for any kind of past solace ('Aber wir verlassen alle Süßigkeit') is doomed to failure, before, at line 8, ('Vielleicht spiel ich im Morgengraun [...]') the lyrical I begins to torment itself with visions of possible futures. A volta can be tentatively suggested at this point, and a very approximate outline of the sonnet can, with some effort and imagination, be coaxed from the fourteen irregular lines that make up the poem. A familiar dialectical configuration also emerges: a busy series of contrasts is conducted throughout — invariably between permutations of harsh reality and of ultimately unfulfilled harbingers of hope, possibilities of escape, acts of recall, what Edmund Blunden called 'saps of retrogression',[73] diggings not forward but backward. A 'resolution' — of a ghastly kind — is achieved in the sense that all of the latter are condemned to inevitable demise. The rhyming plays its part: the metre works in such a way that stress invariably falls on the (masculine) rhyming word, and those rhyming words are always significant both in themselves and also in their relationship with partner words to which they clearly relate through similar or contrasting meaning — the 'Dunst' and 'Feuerbrunst' of the battlefield; 'Umriß' and 'gewiß', where on the battlefield, in the battlefield smoke, no 'contour' can be 'certain'; 'Südland' in all its nostalgic authenticity and its diametric opposite 'Tand' in all its triviality; 'Schlund' and 'zugrund', both heavy and harsh with resonances of destruction. In this way Schnack often associates words, by rhyme or alliteration or assonance, where the meanings are strikingly contrasted or compared: for instance in 'Mund' (human mouth) and 'Schlund' (usually the gaping mouth of an animal or of a man-made beast) and the first line of the poem runs 'Munde [...] Dunkel [...] umkreist [...] Dunst'. Dense verbal texture is typical of Schnack's sonnets. Weinheber, in a paean to the sonnet, recommends precisely this kind of significant, relevant rhyming,

---

73   Edmund Blunden, *Undertones of War* (Penguin, 1987), p. 182.

founded in an 'internal relationship':

> Daß nicht immer der reinere Reim der bessere ist, wissen wir. Aber der schlechteste ist immer der ohne innere Beziehung. Moder — oder, Knie — wie, Komm — vom *sind* keine Reime. Und der beste, der vollkommenste deutsche Reim [...] ist noch immer jener: Herz — Schmerz! Da ist das Ding und die Folge![74]

For Schnack, however, rhyme is much more than an aesthetic desideratum. It is a means of containing what would otherwise be unbearably horrific and a way of securing vital consolations of memory and imagination. Rhyme thus becomes, in Gottfried Benn's terms, a powerful 'ordering principle':

> Bei Goethe stieß ich auf die überraschende Bemerkung: 'seit Klopstock uns vom Reim erlöste' — wir heute würden sagen, daß die freien Rhythmen, die Klopstock und Hölderlin uns einprägten, in der Hand von Mittelmäßigkeiten noch unerträglicher sind als der Reim. Der Reim ist auf jeden Fall ein Ordnungsprinzip und eine Kontrolle innerhalb des Gedichts.[75]

Moreover, the typical rhyme scheme of a Schnack sonnet (abba/cddc/efg/efg) has an intriguing effect: no matter how intense the ebb and flow of despair (in the battlefield reality) and hope (garnered from remembering and imagining), there is rarely utter hopelessness because there is always an answering rhyme. Admittedly it is a distant rhyme and a distant hope — it is only faintly that the rhyme word can sound in our heads, an effect further enfeebled and attenuated by the length of the lines — but the rhyme, long-awaited and invariably memorable, keeps that hope alive and has a literally containing effect. Charlie Louth, in an article on Ernst Stadler, sees not so much hope as an ever closer relationship with prose in the long line of a poetic mode as practised by Stadler (and Schnack). He writes in response to Stadler's review of the poetry of Max Dauthendey:

> He [Stadler] thinks of the expansive line as a kind of receptive instrument, giving him the flexibility to respond to the variety of the inner and outer world with a minimum of constraint, but, as he says himself, there is little to stop those verse-lines becoming prose, and the shaping qualities of rhyme are reduced to an almost inconsequential role. The rhymes hardly function as a heuristic device, and inflect the progress of the poem very little. The longer the line, the easier it is to come up with a rhyme-word and the more nonchalant the rhyming seems: there is a real question of how and whether these lines can be seen and heard as verse at all.[76]

★   ★   ★   ★   ★

There is a crucial difference between Schnack and Dauthendey: while Impressionist poets like Dauthendey used the long line to emphasize not only the limited ability of the senses but also the tendency of external phenomena to move beyond the

---

74   Weinheber, IV, p. 83.
75   Gottfried Benn, *Gesammelte Werke*, I: *Essays, Reden, Vorträge*, ed. by Dieter Wellershoff (Limes, 1959), p. 514.
76   Charlie Louth, 'Enchantment and Loss in Ernst Stadler', *Oxford German Studies*, 41 (2012), pp. 310–26 (p. 317).

boundaries of human perception — at the same time drawing attention to the ephemeral nature of that perception — many Expressionist poets like Schnack in his three earlier volumes (and like Stadler in the collection, *Der Aufbruch*) considered the long line to be the perfect form to contain and body forth their overriding compulsion 'ihr Sein in alle Weiten zu drängen'.[77] And perhaps the fact that the unspooling lines and the often ingenious end-rhymes of the *Tier rang* sonnets, frequently cast as rhythmic prose, are contained within a sequential cycle helps that volume to stay just this side of poetry.

Schnack is a strongly visual poet for whom the outward scene is accessory to an inner theatre, but he does not sacrifice his apprehension of the outer world or his awareness of the physical and the material for the sake of dramatizing his inner world. Schnack's lines do not move forward smoothly: enjambement, asyndetic parataxis, one-word 'sentences', accumulations of hefty substantives[78] which recall the 'Schönheitskatalog' of baroque poets such as Gryphius, listing the parts of their beloved's body, the anxious questioning ('Wer wüsste [...]?'), directed unanswered into the void, a ploy familiar from Rilke who also 'used rhetorical quotations that do not require an answer, many are quite unanswerable'[79] — all serve to take his sonnets away from the conventional form and to bring them closer to prose. This is a by no means uncommon development. Robert Lowell, like his fellow American, Robert Frost, had similar frustrations and strategies in his relationship with the sonnet. In his diary of sonnets, *Notebook 1967–1968*, Lowell laments that

> my meter, 14-line unrhymed blank verse sections, is fairly strict at first and elsewhere, but often corrupts in single lines to the freedom of prose. Even with this license, I fear I have failed to avoid the themes and gigantism of the sonnet.[80]

Lowell, unable to resist the gravitational pull of the sonnet, mostly resisted the temptation of using rhymes and his verse, with some exceptions, flowed free into prose.

Moreover, as the long line bears within itself a tendency to formlessness, it was the ideal compromise for Schnack, still deeply immersed in his Expressionist phase during the writing of *Tier rang*, and for a literary movement which was still too strongly rooted in tradition to renounce completely all allegiance to conventional form, but which at the same time wished to be limited as little as possible by that allegiance. Some kind of check, or, to use Rilke's metaphor, 'Zäune' was perceived to be needed, 'some deliberate cage | Wherein to keep wild thoughts like birds in thrall'.[81] Hence Georg Heym's casting of his vast apocalyptic visions in classically shaped strophes, hence, too, Schnack's apparently unproblematic

---

77 Stadler, p. 138. The relevant lines, from the poem 'Form is Wollust', read: 'Doch ich will mein Sein in alle Weiten drängen [...] Und in grenzenlosem Michverschenken | Will mich Leben mit Erfüllung tränken.'
78 See Jon Silkin, *The Penguin Book of First World War Poetry* (Penguin, 1996), pp. 177–84 for further elaboration.
79 Belmore, pp. 90–91.
80 Robert Lowell, *Notebooks 1967–1968*. (Farrar, Straus and Giroux, 1969), p. 160.
81 These lines are Lord Alfred Douglas's, quoted in Fuller, p. 13.

selection of that most conservative form — the sonnet — to accommodate his otherwise overwhelming visions of frontline horror and to offer refuge to the teeming memories and fantasies which might just balance, if not neutralize, that horror. His sonnets represent meticulous testimony from a very dark place. They are a desolating guidebook to the land of loss.

The objective rules of form — so many lines, so many syllables, so many feet, neat reconciliation — are replaced in *Tier rang* by the poet's subjective rule, which accepts earlier prescriptions as a guide only. Richard Schaukal (see his poem 'Die deutsche Eiche') and Karl von Eisenach (for example, 'Lieder im Kampf 1916') wrote war poems, sonnets, in the classic traditional mode. As well as being much more 'correct' and 'logical' than 'Abendlicher Marsch', they also 'read well': rhythmically and metrically they are consistent and transparent. They are, at least to some extent, 'Klinggedichte' (to use a term familiar from the 'Sonettenkrieg'), but, like Rückert's in an earlier war, they do not begin to capture the reality of living (and dying) on the Western Front. In the end, the nature and extent of Schnack's achievement, over the full stretch of sixty poems and in the face of the threat of inducing tedium by repetition, should be measured in terms of his ability, in the first instance, to seize and sustain his reader's interest in such a familiar (in literary terms) and empirically *unfamiliar* reality. Account should also be taken of his skill in giving a space to chance and senselessness and accident, in exploring the inchoate and imposing form on multiplicity, incoherence and contradiction. His sonnets miniaturize, despite their size, and distil a whole world and, even while compressing it, maximize the true horror of war, thus coincidentally fulfilling one of the prime purposes of the sonnet form: 'Gestaltgewillt, damit das Chaos schweige, | umschlingen sich die streitgeschienten Glieder'.[82] Schnack sacrifices neat poetic control in order to convey something of the disorder and confusion of reality. The soldiers' hectically teeming dreams are matched by random, unexplained battlefield activities: 'Reiter machen sich auf zum Traben' (I, 80). The traditional configuration of the sonnet is constantly expanded in order to accommodate this degree of inchoateness. Samuel Beckett was, of course, not thinking particularly of the First World War when in an interview with Tom Driver in the summer of 1961 he defined the modern writer's responsibilities: 'To find a form that accommodates the mess, that is the task of the artist now.'[83]

★ ★ ★ ★ ★

A second example of Schnack's technique as a writer of sonnets is the poem 'Der Überläufer' (I, 77–78). Among the always unnamed spectral figures in *Tier rang* there emerges one night a deserter, or rather *the* deserter. It is rare indeed to find a First World War poem about desertion and Schnack's 'Der Überläufer' is completely different from the very few others that can be traced. For these reasons alone it is worth considering more closely and quoting in full:

82   Weinheber, II, p. 493.
83   Samuel Beckett, *Drama in the Modern World: Plays and Essays*, ed. by Samuel A. Weiss (Heath, 1974), p. 506.

Nacht; und darein die Gestirne gesetzt mit zitterndem Licht; ein Ton, ein
Ruf, ein Geklirr, verstohlen und knapp, unter der Wolkbank das Meer
Der Scheinwerfer, bleich und gespenstisch; ein Feuer im Grund hinter Wäl-
dern, Flugrauch, der verzog
Mit scharfem Gestank. Ein weites Geschütz anfangend zu heulen in die Fin-
sternis, groß und gewaltig; dann eine Rakete, die flog
In den Raum des Himmels, gewölbt, verschwärzt. Unter ihm lagen sie: tot,
zerrissen, verschwiegen mit lauernden Augen, sprach scharf ein Gewehr
Einer Feldwache, unter ihm kroch einer daher, ging einer hinein in die Stol-
len voll Schlag und kieskollerndem Lärm,
Zerschnitt einer die Drähte, gespannt vor dem Werk ... Und da dies so war
und die Nacht so warm,
Dacht einer der Brunnen und des Gestühls, wo die Glocken hämmerten
morgens, dacht er des Weibes und sah seinen Arm
Voll Lehm und Behaarung, und da er dies dachte, starb der und der, lag
dunkel ein Toter, verwesend, fraßen die Ratten Gedärm ...
Stierte er vor, da wachten die dort drüben in Stollen, in Stein und Verhau und
warfen Raketen ins Brausen der Nacht.
Sah er denn dies: Eine Süßigkeit — Heimat — die Pflugschar — die Schwe-
stern? Hörte er dies: Das Lied eines Mädchens — den Ruf einer Eule?
Noch lag er im Rauch, sehr tief, noch zwischen Tod, noch wurzelnd in Qual;
traf es ihn morgen schweigsam zu sein, erkaltet, mit zerfasertem Leib?
Nebel aus Wald stieg, zog weiß; ein Geroll war hörbar aus Fernen, in steinernen
Sappen lag eine verschlafene Wacht ...
Kriechend auf Bauch und gezogenem Knie; halbstündig barg ihn ein Loch,
bös dunstend von fleischlicher Fäule,
An Wassern vorüber, zwang sich durch Draht und Gestrüpp. Wurde gefan-
gen mit seltsamem Lächeln am Mund, dämmerte Wunder sein Hirn: weiß,
prächtig, gewölbt, geschenkt war er wieder dem Weib.

The very few poems on the subject tend to be about the consequences of desertion,[84]
rather than about the act itself. Probably the best-known example in anthologies of
English war poetry is Gilbert Frankau's First World War poem 'The Deserter'. The
first verse and the last verse (of three verses) read:

> 'I'm sorry I done it, Major.'
> We bandaged the livid face;
> And led him out, ere the wan sun rose,
> To die his death of disgrace.
> [...]
> 'Fire!' called the Sergeant-Major.
> The muzzles flamed as he spoke:
> And the shameless soul of a nameless man
> Went up in the cordite smoke.[85]

84   For example Herbert Read's 'The Execution of Cornelius Vane', <https://www.poetrynook.
com/poem/execution-cornelius> vane [accessed 6 April 2025]; Winifred Mary Letts's 'The
Deserter', <https://en.wikisource.org/wiki/The_Deserter_(Letts)> [accessed 6 April 2025]; and
Francis Ledwidge's 'After Court Martial', <https://www.allpoetry.com/After-Court-Martial> [acc-
essed 6 April 2025]. Detering in Erich Maria Remarque's *Im Westen nichts Neues* (1929) and Private
Arthur Hamp in John Wilson's play *King and Country* are other (prose) examples.
85   Gilbert Frankau, 'The Deserter', in *Up the Line to Death: The War Poets 1914–1918*, ed. by Brian

It would be difficult to think of poetry more different from Schnack's *Tier rang* sonnets. There is dialogue in Frankau's poem whereas not a word is said in 'Der Überläufer'; the jaunty familiarity of the colloquial tone (despite, or perhaps because of, the circumstances) — more Sassoon than Owen, and certainly not Schnack — contrasts starkly with the solemn, stylized tread of *Tier rang*; form and content are mutually supportive with the short snappy lines reflecting the grimly focused business of the day, to be got through as quickly as possible; the very personal and confessional interventions and commentary, the sense of military hierarchy and due deference, the judgemental connotations inherent in 'death of disgrace' and 'shameless soul', none of these finds its counterpart in Schnack's 'Der Überläufer', and the very configuration of 'The Deserter' — three fairly regular and comparatively short-lined quatrains — bears no resemblance to the very long sequences, with no stanzaic breaks, of the German sonnets.

And Schnack's poem is certainly not about an execution. On the contrary, the poem tracks the deserter as he moves across a terrain which came to be known as no man's land, a composition of words barely heard of before the First World War and never an official military term.[86] Although the whole area is littered with bodies, the battlefield is, in fact, abandoned by human beings.[87] Dismemberment, destruction, disappearance, wire, holes, rats — such annihilating effects of the zone are perfectly expressed by the term 'no man's land', as the field of combat is gradually transformed until it becomes virtually impassable, an amorphous mush of terrain which itself will claim new victims. One can only guess at the psychological effect on those on both sides constantly watching it, living alongside it. But the deserter comes on. His nationality is never made clear: the adjectives 'deutsch' and 'französisch' do not appear anywhere in *Tier rang*, and it seems as if he could be moving in either direction between the frontlines before he finally gives himself up. Such anonymity, in personal and national terms, is of a piece with all the poems in this cycle: not a hint of patriotism or nationalism attaches to any of them.[88] The deserter is a (presumably) imagined representative of all those First World War combatants who walked away from the noise of the guns, like Private Arthur Hamp in the equally rare war film about desertion, Joseph Losey's *King and Country* (1964).

What is particularly striking about 'Der Überläufer' is the fact that it depicts two kinds of journey. The first is plainly a description of the arduous struggle to navigate a route across very difficult and dangerous terrain. The second is a

Gardner (Methuen, 1964), p. 85.

86   The Oxford English Dictionary contains a reference to the term dating back to 1320, but it began to be widely used only after the Anglo-German Christmas truce of 1914. It was first used in a military context by Ernest Swinton in his short story 'The Point of View' in the collection *The Green Curve* (1909). It was, interestingly, Swinton who in late 1914 wrote a memo to the War Council in London with his idea of a tank. That idea soon became a reality. 'Niemandsland' does not seem to have been so frequently used at the time, but it certainly came to public notice with the 1931 film of the same name.

87   Ernst Jünger uses the term 'menschenleer' in 'Kriegerische Mathematik', *Der Widerstand: Zeitschrift für nationalrevolutionäre Politik*, 5 (1930), pp. 267–73 (p. 270).

88   Thus once again bearing out Schnack's own comment: 'Das Buch enthält keine hurrapatriotischen Gedichte', Bridgwater, p. 96.

portrayal of the struggle which the deserter has within himself, in his own mind, as he finally resolves to complete the fateful act of desertion. This sonnet then has a double resolving purpose, which the poet handles very deftly. The first four lines of the poem focus on night and on the way in which the darkness is interrupted by the sights and sounds of battle. In lines five and six the deserter is introduced: he is crawling into 'die Stollen voll Schlag' and he is cutting wire. Then comes a hesitation, a hiatus, in which his thoughts seem to turn away from the scene in front of him to his homeland. Horrors intrude, again softened, at least temporarily, by happier consolations. He finds himself still lying there, but the noise of battle reawakens the compulsion to keep moving, to keep deserting, until he ends in enemy arms. It is a stop-start journey mirroring an emotional switchback, in which the portrayal of physical detail and psychological turmoil is expertly achieved. The sequence of events is clear, and the configuration of the poem, even though it is obviously not a classical sonnet, has a volta at line 10, rather than at line 8, followed by a hard-earned resolution.

The poem begins as abruptly as it ends: the monosyllabic 'Nacht' is matched by the equally curt 'Weib', a harshly echoing reminder of the three Expressionist volumes. It is a ghostly scene. Something random, almost arbitrary, is conveyed by a series of indefinite articles — 'ein Ton', 'ein Ruf', 'ein Geklirr', 'ein Feuer', 'ein weites Geschütz', 'eine Rakete', etc. There are stars, but they shed an uncertain ('zitternd') light. The stench, the pandemonium, the fire and the smoke all create an impression of an environment from which one might think any frightened human being would reasonably want to escape. Nothing is stable or stabilized, just like the form. Only the single, simple 'ein Ruf' indicates the possibility of another live human being surviving in this hellish landscape, but the call is uttered into the void and has no apparent human source. Nothing about the form is emollient or forgiving. The sound patterns often involving hard consonants ('Geklirr... knapp... Wolkbank', 'Grund... Flugrauch... verzog... Gestank... Geschütz... groß... gewaltig') serve to reinforce the atmosphere of unrelenting, if for the time being distant, menace. The strangely foreshortened 'Wolkbank' (in line 1), resembling Stramm's habit of 'losing' syllables and contrasting with Schnack's usual practice of retaining the middle syllable (as in 'Wolkenfahrt', 'Wolkenzug', 'Wolkenbank', 'wolkenrund'), in the compound's double abruptness encapsulates this sense of compressed tension and of inhuman activity. Beneath the blackened sky the rifle of a sentry rings out among the dead bodies — or rather, 'a rifle of a sentry speaks': weapons are anthropomorphized at the same time as combatants are dehumanized, and chance and contingency reign unchallenged. All the sibilants in line 4 ('sie [...] zerrissen [...] verschwiegen [...] sprach scharf') rehearse the sound of his bullets. But someone is on the move (line 5), crawling along into the tunnels, up to the wire. 'Kieskollernd' is a striking noun-participle combination: the pounding noise coming over from the battle is enough to set the gravel on the ground shaking and rolling. Equally 'gespannt vor dem Werk' catches the imagination: is it the wire that is drawn tight against the expected assault ('das Werk') or is it the deserter ('einer') who is understandably tense before he reaches the final stage of his 'Werk', the self-imposed challenge of cutting the wire and deserting? Either way the word 'Werk', like 'Wolkbank' before it, has a deeply discomfiting and ironic effect. The repetition of the indefinite article with the weapons of war ('ein Feuer [...] Ein weites Geschütz [...] eine Rakete [...] ein Gewehr') serves to underline the adventitious nature of the hostility confronting the deserter.

In lines 6 and 7 the deserter is moved by the warmth of the night to think of his home, of fountains and church, and, above all, of 'Weib', without any article at all this time, thus drawing attention to the primal and elemental, not of one particular remembered woman, but of women or womankind, of the female and the feminine, the counterpart to 'Tier' and representing the other half of humanity. Reality intrudes again as he catches sight of his mud-bespattered arm. The arm is described as 'voll Lehm und Behaarung' (line 8): 'Behaarung' stresses corporeal being, a very physical presence, while 'Lehm' suggests basic humanity, indicating that all soldiers, even deserters, are ultimately clay. He hears the sounds of men dying and rats eating intestines. The (almost) rhyming combination of 'Lärm'/'Gedärm' and 'warm'/'arm' underscores the incongruity and irony of the conflict in his mind between visions of battlefield reality and dreams of home.

In line 9, 'die dort drüben' (the enemy or his own side?) launch rockets, but once again instant compensation and counterweight are sought in what he imagines he sees, homeland and sisters, and what he imagines he hears, 'das Lied eines Mädchens', 'den Ruf einer Eule'. 'Eine Süßigkeit' (line 10) recalls how in 'Abendlicher Marsch' the marching soldiers of the lyrical I's platoon 'verlassen alle Süßigkeit' while 'Pflugschar' invokes country life and reminds us of the present use of no man's land. Such solace turns out to be an illusion, and he finds himself assailed by thoughts of death and, in a remarkably vivid phrase, 'wurzelnd in Qual'. Abstraction ('Qual') and metaphor ('wurzelnd') in no way diminish either the torment of his experience or the power of the imagery. He wonders if it is going to be his fate (the randomness of the rather odd 'traf es ihn morgen' is clear) to 'be silent' tomorrow. The strange word-order here, like the earlier 'lag dunkel ein Toter' (in line 8) represents his sense of complete disorientation: like the syntax, he is possibly going the wrong way. A thunder of guns in the distance and perhaps the sight of a sleepy sentry set him on his journey again. He hides in a crater, but the smell of decaying bodies (the abstract quality of 'fleischliche Fäule' compounds the horror by dehumanizing even further already dead bodies) drives him on until he is captured — and presumably safe. The verb 'wurde gefangen', oddly dislocated word-order again, placed starkly at the beginning of a sentence, has no subject: anonymity is thus reasserted and preserved. Everyone, friend and foe, interchangeably, is anonymous. The adjective 'seltsam' ('mit seltsamem Lächeln am Mund') indicates a measure of uncertainty and ambiguity in the deserter's actions: whose side is he on? Whose side is he fleeing? And the startling reversal of the normal word-order in the sentence 'dämmerte Wunder sein Hirn' is difficult to interpret partly because 'dämmern' is, very unusually, being used transitively and because 'Hirn' is a neuter noun, thus making us ask what the grammatical subject is. The relief of now being apparently safe enables the deserter to conjure up miracles, miraculous visions, but it is only the inkling, the tremulous outline of a 'miracle', his future safety cannot be guaranteed. 'Wunder dämmerte sein Hirn'/'Sein Hirn dämmerte Wunder' is close to the kind of configuration which is familiar to us from Stramm's two collections *Tropfblut* and *Du*.[89] Indeed, it is the very eccentricity of Schnack's choice which persistently unsettles and dislocates. The visions are indeed miraculous: 'weiß' (in contrast to the dirty, hirsute arm in line 8), 'prächtig' (as opposed to the ghastly landscape he has just traversed), 'gewölbt' (frequently in Schnack associated with the vastness of skies or forests) and, above all, 'geschenkt [...] wieder dem Weib' — restored to womankind (the dative case is called upon to take a heavy emotional and physical weight in a phrase once again catching the eye with its 'wrong' word-order), rather than consigned to the bestiality and inhumanity of war, back to what Blunden calls 'a warm fraternity, a family understanding',[90] a place where he stands a chance of hearing 'das Lied eines Mädchens'. The final word of the poem, 'Weib', still bearing primal force but not without gentler optimism this time, given his present circumstances, counterpoints the memory of the stark opening 'Nacht' and goes some way to extinguishing it. The last line of the poem is by far the longest with its more than forty syllables. It is as if all the intense feelings of relief at escaping and all the deserter's hopes for the future (the smile, the miracle, and, of course, the woman) are all gathered up in the final flourish. Form and content work together for that purpose.

'Der Überläufer' is, quite literally in terms of its subject matter, unique in the sense that in the space of one sonnet it tells the story of a desertion. No judgement, implicit or explicit, is passed, no moral stance is adopted. There is no 'accusation', either against generals or politicians (as in Sassoon's poetry) or even war itself for driving a soldier to such action or against the individual soldier for abandoning his side. There is no 'confession'.[91] There is no lyrical I, there is no one to accuse or to confess. It is a narrative told in the past tense. We the readers watch the events as they unfold, we observe the deserter observing the scene of his desertion. It is almost as if we are on sentry duty watching him scrabble across no man's land, but too sleepy ('verschlafen') to do anything about it. However, the poem allows us to do more than merely watch his movements. We are allowed into his mind, we are invited to sympathize with his humanity (the arm 'voll Lehm und Behaarung' ensures that), and the picture we are given of the anguish and confusion in the deserter's thinking is as convincing and powerful as the depiction of the horrors of the battlefield. A delicate balance is struck. In spite of all the indefinite articles the deserter is not presented as an individual, but nor is he depersonalized. Instead, we enter tentatively into his consciousness. The psychological insights, the tantalizing glimpses of a better time and a better place, are an important mitigation of what might otherwise be intolerably naturalistic descriptions of human devastation. Full weight is certainly granted to such descriptions: these are the kinds of realistic

89   Compare such lines as 'Nacht grant Glas' ('Verzweifelt'), and 'Mutterschösse gähnen Kindestod!' ('Freudenhaus').

90   Blunden, p. 168.

91   This is, of course, a quote from Remarque's preface — 'Dieses Buch soll weder eine Anklage noch ein Bekenntnis sein'.

details, the absence of which constitutes the main substance of Georg Lukács's wholesale rejection of Expressionist writing. But there is also implicit a degree of authorial sympathy which can be seen to lie with the deserter: the very long last line offers hope for his future. That is a hope and a sympathy which are easy to understand. 'Der Überläufer' is thus significant beyond the great rarity of its subject-matter and its unusually clear structure (with its breaks at line 6 and line 10, the latter an obvious volta). It is significant also because in a cycle where the attenuation of personality and individuality is the norm, something of the personal survives, literally and metaphorically.

★   ★   ★   ★   ★

What is most impressive about the sonnets of *Tier rang* is the scale of Schnack's enterprise. There is no question of 'a scanty plot of ground'. Schnack, in this volume, endeavours to capture the world of a paradigmatic sector of a First World War frontline. It is an intimidatingly unbounded world, but the choice of the sonnet as a way to explore this world is intended, if not to bound it, then to make at least some sense of it. We should not be surprised that he resorts to a version, his version, of the sonnet — in the Expressionist circles around *Die Aktion* in which he moved at the time of bringing the poems of *Tier rang* together, the sonnet was a perennially favoured genre. Moreover, unlike Stramm and Trakl (Schnack's only serious rivals in this context, though neither survived beyond 1915) and unlike Rosenberg and Blunden on the English side, Schnack wrote his war poetry retrospectively, thus inadvertently subscribing to the view of Gerrit Engelke, fellow war-poet, mortally wounded at Cambrai on 11 October 1918,[92] that a literary interpretation and reworking of the war is possible only 'wenn nach der Heimkehr in die Gleichgewichtsruhe des Friedens rückwirkend der Krieg durch tiefst gefühlte Reflexion wieder als das furchtbar Außergewöhnliche hinterherfällt'.[93] It is interesting to note that very little war poetry was produced *after* the war, with the notable exceptions of David Jones and Schnack — Sassoon, Graves and Blunden, to name three obvious examples on the English side, all turned to prose to mediate their experiences. In Schnack's case the wait — and he did indeed wait — says nothing, of course, about the quality of the poetry, but it did mean that he had time to gather together a host of scattered poems into the sequence of sonnets which we have today. Neither Stramm nor Trakl nor Engelke had that luxury.

If, in conclusion, an audit is taken of Schnack's contribution to the history of the German sonnet, recalling at the same time A. W. Schlegel's prescriptions for the genre, the following picture emerges. A one-pace choreography of rhythm and tone prevails, but potential tedium, Weinheber's fear for the sonnet cycle, is mitigated by the vigorous narrative and the consistently vivid and shocking imagery. The fifty-five sonnets of *Tier rang* do indeed consist of fourteen lines, those lines are extremely

---

92   Engelke was co-author, with Heinrich Lersch and Karl Zielke, of the collection of war-poems entitled *Schulter an Schulter: Gedichte von drei Arbeitern* (1916).

93   Gerrit Engelke, diary entry for 3 October 1915, 'Tagebuchblätter aus dem Kriege', in *Das Gesamtwerk*, ed. by Hermann Blome (List, 1960), pp. 314–15.

irregular in length, they rhyme, they do not amount to mellifluous 'Klinggedichte', any regular and recognizable metrical pattern is lost in the ungainly lines, little trouble is usually taken over the creation of a volta, especially at the traditional point at the end of the eighth line. But then Schlegel had little to say about volta and metre, focusing above all on rhyme and on length of line. There are certainly not so much single turns as constant breaks in Schnack's sonnets. The traditional sonnet has something happen near its centre where the movement is from consciousness to conscience, but not *at* its centre, because it is in the very nature of a sonnet to disorient the reader by refusing perfect symmetry. A compelling image is invoked or an urgent problem is stated in the octave and examined or resolved in the sestet. One critic calls this strategy a 'picture postcard' effect: we look at the picture, then *turn* it over and read the message.[94] Moreover, for the sake of the sonnet's credibility and authority, this effect should not be underestimated or ignored. In John Fuller's view 'the essence of the [English] sonnet's form is the unequal relationship between octave and sestet'.[95] Schnack's sonnets function differently. There is in each poem of *Tier rang* a constant toing-and-froing of contrasts and commentary, a dialectical pattern, not a single fracture or rupture. The fragmented language of the poems mirrors this configuration: in terms of a prose equivalent that reminds us not so much of Remarque's *Im Westen nichts Neues* but of Ludwig Renn's *Krieg* in which the author endeavours to capture not only the external appearance, but also, through his choice of language, the actual sound and disrupted 'patterns' of life on the frontline. In her discussion of Baudelaire's sonnets in *Les Fleurs du Mal* Sandra Berman argues that there is in them a 'progression from the dream of a happier past to the knowledge of continuing despair in death'.[96] With Schnack it is not a progression, but a perpetual interplay, or negotiation, between a consoling past and a dreadful present with no guarantee of a happy ending or a satisfying resolution.

Mark Elliott's proposal that one of the 'mainsprings of the work of George and Rilke is the dialectic between innovation and tradition' could be equally well applied to the poems of *Tier rang*,[97] but it would be wrong to suggest that Schnack's collection took the German sonnet forward in any significant *formal* sense. The long and irregular lines are rare and innovative, but not quite unique, and there is in any case no particular virtue in writing longer and more irregular lines than anyone else. In its size and scope *Tier rang* is a unique collection of war sonnets: again, their uniqueness says nothing about their quality, but uniqueness is always an interesting claim if only because it invites comparison with predecessors and successors within a huge historical context. Two features are, however, undoubtedly noteworthy: the innovation is happening within the usually sacred precinct of the sonnet and, secondly, the content. This chapter has suggested that in the twentieth century sonnets took on new responsibilities — in Rilke's case to diagnose

94   Levin, p. lxix.
95   Fuller, p. 3. In support of this assertion Fuller quotes J. W. Lever's view that the sestet 'supports the octave as the cup supports the acorn' (*The Elizabethan Love Sonnet* [Barnes & Noble, 1968]).
96   Berman, p. 123.
97   Mark Christopher Elliott, 'German Poetry beyond the Boundaries of the Nazi Era: The Modernist Legacy' (unpublished doctoral thesis, University of Oxford, 2006), p. 95.

contemporary existential contingencies and emergencies, in Reinhold Schneider's and Albrecht Haushofer's to express resistance to tyranny and dictatorship, and it is worth pointing out, in confirmation of Ingo Zimmermann's earlier insight (see the beginning of this chapter), that the poets of the 1930s reasserted the traditional sonnet form after Rilke's (and Schnack's) variations.[98] For its part *Tier rang* addresses the single most catastrophic public event of the early twentieth century and in particular seeks to convey the experience of being subjected to modern warfare. In theory, war seems to be a highly appropriate theme for sonnets with their in-built purpose to seek and attain a reconciliation. But in practice wartime sonnets, or sonnets about war, very rarely dwell on the reconciliation of opposing sides, thus going against the expectations implicit in the genre. In *Tier rang* the conflict dramatized is certainly *not* between Germany and the Allies — neither is mentioned or hinted at — but between the diminishing military self of the lyrical I and the much richer, more confident self of the memories and the remembering. They are not reconciled. By the last poem of the cycle the former is dead and the latter has disappeared. If a sonnet about war cannot reconcile differences or conflicts, it can at least contain experience within a shape that is, in the case of *Tier rang*, stretched almost to bursting point.

There is one further paradoxical reconciliation which is regularly broached by critics and reviewers of Expressionist poetry — between the Expressionist poet's often proclaimed iconoclastic attitude towards form and, in apparent contradiction, his equally frequent recourse to the sonnet genre. Peter Sprengel, for example, writes:

> Man hat oft nach den Gründen der expressionistischen Vorliebe für das Sonett gefragt und eine Paradoxie darin gesehen, daß eine literarische Generation, die für ihre Neigung zum Zerschlagen der Formen bekannt ist, gerade diese besonders straff organisierte Gedichtform kultiviert. Eine mögliche Antwort liegt darin, daß gerade die syllogistische Struktur des Sonetts, sein Charakter als 'Poesiemaschine', einem Bedürfnis der jungen Autoren entsprach: nämlich der Betonung der Unausweichlichkeit, Monotonie und Determiniertheit, ja der unterschwellig mechanischen Qualität des modernen Lebens.[99]

Sprengel is referring in this context specifically to the life and work of Georg Heym in prewar Berlin, but his words are pertinent, at least from one angle, to Schnack's war poetry. For nearly 3,000 years, since Homer, war and love have been the primary themes of western literature. But war is, in theory, an extremely unpromising subject for writers of prose and poetry because they must at some point confront a central contradiction. In any serious account of the experience of war only truth has real value, but the truth about war is that it contains nearly unbearable levels of repetition, boredom and meaninglessness. Ludwig Renn's heavily autobiographical and painstakingly faithful account of the infantry soldier's daily grind on the Western Front in his *Krieg* is vulnerable to the charge of tedium-inducing monotony. For the average combat soldier war is indeed tedium only

---

98   With the exception, it seems, of Wolfgang Borchert. See Elliott, p. 153.
99   Sprengel, pp. 604–05.

occasionally punctuated by moments of extreme violence, and writers tend to get round this by focusing on the violence, typically at a moment of heroism. They then endeavour to contain within the bounds of a classical form the chaos and the horror, what Blunden called 'the stream of mechanized fury'[100] issuing from the violence. Perhaps rather simplistically one needs to look no further for an explanation of the paradox than to repeat that, in composing *Tier rang* as a cycle of sonnets, Schnack was choosing to join a very rich and versatile tradition which has been constantly recruited and reinvigorated over the centuries by the vast majority of Germany's (and Europe's) greatest poets.

 Tier rang spares us no details of what happened on the battlefields of northern France: exploiting the sonnet's capacity to enter the psychological recesses of the poet's mind, it also expresses an existential crisis, one that ends not in poetic triumph or a reconciliation of life and death, as in Rilke's *Sonette an Orpheus*, but in the dissolution of the self under the impact of modern warfare. The next chapter will focus on the sonnets of *Tier rang* purely as war poems and will examine both the development of the fate of the lyrical I and the nature of the warfare to which the I is exposed.

---

100 Blunden, p. 31.

CHAPTER 6

Anton Schnack — War Poet

Ahmt nicht
Früherem nach, Einstigem. Prüfet,
ob ihr nicht Schmerz seid. Handelnder Schmerz.[1]

This chapter will show how the narrative of the lyrical I's life develops when the unrestrained hedonism portrayed in the three earlier Expressionist volumes gives way in *Tier rang* to the harsh realities of living and dying on the frontline. This will mean examining the physical and psychological pressures which imposed themselves on all the combatants and suggesting ways in which the nature and extent of those pressures were at the time unique and unprecedented. A detailed analysis of one of the key poems in *Tier rang*, reinforced by references to many others, should then reveal how, by tracing the journey of the lyrical I to the 'gateway of death',[2] Schnack responds to the challenge of depicting the realities of trench warfare. Reference to earlier German war poetry, particularly that of patriotic poets such as Theodor Körner and Detlev von Liliencron, will highlight what is potentially Schnack's major achievement in realizing and demonstrating that a new kind of poetry was required, in other words that tradition was to be used as a springboard, not as a resting place.

Only a shockingly new form, as in the case of August Stramm, or a rupture of an old form, as we have seen with Schnack, would be adequate to do justice to a radically new content. The focus in this chapter will, therefore, shift from considerations of form to the question of content in an attempt to gauge the quality of the sonnets of *Tier rang* purely and simply as poems about war. A caveat should be introduced at this point: there has often been a tendency among critics, reviewers and readers to value war poetry *solely* for the reality it apparently conveys: Patrick Bridgwater inclines rather in this direction.[3] Part of Schnack's achievement, it will be suggested, is that, if he cannot offer warmth and redemption to counterbalance the unrelentingly cold hardship of life in the trenches and on the battlefield, he regularly invokes the solaces of remembering and the condolences of nostalgia as potential sources of emotional reassurance. The last of Rilke's 'Fünf Gesänge' enjoins those whom he calls 'Freunde' to repudiate the past: the first

---

1   Rainer Maria Rilke, 'Fünf Gesänge', in *Werke: Kommentierte Ausgabe in vier Bänden*, ed. by Manfred Engel and Ulrich Fülleborn (Insel, 1996), II/2, p. 110.

2   The title of the final poem in the cycle is 'Am Tor des Todes', I, 97.

3   Bridgwater, 'The German Poets of the First World War', pp. 14–17.

contains the words 'Herzen voll Heimat',[4] a phrase which again is relevant in this context.

Everything conspired on First World War battlefields to ensure that individuality and a sense of selfhood were diminished and threatened with extinction. Any individual combat soldier on the German or the Allied side must have spent his days and nights prey to the dreadful awareness not only that he was a disposable pawn in someone else's plans and on someone else's map (Edmund Blunden writes of armies being 'adjusted in coloured inks on vast maps at Montreuil or Whitehall'[5]), but also that it would not make an iota of difference to the outcome of the battle if he lived or died or even summoned an act of heroism. He was powerless to speak, to leave the scene or to assert his identity, coerced by vast unlocalized forces, at the mercy of a rigid chain of command and a mighty military tradition, and bound by a uniform which symbolized selfless respect for that tradition and unquestioning obedience to authority.

Of course, the soldier had weapons available to him, particularly guns and bayonets, but in using them he was yielding control to impersonal, mechanical forces and thus forfeiting some part of his humanity and his very selfhood. The development of weapons over the preceding century serves to underline the increasing impersonality of First World War ordnance. At Waterloo in 1815 it had been principally muskets (firing only two shots a minute), grossly inaccurate pistols, lances, bayonets, sabres, the solid shot of six to twelve pounders (easily visible and avoidable) and much single combat arising directly from cavalry charges: a considerable degree of personal, single engagement was thus maintained and ensured. Some fifty-five years later, in the Franco-Prussian War, the situation began to change: while both armies still relied on their cavalry, there were also thousand-pound Krupp cannons, much more efficient breech-loading rifles and the mitrailleuse, a precursor to the machine-gun. Within forty years the nature of warfare then changed again, this time radically. Anonymity, depersonalization and distance were more or less guaranteed by extremely efficient sniper rifles, tear-gas grenades, shrapnel, poison gas (first used at the Second Battle of Ypres), tanks (first seen in late summer 1916), flame-throwers, planes, Zeppelins, much heavier artillery and, above all, machine-guns firing 600 shots a minute. There was comparatively little single combat, not least because cavalry charges were now outmoded: horses, previously a soldier's great friend as physical support and as a reminder of 'bucolic interludes' and 'Arcadian recourses',[6] were reduced to carrying transport. The mysterious horsemen who ride in and out of *Tier rang* have a spectral, insubstantial quality in line with Schnack's own estimate of his volume: 'Mein erstes großes Werk war traurig und gespenstisch und nannte sich Tier rang gewaltig mit Tier [...]'.[7] Two abiding images in the volume are of dead horses' legs poking into the sky[8] and of the lyrical I in the penultimate poem of the cycle hurling death

4   Rilke, 'Fünf Gesänge', p. 107.
5   Blunden, p. 181.
6   Fussell, pp. 231–35.
7   Schnack, Manuscript Department Marbach.
8   'Flucht', 1, 88.

randomly 'in das Gewühl'.[9] Having quoted from Schnack's poem 'Die Batterien' (I, 66) to illustrate how in Expressionist war poetry 'die Vermenschlichung (Personifizierung) von Geräten, also die Entmenschlichung' becomes ever more dominant, Uwe Wandrey writes:

> Kanonen sprechen und rufen nach Steinen, Mauern und auch nach Menschen, d.h. sie fordern sie. Aus dem handelnden Subjekt wird ein be- und mißhandeltes Objekt. Das Subjekt ist seinem Werkzeug entfremdet. Die tatsächliche Wirkung der Batterien [in Schnack's poem], die Tötung von Leben, wird euphemistisch mit der Vorstellung von Rufen und Sprechen umschrieben. Hier wird womöglich ungewollt ausgesprochen, wohin die Überlassung der Kontrolle an andere, an Maschinen und Apparate, führt: zur physischen Vernichtung des entmündigten Subjekts.[10]

As he yields control to industrialized, mechanical weaponry and artillery, the human subject loses identity and individuality, and that death-dealing weaponry, arrogating the human attributes of 'Sprechen' and 'Rufen', ends by destroying the human subject who is now deprived of all rights of decision ('entmündigt') and thus becomes a husk or, to repeat Schnack's own image, a ghost. An ironical reversal takes place: weapons are anthropomorphized and given names (as in the case of the two legendary, monster German machine guns, Blighty Albert and Quinque Jimmy, in Blunden's account of what he calls 'trench education')[11] at the same time as human beings lapse into anonymity. This is a conclusion which is familiar to us from Stramm's letters and such poems as 'Patrouille' ('Die Steine feinden | Fenster grinst Verrat | Äste würgen'): it also points to one of the main proposals of this chapter, namely that through the nineteenth century the individual soldier, as depicted in war poetry, became less and less visible, more and more vulnerable, until by the end of the First World War, and certainly by the end of *Tier rang*, he had disappeared altogether.

By all the accounts we have, in poetry and prose, in letters and diaries, the frontline soldier felt isolated and lost in a battlefield,[12] a killing zone, a 'sullen swamp'[13] which grew larger and larger as battle metamorphosed inexorably into 'siege'.[14] He felt separated from those behind the frontline who were planning

---

9   'Handgranatenwerfer', I, 96.
10   Wandrey, p. 88.
11   Blunden, p. 29.
12   There is, of course, a multitude of books on the subject including: Edmund Blunden, *Undertones of War* (Penguin, 1987; first published 1928); Matthew Hollis, *Now All Roads Lead to France: The Last Years of Edward Thomas* (Faber & Faber, 2011); Richard Holmes, *Tommy: The British Soldier on the Western Front 1914–1918* (Harper Collins, 2004); Siegfried Sassoon, *Memoirs of an Infantry Officer* (Faber and Faber, 1930); Paul Fussell, *The Great War and Modern Memory* (Oxford University Press, 1975/2000); Niall Ferguson, *The Pity of War* (Basic Books, 1999); and John Keegan, *The Face of Battle* (Viking, 1976; Pimlico, 2004). Ludwig Renn's *Krieg*, Erich Maria Remarque's *Im Westen nichts Neues*, Ernst Jünger's *In Stahlgewittern* and, particularly, his *Das Wäldchen 125: Eine Chronik aus den Grabenkämpfen 1918* and Thomas Weber's *Hitler's First War* (Oxford University Press, 2011) tell what amounts inevitably to a very similar story from the German side.
13   The phrase appears in Siegfried Sassoon's poem 'On Passing the New Menin Gate', in *The Penguin Book of First World War Poetry*, ed. by Walter, p. 247.
14   John Keegan suggests that 'siege' rather than battle is a more appropriate word to describe First

the campaign and, therefore, shaping his fortune. Far from home he sometimes believed, and was surely right to believe, that those back at home had no idea how he was living or even whether he was alive. Crouching for much of the time below ground, he could barely make out the course of the most local skirmish, let alone the progress of the battle as a whole: only dispatch riders like Corporal A. Hitler had that privileged information. This phenomenon, called Stendhal's Paradox (a concept coined after the Battle of Waterloo from the disorientated perspective of Stendhal's hero Fabrice del Dongo in *La Chartreuse de Parme*) whereby the soldier who is directly involved in the battle sees least of what is happening around him, became a commonplace in the Great War. He rarely saw or met the commander of his regiment who, given the completely changed circumstances of First World War combat, could not be expected to keep a close eye on unfolding events by riding up and down just out of range of enemy guns as Wellington had done 100 years before at Waterloo. Even worse in a way, the soldier in the trenches rarely saw an enemy whom in any case he had not chosen to fight and against whom he had no reason to harbour personal ill will. At any moment of every day he risked being killed, and was expected to do his share of the killing, sometimes from a distance, however fiercely his conscience and his deepest feelings might resist the very idea. He was, moreover, at the constant mercy of targeted *and* random shells and bullets, splinters and shrapnel. With the virtual disappearance of hand-to-hand fighting (at least, in comparison with earlier conflicts) he lost the inspiration which came from the consciousness that he was defending himself in single combat. Only occasionally were there opportunities for individual heroism such as the kind of outstanding bravery shown less than forty years previously at the Battle of Rorke's Drift in the Anglo-Zulu war when 139 British soldiers held out against 4,000 Zulu warriors, and eleven Victoria Crosses were awarded. It is sometimes claimed that the use of the bayonet was a modern form of hand-to-hand fighting, and when it comes to bayonet casualties in the First World War, the statistic of 1.02% of total casualties has been quoted.[15] Considerable debate, however, surrounds that figure. Rob Engen, for example, writing in the *Journal of Military and Strategic Studies*, uses his paper to try to demolish the claim of 'popular historians such as Pierre Berton' who claim that the bayonet is 'as useful as a cutlass' on the modern industrialized battlefields of the Great War.[16] Engen concludes that, on the contrary, the morale-boosting effects of the bayonet were incalculable and that 'the "offensive spirit" engendered by the bayonet was held in high regard by commanders and theorists'.[17] At all events, most of the action on a battlefield, especially on a First World War battlefield, is carried out anonymously, as if the fighting were happening without the volition of the participants.

and Second World War fighting. See his *The Face of Battle*, p. 303.

15   For example by Byron Farwell (*Mr Kipling's Army: All the Queen's Men* [Norton, 1981]) and Tom Wintringham (*Weapons and Tactics* [Faber and Faber, 1943]). Richard Holmes (*Tommy*, pp. 382–83) suggests an even lower figure of 0.32%.

16   Rob Engen, 'Steel against Fire: The Bayonet in the First World War', *Journal of Military and Strategic Studies*, 8.3 (2006), pp. 1–21 (p. 1). The Pierre Berton reference is to *Vimy* (Anchor Canada, 2001), p. 117.

17   Engen, p. 21.

But it was much more than a question of relentless physical threat. The First World War soldier was often alone and isolated on sentry duty or engaged in perilous night-time raids. His fellow soldiers in his company, undergoing the same physical deprivations and psychological torment, overwhelmed by fatigue and despair, were almost certainly unable to offer much long-term emotional comfort because they, too, could be killed one by one, by enemy fire (the experience of Paul Bäumer's platoon in *Im Westen nichts Neues*) or literally pulverized in a group by a stray shell: Robert Graves speaks of 'life's discovered transitoriness' and of 'premature fate-spasm'.[18] It is no coincidence that Schnack's *Tier rang* contains no reference to 'Freund(e)', 'Kamerad(en)' or to 'Gemeinschaft'. Comradeship, however powerful (as in Bäumer's platoon), however desperately sought, was inevitably compromised by a sense of ephemerality and contingency. Writing a month before he died to Walter de la Mare on 9 March 1917 from Arras, the English war poet Edward Thomas laments: 'One is absolutely friendless here [...] You say it would be good if we could have a talk, but, you know, I fancy it would not do to have a real friend out here.'[19] Comradeship was encouraged by the authorities, but it was something of a myth, and Schnack, in his evocation of isolation and impersonality, perhaps comes closer to the experience of many soldiers. Furthermore, the First World War soldier was caught, again literally, between ripped earth and louring sky ('the common sky | That sagged ominously upon the earth'),[20] between spasms of violent action and sloughs of sense-numbing inactivity and tedium, between a constantly assailed determination to cling to life and the dread of dying or being maimed when, he knew, medical care was bound to be perfunctory and primitive.

It can, of course, be argued that much of what has been said about the situation facing participants in the First World War could equally well apply to, for example, nineteenth-century battles like Waterloo, Sedan and Gettysburg. To some extent that would be true, but everything about the 1914–18 war was on an unimaginably larger and more lethal scale: Wilfred Owen's phrases 'carnage incomprehensible' and 'human squander' do indeed seem most appropriate to the twentieth-century conflict.[21] John Keegan charts the evolution of what he calls 'the impersonalisation of battle' from medieval times to the present day, referring at the same time to the combatants' 'sense of littleness, almost of nothingness, of their abandonment in a physical wilderness, dominated by vast impersonal forces'.[22] 'Wir sind Verlorene [...] Klein wie Zwerge', Schnack writes in the poem 'Im Graben' (1, 68) and later, having dispersed the lyrical self into a 'wir', isolates that self in its smallness: 'Ich werde eingehn in den Tod [...] schmerzlos, seltsam klein' (1, 81). In his study of First World War literature Alfredo Bonadeo refers to what he calls the inevitable 'loss or shrinkage of the human self' in the battlefield.[23] The tranquillization of bad

18   In his poem 'Recalling War', in *The Penguin Book of First World War Poetry*, ed. by Walter, p. 263.
19   Hollis, p. 327.
20   Wilfred Owen, 'Mental Cases', in Walter, *The Penguin Book of First World War Poetry*, p. 263.
21   Ibid., p. 218.
22   Keegan, p. 322.
23   Alfredo Bonadeo, *Mark of the Beast: Death and Degradation in the Literature of the Great War* (University Press of Kentucky, 1989), pp. 4–6.

memory (though the lyrical I in *Tier rang* constantly strives to invoke flurries of good memories), the extinction of individual personality, the relentless feeling of intense insecurity, of living and dying in an atmosphere of crisis and emergency and being potential prey for 'the foul beast of war that bludgeons life'[24] — all this serves to diminish the I. At the end of his study of Agincourt, Waterloo and the Somme, Keegan offers the following audit of the First World War soldiers' unprecedented fate:

> it ['the new warfare'] marooned them, as it were, on an undiscovered continent, where one layer of the air on which they depended for life was charged with lethal metallic particles, where man in consequence was forced to adopt a subterranean dwelling and an abject posture, where the use of day and night was reversed and where, by a bizarre modification of Erewhonian logic good health was regarded as a burden, but wounds as a benefaction to be sought and enjoyed. It was as if the arms-manufacturers had succeeded in introducing a new element into the atmosphere, compounded by fire and steel, whose presence rendered battlefields uninhabitable.[25]

It is wholly characteristic of *Tier rang* that it contains no berating of arms manufacturers or of war profiteers (unlike *Im Westen nichts Neues*),[26] of generals or politicians, unlike the poetry and prose of Siegfried Sassoon. Instead, Schnack's focus remains permanently fixed on the new circumstances of the battlefield. And here soldier becomes first beast ('Tier rang gewaltig mit Tier', I, 86) and then victim, countryside becomes literally no man's land as nature herself is dragged into the conflict and peacetime values become inverted, even perverted and certainly 'verdorben', to use Schnack's preferred descriptor for the moral degradation wrought by war.

As well as the new weaponry, the considerably expanded killing zone and the ever more protracted nature of First World War battles — all of which had a hugely injurious impact on the physical and psychological well-being of the combatants — there was one further significant factor in these new twentieth-century circumstances. In earlier wars it is a reasonable assumption that, while many individual soldiers were mercenaries, others were borne along on a wave of patriotism and nationalism. They might well have believed in the rightness of the national cause or at least accepted it unquestioningly, and if they had been poets, they would have proclaimed that rightness. The First World War soldier, after the first few months of the war, was no longer sustained and inspired by such thoughts and no longer voiced them. The consequence was that he did not feel himself to be part of a going concern, a participant in an enterprise whose purpose was clearly discernible and generally accepted, nor did he have a model of a better life because he suspected that his enemy (what enemy?) was equally badly off. Once that

---

24   Siegfried Sassoon, 'The Dream', in *Collected Poems 1908–1956* (Faber and Faber, 1961), p. 94.
25   Keegan, p. 306. Keegan's *The Face of Battle* has been particularly useful for much of the technical, factual and military information in this chapter.
26   See the conversation between Kat and Tjaden and others (but not Paul Bäumer, who sits in on the heated debate, but says nothing) in chapter 9 and Bäumer's own, very rare, reference to wealthy 'Fabrikbesitzer' in chapter 11.

emotional and psychological link, between individual soldier and national cause, is lost, vital self-validation is also forfeited.[27] It is true that he had *memories* of a better life, but those memories were ultimately flawed because he knew that he was going to die and that his memories would thus die with him:

> Ich werde eingehn in den Tod wie in ein Tor voll Sommerkühle,
> Heuduft, Spinnweben; ich werde nie mehr wiederkommen
> Zu bunten Schmetterlingen, Blumen, zu den Frauen, zu einem Tanz
> und einem Geigenspiel,
> Ich werde irgendwo zu Steinen niedersinken mit einem Schuß im Herzen [...]
> ('In Bereitschaft', I, 81)

The certainty of his death was not palliated for the lyrical I in *Tier rang* by a conviction that he was dying for a worthwhile cause: indeed no cause, no political aspiration, is ever invoked. And Schnack makes his own 'unpatriotic' stance abundantly clear when he writes: 'Das Buch [*Tier rang*] enthält keine hurrapatriotischen Gedichte, sondern es ist vielmehr ein Buch des Weinens und der Trauer.'[28] He was by no means the only writer to realize that in the special circumstances of the First World War the patriotic insistencies of earlier German war poetry were outmoded and inappropriate. Kasimir Edschmid's retrospective résumé reads:

> er [der Krieg von 1914] war eine Umwälzung aller Anschauungen und Begriffe. Er war nicht ein patriotischer, nicht ein abenteuerlicher und nicht ein romantischer Krieg, wie frühere Kriege oft erschienen waren. Er hatte keine Pause und kein Ethos. Der letzte Krieg 1870/71 hatte praktisch die Lebensgewohnheiten und die seelische Einstellung des Volkes kaum anders als in patriotischem Sinne berührt. Dieser Krieg von 1914 aber war eine Ewigkeit an Zwang, Not und Verbrechen an der Menschheit.[29]

It may in some cases have taken a little time to identify the nature of the seismic change: writing to Katharina Kippenberg in May 1917 and looking back to August 1914, Rilke recalls how at that time the war could be seen as one of those conflicts 'wie man sie aus der Geschichte geglaubt hatte, für eine chevaleresque Freiheit zu historischem Handeln'. But no longer: it must now be viewed as 'diese nichts als monströse, ihrer Natur nach verdorbene und schlecht gewordene Weltkatastrophe':[30] Rilke, like Schnack, draws attention to the 'verdorben' nature of war. The chivalric imagery of the old century is glaringly absent from *Tier rang*, as is any suggestion of patriotic or nationalistic fervour. Into the void where patriotism and strong convictions (for instance about chivalry and honour) used to be, cynicism and sarcasm, irony and indignation, even black humour and mockery could easily intrude, as happened with Sassoon and began to happen with Alfred

---

27   See Hoffmann von Fallersleben's letter to Karl Hirsche of 24 September 1870 in which he writes: 'Der einzelne ist nur noch etwas, indem er sich am großen Ganzen beteiligt, für des Vaterlandes Einheit und Freiheit sein Bestes tut' quoted in Walter Pape, 'Hurra Germania — mir graut vor dir', in *German Unification and the Change of Literary Discourse*, ed. by Walter Pape (De Gruyter, 1993), pp. 107–34 (p. 114).

28   In a letter to Patrick Bridgwater dated 1 November 1960. Quoted in Bridgwater, p. 96.

29   Kasimir Edschmid, *Lebendiger Expressionismus* (Desch, 1961), p. 206.

30   Rilke, letter of 24 May 1917, in *Briefe*, ed. by Nalewski, I, pp. 619–21.

Lichtenstein.[31] With Schnack, however, the tone remains steadfastly melancholy and at times desperately forlorn: *Tier rang* indeed proves to be 'ein Buch des Weinens und der Trauer'.

Brief reference to two nineteenth-century predecessors most closely associated with patriotic war poetry should help to demonstrate how far Schnack moved away from any hint of 'Hurrapatriotismus'. Theodor Körner, Germany's most famous patriotic poet of the Napoleonic era, is one obvious example: after all, when in his 'Gebet vor der Schlacht' Lichtenstein seeks to mock and parody (after the style of Heinrich Heine) the heroic mode of much nineteenth-century war poetry, he takes as his targets 'Bundeslied vor der Schlacht' and 'Gebet während der Schlacht', both of which appeared in Körner's volume of war poetry *Leier und Schwert* (posthumously published in 1814). Körner was urged by his father to help restore Prussia's honour after so many humiliations at the hands of the French, if necessary by dying a hero's death, and to direct his undoubted poetic talents to that same purpose.[32] Just fifteen when Prussia was defeated in 1806 at Jena and Auerstedt and barely eighteen when Napoleon defeated the Austrians at Wagram in July 1809, Körner restrained any expression of his intense patriotism until 'Zwölf freie deutsche Gedichte' of *Leier und Schwert*. These poems are inspired by, and issue from, the poet's own jubilant commitment to battle: they are a rousing call to duty for like-minded compatriots, and, as Körner's own 'Zueignung' makes clear, their purpose is to recruit 'den verweg'nen Zitherspieler', indeed all poets and singers and lyre-players, to the national cause. Once the lyre has fallen silent, the sword will take over with its superior song:

> So bleibt mir hold! — Des Vaterlandes Fahnen,
> Hoch flattern sie am deutschen Freiheitsport.
> Es ruft die heil'ge Sprache unsrer Ahnen:
> 'Ihr Sänger, vor! und schützt das deutsche Wort!'
> Das kühne Herz läßt sich nicht länger mahnen,
> Der Sturm der Schlachten trägt es brausend fort;
> Die Leier schweigt, die blanken Schwerter klingen.
> Heraus, mein Schwert! magst auch dein Liedchen singen.[33]

There are early signs here, as was noted with First World War poetry, that power is being ceded by the human subject to weapons, but little else is comparable. The lyrical I casts himself as his nation's spokesman, the tone is bardic, dynamic and yet intimate. Exclamations and imperatives jostle alongside urgent entreaties and insistencies. The relentlessly jaunty, swashbuckling tone of the twelve poems, the conventional rhyming and the pounding iambic metre ('Es wogt der Kampf,

---

31   Lichtenstein wrote only six war poems (the best-known being 'Romantische Fahrt', 'Gebet vor der Schlacht' and 'Die Schlacht bei Saarburg') between the outbreak of war and his death from wounds sustained at Vermondovillers on 25 September 1914. See Hartmut Vollmer, *Alfred Lichtenstein: Zerrissenes Ich und verfremdete Welt* (Alano, 1988), pp. 167–81.

32   Körner was duly killed just short of his twenty-second birthday on 26 August 1813 at Rasenow bei Gadebusch north of Schwerin.

33   Theodor Körner, *Körners Werke*, ed. by Hans Zimmer, 2 vols (Biographisches Institut, 1893), I, p. 67.

es brüllt der Tod, | Die Wunden klaffen blutigrot'[34]) do nothing to lower the temperature of the poet's ardour. The important point about nineteenth-century war poetry is, however, not just that it uses patriotic language, but that it is mostly abstract and remote from the actual experience of fighting. Körner's poems tend to consist of a sequence of metaphors and abstractions which serve only to obscure the reality of fighting — 'des Vaterlandes Fahnen', 'am deutschen Freiheitsport', 'die heil'ge Sprache unsrer Ahnen' and 'der Sturm der Schlachten' are obvious examples in the above lines quoted from the 'Zueignung'. In practice there are in *Leier und Schwert* very few descriptions of battlefield action. For example, in 'Auf dem Schlachtfelde von Aspern 1812', Körner quickly reveals that he was not even present on 21–22 May 1809 — he visited the scene three years later with his friend Wilhelm von Humboldt.[35] Like Ewald von Kleist before him and a host of Romantic poets after him, Körner did not see the reality of war beyond the mirage of misleading associations and slogans: words like 'Deutschland' and 'Vaterland' assumed a patina of mysticism and became the rallying point for writers like Körner who felt that they could not fight in a war — or, at all events, write about it — without invoking some kind of transcendental or metaphysical sanction for it. It is no surprise that Gerrit Engelke, living and eventually dying on the frontline in the First World War, is completely dismissive of those of his colleagues who simply produce 'die alten Phrasen' in the 'weary' style of Theodor Körner. As early as November 1914 Engelke makes his feelings on the subject abundantly clear to his great friend Jakob Kneip:

> Die augenblickliche Kriegspoesie ist matt. Wir sitzen ja auch alle noch ganz im Wirbel drin und können natürlicherweise noch gar nicht zum Vollkommenen und zu schöpferischen Eindringlichkeiten kommen. Man kann jetzt eigentlich sofort die gewöhnlichen und die besonderen, weil bedeutenden Dichter erkennen. Die ersteren setzen die alten Phrasen, mit denen schon die Körner usw. gewirtschaftet haben, neu zusammen und 'erringen' den Beifall der begeisterten deutschen kompakten Majorität: die anderen bemühen sich, den großen Ton zu finden, der eben nur diesem Kriege, dieser Zeit gerecht wird, erreichen es teilweise; nur wenige schaffen vollkommene *Kunstwerke*.[36]

Incidentally, Engelke, like Schnack, made no attempt himself to publish a volume of war poetry *during* the war (in fact, he deemed it inappropriate to do so): only by waiting, he believed, did he have a chance of creating 'a perfect work of art'. Unlike Schnack, he did not survive long enough to compile such a volume: he died from his wounds one month before the armistice.

It is not unusual for the bulk of lyric poetry of the Franco-Prussian War to be denigrated, even dismissed out of hand. Helene Adolf in her survey of late nineteenth-century verse maintains that the 1870–71 war is caught awkwardly 'zwischen den Feldzügen früherer Zeit, die persönlichem Wagemut noch Raum

---

34   Ibid., p. 79.
35   His actual words are: 'Daß ich damals nicht bei euch ['Manen der gefall'nen Helden'] gestanden! | Daß, wo Brüder Sieg und Freiheit fanden, | Ich, trotz Kraft und Jugend, doch gefehlt!' Ibid., p.74.
36   Gerrit Engelke, letter to Jakob Kneip dated 18 November 1914, in *Das Gesamtwerk*, ed. by Blome, p. 378.

ließen, und der Schlachtenführung von heut, in der der einzelne verschwindet'.[37] Adolf's principal thesis — the quickening disappearance of the personal and the individual under the impact of modern warfare — is familiar to us, but there is one poet who should be rescued from her generally disparaging assessment because he did succeed in bridging the gap which she identifies in her survey. Detlev von Liliencron joined the Prussian army as a 'Fähnrich' and fought with considerable distinction in 1866 and 1870–71, and although he subsequently had to give up his commission and leave the army because of gambling debts, his deep sense of patriotism never wavered. We learn, for example, that when his 'Geldgeschichten' became too great for him, he simply donned his uniform and grasped the handle of his sword — 'das hat mir oft wieder Mut gegeben zum Weiterleben'.[38] But Liliencron's is an intriguingly new kind of patriotism in contrast to Körner's. In his poetry he never glamorizes war; he does not sing of battle or victory to glorify the army or to inspire patriotism in others. He sees the battlefield as an arena in which the soldier can reach for the best and the noblest of which he is capable, and, as a poet, he appears to revel in voicing that thought. He wrote few manifestly patriotic poems for he was interested, above all, in the act and the art of soldiering, and fighting for his country gave him the opportunity to practise the art without, at the same time, feeling bound to proclaim allegiance to his fatherland. He sticks to the anecdotal, the characteristic detail of events which he himself, an immensely brave soldier, has experienced and witnessed. His *Adjutantenritte* (1883) represent the most distinguished literary response to the war by an actual combatant. In line with the experiments of the Naturalists of the 1880s and 1890s there is no sparing of gruesome details: the naturalistic descriptions bring us close to, indeed onto, the battlefield. War is seen as a primitive human experience, as an elemental happening, as an awesome natural power, but also ironically as the progenitor and protector of a guaranteed peace. The poems of *Adjutantenritte* present themselves as series of alternately shocking and exciting impressions, a 'worm's-eye' view of the battlefield in striking contrast to the more usual tendency to portray battle scenes from the distant, elevated vantage-point of the 'Feldherrnhügel' or in the aestheticized, often rhetorical terms of the non-combatant home front. We are moving from the facile 'Hurra Germania' ethos of much 1870–71 poetry towards the ambience of 'Tier rang gewaltig mit Tier'. Liliencron's long poem, 'Der Haidegänger', like the poems in *Adjutantenritte*, offers many examples of his willingness to confront and describe carnage:

> Trägt eines Feindes abgehaunen Kopf
> Meine Linke, den wolligen Haarschopf,
> Längsseits der Decke! Tröpfelt neben meinem Pferde
> Aus dem verzerrten Haupte das Blut auf die Erde!
> Etwas vorgebeugt, den Helm im Nacken,
> Den Schweiß abtrocknend von Stirn und Backen,

37   Helene Adolf, in *Deutsche Literatur: Dem neuen Reich entgegen 1850–1871*, ed. by Heinz Kindermann (Reclam, 1920), pp. 12–13.
38   These are Liliencron's own words quoted in Harry Maync, *Detlev von Liliencron: Eine Charakteristik des Dichters und seiner Dichtungen* (Schuster und Loeffler, 1920), p. 66.

> Reit ich im Schritt, die Augen gradaus,
> Immer gerichtet aufs Tempelhaus.[39]

The harshness of these lines, whose irregular length (varying from ten to thirteen syllables) already indicates the beginning of a break from the strictly regimented verse of Körner and Rückert, could hardly be more explicit or particular, a combination of deeply personal 'Erlebnis', uncompromising realism and a fierce determination to continue to do his duty — 'die Augen gradaus, | Immer gerichtet aufs Tempelhaus'. The lyrical I engages in no excessive jubilation that his enemy is dead, but he appears to feel a certain satisfaction that he has worked hard to earn his triumph. However, it surely was not at all common in the Franco-Prussian War to cut off an enemy's head and parade it like a trophy: at this point Liliencron is departing from realism in order to depict war as primitive barbarism. In the poem 'Krieg und Friede' attention shifts from a description of man-to-man fighting to the lyrical I's own struggles and ends with the focus on one badly injured horse. The suffering of animals is rarely mentioned in war poetry, but in this case the physical details of the injury and of the animal's distress leave nothing to the imagination — 'Ich seh der Vorderhufe Blitz, | Blutfestgetrockneten Sporenritz, | Den Gurt, den angespritzten Kot, | Der aufgeblähten Nüstern Rot'.[40] With Liliencron begins a subtle change in the focus of war poetry — from that which upholds to that which denies the value of war. Lamentation, bardic calls to arms, heady exhortation, all staples of war poetry until Liliencron, find few echoes in such poems as his 'Krieg und Friede'. The physical character of war — that it involves killing other people and being killed — was at best only uneasily present in the poems of Körner, and never fully acknowledged. This kind of imperfect honesty is not repeated in Liliencron's war poetry: he is frank about the brutal killing which war involves and requires and thus points the way to the 'bundle of poems' which Schnack brought back from the frontline in late February 1916 and assembled in *Tier rang*.

A final point of comparison between Schnack and Liliencron is that, for both poets, the experience of seeing at first hand the devastation wrought by war was a bitter reality check after youthful excesses — in Liliencron's case in the gambling rooms of Kiel, Mainz, in fact wherever he was garrisoned, in Schnack's on a hedonistic Gap Year in Bolzano, a phase of his life vividly portrayed in his three Expressionist volumes. The lyrical I in Liliencron's poem 'Rückblick' suggests that war imposed a necessary purpose and direction:

> Weiter nun in bunten Reihn
> Zog mein wüstes Leben.
> Wenig Taten, vieler Schein,
> Wenige Spinneweben.
> Würfel, Weiber, Wein, Gesang,
> Jugendrasche Quelle,
> Und im wilden Wogendrang

---

39   Detlev von Liliencron, 'Der Haidegänger', in *Gesammelte Werke: Gedichte II* (Deutsche Verlagsanstalt, 1923), p. 200.
40   Liliencron, 'Krieg und Friede', ibid., p. 65.

> Schwamm ich mit der Welle.
> [...]
> Schwamm ich viele Jahre lang
> Steuerlos im Leben,
> Hat mir heut der scharfe Gang
> Wink und Ziel gegeben.[41]

Some forty years later when the lyrical I in Schnack's 'Fahrt nach dem Westen', the first poem in *Tier rang*, sets out for the frontline, weary, anxious and disillusioned after earlier excesses, he too, but very painfully, has a clear direction. Yet any thought of a purpose, let alone of ultimate triumph and of personal redemption, is overwhelmed by a dreadful foreboding that 'der scharfe Gang' of this new war will bring only catastrophe and destruction.

★   ★   ★   ★   ★

In the previous two chapters the sonnet form and the cyclical configuration of *Tier rang* were examined. So far in this chapter the special and radically changed circumstances of warfare in the early twentieth century have been described and some of the characteristic qualities of the tradition of patriotic German poetry as it responded to nineteenth-century armed conflict have been outlined. Having already looked in general terms at the form of *Tier rang*, almost sixty sonnets embedded to mutual advantage within the framework of a cycle, this chapter will now focus on the particular by analysing what is potentially one of the most significant poems in the volume. This should enable us, after a setting in context of the selected poem, to answer the two questions with which we began: namely, how successful is Schnack in conveying in *Tier rang* life on the frontline and the psychology of the individual soldier who fought there? And to what extent does Schnack's war poetry, as exemplified by this example and by references to other poems, move on from traditional war poetry, using that tradition, as intimated earlier, *not* as resting place, but as a springboard? As a way of introducing both the context and the poem, it is necessary to continue to use the concept of the self.

Even though Schnack was on the frontline for less than three months, the war unsurprisingly made a deep and lasting impression on him and appears to have left an unhealed scar on his memory.[42] It should be pointed out in this context that the incidents on which Wilfred Owen's war poems are based took place in the first few months of 1917 during which Owen saw, or participated in, action for 'only' about thirty days: a month of horrors was enough to make an indelible mark and to shape his poetry.[43] In the autobiographical sketches and essays which go to make up much of his published prose work Schnack rarely refers directly or explicitly to the war, but it is there, casting a long shadow over his post-war life. When he does allude to it, it is invariably with reference to lost friends or classmates:

---

41   Liliencron, 'Rückblick', ibid., pp. 44–45.
42   This was gleaned from conversations with his niece in August 2011.
43   See Dominic Hibberd, *Wilfred Owen: A New Biography* (Weidenfeld & Nicholson, 2002).

> Der Strudel des gewaltigen Krieges von 1914 gurgelte plötzlich durch Europa, die Knaben von einst waren Jünglinge geworden und zogen in die Feuerhöllen von Verdun, an der Somme oder an der Aisne. Ich war der Einzige von den Kameraden des sommergrünen Eichenwaldes, der in einen schwarzen und bitteren Frieden zurückkehrte.[44]

The essay in which this extract appears was published in 1941, some twenty years after the compilation and publication of *Tier rang*. In it Schnack feels able to use the word 'Kameraden', which does not emerge in the sixty poems of the cycle. This prose essay is presumably addressed to a readership for whose benefit he has to adopt some of the familiar terms in which the 'Fronterlebnis' was stylized and subsequently mythologized. Friends and friendship go missing in the poetry (where they are confined to his remembering), as they went missing on the battlefield: they reappear in the prose where they are invested with the kind of deeply personal, individualized presence which progressively vanishes in *Tier rang*.

What also made a deep and painful impression on Schnack was the sight of defeated German soldiers returning from the war. In a sketch about himself not included in the second volume (*Prosa*) of Vollmer's edition Schnack writes: 'Tagtäglich zogen in den Oktobertagen müde niedergeschlagene feldgraue Männer vorbei, aus Mannheim und der Pfalz kommend, die Gewehre geschultert, hinkend, fußlahm, traurig. Es waren die Geschlagenen des ersten Weltkrieges. Niemals werde ich diesen Eindruck vergessen.'[45] The detailed physicality and the visual strength of these lines, together with references to the soldiers' mental and emotional state, are mirrored two years later in the verse of *Tier rang*.

★   ★   ★   ★   ★

The cycle presents itself as a journey first by train, then on foot, to the frontline in north-eastern France. Schnack himself made such a journey in November 1915. The impact of the war on the countryside soon becomes clear — a church in ruins, a house riddled with bullets, a dead man who 'lag da wie eine Einsamkeit, wie ein Gelage Steine' ('Der Tote', I, 49), the last two phrases underlining the abstract and impersonal nature of the observer's response to the scene. The soldiers, now marching towards Verdun, pass through towns and villages in Lorraine — Montmédy, Dun, Ivoiry, Brieulles, Montfaucon, Epinoville. They cross the river Meuse and bivouac in the Argonne Forest. As Schnack takes us on this march, he deploys a level of precise geographical detail which is new to German war poetry.[46]

The Battle of Verdun was launched on 21 February 1916. The twenty-third poem of the cycle, 'Nacht des 21. Februar', duly records how the lyrical I is filled with barely controlled premonitions of death, but is cast in a self-observing role again:

---

44   Anton Schnack, 'Die Feuertaufe', II, 170. This essay, really little more than a rueful reminiscence, appeared in the *Krakauer Zeitung* of 16/17 March 1941.
45   From 'Anton Schnack über sich selbst', quoted in Glöckler, p. 15.
46   While this is 'precise', the town of Cierges (I, 58–59) appears in the inventory of places either glimpsed or passed through. Cierges is in Picardy, not Lorraine, and so it is not clear how Schnack's company could have got there at this point in the campaign.

'Ich sah mich sein: tierhaft, besorgt, von Angst, daß er mich würfe, der Tod, mit einem Stein ins Antlitz, das einst roch Nächte, süßlich, südlich, heiß, | das einst gebräunt war' ('Nacht des 21. Februar', I, 64–65). The relative clause reminds us of the orgiastic scenes so graphically described in Schnack's earlier volumes, the unusual transitive use of 'roch', with no intervening preposition, underscoring the direct physical encounters of those volumes, the preference of 'Antlitz' to 'Gesicht' indicating a certain distancing among the cluster of assonances so typical of Schnack ('sein [...] einem Stein [...] einst [...] heiß [...] einst'). There is in this fear a powerful existential element which was largely absent from Körner's and Liliencron's war poetry. In the next poem, 'Nacht im Januar' (I, 65–66), fear and horror become more physical and sensory again as it is the smell of gunfire and rotting corpses which catches the lyrical I's attention.

For the moment the sequence of events as depicted in *Tier rang* may well mirror Schnack's own experiences:

> Starr, steinhaft; nur dann und wann Geruch von Feuern, fern, verloschen,
> ausgetan, allein;
> [...]
> Da überall sie [dead soldiers] schlafen, schwer Träumende und todesgelbe
> Reife, (I, 65)

Then, oddly, at this point the chronology goes into reverse with the poem 'Nacht im Januar'. Perhaps this kink in a hitherto geographically and chronologically accurate sequence has to do with Schnack's own fate. He was injured at the end of February and sent back from the frontline:[47] this suggests that everything from, say, 'Die Batterien' (I, 66) onwards has its origins in his imagination. The gunfire, the events in trench and shaft and shell hole, the barbed wire, the observation post, the smoke, the gas, the French prisoners, everything in the final thirty-five sonnets is imagined. Even if it is assumed that Schnack stayed on the frontline right until the end of February, he would have had just one week there once the Battle of Verdun had begun. Moreover, we know that after a ten-hour artillery bombardment which initially pulverized the French lines, there followed an irresistible German advance for well over a week. Schnack's regiment could not have been subjected to an attack (as described in 'Der Angriff', I, 85–86), nor could he have witnessed, or participated in, a retreat or a flight into the mountains of north Italy, the subject and scene of a group of poems at the end of the cycle. By 28 February 1916 Schnack was at home in Alzenau (Franconia) and was never to return to the front. The fact that fewer than half the sonnets in *Tier rang* are based on first-hand experience says nothing, of course, about their quality or about the quality of the remaining majority. The example of Erich Maria Remarque, author of *Im Westen nichts Neues* and *Der Weg zurück*, comes to mind: having arrived at the front in Flanders on 26 June 1917, he was wounded just over a month later and taken to a hospital in Duisburg where he spent, effectively, the rest of the war. And a recently republished anthology of war poems written by women who clearly could not have been present on the battlefield contains at least two poignant poems about trench warfare.[48]

---

47   See the chronology of Schnack's life in Vollmer, I, pp. 474–77.
48   See Maud Anna Bell's 'From a Trench' and Sybil Bristowe's 'Over the Top', in *Scars upon my*

In the course of just over three months, on his journey through Lorraine, Schnack could certainly have seen enough (but no actual combat) to inspire his imaginative powers and to provoke his worst fears about what was to come. Then, given that *Tier rang* was not published until 1920, he could doubtless have read reports and listened to returning soldiers in 1918–19 in order to supplement his material and to fill out the picture of frontline warfare. One reason that the lyrical I, a strongly autobiographical persona in Schnack's poetry, seems to adopt more and more of an observer's role and that human agency progressively diminishes is simply that Schnack was no longer there and he ceases abruptly to rely on first-hand experience. Instead, a pattern of extraordinarily powerful and convincing imagining takes over, a pattern in which man becomes animal and things (or corpses) are on the move and dominate a shattered landscape. The vigour of his imagination does not seem to have waned over the years: in an essay written in 1943 he relates a strange incident in which, on a walk in the Main valley, he sees an old school friend coming towards him kicking a football: 'Aber es kann nicht sein — Aulenbach ist schon lange tot. Ich erinnere mich, daß er im Jahre 1916 an der Südtiroler Front [where Schnack could not have been] gefallen ist.'[49]

There is no relaxing of tension after the poem 'Nacht des 21. Februar' (1, 64–65). On the contrary, everything leads inexorably to the apocalyptic scene portrayed in 'Am Tor des Todes'. And on the way to that dénouement the lyrical I witnesses, and is caught up in, a whole series of brilliantly executed tableaux — of men trapped in shaft and trench, of rockets and planes climbing into the sky, of gas spreading poisonous clouds, of victims caught in the wire, of smoke constantly blacking out sky and horizon, of dismembered corpses lying out in no man's land, of *the* deserter (representing all deserters[50]) making his arduous way through the trenches, of sentries on precarious watch and of mysterious horsemen criss-crossing the eye-line. No nationality or identity, let alone a personality, is ever attached to these figures: a 'spectral' quality, to use Schnack's own word,[51] prevails in this apparently endless sequence of 'Nächte ganz zerrüttet von Schreien, von gewaltigen Todesschreien, gebrochen aus der Tiefe kommend, irr und wehklagend' ('Schreie', 1, 83). A kind of existential alienation accompanies the physical devastation. War, as depicted in these tableaux, is already on a much larger scale, much noisier and clearly much more dangerous than any previous conflict. The war of movement and early trench combat which until Christmas 1914 had retained many of its traditional military forms changed at Verdun and on the Somme into mass slaughter: in *Tier rang* it ends 'Am Tor des Todes'.

Of all the sixty poems in *Tier rang*, 'Am Tor des Todes', the last in the cycle, has been chosen for closer analysis, not only because it is astonishingly powerful

Heart: Women's Poetry and Verse of the First World War, selected by Catherine Reilly (Virago Press, 1981), pp. 10–11 and 13.

49   II, 528. The essay, entitled 'Maintal bei Miltenberg' in the section 'Blick in die Tiefe' in the 'Prosasammlung', first appeared in the *Kölnische Zeitung*, 2. Morgenblatt, 18 November 1943.

50   See the poem 'Der Überläufer', 1, 77–78.

51   See Schnack's comment, already quoted in this chapter: 'Mein erstes großes Werk war traurig und gespenstisch[...].'

in itself and is wholly characteristic of its predecessors, but also because it depicts, dramatically and graphically, the final climactic stage of the lyrical I's doomed journey. For the sake of convenience, the poem's very long lines have been broken into three sections but it is quoted in full. From the outset the depersonalization or, rather, to use John Keegan's word, the 'impersonalization' of battle should be stressed. Of course, that sense of impersonalization is heightened further if the focus shifts to the *aftermath* of battle and the lyrical I is confronted not by fighting and dying, but by death and battle's detritus.

There is, in fact, no lyrical I in 'Am Tor des Todes': the reality of war is, after all, that the lyrical I, like everyone else, stands an extremely good chance of being eliminated. There are forty-six verbs in the poem, eleven are infinitives (seven linked with 'zu' and having no subject as in line 3 below 'Mit ihnen zu spielen [...]'). There are eight past participles (either standing alone or, in the case of 'verworren', used as an adjective) and nine present participles (five standing alone, four with modified adjectival endings). There are, therefore, just eighteen main verbs with a subject. Only three are human subjects — 'man', 'Bauern' and 'Jäger' who join the action as figures in the landscape conjured up late in the poem. None of these three operates in the 'real' world: 'Bauern' and 'Jäger' are summoned up from memory *not* to bring immediate comfort, but to become players in a longed-for future if only the dreadful present time can be survived. 'Man' as the subject of a verb in the conditional tense also has only a very tenuous hold on the present and is likewise caught up in optimistic speculation ('Dunkles könnte man sinnen').[52] Otherwise the subjects are 'things' or, at least, neuter — 'alles', 'dies', 'seltene Tage', 'der Tod'. The only animate objects, as we shall see, are 'Fliegen, die an der Verwesung sind mit grünem Rücken und goldenen Fühlern' — see line 4 below. The astonishingly consistent impersonality of the verbs forces one to dwell on the ugliness of the experience and of the depicted scenes. In contrast, the first poem in the cycle, 'Fahrt nach dem Westen', has sixteen main verbs with nine human subjects.

The overriding dehumanization of 'Am Tor des Todes' is called into question by its very first word, 'Seltsam':

> Seltsam: hinabzusteigen in die weißen Knochen der Toten, die schon
> jahrelang unter dem Himmel sind, frei und unbegraben, bläßlich dämmernd;
> und weit zu gehen,
> Weiter in die Tiefe der Landschaft, hinab ins Blaue, hinein in die schwere
> Luft, julisommerlich, über das Gras voll gelblicher Knochen, von Regen-
> güssen gereinigt,
> Mit ihnen zu spielen klirrend wie mit klingenden Stäbchen — zu lauern an
> dem Gitter der Drähte mit drückendem Schmerz im Schädel, gepeinigt
> Von den Fliegen, die an der Verwesung sind mit grünem Rücken und
> goldnen Fühlern — in die Augen eines Toten zu sehen,
> Groß und unendlich tief, entblößt, mit der Reihe der Rippen, unbeschädigt,
> glänzend und klappernd im Wind. [...] (1, 97)

---

52 'Dunkles' here means something mysterious, rather than melancholy or bleak, as succeeding lines (8–10) make clear.

'Seltsam' at the beginning of a sentence promises a reflective, summative conclusion to the cycle and, therefore, presumably, a ruminating persona. However, the immediate use of an infinitive ('Seltsam: hinabzusteigen') involving no human agency suggests a generalizing statement rather than an account of a personal journey onto the battlefield. It seems that the bones of the dead have been gathering for many years on the surface of the ground. Unburied, they look seductively cleansed in the same deceptive way as 'die schwere Luft' could be that of a July day in summer and the descent is 'hinab ins Blaue'. Such apparently alluring features are swiftly contradicted by the third impersonal infinitive ('zu spielen') and by a fourth ('zu lauern an dem Gitter der Drähte'). Two sickening images intrude. It turns out that the air is not heavy with the sounds of summer, but with flies feeding on rotting bodies (reduced to the abstract noun 'Verwesung'): the fact that the flies' backs and antennae are green and golden compounds the horror of the image. 'Grün, golden' — the combination is the more shocking since these adjectives are often paired in Romantic poetry, most notably in Mörike's famous 'Auf eine Lampe' ('Auf deiner weißen Marmorschale, deren Rand | Der Efeukranz von goldengrünem Erz umflicht') and in the final four lines of his 'Im Frühling' ('in golden grüner Zweige Dämmerung').[53] Indeed the impact of the gruesomely realistic prepositional phrase 'an der Verwesung' is arguably the most shocking in the poem, if not in the whole cycle. The air is also heavy, it seems, with the sound of the wind blowing through the 'Reihe der Rippen' of presumably the same corpses: again, the parenthetical comment that the ribs are 'unbeschädigt, glänzend' somehow accentuates the gruesomeness of a scene for which we have already been prepared by the reference to playing with yellowish bones and making them sound like 'klingend[e] Stäbchen'.[54] The horror is not alleviated by the final 'strangeness' — 'to look into the eyes of a dead man': with its five dependent infinitives the word 'Seltsam' which launched the poem dominates and shapes the opening lines. As if in reproach to God for apparently ignoring the desperate plea for help with which the poem 'Schreckliche Vision' ended ('[...] jetzt in den Winden der Nächte [...] ruf ich ihn an, den Gott, unbekannt, der Rätsel größtes', [I, 95]) all that is left on the battlefield is reduced to 'göttlicher Tand':

> [...] — Vieles ist da, göttlicher Tand:
> Schutt und Kupfer der Knöpfe, riechendes Leder, eine wunderliche Hand,
> klein und ohne Fleisch, knäblich, schwach und gekrümmt nach innen,
> Als wollte sie Gras rupfen, junge Blumen; als wollte sie sich anklammern an
> die ewige Erde... Dunkles könnte man sinnen,
> Verworrenes Zeug, seltsame Gedanken, Einstmaliges: von einer Süßigkeit,
> die sie genoß, von einem Mädchenhaar, das durch sie glitt, von einem
> silberhellen Sand,

---

53 Earlier, in Klopstock's 'Die Frühlingsfeier', the poem invoked in Goethe's *Werther* at a moment of intense emotion when Werther and Lotte experience a thunderstorm, the 'Frühlingswürmchen' is described as 'grünlichgolden'.
54 One thinks of the scene depicted by the prophet Ezekiel: 'The hand of the Lord [...] put me down in a plain full of bones [...] and as I prophesied there was a rustling sound and the bones fitted themselves together.' Ezekiel 37. 1–9. Blunden, too, in his first visit to the Old British Line, comes upon 'a great many bones, like broken bird-cages'. Blunden, p. 27.

Den sie am Meere siebte, von einer Vogelfeder, die sie hielt, gelb, mit grünen
Streifen; seidene Tage werden wach, weit drunten im Süden,
Weit nördlich an schaumiger Küste, klippig, mit grauen Möwenflügen...
Alles verrinnt, auch dies; [...] (I, 97)

'Tand' is a word regularly used by Schnack to encompass anything that is
meretricious or spurious. But among the detritus is 'eine wunderliche Hand'
which, fragile as it might be, intimates a fleeting moment of hope and tenderness
— at least it is alive — until one notes that its rhyming word is 'Tand' and that
the three pathetic gestures ascribed to it, tugging grass, plucking flowers, clinging
to the earth, are prefaced and compromised by 'als' (ob) each time. Moreover, the
'blau[er] Samt' (I, 45) of Ursa Minor and the Plough in 'Fahrt nach dem Westen'
has now metamorphosed into the 'riechendes Leder' of a corpse's tunic, and the
'süße Hand' of the earlier poem, a metaphor then for a ship gliding down the river,
has become a weak and fleshless limb. Once again, the cyclical configuration of
the sonnets allows repetitions and identifications to emerge from (literally) first
poem to last, with the result that the final destination of the lyrical I's journey
remains irreversible and never in doubt. Repetitions within 'Am Tor des Todes'
itself also help to impose a symmetry — 'Selten(heit)', bones, light and dark, the
colour yellow, barbed wire, birds, all recur and combine not only to restore a
kind of order, but also to create an atmosphere of inevitability. Likewise, at line 8,
'verworrenes Zeug' now replaces 'seltenes Zeug' in the earlier poem, with 'Zeug',
as peremptory as 'Tand', suggesting something material and completely, almost
dismissively, impersonal. The heavily neuter endings on 'Dunkles', 'Einstmaliges'
(both capitalized to accentuate their abstraction) and 'verworrenes' serve to renew
the sense of impersonality. The tantalizing images of a girl's hair and a bird's feather
are illusory, for we remember that at least twice in 'Fahrt nach dem Westen' groups
of women had featured, but are now reduced to the synecdoche of a girl's single
hair, and that the last time birds had been mentioned (in 'Handgranatenwerfer', I,
96) they were linked with grenades and stones. The positive images and memories
are thus very tenuous and vulnerable, and it should also be noted that, while
throughout the cycle there is a repeated contrast and interplay between consoling
memory and forbidding present, here in 'Am Tor des Todes' what we are given are
at a further remove — the imagined memories of an unknown dead man killed
by the lyrical I's deftly hurled grenade. For one phrase (the 'silberhell[er] Sand'),
for one sentence ('seidene Tage werden wach, weit drunten im Süden, | Weit
nördlich') the images conjured up are again very briefly positive and optimistic,
but that optimism is swiftly extinguished by reference to 'grau[e] Möwenflüge[n]'
and the utterly deflating 'Alles verrinnt, auch dies'. The hope invested in the earlier
image of the hand clinging to, or wanting to cling to, 'die ewige Erde' is difficult
to separate from the certainty that everything 'seeps away' into the sand, just as in
the last section of the poem the bones on the battlefield are 'verwandelt [...] in Erde'.

Nur der Tod ist ewig, nur die Erde und die Glocke des Himmels darüber.
Auch dies wird wieder schweigen: Schüsse und der dumpfe Ruf
Ferner Sprengungen. — Auch sie werden verwandelt, die Knochen, aus ihrer
weißen Schönheit in Erde, einstmals, wenn Jäger wieder mit Rüden

Durch die Kohlfelder jagen, wenn Bauern über die Äcker johlen hinter den
schwarzen Raben, schwerfällig, hungrig ... Oh, Seltsamkeit: hineinzu-
steigen in das Paradies
Veraltender Gebeine, gelb und mit bläulichem Schimmer, Jahre schon lie-
gend unter dem Mantel der Sterne; oh seltsam: zu lauern am Netz der
Drähte gegen die Finsternis, die im Schoß eine scheußliche Schrecknis
uns schuf ... (I, 97)

The switchback of emotions provoked by the poem persists to the end. It may
be that 'nur der Tod ist ewig', but so are 'die Erde und die Glocke des Himmels
darüber'. Moreover, one day, the guns will fall silent and the bones of the dead (now
described as being 'aus ihrer weißen Schönheit' rather than simply 'weiß[en]' as in
the first line of the poem) will be absorbed back into organic matter and human
beings will repopulate the fields as country life is restored. The glimpse into the
future, of life after the war, is ambivalent. If 'Jäger' and 'Bauern' are metonyms
for rural life, 'Rüden' and 'schwarze[n] Raben' are no less so for aggression and
hunger. A certain comfort is to be derived from the admittedly bizarre image of
'hineinzusteigen in das Paradies | Veraltender Gebeine' and, more so, from the
image of years coming to rest 'unter dem Mantel der Sterne'. It is also significant
that the 'Netz der Drähte', repeating the earlier 'Gitter der Drähte', is now ranged
'*gegen* die Finsternis' (my italics), as if some kind of opposition is being set up against
the darkness, and one final reference back to 'Fahrt nach dem Westen' emerges
in the very last clause of the poem: the 'junger Frauenschoß' of the earlier poem
has, grotesquely, become the womb of darkness accommodating 'eine scheußliche
Schrecknis'. Ambiguity, however, prevails to the end: what is the grammatical
subject of the last verb 'schuf'? Is it the 'Finsternis' that has created 'eine scheußliche
Schrecknis' or is it the latter that has created the 'Finsternis'? And which of them
has the 'Schoß'? The whole effect of this ambivalence is compounded not only by
the tongue-twisting nature of the proliferating sibilants ('oh s̲eltsam [...] Fins̲ternis̲,
die im S̲choß eine s̲cheußliche S̲chrecknis̲ uns̲ s̲chuf...'), but also by the way in
which the poem, and therefore the whole cycle, just trails away without reaching a
conclusion.[55] Battles have gone on, will go on indefinitely. Such was the particular
reality which the First World War embedded in the consciousness of its participants
and which Schnack has succeeded in encompassing in *Tier rang*. The original descent
into hell which 'Fahrt nach dem Westen' signalled seems to have been superseded
by the possibility and prospect of a happier entry into an undefined place. The fact
that the lyrical I has now vanished completely from the scene means that it is not
clear, however, who could take advantage of any offer to be involved in a future
redemptive journey.

★   ★   ★   ★   ★

55   For a full discussion of this phenomenon see Barbara Herrnstein Smith, *Poetic Closure: A Study
of How Poems End* (University of Chicago Press, 1968).

The original purpose of this chapter was twofold: to demonstrate how Schnack sets about achieving in *Tier rang* a volume of poetry powerful enough to represent a particular catastrophic phase of early twentieth-century European history and to examine how, in the process, the lyrical I of Schnack's three Expressionist collections develops and matures. It would be facile to suggest that, because Expressionist poets were used to depicting 'Großstadt' ugliness, they were somehow more open to the ugliness of life in the trenches[56] or that the frequently proclaimed iconoclastic tendencies of Expressionism lent themselves to understanding and communicating the realities of modern armed conflict.[57] However much truth there is in either of these propositions, any convincing war poet, Expressionist or otherwise, still has to engage in a great deal of innovative imagining as well as find the appropriate words and poetic forms if they are going to do justice to the tragedy of war. It is difficult to believe that a poet could capture the ghastly aftermath of a First World War battle more impressively than Schnack does in 'Am Tor des Todes', and the same conclusion applies to his coverage, in the preceding fifty-nine poems, of the events leading to that aftermath, whether it be the description of shattered towns and villages (for example, 'Zerschossenes Haus' and 'Zerstörte Kirche', I, 47–48), an anxiety-plagued night round a campfire ('Am Feuer', I, 49), the first sight of the river Meuse ('Maas', I, 51–52), the first sound of artillery uttering 'gewaltiges Zeug' ('Die Batterien', I, 66), a wretch caught in the barbed wire ('Am Drahtverhau', I, 70–71) or a panic flight into the mountains ('Flucht', I, 87–88). We know from the facts of his life that Schnack had to fall back on his imagination for much of his material, but it does not follow that a poem of first-hand witness will necessarily be better or more poignant than one of second-hand witness. Tennyson was not present on 25 October 1854 at the Battle of Balaclava: he had only his mind's eye to see the 'Charge of the Light Brigade' and thus to pay tribute to the British cavalry, but his imaginative powers and his absorption in Arthurian legend enabled him to feel, and make us feel, the desperate fury and the wild excitement of that fateful charge. Similarly, Thomas Hardy had never seen a Boer War burial party, nor was he present at the Battle of Magersfontein on 11 December 1899, but his lifelong absorption in the little world of Wessex enabled him in 'Drummer Hodge' to take his place, imaginatively, at the boy's graveside, mourning as for the son he never had. For his part, Schnack *did* have the benefit of spending three months at or near the frontline, and his absorption in the tranquil routines of life in the beautiful countryside of Franconia enabled him to gauge, by contrast, the full horror of what he encountered during that brief posting in northern France. He then took four years to shape both the experience and the stark contrasts into the poems of *Tier rang*, for the special circumstances of the First World War required those who wished to give that war its due to change their identity from being poet-soldiers (poets first and soldiers second, like Körner and Liliencron) to being soldier-poets (like Owen and Rosenberg, Stramm and Schnack).[58]

---

56   See Löschnigg, pp. 18–19.
57   See Wandrey, p. 214.
58   George Walter set out this distinction. He capitalises 'Soldier Poets' (also 'Trench Poets'). See

Given those circumstances, there is little doubt that the lyrical I is doomed from the outset, and he knows it, but our interest in his fate is sustained over the length of the volume because his constant recourse to consoling memory not only keeps him going, but also, at the same time, by softening our sense of inevitability, keeps us absorbed in his story. Schnack's success in achieving this is enhanced by the fact that he surmounts a difficulty which confronts all war poets, namely that the elements of engaging in any war — setting out, journey to the line, initial fears, first sights and sounds, confirmed dread, even the individual skirmishes or battles themselves — are not going to vary much and will test a poet's inventiveness and innovative skills to their limit. Scale and intensity, as we have seen, changed hugely between 1870–71 and late 1914, and it is to Schnack's great credit that his poetic response is coherent, where incoherence prevailed, and sensitive, where numbness was the typical emotional and mental state. The cycle derives its coherence from a geographical and historical logic, a strictly linear development and an allegiance to faithful depiction of real life-and-death battlefield phenomena, but also from the sense of a self shrinking from scrutiny and then ineluctably losing control in intolerable circumstances. It is certainly possible to point to isolated individual poems of similar quality, as Bridgwater does with Heinrich Lersch's 'Massengräber', but this is a cycle which sustains an exceptionally high quality and lexical richness over the length of almost sixty huge sonnets.

We have seen how one of Schnack's immediate predecessors, Detlev von Liliencron, particularly in his *Adjutantenritte* and in the long poem 'Der Haidegänger', endeavoured to confront the horrors of the battlefield and composed realistic, almost naturalistic battle scenes, but Schnack takes the process on by several stages. He brings us closer to the experience of the front, without necessarily quite getting there, since the lyrical I is not, in the final analysis, the biographical Schnack and since his choice of material is selective. The physical experience is vividly depicted, but the people who are living the experience — whether the lyrical I or his comrades — become ever more elusive. At the same time his poetry has none of the jaunty, sublimely confident spokesman-cum-intercessor tone characteristically adopted by German war poets from Ewald von Kleist and Johann Wilhelm Gleim onwards. Schnack in *Tier rang* no longer sees as self-evident a comforting bond between the lyrical self and the Fatherland, cherishes no unshakeably loyalist feelings of support for the nation's cause and leaves the big words ('Freiheit', 'Ehre', 'Opfer', 'Vaterland') completely out of account. He has apparently no interest in history or politics, military strategy or final outcome. Nor does he hope or expect that his poetry might influence the course of events or the decision-makers. True to his word, neither patriotism nor nationalism attaches to his verse, and when love for his homeland does become evident (as in the poem 'Ich trug Geheimnisse in die Schlacht' with its invocations of 'Franken', 'Volkslieder aus den Höfen', 'Bamberg' and 'Beethoven'; I, 84) it is always from a narrowly parochial, intensely personal perspective steeped in a gentle, apolitical nostalgia 'garnering his memories

his *The Penguin Book of First World War Poetry*, pp. xvii–xviii.

against the morrow'.[59] If anything, Schnack, like Edward Thomas, offers a literal patriotism. He may become misty-eyed as he recalls the farmers and huntsmen in the forests of Franconia, but there is nothing mystical or transcendent about his praise of his 'Heimat'.

Any references of this kind are a code to hint by antithesis at the indescribable, and it is an important part of Schnack's achievement that he renders justice to both sides of what Paul Fussell in his famous study of the First World War calls an 'insistent polarity',[60] the reality of trench warfare and the reality of memories of the past and hopes for the future — after all, a hand reaching for grass and young flowers, a girl's single hair and a bird's green and yellow feather survive into 'Am Tor des Todes' alongside the yellowish-white bones, the flies bloated on corpses and the network of barbed wire. While Schnack's poetry is notable for such discomfiting detail and precision, its tone is never maudlin or melodramatic or gratuitously shocking. Nor does it succumb to what had frequently been war poetry's greatest weakness — easy, posturing eloquence. Uwe Wandrey concludes his study of Expressionist poetry's response to the First World War by claiming 'daß eine inhaltlich-realistische Erfassung der Kriegsrealität nur in den seltensten Fällen geleistet wurde'.[61] It is the contention of this chapter that Schnack's volume of war sonnets is one such 'rare case' and the fact that it gives more than simply a realistic account makes it worthy of a place alongside the very best poetry of the First World War. 'Against ruthlessness, remembering was the only defence.'[62] Both the ruthlessness and the remembering vie successfully for a place in *Tier rang*.

---

59   The phrase is Lilian M. Anderson's. See her poem 'Leave in 1917', in *Scars upon my Heart*, ed. by Reilly, pp. 3–5.

60   Fussell, pp. 79–80.

61   Wandrey, p. 252.

62   The sentence is Salman Rushdie's from his book *Joseph Anton* (Cape, 2012). He is referring, of course, not to the First World War, but to the fatwa which was imposed on him in 1989. Quoted in the *Daily Telegraph Review*, 22 September 2012.

CHAPTER 7

The Later Poetry

Anton Schnack zu lesen macht kein
Herzklopfen, aber es macht Spaß, es macht
aufmerksam auf vergangene Lebenszusammenhänge,
auf die Wanderwelt des Alltags [...][1]

Between 1920, the year in which *Tier rang* appeared, and 1953 when his last collection was published, Schnack produced the four slim volumes of poetry on which this chapter will focus. *Die Flaschenpost* (1936) was followed by *Der Annoncenleser* (1947), *Mittagswein* (1948) and *'Jene Dame, welche ...'* (1953), which was, in fact, an extended new edition of the 1947 volume. Hartmut Vollmer, who in his splendid two-volume edition of Schnack's complete works has done more than anyone to bring Schnack to contemporary attention, has comparatively little to say in his Nachwort about the four early volumes, including *Tier rang*. These volumes are certainly *not* dismissed,[2] but they are seen as very much of their time and as prefaces to what proves to be the more congenial, comfortable verse of the later volumes. It has been an assumption of this book from the outset that *Tier rang* represents the summit of Schnack's poetic achievement, but Vollmer's implicit advocacy and the fact that the later volumes amount to half of Schnack's lyrical output surely indicate that they merit serious examination. There is an almost audible sigh of relief when the main speaker, on the occasion of the celebration of what would have been Schnack's hundredth birthday, moves very swiftly on from the implicitly heavy and 'superannuated' early poetry to the much lighter later verse and, more particularly, prose:

> Das Zuviel an Drang und Bild und Wort, das in jenen langzeiligen, fast wie Prosa wirkenden Versen [in *Tier rang*] steckt, gehört heute der Vergangenheit an, war damals aber gültiger Ausdruck der Zeit. Ähnlich steht es um die kurz darauf erschienenen Sammlungen 'Strophen der Gier' und 'Die tausend Gelächter.'[3]

---

1   Rolf-Bernhard Essig, 'Blaue Beeren: Die Werke des Fränkischen Schriftstellers Anton Schnack', *Süddeutsche Zeitung*, no. 97, 27 April 2004, p. 14.

2   After all, Vollmer subsequently describes *Tier rang* as 'ein so sprachgewaltiger Gedichtband' undeservedly neglected and worthy of a place among the major achievements of Expressionist poetry. See his letter to me dated 15 August 2011 quoted in Chapter 1.

3   The speaker was Ursula Stickler. The celebration was held in the Kahler Festhalle on 19 July 1992. A report of the event can be found in the *Hanauer Anzeiger* 23 July 1992. A full transcript of her address is available in the town hall archive in Kahl.

Schnack's nephew, Ralph Glöckler, explains the fact that only one volume of poetry was published between 1920 and 1936 by suggesting 'daß Anton Schnack nach den expressionistischen Kriegsgedichten verausgabt war'.[4] Hartmut Vollmer was quick to deny this: 'Ich denke nicht, daß Schnack nach diesem Band [*Tier rang*] dichterisch "ausgebrannt" war. Nach den gewaltigen Schrecken des Ersten Weltkriegs und wohl auch nach den "verbrauchten" Stilformen des Expressionismus wurde allgemein eine literarische Neuorientierung notwendig.'[5] Vollmer then goes on to aver that the new direction taken by Schnack situates him alongside Alfred Polgar, Franz Hessel and Robert Walser as, once again, a 'Meister der Kleinen [sic] Prosaform'.

This is not to say that the later poetry is without interest or merit, but the interest and the merit reside perhaps in the poetry's 'zeittypisch' qualities, rather than in anything uniquely remarkable or intrinsically valuable. Oskar Loerke's *Der Silberdistelwald* and his *Der Wald der Welt* had appeared in 1934 and 1936 respectively, Wilhelm Lehmann's *Antwort des Schweigens* in 1935, the same year as Peter Huchel was thinking seriously of publishing *Der Knabenteich*, while Werner Bergengruen's *Der ewige Kaiser* appeared two years later in 1937. Schnack's *Die Flaschenpost* (1936) thus inserts itself among four much better known collections of poetry by writers whose responses to the unique challenges set by the presence in power of the Nazi regime were, as it turned out, very different from Schnack's. Brief references will be made to these other contemporary writers, but the principal focus of the chapter will be Schnack's collections published subsequently to *Tier rang*. First, however, it is necessary to present an account of Schnack's life during the Weimar Republic and the Third Reich. Much of this information comes from personal contact with surviving members of his family and the archive at Marbach where he deposited his private papers.

From 1920 to 1925 Schnack worked in Mannheim as a theatre-critic and editor of the arts section of the *Neue Badische Landes-Zeitung*. Then for five years he travelled with his wife Maria to the Lake Garda resort of Malcesine north-west of Venice, to Danzig on the Baltic Sea, to Dalmatia, to Ragusa (Dubrovnik) and to southern France. For the next seven years (before settling in Frankfurt am Main for the duration of the Second World War) he kept moving, but confined himself to towns and cities in Germany. Throughout the period between the two world wars a powerful urge to travel was matched by an equally strong longing to return home and settle there into an unassuming domestic routine. Vollmer writes of 'die existentielle Spannung zwischen Heimweh und Fernsucht, "Weltfahrt" und Rückkehr in die geliebte Heimat' as evident in *Die Flaschenpost*,[6] while an anonymous reviewer, on the occasion of Schnack's seventy-fifth birthday in 1967, ends his article by portraying Schnack as 'ein weltbefahrener Franke, der nie vergaß, wo er zu Hause ist'.[7] In one of many nostalgic essays which he composed in the

4   In a letter to me dated 29 November 2010.
5   In a letter to me dated 15 August 2011.
6   I, 457.
7   *Fränkisches Volksblatt*, no. 164, 20 July 1967.

1930s, Schnack recalls how as a boy he and his school friends shared this compulsion to travel: they would race out of their school in Dettelbach, leap into the river Main and follow the 'Meekuh' in order to capture 'einen Fetzen des Glanzes [...], der im Kielwasser des Schleppers glitzerte, denn dort, woher der düstere und lärmende Schlepper kam, war nicht ein verwinkeltes und enges Frankenstädtchen, sondern die unendliche und abenteuerreiche Welt, die Ferne [...]'.[8]

Indeed, after the Second World War, he settled for the rest of his life in the small town of Kahl am Main not far from Aschaffenburg. Unlike his brother Friedrich, who spread his wings as far as Würzburg and travelled widely in a public role as an ambassador for that city, and unlike, too, Max Dauthendey (much admired by Schnack[9]), who sent anguished letters back to Germany throughout the First World War from Java (before dying there in August 1918), Schnack seems to have led a reclusive life within the borders of his country and, eventually, his province, avoiding the public gaze, very rarely commenting on public events. In the final paragraph of one of the last prose pieces he wrote he rejects the notion that he might be deemed parochial or geographically narrow: 'Ich bin kein Provinzler'[10]. But there is no denying that in the 1930s and afterwards he did most of his travelling in his imagination. Reviewers of his later work (that is, everything after *Tier rang*) are not sure whether to see him as a latter-day 'Sindbad, den kühnphantasierenden Seefahrer' or 'den frommen, heiter Liebenden Frankens'.[11] To his close family he was a sometimes disturbing mixture of 'Weltbürger', 'Heimatdichter' and 'Eigenbrötler, der die Öffentlichkeit ablehnte und kein Interesse an Weltereignissen hatte',[12] and who decorated his study in Kahl with maps of countries he longed to visit — 'die Landschaften jenseits der tristen Alltäglichkeit, die weiten Ebenen Amerikas, die Sandwüsten Afrikas'.[13] Nothing, except on the page, came of this fantasising, which, as we have seen, was recruited to good effect in *Tier rang*. *Die Flaschenpost* is founded in the gentle collision between 'Heimweh' and 'Fernsucht' — 'gentle' because it was usually not Schnack's style, nor was it in his nature, to 'stir things up'.[14]

Werner Bergengruen saw it as a moral duty to 'participate in the life of my time',[15]

8   Anton Schnack, 'Ich vergesse dich nicht, große Flußorgel', *Münchner Neueste Nachrichten*, 22 August 1938, II, 157.

9   I, 463.

10   Published posthumously in: *Spessart*, November 1976. This essay can also be found in II, 576, under the title 'Hymne an eine Landschaft'.

11   Maria Forster-Rettelbach, 'Sindbad, der Seefahrer von Franken Anton Schnack', *Main-Echo*, no. 67, 2 May 1960.

12   These are his niece's (Frau Ursula Stickler's) words to me in a conversation held in her house in Kahl in August 2011.

13   See p. 8 of the Regionalstudio Mainfranken transcript.

14   See, for example, Brecht's lines 'Ganze Literaturen | In erlesenen Ausdrücken verfaßt | Werden durchsucht nach Anzeichen | Daß da auch Aufrührer gelebt haben, wo Unterdrückung war.' See his 1939 poem 'Wie künftige Zeiten unsere Schriftsteller beurteilen werden', in Bertolt Brecht, *Gedichte VI: Gedichte im Exil* (Suhrkamp, 1964), p. 15.

15   His actual words, written in 1943, are: 'Ich habe mich am Leben meiner Zeit teilgenommen und doch getrachtet, mich an dieses Leben nicht zu verlieren.' Quoted in Werner Wilk, *Werner Bergengruen* (Hess, 1968), p. 63.

even admitting (perhaps with a certain element of retrospective self-justification) to the label 'engagé'.[16] Schnack, on the other hand, in poetry and prose, regularly cast himself as an interested, but wholly passive, observer: 'Ich liebe die Beschaulichkeit, von einem Punkte aus zu lauern in das Chaos des Lebens, in die große Flut des Lebendigen [...] Ausdauer fehlt den Krebsgeborenen, er zieht sich leicht zurück.'[17] 'Beschaulichkeit', a life of contemplation, was often expanded into something more intense, for instance when he drew up outline hopes and plans for the ideal, idyllic November: 'Eremit werden. Also Einsiedler, Klausner, Weltflüchtling. Einkehr bei sich selbst halten. Zu diesem Zweck kleines Blockhaus am Waldrand abgelegener Gegend sich zulegen, mit Zugbrücke, breitem Wassergraben und umstachelt von einem Gürtel undurchdringlicher Weißdornhecken.'[18] *Flirt mit dem Alltag*, from which this excerpt is taken, was written in 1956, but it encapsulates Schnack's life-long craving, even after or especially after spells of travelling, to return home and to retreat to a domestic idyll. One of the reasons why *Tier rang* is such a powerful volume is because Schnack's portrayal of the horrors of trench warfare is offset by poignant memories of happier circumstances, principally at home. His childhood may have been 'geprägt von einer tiefen Heimatverbundenheit einerseits und einer großen Sehnsucht nach der fernen Fremde andererseits',[19] but by the mid-1930s, when *Die Flaschenpost* appeared, the bond which he felt for his homeland held sway and there seems to have been no longing for the foreign travel of the earlier decade. By nature, by temperament, he was suited to, and drawn by, the quiet life, and that natural instinct, under pressure from public events, became a self-centred, meticulously sustained retreat from what Margaret Schlegel in E. M. Forster's *Howard's End* calls 'a great outer life [...] a life in which telegrams and anger count':[20]

> Ich kenne Menschen [...] die weichen aus. Die haben keine Freude an polizeilichen Anmeldungen, kein Vergnügen an amtlichen Bescheinigungen, Erkennungsausweisen und Wehrpässen. Menschen, die einen Blick in das Paradies der Freude getan haben, wollen nur sich selbst und ihren Träumen gehören. Ganz allein sich selbst. Auch ich, Herr aus Franken.[21]

Schnack calls himself 'Herr aus Franken', not 'Herr aus Deutschland', for there is indeed nothing patriotic, let alone chauvinistic, about his love for his homeland: what inspires him is 'Heimatgefühl', not 'Vaterlandsgefühl'. It is the kind of literal patriotism noted in the earlier analysis of *Tier rang*. 'Heimat' is then narrowed down to 'Hof' when Schnack, as early as 1927, describes the state of mind which will shape his attitudes and emotions in the 1930s:

> Ich liebe die Abgeschiedenheit des kleinen Hofes, dem ich aus dem vergrämten Fenster mitten ins graue Herz schaue, das leblos und vertrauert zwischen den

16   Werner Bergengruen, *Dichtergehäuse* (Arche, 1946), p. 195.
17   Quoted in Glöckler, pp. 7–8. Undated, but these words are appropriate for virtually any period of his life.
18   II, 344.
19   I, 452–53.
20   E. M. Forster, *Howard's End* (Vintage Books, 1921), p. 27,
21   I, 462.

Steinbarrikaden der hohen Häuser liegt. Seine Abenteuer sind die Abenteuer des kleinen Lebens, des unauffälligen Gleichmaßes, der stetigen Wiederholung und des schweigenden Verzichtes auf die Buntheit und Vielfältigkeit des Straßenglanzes.[22]

This passage contains echoes of a Stifteresque approach to life: when one reads of Schnack's playing the role of a 'Grandseigneur in seiner gelben, efeuumrankten Ritterklause',[23] it is difficult not to think of Risach's 'Rosenhaus'. The primal experience of inner emigration did not, of course, start in the 1930s. Probably its most notable literary paradigm is, indeed, Stifter's novel *Der Nachsommer*:

Ich habe wahrscheinlich das Werk [*Nachsommer*] der Schlechtigkeit willen gemacht, die im allgemeinen mit einigen Ausnahmen in den Staatsverhältnissen der Welt, in dem sittlichen Leben derselben und in der Dichtkunst herrscht. Ich habe eine große, einfache, sittliche Kraft der elenden Verkommenheit gegenüberstellen wollen. Was Wunder, daß die Verkommenheit stutzt, ja erzürnt ist. Aber es schadet nicht. Ist mein Vorbild menschlich gut, so wird es geduldig stehen bleiben, die Lästerer werden schweigen und allgemach zu ihm übergehen.[24]

Instead of 'Gegenbild' we find 'Vorbild', but there is no doubt that Stifter's model prefigures the phenomenon of inner emigration nearly one hundred years later. However, the moral (and moralizing) purpose of that model, the explicit reference to contemporary 'elende[n] Verkommenheit' and the readiness to court and expect a hostile reaction, all are far removed from Schnack as he apparently endeavours to write as uncontentiously as he can — out of harm's way, as it were. In so doing, he ran the same risk as Lehmann and Loerke did in terms of making himself vulnerable to 'der gefährliche und zweideutige Trost der Geborgenheit im Provinziellen'.[25] Adorno's substantive 'Geborgenheit' is one of the key elements of the vow which 'the boy', a thinly disguised Anton Schnack, takes in the autobiographical prose piece *Der verschollene Onkel* (1941):

Da gelobte sich der Knabe, niemals aus der Geborgenheit der Heimat zu gehen, sondern in ihrer schönen und vertrauten Landschaft zu bleiben als ein Lehrer oder Arzt, in irgendeinem Dorf, das unter dem schwarzen Schatten des großen Waldes liegt oder zwischen Baumalleen und Weinhügeln versteckt ein ungefährdetes und beschauliches Dasein führt.[26]

The poems of *Die Flaschenpost* reflect Schnack's determination to pay tribute to the beauty and variety of the landscape of a beloved corner of his homeland. They also reflect what Walter Höllerer has identified as the characteristic pose of the lyrical self created by Anton Schnack — someone standing at a window looking

---

22   II, 403.
23   See p. 2 of the Regionalstudio Mainfranken transcript.
24   Letter to Gustav Heckenast, 11 February 1858, in Adalbert Stifter, *Briefe*, ed. by Friedrich Seebaß (Wunderlich, 1936), pp. 197–99.
25   T. W. Adorno, 'Die auferstandene Kultur' (1949), in *Gesammelte Schriften*, ed. by Rolf Tiedemann, 20 vols (Suhrkamp, 1986), XX/II, pp. 453–64 (p. 455).
26   II, 162–63.

outside, for outside is where all the adventures are happening.[27] And the window in question is often a window of a house in a small town looking out into the world. This should not surprise us because, after all, Schnack had adopted a similar vantage point in the war poetry of *Tier rang* — close enough to the main action to see and report and then reimagine all the details, far enough away to avoid direct participation. Moreover, Schnack, it will be recalled, earned his living as an editor, journalist and reviewer for numerous publications.[28] It is true that this role would inevitably have kept his name in the public eye, but it also reinforced what seems to have been a natural instinct to want to observe and report rather than to be directly involved. And it was always a very local and localized public for which he wrote, commenting on other people's cultural activities rather than on social and political matters of national or international significance. He set his life and his practice as a poet outside active involvement in social processes. When the first German nuclear power plant was built in Kahl, unlike his brother Friedrich, he made no public protest. When East German soldiers placed mines on the border between Kronach and Coburg he stirred briefly from his retreat, but referred to the incident only indirectly, as usual camouflaging the implications in a nostalgic glow: 'Wo ich einst spielte, wenigstens eine Zeitlang, kannte man keine Minenfelder; wir wußten in unserer seligen Arglosigkeit nicht einmal was Minen waren.'[29]

None of this meant, of course, that he detached himself wholly from a wider public life. After all, as we have seen, in a very bizarre and uncharacteristic intervention, he dedicated his poem 'Lied an Frankreich' to Charles de Gaulle and Konrad Adenauer as architects of an eventual rapprochement. Furthermore, he spoke of *Tier rang* as 'ein lyrisches Antikriegsbuch', which brought all kinds of hostile, public criticism upon him: 'Ich wurde von vielen bürgerlichen Blättern mit Dreck beworfen.'[30] However, it has not been possible to find any examples of these allegedly vitriolic responses. Later, in 1926, there was a very strange incident in Italy where, as a result of a hostile article (or was it a poem?) which he wrote about the Italian tourist trade, he was driven out of the country by the Fascist authorities — or was he arrested? Details are unclear and conflicting.[31] Three years later, on 6 June 1929, he published in the magazine *Querschnitt* the poem 'Aschaffenburg' whose last line reads: 'Aber dafür kannst du für ein Viertel Praliné mit allen Mädchen Gemeinschaft haben'.[32] For thus allegedly maligning the reputation of the young women of Aschaffenburg Schnack found himself (by his account) assailed by the municipal authorities and spurned by everyone else: 'Alle zeigten mir die kalte Schulter. Auch der Ullstein-Verlag. Man wollte [he means: 'ich wollte'] Auseinandersetzungen mit den heraufkommenden Nationalsozialisten vermeiden.

---

27   Walter Höllerer, 'Anton Schnack', *Weltstimmen: Weltbücher in Umrissen*, 3 (1953), pp. 97–102.
28   For example for the *Darmstädter Zeitung*, the *Neue Badische Landes-Zeitung*, *Simplicissimus*, *Querschnitt*, *Die Dame* and many others.
29   See page 11 of the Regionalstudio Mainfranken transcript.
30   See 'Anton Schnack über sich selbst' (n.d.), Manuscript Department, Marbach.
31   Ibid.
32   I, 314.

[...] Ich setzte mich daraufhin nach Südfrankreich ab [...].'[33] The incident was reported in the *Beobachter am Main*, 9 July 1929, under the rather sensationalist heading 'Eine schmachvolle Beleidigung der Aschaffenburger Mädchenwelt!' He did not escape unscathed: it seems that the local Nazi party condemned him in a local meeting as a 'Schmutz- und Schunddichter'.[34]

Again it is not clear whether he was then driven out of the town and forced to retreat to southern France or whether he simply felt so uncomfortable and unsafe that he took refuge for a while in Le Lavandou and Marseilles. It should be acknowledged that, whenever Schnack gives an account of his brushes with authority, it is not difficult to detect a note of self-dramatization, perhaps even of a persecution complex in two of his reminiscences: 'Ich bin immer angegriffen worden. Ich bin von den Katholiken, von den Protestanten, Stahlhelmern, Deutschnationalen, Nationalsozialisten u.s.f. angegriffen worden, so daß ich auch nach dem Kriege wieder angegriffen werde.' And, later, 'Das Gedicht ['Aschaffenburg'] fegte im Jahre seines Erscheinens einen Skandal auf und hetzte mir den Nationalsozialismus auf den Hals.'[35]

There is no documentary evidence of these 'constant attacks'. At this distance no one can be sure whether his life or his family's lives were ever in danger, but what is certain is that Schnack was sufficiently shocked by the public response to engage in his own version of an 'outer emigration' and that the incidents in Italy and Aschaffenburg happened seven and four years respectively before the Nazis came to power. There was then a gap of fifteen years before Schnack again attracted the attention of the authorities — again apparently for minor misdemeanours. First he gave a hostile review to a book by Dr Erich Ebermayer and then he was taken to court by the 'Verband der Klavierhändler' because that union disapproved of his poem 'Klavierunterricht'.[36] These incidents, like the earlier two, were low-key skirmishes rather than full-blown conflicts. But the events in Italy and Aschaffenburg alone were clearly sufficient to encourage him, like so many other politically non-aligned intellectuals, to withdraw in the 1930s from the realm of political discourse into a private realm in which very conventional attitudes were struck and traditional stylistic influences cultivated. In Schnack's case his retreat seems, in retrospect, as much a conscious strategy as an emotional withdrawal. He planned to write a romantic, fantastic novel depicting the general contemporary malaise and fear about the future: its title was to be *Der barbarische Ausflug*, 'aber dann kam das Drama Hitler'[37] and it was never published. Instead we have the novel *Der finstere Franz* (1937), the story of how Jean David becomes the notorious pirate François d'Olonois, engages in bloody battles with the Spaniards and ends up losing the fair Raphaela to the noble and dignified Guy de Montbars. Any attempt to equate d'Olonois with Hitler seems absurd: François may be a monster, but he has soot-black hair falling to his shoulders and the wrong kind of moustache —

33   Letter of 15 December 1969 to Dieter Hoffmann. See I, 472.
34   Ibid.
35   See 'Anton Schnack über sich selbst' (n.d.), Manuscript Department, Marbach.
36   See I, 241–42. Again it is hardly an incendiary poem.
37   A. Schnack, 'Biographie', an undated essay available in the Manuscript Department, Marbach.

'ein schmaler gezwirbelter Schnurrbart, der sich um die Oberlippe ringelte'.[38] Nor was it Schnack's intention that his novel should ever be interpreted as the kind of political allegory which Bruno Werner attempted and achieved in his remarkable novel *Die Galeere* (1943–47).[39] In an angry exchange of post-war correspondence with a literary reviewer who suggested that *Der finstere Franz* was atypical of Schnack's other work, Schnack retorted that on the contrary it was merely meant to be of a piece with his other writings, a transposition of 'eine bluttriefende Seeräubergeschichte aus dem Kolportagenhaften ins Dichterische'.[40] The year 1953 would, one might think, have been an ideal time to claim, in retrospective self-justification, that he had written an anti-Nazi novel. Nor did a close friend see the novel as anything other than what it was, chiding Schnack for wasting his talents on such a project. Writing just before Christmas 1937, Willibald Omankowski, critic and reviewer, began by stating how much he enjoyed the work, but then added that he had a particular New Year's wish:

> Und nun möge Ihnen das neue Jahr einen schönen, stillen, dichterischen Roman schenken, dem sich Ihre große Könnerschaft nicht an Räubergeschichten vertut (nicht böse sein, bitte!) sondern die seelische Landschaft gestaltet, die die anderen, die noch in Deutschland geblieben sind, nie gestalten können.[41]

As far as we know, Schnack did not take up Omankowski's New Year challenge. Nor did the authorities or the censors make any move against the author of *Der finstere Franz*. The Nazis had guaranteed a 'politikfreie Sphäre' in the early years of their rule: this perpetuated the illusion of freedom of expression for accomplished literature which was not of a political nature, and so the story of François d'Olonois, never seen by its author or, apparently, by its readers in the same light as, say, Bergengruen's *Der Großtyrann und das Gericht* (1935) in terms of historical camouflage, slipped past the censor without any recorded objection or difficulty.

How, in fact, did the Nazi authorities respond to Schnack's work? And how did he behave in response to their demands and expectations? Schnack's name appeared among the eighty-eight writers who, within a few months of Hitler's coming to power, signed a vow of loyalty to the Führer. His own account of the event reads as follows: 'Im Herbst 1933 erschien in deutschen Zeitungen entweder vom Schutzverband Deutscher Schriftsteller oder Reichsverband DS eine sogenannte Treuekundgebung für Hitler. Auch mein Name stand darunter, ohne daß ich Gelegenheit hatte dazu Stellung zu nehmen.'[42] It is not altogether clear what that final disclaiming clause might mean, nor can one be wholly certain as to

---

38   A. Schnack, *Der finstere Franz* (List, 1937), p. 143.
39   It *is* a truly remarkable work. It follows the fortunes of Georg Forster who, like Schnack, like Werner himself, is a theatre- and art-critic with First World War front-line experience. It offers a panoramic view of the impact of the Nazi regime on a whole host of different personalities, neither absolutely good people, nor absolutely bad. The pictures of a destroyed Dresden are unforgettable. In the end, the captain of the Galeere is overwhelmed by the crew. See Albert Morhof's excellent review 'Im Zeichen der Galeere', *Freude an Büchern*, 2 (1950–51), pp. 310–11.
40   See a letter dated 30 December 1953 to Franz Lennartz, Manuscript Department, Marbach.
41   Letter from Willibald Omankowski, dated 23 December 1937, in the same department.
42   See the document 'Lebenslauf Anton Schnack' (n.d.), Manuscript Department Marbach.

how significant the declaration of commitment was. After all, Loerke's name was among the eighty-eight alongside the more predictable names of Gottfried Benn, Hanns Johst, Heinrich Lersch, Ina Seidel and Will Vesper, but what diminishes the document's credibility is that many writers signed up only in order to protect their publishers[43] and perhaps also because they did not believe that the Nazi regime would last long. Apart from that one rather cryptic 'ohne daß ich Gelegenheit hatte dazu Stellung zu nehmen' there is no record of how Schnack felt, at the time or subsequently, about the whole affair. He was, however, not allowed to forget it. In 1950 Ossip Kalenter, President of the PEN Centre of German-Speaking Writers Abroad, wrote in a faux jovial vein which barely concealed his serious intent:

> Da man hier empfindlich ist, lieber Antonio, sagen Sie mir bitte vielleicht gelegentlich ein paar Worte über eine Sache, mit der Ihr Name hier draußen [in Zürich] seit 1933 häufig in Verbindung genannt wurde: das blöde Sondertreuegelöbnis der 88: Sie wissen sicher, was ich meine. Mir müssen Sie nicht erklären, daß Sie kein Nazi waren. Ich weiß es. Ich kenne auch in großen Umrissen Ihre Affäre Ebermayer [...] Und Bruno E. Werner gab ja in seiner 'Galeere' eine Erklärung dafür ab, wie es zu jener Hitler-Huldigung und den Unterschriften kam [...] Aber ein paar Worte von Ihnen wären schon gut. Entschuldigen Sie, daß ich daran rühre. Aber man ist hier draußen durch solche Dinge schrecklich irritiert.[44]

Schnack's reply, if he gave one, to this direct request for an explanation is not on record, though he does concede that he was allowed to continue writing virtually without harassment: 'Ich konnte (mit einigen Ausnahmen) in der Linie meiner früheren Grundhaltung weiterarbeiten. Allerdings nur wenig und gehemmt durch innere und äußere Umstände und Einflüsse. Vom Regime blieb ich im großen und ganzen unbehelligt [...]'.[45] In 1934 Schnack received a pass from 'die Reichskulturkammer Berlin' headed 'Reichsverband Deutscher Schriftsteller in der Reichsschrifttumskammer' giving him the right 'die Tätigkeit eines Schriftstellers auszuüben'.[46] Rosenberg's 'Hauptamt für Schrifttumspflege' worked to various criteria: Kasimir Edschmid and Joachim Ringelnatz were deemed to be 'bedingt negativ', Paul Alverdes and Friedrich Georg Jünger were 'bedingt positiv', Bergengruen, Loerke and Wiechert were 'unnachsichtig verurteilt', while Schnack was judged 'überholt — mit Einschränkung'.[47] The 'Einschränkung' never amounted to outright rejection or the censor's ban. Schnack also earned the label 'unerwünscht aber geduldet', but once again the label did not mean very much in practice:

---

43   Joseph Wulf, *Literatur und Dichtung im Dritten Reich: Eine Dokumentation* (Mohn, 1963), p. 96.
44   Letter from Ossip Kalenter, 14 December 1950, Manuscript Department, Marbach.
45   See the document 'Lebenslauf Anton Schnack'.
46   In the Manuscript Department, Marbach: see the file called 'Zugehörige Materialien — Urkunden, Zeugnisse, Ausweise', containing a pass issued to Anton Schnack by the Reichskulturkammer Berlin (Ausweis 1813), dated 26 June 1934. Schnack's 'Fachschaft' is given as 'Erzähler', not 'Dichter'.
47   Dietrich Strothmann, *Nationalsozialistische Literaturpolitik* (Bouvier, 1963), pp. 248–50.

> Das Etikett 'unerwünscht' allein gibt jedoch kein stichhaltiges Urteil über eine mögliche Oppositionshaltung der Verfasser. Unter den Autoren 'unerwünschter' Werke befanden sich neben Autoren der Inneren Emigration wie Loerke, Lehmann oder Wiechert auch Schriftsteller, deren internationalen Rang die Faschisten kulturpolitisch zu nutzen versuchten wie G. Hauptmann und sogar faschistische Autoren wie R.C. Muschler, von denen einzelne Werke 'unerwünscht' waren.[48]

Quite simply Schnack did not present, and was seen not to present, much danger to the regime, and to all appearances that was the way he wanted to be viewed — as an unpolitical, detached professional writer dedicated to producing innocuous poems and articles for magazines and to composing the (very) occasional volume of poetry, a stance summed up by one reviewer's assertion that 'Schnack gab den grauen Bildern des Alltags kein Daseinsrecht'.[49] Another reviewer reduces Schnack's 'Methode, als kreativer Intellektueller das Dritte Reich zu überstehen' to the stark assertion: 'Schnack kaprizierte sich auf das Verfassen von unverfänglichen Romanen und Reiseliteratur.'[50]

When released from American captivity in 1945 he had to complete a questionnaire entitled 'Military Government of Germany' and gave answers to a series of personal questions. When asked about his membership of any political party or section of a party — the NSDAP, the Allgemeine SS, the Waffen SS, the Sicherheitsdienst der SS — he answered in the negative: he did not vote in the March 1933 election; he was a member of the Reichsschrifttumskammer from 1934 to 1945, and of the Reichspressekammer for a few months during 1943. To the question 'Sind Sie jemals aus [...] irgendeiner Stellung auf Grund activen oder passiven Widerstandes gegen die Nazis oder ihre Weltanschauung entlassen worden?' the answer was also 'Nein'.[51] The abiding sense conveyed by Schnack's brief references to his role in what occurred is of a man determined to settle for the quiet life: a harsher interpretation would be that his answers give the impression of a man so sensitive to criticism, so attuned to acquiescence that he eschewed confrontation in circumstances where his pride might have forced him into it. Rolf-Bernhard Essig, reviewing Hartmut Vollmer's two-volume edition of Schnack's work, makes a similar point in different words:

> Mit den Nationalsozialisten gab es keine Auseinandersetzung und keine Gemeinschaft, sieht man von der kollektiven Ergebenheitsadresse des Schriftstellerverbands an Hitler ab. Man kann dem Autor Schnack diese Indifferenz vorwerfen, dazu Blindheit und Egozentrik. Er blieb sich selber selig und treu, publizierte weiter seine Petitessen-Sammlungen. Spuren der Ereignisse vor, in und nach dem Zweiten Weltkrieg sucht man darin so gut wie vergeblich.[52]

---

48   Ralf Schnell, *Literarische innere Emigration 1933–1945* (Metzler, 1976), pp. 30, 175.
49   See p. 11 of the Regionalstudio Mainfranken transcript.
50   Luise Glaser-Lotz, *Rhein-Main*, no. 177, 2 August 2003, p. 60.
51   §E of the questionnaire entitled 'Military Government of Germany' is the one which contains the relevant questions and answers.
52   Essig, 'Blaue Beeren'.

This did not prevent the (anonymous) author of the article 'Der Ruch der treuen Gefolgschaft' in a very recent edition of the *Main-Echo* claiming that 'bis dahin [May 1945] gefeierte Autoren' (including Anton and Friedrich Schnack) disappeared 'aus dem nationalen Interesse — nicht zuletzt, weil sie während des Dritten Reichs Partei für das NS-Regime ergriffen'.[53] In his reply to my letter querying this assertion, the present mayor of Kahl, Jürgen Seitz, wrote: 'Anton Schnack hat sich niemals politisch betätigt, und war kein Parteigänger.'[54]

It is hardly surprising that the most official step in assembling writers who had survived the Third Reich without undue moral compromise was taken explicitly without a programme of action. Founded in the Frankfurt Paulskirche in 1949, the Deutsche Akademie für Sprache und Dichtung borrowed as its rationale the maxim of the French Academy, proclaiming its desire to become 'the highest body in the sanctioning of the current usage of language'. It maintained the legitimacy of those who had opposed Hitler and received full support from the highest official of the new republic, Theodor Heuß, who himself was a member, and it offered a prestigious forum for writers who tried to revitalize literary life by calling on traditions that harked back to the 1920s and before. The list of its forty-nine founding members reads like a proclamation that inner emigration was the basis for this kind of official recognition: Werner Bergengruen and Wilhelm Lehmann are there, as are Reinhold Schneider, Erich Kästner and Elisabeth Langgässer. Friedrich Schnack's name appears, but his brother's does not. Anton's strategy of keeping a low profile and consistently publishing only 'Petitessen-Sammlungen' had obviously worked.

★   ★   ★   ★   ★

Die Flaschenpost (1936) was the only collection of poems which Schnack published between 1920 and 1947. It is a title rich in allusions, implications and associations, and it raises expectations, especially given its social and political context where writers could hardly avoid addressing political and moral pressures and where 'speech and silence alike took on the force of a moral response to the political events'.[55] As a metaphor, 'message in a bottle' suggests a communication between an author who encloses his words in a container and a reader who, he hopes, will find and open it. The strong implication is that the writer is in a critical state of isolation and despair. The possibility of direct oral communication in a space which would enable author and recipient both to see and hear each other has, for whatever reason, had to be ruled out, but there is, in any case, no guarantee that the message will find a reader. Traditionally a message in a bottle is sent by a person who has been shipwrecked and then washed up on some desolate island. That message will invariably contain vital, rational, potentially life-saving information, but will be grounded in emotional desperation. The act of communication in such circumstances is borne not by any

53   *Main-Echo*, 22 August 2012.
54   In a letter to me dated 4 October 2012.
55   Elliott, p. 267.

sense of confidence, but by a forlorn hope.[56] It is possible to express that hope more optimistically. Paul Celan, for example, sees all poetry as being potentially a kind of 'Flaschenpost' because all poems are inherently a dialogue: 'Das Gedicht kann [...] eine Flaschenpost sein, aufgegeben in dem — gewiß nicht immer hoffnungsstarken — Glauben, sie könnte irgendwo und irgendwann an Land gespült werden, an Herzland vielleicht.'[57] Schnack is, above all, a literal poet in the sense that he has no time for, or, apparently, interest in, the allusive and the oblique. At pains not to give any offence, especially after the Aschaffenburg incident, and, it seems, in denial about what is happening beyond the narrowest confines, he sends his 'Flaschenposten' *not* from some life-threatening situation, but from his and his family's joyfully remembered life-sustaining past. His messages, the poems of *Die Flaschenpost*, amount to unambiguous transparencies and snapshots of the past, and there is no invitation to the reader, either implicit or explicit, to move beyond the obvious, the superficial and the literal. The compulsion to get away, matched in intensity by a longing to stay put, proves not to be, for example, a flight from personal adversity or national crisis, but a rehearsal of the Romantic yearning, best embodied by Eichendorff's *Taugenichts*, to set out for some distant, exotic land. It is not a question of a message sent against the odds, because there are, it seems, no odds except those presented by hostile climatic conditions.

Schnack is certainly well aware of the traditional significance of 'a message in a bottle': two of the poems in the *Flaschenpost* collection concern such messages. The first, 'Die Flaschenpost des Kolumbus',[58] sent by Columbus from the Azores in February 1493, does not arrive at the court of the King of Spain, whereas in the second, 'Die Flaschenpost des Matrosen Wengfield',[59] the message is found and deciphered by a ship's pilot: 'Alles vermache ich Mary!'. Moreover, Robinson Crusoe, the protagonist of Defoe's 1719 novel, a castaway for twenty-six years on a tropical island near Trinidad, is a recurring figure in Schnack's prose work: a 1946 collection of essays bears the title *Die Angel des Robinson*. In a biographical sketch published three years later Schnack relates how in his youth he often imagined Crusoe's rather ineffective fishing net and took pity on his hero in the latter's 'peinigende Inseleinsamkeit' from which, incidentally, he did not send a 'Flaschenpost':

> Und um den Fischsegen zu beschwören, schrieb ich auf ein kleines Stück Papier Verse meiner Sorge, schrieb ich meine Bitte an den Beherrscher der Meere und warf es in den Mainfluß, damit das Blatt aus der Knabenhand ins ferne Meer reise:

---

56   For a fuller discussion of the term, see Karen Leeder (ed.), *'Flaschenpost': German Poetry and the Long Twentieth Century*, special issue of *German Life and Letters*, 60 (2007), 277–466. Katrin Kohl's essay 'Sprache als Metapher in der Lyrik des zwanzigsten Jahrhunderts' (pp. 329–47) is particularly relevant.
57   'Ansprache anläßlich des Literaturpreises der Freien Hansestadt Bremen' (1958), in Paul Celan, *Gesammelte Werke*, ed. by Beda Allemann and Stefan Reichert, 5 vols (Suhrkamp, 1983), III, p. 186.
58   I, 176–77.
59   I, 177. It has not been possible to discover who Sailor Wengfield might be. He does not reappear in Schnack's work.

> 'Möge der dreizackbewehrte Neptun
> dem armen Robinson gnädig sein!'[60]

These lines refer directly to a trip Schnack made to Ragusa (Dubrovnik) in 1927 and there is no reason to take them at anything other than face value. The poems of *Die Flaschenpost* should be interpreted in the same way, as messages hurled by a boy's hand into the river Main and then carried out to sea. After all, this is precisely what happens, according to Vollmer, in *Die Angel des Robinson*: 'Der Schriftsteller-Robinson angelt sich — metaphorisch gesprochen — zauberhafte Prosastücke aus dem weiten Weltenmeer seines Lebens und bietet sie, an Land (ins Buch) gezogen, dem Leser zur genußvollen Lektüre an.'[61] In a footnote to his own commentary Vollmer adds: 'In ähnlich metaphorischer Bedeutung ist der Titel des 1936 erschienenen Gedichtbandes *Die Flaschenpost* als ein "Heranspülen" von poetischen Lebenszeichen zu verstehen.'[62]

In *Die Flaschenpost* Schnack is primarily concerned with his own immediate past. It is undeniably an autobiographical collection: Schnack is relating his own life, rosy-hued and idealized it is true, but grounded in his own affections and reminiscences. At the same time, the lyrical I of the poems offers a space and an opportunity for the poet to release his yearning to travel:

> Ich gehöre zu den Schiffsmatrosen,
> Länderhungrig, meerbetört,
> Nackte Brust, verschmierte Hosen,
> Gelber Taifun röhrt.
> Inseln, Knabentraum,
> Grün im Brandungsschaum.
>
> Wo die alten Weltentdecker fuhren,
> Fahr' ich nun.[63]

By the last stanza he sees that his childhood dream has not been realized, but he can take consolation from the fact that ships are still sailing the oceans, will always sail the oceans, though he himself is not on board:

> Immer fahren Schiffe auf den Ozeanen:
> Ich bin nicht an Bord.
> Und es pfeifen Dampfer, die an Abfahrt mahnen:
> Und ich bin nicht dort.
> Und ich bin nicht dort:
> Paradiesvertreibung, Trauerwort!

The melancholy ending of this poem — 'Trauerwort' rhyming with the reiterated 'nicht dort' — is *not* typical of the cycle because Schnack usually focuses his attention on keeping the paradise of childhood alive by consigning it to memory. He can then, as it were, re-enter that paradise and invite us to join him there. In *Tier rang* he had also used memories of deeply personal occasions and of significant people

---

60   'Ragusäische Fischernetze', II, 515–16.
61   I, 460.
62   Ibid. See footnote 49 on I, 472.
63   'Schiffsbewegung der Hornlinie', I, 180–81.

from his past as sources of consolation, as attempts to make the horrors of Verdun more tolerable. But there is a crucial difference: it is made plain in *Tier rang* that those memories are mortally threatened. With the inevitable extinction of the self the precious memories will die too, erased by an all-powerful external agency.[64] The purpose of *Die Flaschenpost* seems to be to strive to preserve the memories of the idyllic parts of his childhood and his boyhood dreams, but 'only' against the depredations of time, with no hint, even by implication, of the countervailing forces of the outside world. In other words, the poems of the collection are enveloped in a haze of benign nostalgia. The consolation conveyed ends up being only just short of sentimentality, the harmony achieved is not readily distinguishable from conformism, and if the sense of goodness and optimism communicated is not shallow, it is certainly untested by evil and setback. The perennial dilemma for Schnack — how to balance his abiding allegiance to his homeland and a longing to be a latter-day Crusoe — is resolved comparatively painlessly: of all Franconia's geographical attractions rivers feature most prominently in *Die Flaschenpost*, for rivers take travellers away *and* bring them back.

The collection consists of forty-seven poems divided into four roughly equal sections — 'Jugendlegende', 'Buch der Familienbilder', 'Weltfahrt' and 'Heimkehr'. The headings indicate the stages of the poet's life: by 1936 his days of wide-ranging travel were long over and he was back home. The contrast between *Die Flaschenpost* and its predecessor, *Tier rang*, is stark. Obviously, sixteen years on, the subject matter is different, although the First World War, or rather war in general, receives two or three slight references. Formal differences are even sharper. There are no sonnets in the later collection, and while the line lengths vary considerably in *Die Flaschenpost*, none is longer than twenty-two syllables and thus falls far short of the standard shape of the poems in *Tier rang*. Rhyming, some as ingenious as ever, remains very important to the poet: only 'Indianer' (I, 156) does not rhyme.

In the 'Jugendlegende' section of *Die Flaschenpost*, as Schnack takes us through memories of his childhood games and wanderings along the Saale, of his schooldays and schoolfriends, he draws up a gallery of other key figures working in the Franconian countryside and on Franconia's rivers — huntsmen, boatmen, fishermen, foresters, farmers, the 'Flur- und Weinschütz', all creating within him a deep respect for rural authority, for their special knowledge and expertise, for the traditions they represent, for the way in which their continuing existence is a unique link with the past. They are vigilant guardians of something precious; a kind of eternity attaches to them and to the jobs which they do. 'Der Flur- und Weinschütz' is singled out for particular praise:

> Kenner aller Spuren in dem Lehm der Fluren,
> Wissender und Weiser, liebte alle Reiser,
> Wetterwechsel wurde ihm geheimnisvoll gewahr. (I, 158)

Schnack's almost religious reverence for the countryside and for those who preside over it and look after it is evident, but it is certainly the countryside of his childhood, it is *his* countryside, appropriated by his remembering. Other more exotic figures

---

64   See the poem 'In Bereitschaft', I, 81.

take their place alongside the local heroes. His school atlas and his stamp collection
set him thinking about smugglers, pirates, even a gold-digger. Stamps inspire him:

> Schicksal war eingebrannt der Marke,
> Schicksal schrie aus dem Bilderfeld.
> Dem Knaben war sie Träumerbarke:
> Sie fuhr ihn in die weite Welt.
> ('Die Briefmarke', 1, 161)

The promise of danger and excitement is almost irresistible, and it is perhaps the
'Handwerksburschen', the travelling journeymen, residual figures from a Romantic
Novelle by Eichendorff or Keller, who personify the vagrant spirit which so appeals
to him: 'Denn Handwerksburschen waren wunderbar: | Sie zogen durch das ganze
Jahr' ('Fränkischer Gendarm', 1, 158). It is with mixed emotions that the lyrical self
regards the journeymen's nomadic life, for *his* homeland always calls him back. It
is also with mixed emotions that he sees another boy playing the games he used
to play, but at least that means that there is a kind of unbroken continuity, that
something invaluable is being preserved:

> O and'rer Knabe mit den and'ren Haaren,
> Auch du wirst sie [Die Fränkische Saale] in deinem
> Herzen stets bewahren. ('Die Fränkische Saale', 1, 154)

In the second section, 'Buch der Familienbilder', attention switches from childhood
memories of the Franconian countryside to family members, real and imagined.
The poet's task is clear — to establish and consolidate links with his past and to
honour his ancestors:

> Ich sah die Hessen und die Franken,
> Die Niedersachsen aus dem Moor,
> Ich sah die Dicken und die Schlanken,
> Die Kerngesunden und die Kranken;
> Aus allen sprang ich jäh empor.
> ('Buch der Familienbilder', 1, 164)

A gold-digger from Hessen, a cavalryman with the Bavarian Uhlans, the huntsman
with the robber's skin, the uncle on the father's side who has gone missing — he
is proud to be their heir. There is even a hint of scandal in the family's history,
between a 'Magd' and a 'Bursche': 'Die Mägdekammer wurde nachts nicht
zugeriegelt, | Die Burschentritte schlichen leiser.' ('Legende aus dem Ahnenbuch',
1, 168.) The maid came to a tragic end by drowning herself, but the opportunity is
taken to keep her story alive, to shake the dust from the history books, by claiming
it as part of his past. Myth, legend, folksong, ballad, runes, fairy tales — all figure in
the portrayal of his ancestors, and once again it is the forests, 'forests of the fathers',
forests trodden by his forebears, which are the natural source of all these messages
and magical narratives from the past:

> Aus den Wäldern, die Deutschland bedecken,
> Kommen die Märchen der Kinder,
> Die stillen, süßen, die kaum erschrecken:
> Schneewittchen glänzt im Waldwinter. ('Wald der Vater', 1, 169)

After all, he knows a great deal about the ancient forests because his predecessors lived and worked in them. Carrying on as their heir, he feels thoroughly at home in those same forests:

> Ich weiß noch viel von der Zeit in den Wäldern,
> [...]
> In den Wäldern, unterm Schattengewölbe der Bäume,
> Im Rauschen und Wipfelgebrause,
> Glühen Uraugen und glückliche Ahnenträume:
> In den Wäldern bin ich zu Hause. ('Wald der Väter', I, 170)

And being at home in these forests, not just in the forests of Franconia, he has learnt a lot about them, about the routines of the people who have lived and worked in them down the ages (this is the force of 'Uraugen' and 'Ahnenträume'). If this sounds far-fetched and bizarre, it is matched by what he claims for his maternal past. In the poem 'Die Mütter' (I, 164–65), he does not, as one might have expected, refer to 'meine Mutter': instead, he seems to be saying that through the ages, down the length of his family's past, all the mothers have wept over him and watched over him and they are still indissolubly linked to him. By implication he is more closely bonded to 'Mutter', than to fathers who are traditionally combative and violent, all the more so because she has 'conquered death' and is, therefore, presumably living on in him ('Mutter ist Blume, aus Demut gemacht, | Mutter besiegt den Tod', I, 164). Schnack thus seeks to place himself in a long line of his forebears and to insist that they survive in him, in the same way as he implies that the magic and the myths of the primordial forests are still accessible to him. 'Bild vom Väter' (I, 165–66) also contains a poignant picture of a father who missed out on the travelling which, by implication, his son enjoyed:

> Was blieb ihm [dem Vater] von seinem Leben?
> Was hat Leben ihm gegeben?
> Dunkles Blatt der Efeureben,
> Sah er je das ungeheure Meer? (I, 166)

But even such a downbeat portrait is part of a project to show that time can be defeated and to imbue life with a sense of continuity and permanence. The family line stretches back a long way. With a little imagining it can be glamorised and dramatised, even manipulated. Bold assertions can be made: it lives on in him, he claims, and the Uhlan horseman is not (yet) dead:

> Straffes Mannsgesicht,
> Rotgegerbt von bösen Regengüssen,
> Pulverschwarz von Karabinerschüssen,
> Tot bist du noch nicht! ('Der ein Reiter war', I, 167)

The third section, 'Weltfahrt', is a series of paeans to the pleasures of travel to places Schnack knows from personal experience and to destinations conjured up by his imagination. He is a time-traveller and identifies himself with the great explorer Columbus. The preferred mode of transport is certainly boats and all that they connote of wild seas, pirates, sunken islands, exotic spices and gigantic fish   after all, 'Krebsgeborene haben Glück auf Wasserreisen' (I, 175–76), and Schnack, born on 21 July, was a 'Krebsgeborener' himself. 'Real' places — southern France, Berlin, Würzburg, Munich — jostle alongside undefined equatorial and tropical countries and magical lands like Atlantis. 'Das Fabelland' is a favourite destination. He is certainly happiest on the move because potentially magical encounters beckon:

> Holde Abenteuer wandern mit,
> Mädchenblicke, weich wie Samt,
> Küsse trägt hinweg der Schritt
> Von der Liebe, die vorübergehend flammt
> Und die keine Abschiedsschmerzen litt.
> [...]
> Und die Wanderschaft wird wunderbar.
> Und vielleicht, daß dir ein Gott begegnet,
> Der dich küßt auf das verstaubte Haar.
> ('Mond im Krebs oder Waage ziehe man über Land!', I, 183)

It is not just with fictional heroes that Schnack identifies himself. The last poem in this section, 'Der mit Konradin geritten ist', takes us to a very different time and place, namely thirteenth-century Germany, and tells the story of the knight Konradin, born in Bavaria, riding south to fight 'das Königskind der Hohenstaufen' and losing his life in the campaign. It is not clear, we are told, who or what was to blame for his death. In the final stanza, switching to the present and thus somehow saving the hero across the centuries, the lyrical I wonders if indeed Konradin lives on:

> Weiß ich, ob nicht froh im südlichen Sorrent
> Kinder spielen unterm Staufenwappen,
> Weiß ich, ob nicht von dem Schwabenknappen
> Ein verblaßtes Blau in ihren Augen brennt! (I, 184–85)

The return to a long distant past, in this case medieval Germany, is not quite unique in *Die Flaschenpost*: there is also a fleeting reference to ancient history in the poem 'Die Brücke' (I, 194–95), to 'ein Römerstein. | Er war blutrot, verrufen und gemein' on an unnamed bridge. But it would be potentially unjustified to attempt to load essentially slight poems with excessively heavy interpretation. Even if, as the poem 'Der mit Konradin geritten ist' suggests, Konradin's spirit is still alive, there is no question, as there was no serious question with the novel *Der finstere Franz*, of this poem representing some kind of historical camouflage or allegory with Konradin resuscitated as a latter-day hero nobly sacrificing himself in a good cause for his country. Konradin's name and fate are invoked simply to lend a quota of exotic glamour and to make the point that, in the poet's world, a heroic past never dies. But that past is not shown to have any relevance to present circumstances in Germany in the mid-1930s. An SOS is not being sent.

In section IV, 'Heimkehr', the joy the lyrical I feels on his return to his homeland is even greater than the expectation he felt on setting out on his world travels. He can barely wait to see familiar sights, especially during the month of August:

> Göttlicher August,
> Blau und heiß vom Sonnenkuß,
> Wälder, Meer und Heimatfluß
> Sind Geschenke seiner Lust. ('Lied an den August', 1, 191)

And there is always the promise of romance now that he is back home:

> Eine Türe geht am Nachbarhaus:
> Mädchenliebe hat an mich gedacht. (1, 191)

In a way, he suggests, he did not actually ever leave his homeland because his memories of particular places, sights, smells, wine-fuelled celebrations and quince and other local fruits were so intense that, as it were, he took them all away with him. When he returns he identifies so strongly with them that he virtually becomes them. Everything else may be cursed by time passing, but because an aura of eternity attaches to all the features of his homeland. He singles out particularly the river Main, the days he spent playing on the banks of that river in his childhood will also be magically preserved in perpetuity:

> Ich ging nie von dir fort,
> Fort ging das Rad der Zeit,
> Verflucht, geweiht.
> Aus Tagen wurde Ewigkeit,
> Doch du und ich sind noch das gleiche Wort!
> ('Dem Main gewidmet', 1, 188)

'Zeit' — 'geweiht' — 'Ewigkeit': time, hallowed, eternity. He takes great solace from the fact that the river has roared since time immemorial through the weir, that girls have always, it seems, sung in the clover fields and that fishermen have always slit open the belly of the white fish. He himself is 'eternities old' like the river:

> Du bist mir gut bekannt von je und eh;
> Denn ich bin wie du ewigkeitenalt. (1, 187)

Sometimes, though, he needs to jog his memory, and he does this by asking himself questions to which he always finds ready answers:

> Mancher Wein stand vor mir ganz allein.
> Wo und wann? Die Stunden waren bitter,
> Leben schien Gefangenschaft und Gitter
> [...]
> Doch es löste sich die dumpfe Schwere
> Und ich dachte an die großen Meere. ('Worte vom Wein', 1, 189)

Bread in particular becomes a symbol of a permanent tradition: the smell of it being baked, the sight of mother cutting it, the way in which it has become a universal staple of human diet, the fact that it is a perennial and necessary companion on all his wanderings and adventures — all this combines to make it a particularly treasured memory (see the poem 'Worte vom Brot', 1, 188–89). Plants and fruits and animals are named, not with Wilhelm Lehmann's painstakingly scientific professionalism and exhausting thoroughness, but regularly enough to bring life to the natural landscape — grapes, sloes, mushrooms, apples, brambles, raspberries, larks, crickets, deer. However, he reserves his warmest praise for wine, grapes, vineyards and the celebrations which go with them. A fleeting reference to the First World War, barely more than a quizzical aside ('Was ist mit dem Mitabsolventen Johann Aloisius Bull? | Ist er gefallen im Kriege oder wurde er in fremden Ländern Konsul?', 'Das Gedicht vom Nachdenken', I, 149), does nothing to disturb the domestic idyll, and the two allusions to poverty in the poem 'Fränkischer Gendarm' (I, 157–58) cannot be said to bear any relationship to contemporary deprivations.[65] These are, at all events, erased by the glorious confidence of the last poem in the collection. Having sought throughout the volume to show that the landscapes of his childhood and the people who moved through them are securely enshrined in a kind of eternal recurrence, Schnack declares that poetry too will accompany natural phenomena into eternity:

> Sie [Gedichte] werden sein, solange sich Jahre erneuern,
> Solange Wasser ein Tal durchfließt,
> Solange Gewitter Blitze in die Sommernacht feuern
> Und Regen aus Novemberhimmeln grau sich gießt:
> ('Verteidigung der Gedichte', I, 198)

Poems will be ubiquitous and for all time. 'Verteidigung der Gedichte' is the most moving, impressive poem in *Die Flaschenpost* because the lyrical I does not intervene, does not narrow the perspective and thus a kind of untypical universality attaches to the poem's 'message':

> Wo ein Herz sich öffnet, wo ein Herz zerbricht,
> Blüht das Gedicht. (I, 198)

Ironically, however, this final couplet points to an essential weakness in the collection. *Heart*-felt emotion is rarely evident in a series of poems which often bear the hallmarks of a mixture of tourist brochure,[66] geography lecture and avuncular reminiscence. They are innocent of irony and satire, content to trace the contours of a benevolent, acceptable world and unlikely to set the pulse racing.

The form of the poems in the collection is very varied — rhyming couplets, regular and irregular quatrains, five-six-seven-line stanzas rhyming abaabccc. 'Indianer' (I, 156–57) is the exception with its sprawling lines culminating in a nine-line block of unrhyming lines. Everywhere else there seems to be a determination to keep line and rhyme well under control, and a clear shape is always discernible. What is most evidently carried over from the *Tier rang* cycle is his astonishing ingenuity in creating unusual, eye-catching rhymes, often triple rhymes. There are innumerable examples of this virtuosity: 'getuscht', 'bebuscht', 'hindurchgehuscht'; 'raubfischkühn', 'glühn', 'grün'; 'Einsamkeit', 'Sintflutzeit'; 'Schlangenhäuten', 'Kaufleuten'; 'Donauwörth', 'gehört'; even 'Liverpool', 'Wirtshausstuhl'. Sometimes huge compound nouns are marshalled into rhymes: 'Urwaldfaktorei', 'Papageischrei'; 'Bergwerkstollen',

---

65   For example, the lines 'Die grauen Schuhe [of the young journeymen] zeigten nackte Zehen. | Sie waren ärmer als die Kirchenmaus. | Er [the local policeman] ließ sie ungeschoren, unbesehen' in the poem 'Fränkischer Gendarm' (I, 157–58).
66   The anonymous obituarist in the *Frankfurter Allgemeine Zeitung*, 11 October 1973 calls Schnack 'ein Reiseschriftsteller'.

'Lawinenrollen'; 'Hochstaplergesicht', 'Mitternachtslicht'. Occasionally a large compound noun is made to sit rather ludicrously alongside a very short substantive — 'Schlapphutwirte', 'Hirte'. In the six five-line stanzas which make up the poem 'Die Regengüsse' the last word of the first line rhymes each time with 'Regenguß', the final word of the last line (I, 196–97). There are, on the other hand, examples of poor rhyming: 'Kleider', 'Reiter'; 'blasen', 'durchmaßen'; 'geblasen', 'Straßen'. The effect is not, as one might have expected from such extended confections, one of ponderous unwieldiness, but rather of innocuous and humorous whimsicality.

A predilection for verbs, especially past participles, beginning with the prefixes 'ver-' and 'zer-' is also a familiar habit noted in the earlier volumes — 'vermorscht', 'verkrallt', 'verkratzt', 'verwacht', 'dornzerrissen', 'wutzerkrallt', 'zersprungen' are a few of the more idiosyncratic examples. Carrying their traditional resonances of decay, decline and disintegration, they indicate the effect of time passing, one of the themes of the volume, and are often conspicuous among poems which are essentially optimistic and enthusiastic. In order to underline the local nature of some of the sights and sounds which inform the poems of *Die Flaschenpost*, Schnack does not hesitate to use unusual vocabulary — 'Schmöker', 'Vogelzeh', 'knarzen', 'Wasserschwappeln' (rhyming with 'Zappeln' and 'Pappeln'), 'gewunken', 'gepriemt', 'stakten', 'affenbehend', 'Spelz'. Some of the compound forms — 'abenteuerglanzgespeisten', especially as it overwhelms its noun 'Tage' — seem ludicrous ('Dem Main gewidmet', I, 187), and while one can admire the trio 'vogelkalkbedeckt', 'versteckt' and 'bedeckt' ('Die Brücke', I, 195), 'schwarzbestaubt' and 'pappelblattbelaubt' ('Die Brücke', I, 194) probably tip the balance into indulgence. At its best, though, Schnack's inventiveness in this regard is a strong feature of his poetry and remains so through all his volumes of verse.

There is, as has been argued, nothing behind and beyond Schnack's poems in *Die Flaschenpost*. When in the poem 'Die Flaschenpost des Kolumbus' we read

> Hinter allen Wogen schien das Ende,
> Hinter allen Wolken brauste Nacht. (I, 176)

we can take the couplet only at face value: we know by now that these lines stand for themselves alone and have no mysterious, insinuative shadow-life. There is no sense of an encoded message and there are no layers of possible meanings because the web of resonances and illusions around 'message in a bottle' is not exploited. In their compendious study of 'Verdeckte Schreibweise' during the Nazi regime Heidrun Ehrke-Rotermund und Erwin Rotermund list the methods used by some writers to deceive the Nazi censors — 'Schreiben zwischen den Zeilen', 'verschlüsseltes Schreiben', 'Camouflage', 'Tarnung', 'sublime Rede' and 'Darstellung in Chiffren'.[67] Few, if any, of these ploys can be detected in the poems which Schnack wrote in the 1930s, because, we assume, he had no desire to challenge the authorities, whereas the verse collections of the four writers referred to at the beginning of this chapter are characterized by more or less subtle techniques of misdirection, indirection and suggestion. Bergengruen's poetry, for instance,

---

67   See Heidrun Ehrke-Rotermund und Erwin Rotermund, *Zwischenreiche und Gegenwelten: Texte und Vorstudien zur 'Verdeckten Schreibweise' im 'Dritten Reich'* (Fink, 1999), p. 11.

is backed by a strong political consciousness kept under wraps with increasing difficulty: the title of his 1937 volume *Der ewige Kaiser* is deliberately significant while his 1935 novel *Der Großtyrann und das Gericht* offers a blatant 'Gegenbild' to Nazism.[68] Loerke's poetry is founded in personal anguish ever more eloquently expressed and yet all the time escalating almost beyond control and then into that final, fatal heart attack. His diaries represent one of the best accounts we have of what Hans Carossa calls 'der schauerlichste Hakenkreuzkitsch',[69] the insidious, attritional impact of the regime on the daily life of an essentially honourable man, while his poetry, more subtly,[70] charts the same creeping personal and national decline. Wilhelm Lehmann's *Antwort des Schweigens* (1935) and *Der Grüne Gott* (1942) are characterized by an expert, almost scientific appreciation of nature, by a conviction that the natural world lives by its own independent time-scale and that it thus offers a precious environment to myth, symbol, legend and magic, as well as being a more congenial setting for the modern self. Peter Huchel's poems issue from the discomforting ambiguity of his role of dissenting collaborator in Nazi Germany: by all accounts (for example, his own after 1945) he wanted to dissent, by all appearances he was collaborating.[71] Though his poetry may seem remote from political realities, it expresses feelings of loneliness and fear, even dread, which are an implicit response to the politics of his time.[72]

In their very different ways all four of these contemporary poets offer 'ideelle Alternativen zum herrschenden Regime [...] Gegenwelten [...] die Qualität eines zeitenthobenen tieferen Seins (Heilsgeschichte, mittelalterlicher Reichsgedanke, überdauernde Naturordnung, antiker Mythos, humanistische Bildungsidee)'.[73] Of course, thanks to what Christian Adam calls the 'Kompetenz-Wirrwarr' prevailing between Rosenberg's and Goebbels's offices and the absence of any coordinated party policy on censorship,[74] a less discreet kind of poetry was possible — for example, Friedrich Georg Jünger's 'Der Mohn',[75] some of Reinhold Schneider's sonnets, Rudolf Hagelstange's (admittedly later) *Venezianisches Credo* (1945) and Georg Kaiser's astonishing poems 'Das Batzenschwein' (Goering) and 'Rosinen im Kot' (the Reichsschriftumskammer).[76] In these cases the full force of the prepositional prefix in 'Gegen-welt' and 'Gegen-bild' comes into focus.[77]

68   See also Bergengruen's allegorical poem 'Arges Haus' (1936).
69   In a letter to Hedwig Kerber, 10 June 1933, in Hans Carossa, *Briefe II 1919–1936*, ed. by Eva Campmann-Carossa (Insel, 1978), p. 288.
70   Although there is nothing at all subtle about the heavily ironic 1934 poem 'Genesungsheim' in Oskar Loerke, *Die Gedichte*, ed. by Peter Suhrkamp (Suhrkamp, 1958), p. 440.
71   See Stephen Parker's *Peter Huchel: A Literary Life in 20th Century Germany* (Peter Lang, 1998) for an excellent account of Huchel's life and work.
72   Not only the famous 'Havelnacht', Peter Huchel, *Die Gedichte* (Suhrkamp, 1984), pp. 88–89, but also 'Deutschland' (ibid., p. 99).
73   Ehrke-Rotermund and Rotermund, p. 9.
74   Christian Adam, *Lesen unter Hitler* (Galiani, 2010), pp. 15 and 19.
75   See Rotermund, pp. 513–19 for an analysis of Jünger's 1934 poem.
76   In these poems, published in 1936, Hitler appears as 'Der Kaulbarsch', Goebbels as 'Das Scheißhuhn', Rosenberg as 'Der Mistbock' etc. Georg Kaiser, *Werke*, IV, ed. by Walther Huder (Ullstein, 1971), pp. 667–69.
77   For general background information on the question of 'Innere Emigration', see Ehrke-

And Schnack? It can be argued that, despite his predilection for what he subsequently called 'eine Literatur der Unbekümmertheit',[78] he too offered a kind of counter-image in *Die Flaschenpost*: there is, after all, a constant quest for solace in nature, a regular retreat to the past and an occasional historical reference. But there is a crucial difference between, say, Schnack's depiction of nature and Lehmann's. For Lehmann nature represents something 'other', independent, a timeless monolith, indestructible, accessible (if at all) only to the detached expert, the natural scientist, and man is at best a privileged visitor with no proprietorial claims on nature. With Schnack it is solely a question of *his* past and *his* experience of nature within a very limited chronological and geographical frame, of creating 'mein kleines geistiges Reich'[79] so that we end up with a sequence of attractive vignettes and pastels, nothing approaching a mirror of his times and rarely, it seems, issuing from deep emotional engagement. The memory and the response invoked are always Schnack's own, he does not shift beyond the personal, and the lyrical self is inserted into all depictions of an idealized nature. The unambiguous message of *Tier rang* was, however, that under pressure, in crisis, the self is not only embattled, but highly vulnerable: nature and indeed memory thus viewed cannot be timeless. If we impose that message on *Die Flaschenpost* — that in dire circumstances, be it the First World War or the 'verruchtes Jahrzwölft',[80] the self is in mortal danger — the later collection gives us neither a desperate self nor intolerable circumstances. Its gently nostalgic quest for timelessness has not stood the test of time.

★   ★   ★   ★   ★

Although *Der Annoncenleser* was originally published in 1948, an extended new version of the volume, *'Jene Dame, welche...'*, was produced in 1953[81] and so the volume *Mittagswein* (1948) will be considered next. *Mittagswein* consists of thirty-four poems, seven undated, written in a wholly familiar form. As always lengths of lines vary though poems composed of couplets or more or less regularly shaped quatrains (and five-line stanzas) predominate. There are no sonnets. Every poem without exception rhymes, and there is no relaxing of Schnack's customary prosodic ingenuity. The earliest ('Herbstliche Nacht', I, 221–22) is dated 15 September 1924, the latest ('Das Gedicht vom Marmor', I, 211–12) 9 February 1944. Seven were published before 1936, that is before *Die Flaschenpost*, and some of these (for example 'Schiff meiner Sehnsucht', I, 218–19) would fit seamlessly into that volume. What

---

Rotermund and Rotermund; Bergengruen (especially his *Dichtergehäuse* and *Schreibtischerinnerungen* (Nymphenburger, 1961)); Alfred Andersch, *Die Kirschen der Freiheit*, ed. by C. A. H. Russ (Heinemann, 1979); *Flight of Fantasy: New Perspectives on Inner Emigration in German Literature 1933–1945*, ed. by Neil H. Donahue and Doris Kirchner (Berghahn, 2003); *Die deutsche Literatur im Dritten Reich*, ed. by Horst Denkler and Karl Prümm (Reclam, 1976); and Ralf Schnell, *Literarische innere Emigration* and the same author's *Dichtung in finsteren Zeiten* (Rowohlt, 1998).

78   A. Schnack, 'Literatur-Prognose', *Freude an Büchern*, I (1953), p. 6.

79   The phrase is Carossa's, who may, of course, not be aware of the irony implicit in these words. See Carossa, *Briefe II*, letter to Katharina Kippenberg, 17 May 1933.

80   Werner Bergengruen, *Schreibtischerinnerungen* (Nymphenburger, 1961), p. 76.

81   I, 433.

is particularly interesting, however, is that twenty-one of the twenty-seven dated poems were published in *Simplicissimus*, a magazine founded in Munich in 1896, which had begun as a cultural review, but had quickly become a hugely popular satirical publication. It attracted contributions from, among many others, Heinrich and Thomas Mann, Rilke, Hugo von Hofmannsthal, Robert Walser, Frank Wedekind (known as Hieronymus Jobs) and, later, Joachim Ringelnatz, Käthe Kollwitz, Kurt Tucholsky ('Theobald Tiger') and Erich Kästner. Its principal targets, usually caricatured in striking visual images, were the bourgeoisie (especially rather obese businessmen), the church, the military, officialdom, Wilhelminian politicians and various political groupings. It spared no one: it was banned in Austria-Hungary. By 1929 it was assailing extreme political factions on the left and the right, not least the National Socialists: the cover of the Fasching edition of 19 February 1933 headed 'Sabotage' is an illustration of an orgy composed of clowns and masked figures, all looking suspiciously like the recently anointed Adolf Hitler. However, within weeks of Hitler's becoming Chancellor *Simplicissimus* was 'gleichgeschaltet' and, to the horror of such emigrants as Heinrich Mann, consistently toed the party line until (and including) its final publication on 13 September 1944.[82] For those eleven years it delivered propaganda for Nazi Germany, developing a paranoiac hatred of everything foreign and, in 1939, supporting the war effort. Of the twenty-one poems in *Mittagswein* which were published in the magazine none was published before 1933. Schnack's habit of avoiding, or, rather, not appearing in, *Simplicissimus* in its peak satirical years is reflected throughout his work: none of the poems in the three early Expressionist volumes, in *Tier rang* and the fifty-five 'verstreut veröffentlichte expressionistische Gedichte'[83] appeared in the magazine. Twenty of the thirty-three poems of *Die Flaschenpost* were there, all after January 1933, and of the ninety-three uncollected poems forty-six were published in *Simplicissimus*, but only six before January 1933.[84] It is difficult to avoid the conclusion that, unsurprisingly, editors of *Simplicissimus* selected Schnack's poems, and he put poems forward to them, only when it was mutually expedient to do so. As a writer he naturally wanted to see his work published, but the fact remains that of his 409 published poems only six found their way into Germany's premier satirical magazine when it was at its most aggressive. His essentially quietistic attitude to world events barely faltered.

Not that *Mittagswein* manifests any of the xenophobic tendencies evident in *Simplicissimus* between 1933 and 1944. In fact, the collection is founded in a localized conservatism which reveals itself in two familiar ways. First, there is the abiding love of Franconia and the unquestioning reverence for nature, or rather, for those natural phenomena such as rivers, hills, mountains, the West Wind, forests and the tracks which migrating birds follow, all of which, for Schnack, betoken eternity. Such phenomena have been there since time immemorial ('urweltlich', 'Urmeer',

82   Ruprecht Konrad sums up the death-throes of the magazine thus: 'In geduldeter Belanglosigkeit siechte der *Simplicissimus* dahin [between 1933 and 1942].' See his 'Nationale und internationale Tendenzen im *Simplicissimus* (1896–1933)' (unpublished doctoral thesis, Ludwig-Maximilians-Universität-München, 1975), p. 200.

83   I, 101–46.

84   I, 299–419.

'Urzeitenbooten' occur in these descriptions of nature), they have always been there and always will be:

> Im Unmaß steiler Absturzseiten [of Mount Göll]
> Rauschen des Urmeers große Gezeiten,
> Donnern Lawinen der Ewigkeiten.
> ('Der Hohe Göll bei Berchtesgaden', 1, 215)

The mountains and forests of Bavaria have traditionally accommodated gods and mythological figures, creatures of legend and fantasy who, like present-day inhabitants (hunters, climbers, shepherds, fishermen, farmers, gatherers of timber, all outdoor types), symbolize eternal natural values and survival in a threatened world. The eternal laws which govern nature are seen once again, implicitly, as a refuge and solace against life's crises and time's erosion. The conservative in Schnack rails against time's passing:

> Ach, wie schnell die Tage kommen und vergehen!
> ('Beeren des Herbstes', 1, 224)

In the same way as snow and rain (the subject of a number of poems in the collection) have always fallen, rivers particularly (the Main, the Inn, the Saale and the Salzach) are for the poet symbolic of eternity. They take the traveller away and are always there to bring him back, but, even more significantly, they renew and immortalize themselves by flowing into vast oceans:

> Der Inn verschlingt wütend die Salzachschlange
> Auf seinem Donaudrang,
> Vereint, aber zankend, und Wange an Wange
> Stürzen sie sich im Überschwange
> In die grünliche Donau, die mütterlich bang
> Sie aufnimmt in ihren großen Gesang.
> ('Die Salzach im Bayrischen', 1, 216)

The image here is clear: the larger river, the Danube, instinctively absorbs the smaller (the adverb 'mütterlich' and the accusative case in the last phrase underline the solicitous nature of the phenomenon), and the larger river itself will ultimately flow into one of the world's oceans (the 'Urmeer'),[85] thus achieving immortality. It is quite simply the natural order of things, and the lyrical I, following the example of one of his deeply admired and envied journeymen ('Handwerksburschen'), longs to travel the same river to foreign lands and, perhaps, find the same kind of immortality himself ('Es zuckt mein Herz von seiner Wandergier', 'Der Handwerksbursche in der Familie', 1, 209).

The second aspect of the lyrical I's conservatism is the familiar recourse to remembrance of times past. Details of life in Hammelburg where Schnack went to the Lateinschule for eight years, time spent wandering through the lanes, skating, observing the way in which the snow magically covers both city and landscape, and reciting bedtime prayers — all feature in these tranquil, studiously uncontroversial reminiscences, as do particular places, a timber yard, an inn in an Alpine pass and a farmer's garden with comically shaped cucumbers ('Gurke in einem bayerischen

---

85   See the poem 'Der Hohe Göll bei Berchtesgaden' (1, 214–15).

Bauerngarten', I, 216–17), and mysterious figures like the spectral trapper whom Schnack claims as an ancestor in 'Der Trapper Schnack' (I, 207–08). All the time homage is paid to nature in its eternal aspects — the way fruits (hazelnuts, rowan berries, damson plums ['Zwetschgen'] and grapes) appear every year, the reliability of the seasons ('Der Oktober', I, 222–23), the annual harvests and local, domestic routines. At this point Schnack's poetry can be seen to be approaching Lehmann's and certainly to be returning to many of the images familiar to us from *Die Flaschenpost*. As with the poems in that collection, the poet's ambition is modest, the emotional range is narrow, the reader's pulse (and the poet's) does not quicken, the quest for eternal values is insistent, but controlled. In the poem 'Alter Stich vom April' (I, 220–21), the description of human and of nature's activity in and around an old engraving ends: 'Ewig ist das Bild'. The images and themes in Mörike's famous 'Auf eine Lampe' are clearly discernible here.

But discordant notes are struck in the repeated image of a beautiful surface hiding something sinister, of something lying beneath — be it a frozen lake concealing 'ein Sumpfgeist' (presumably a creature from a homely yet demonic natural mythology) and a 'Schwedendolch' (presumably a relic of the Thirty Years War)[86] or the snow covering 'das Grab des Mädchens, das der Liebende umschlang' ('Was der Schnee bedeckt', I, 229) or rivers peopled by frozen corpses ('Die Flüsse', I, 220). Moreover, it is extremely tempting to read a great deal more into what I regard as the collection's best poem (published in 1936), 'Gewitter über Franken'. It is apparently 'only' a description of a monstrous black cloud building up over a silent Franconian landscape: the trees, the hills, the fields, the streams, the damson plums, all the things which, the poet confesses, he loves will not be able to bear 'kalte, schräggepeitschte Hagelhiebe'. 'Mir ist in Franken vieles teuer' is repeated, but the threat is huge, and the language is dynamic. The visual power of Schnack's imagery, the threatening edge to the language (in the harsh consonants, the k, z, t, g sounds) and the tension as the ground below waits for the storm to break are unmistakable:

> Das große Wetter ist zerrissen
> Und aufgelöst in weiße, fliehende Wolkenkissen.
> Es hat den Bauernzaun, dahinter Lilien stehen, hin- und hergerüttelt,
> Die dürren Äste von den Straßenpappeln abgeschüttelt. (I, 232)

The determination to keep the rhyming going when a natural phenomenon is wreaking havoc on nature is wholly typical of Schnack's methods. While we may balk at such confections as 'schnabelabgestreift' ('Der Regen', I, 228) and 'pelzvermummten' ('Der Trapper Schnack', I, 207) and reel in front of the monstrous compound 'feuerspandurchfunkelt' (ibid.), the ingenuity of devising 'lichtgerändert' rhyming with 'blitzbebändert' ('Gewitter über Franken', I, 231), 'hergerüttelt' with 'abgeschüttelt' ('Gewitter über Franken', I, 232) and the triple rhyming 'gesäumt', 'mondüberschäumt', 'träumt' ('Holzplatz in Bayern', I, 217), and many more, deserves acknowledgement. Bearing in mind all we know of Schnack's obstinately guarded seclusion and apparently inflexible apolitical stance,

---

86   See the poem 'Der zugefrorene See', I, 204–05.

perhaps we should leave 'Gewitter über Franken' to be what it claims to be, and, in practice, becomes — a magnificent depiction of a storm brewing and breaking over Franconia, with, in its last couplet, the promise of an exhilarating renewal. For the same reason, the much earlier 'Herbstliche Nacht' (I, 221), mysterious, melancholy, slightly sinister, recalling Georg Trakl in tone and imagery, prefiguring the unease which resonates in the poetry of Peter Huchel, is of sufficiently high quality to stand on its own terms.

★   ★   ★   ★   ★

Der Annoncenleser (1947) consists of twenty-nine poems: beneath the title of each one is a brief telegrammatic description of what is being sought, offered or announced. As it turns out, the poems in this volume are not only about advertisements or about the people and things being advertised: they are also about the 'reader' who uses that material to set his imagination or his memory free. Whatever advertisements, by their very nature, lose in lyrical eloquence, they gain in factual pragmatism and potential usefulness. By resorting to this form Schnack is aligning himself with the 'Gebrauchslyriker' of the 1920s and 1930s, key members of the 'Neue Sachlichkeit' movement, and thus joins the company of better known proponents such as Bertolt Brecht, Kurt Tucholsky, Joachim Ringelnatz, Erich Kästner, Walter Mehring and Mascha Kaléko. Of these Mehring certainly introduced advertisements into his poetry,[87] but there do not appear to be examples of a writer using them for the same purpose as Schnack — to comment on, and draw conclusions from, a series of self-created advertisements over the extent of a whole collection of poems. In another way, too, his poems are very different from those of his contemporaries. 'Gebrauchslyrik', written at a particular time for a particular purpose in the name of a given cause, was intended to be of practical use and was invariably concerned with specific social and political problems to which the poet, writing in easily accessible and clearly comprehensible image-free unsentimental verse, wished to draw his readers' attention. The tone could be sardonic and heavily ironic (as with Brecht), wry and humorous (as with Kästner) or fiercely comical and bitter (as with Ringelnatz and Tucholsky). The authorities might, in fact, be the first to pay attention, as was the case with Mascha Kaléko's best-known work, *Das lyrische Stenogrammheft* (1933). Her depiction, laced with sharp political comment, of the drab lives and the economic and financial suffering of ordinary people in Berlin was immediately seized and burnt by the Nazis, who banned her from further publication.

Schnack's purpose in *Der Annoncenleser* seems to have been completely different: the twenty dated poems follow the customary pattern — thirteen were published in *Simplicissimus*, only two before the watershed of January 1933,[88] and only two later than 1938.[89] According to Hartmut Vollmer, Schnack was very aware of the cultural

---

87   Midgley, pp. 72–73.
88   'Todesanzeige' (9 March 1931), I, 269 and 'Kegelbahn' (25 May 1931), I, 263–64. Neither carries more than a slight political or satirical edge: the latter hints at Schnack's awareness of environmental damage.
89   'Möbliertes Zimmer zu vermieten' (4 February 1943), I, 242–43, and 'Wer erteilt Unterricht' (24

and emotional devastation wrought by the Second World War:

> Er [Schnack] selbst war sich 1947 bewußt, daß es vorläufig 'in Deutschland
> keine einheitliche literarische Schicht mehr' gibt und daß 'die große Masse
> des Volkes' 'seelisch zerstört, entwurzelt und deprimiert ist'.[90] Vor diesem
> Hintergrund versuchte er, der 'seelischen Zerstörung' entgegen zu schreiben,
> das vernichtete Gefühl glücklicher Existenz zurückzurufen und den Blick für
> die Schönheiten und Merkwürdigkeiten des Lebens phantasieerregend wieder
> zu schulen.[91]

Schnack's response was *not* to write and publish verse in the immediate aftermath
of the war, but to rehash poems written principally in the 1930s. The first of the
poems in the volume is, in fact, an advertisement for what is to follow. It is called
simply 'Gedichte angeboten':

> Ich biete zur öffentlichen Beachtung Gedichte über Zeitungsinserate an,
> Gedichte, die reden vom Leben.[92]

'Poems which speak of life'? This is immediately qualified:

> Gedichte, die beben.
> Beben von den Wundern der Alltäglichkeit, des Gegenständlichen und
> Nahen;
> Gedichte, denen Spott gleich wichtig ist wie Ekstase und frohes Bejahen.

The usual limit is imposed: only 'Wunder[n]' will be regarded as appropriate
material, and, when it comes to it, 'frohes Bejahen' (but not 'Ekstase') outweighs
incursions of 'Spott'. The tone of the volume is indeed one of jaunty optimism
mingled with considerable pathos. The final couplet of the poem indicates where
the emphasis is going to fall:

> Hat es [das Leben] trotz Sorgen, Armut und Plunder
> Nicht auch Geheimnisse, Freuden und Wunder!

This is a statement, a joyous declaration, not a question. For Schnack the 'small ad'
columns of newspapers are alluring and fascinating: they are microcosms of life; they
contain the whole of (a certain section of) society, the well-off middle class with a
rare incursion from the lower classes; they often reveal the quirky sides of human
nature and human aspirations; they appeal in their fragmentary and abbreviated
format to a temperament which prefers the disparate to the coherent and the essay to
the novel. They are the perfect miniature quarries for his imagination and humour
to seek out inspiration and trigger a response.

  Advertisements, unless they are merely announcements of coming events (births
or marriages or concerts), tend to involve possession and loss, items for sale or
people and objects missing and being sought. It is a sense of what has been lost
or missed which predominates in *Der Annoncenleser*. While the 'reader' reflects

November 1943), I, 239–40. Neither refers, for example, to the Second World War and Germany's
part in it.
90   Vollmer gives as his references for these phrases: Anton Schnack: 'Versuch meine Arbeitsweise
zu beschreiben'. Unveröffentlicht, zitiert nach Glöckler (p. 102). I, 472.
91   I, 461.
92   I, 237.

on missing or coveted objects ('eine goldene Brosche mit fünf Aquamarinsteinen und schwarzbunter Chiffonschal am Dienstag in Regensburg bis zur Donaubrücke verloren'[93] — the amount of invented detail is always impressive), he more frequently uses the opportunity to hark back to memories of his own childhood. At least a third of the poems in the collection are heavily self-referenced in this way, but there are also depictions of other people's more desperate human situations: the mother pleading for a job for her fourteen-year-old son ('Der Schuhmacherlehrling', I, 244–45), the children's nanny craving children of her own ('Herhören: mein Herz klopft oft erhitzt, bedrängt, | Bedrängt wodurch, bedrängt wovon? | Warum ist's nicht mein eig'ner Sohn, | Der sich um meine Schultern hängt, | Warum nur fremde Gören?'[94] — the use of the dialect word 'Gören' does nothing to dilute the pathos of this), the woman in her 'early thirties' advertising for a husband ('Heiratsgesuch', I, 248–49) and Frau Elli Kallischan announcing the death of her 'innigstgeliebter Mann' ('Todesanzeige', I, 269). It is no accident that the compound 'Sehnsuchtsschrei' appears twice in these pages.[95] Missed opportunities, the almost-but-not-quite love story, thwarted hopes (swapping glances with a 'J. Frl' on the Nuremberg–Munich express on the 20 July[96]), even personal tragedies ('[...] den armen Kegeljungen, | Den, während er sich bückte, stachen beide Lungen', 'Kegelbahn', I, 264), all appear alongside causes for greater optimism — the joys of sailing, listening to music and sampling different kinds of tea.

Often, too, the tone of the more poignant poems is lightened by a humorous detail — the woman in 'Heiratsgesuch' is looking for a 'prof. Witwer mit Wohnung [...] Trinker und Abenteurer ausgeschlossen' in a pointed reference to Schnack's own personal and poetic past ('Heiratsgesuch', I, 248–49). Indeed, lightly humorous and whimsical touches are a frequent feature: having praised the virtuoso performance of four black jazz pianists the reader of the advertisement asks 'die Frage, ob *der* auch so freundlich sein Gehör wie ich ihnen zuwendet, | *Der* von dem Haus, wo sie *üben*! ...' ('Jazz auf vier Flügeln', I, 260). And as for the elderly men in the bowling alley, bending with difficulty, we learn that 'Der Ehe-Eros hat sie längst verlassen. | Sie sind befriedigt, mit der Kellnerin zu spaßen' ('Kegelbahn', I, 263). Meanwhile it is noted that it is a Herr Streichhölzer who is trying to 'ignite' a relationship with the young lady on the Nuremberg–Munich express and that the impresario, advertised for in the poem 'Impresario gesucht', should be 'pol. unbel.', presumably 'politically clean' (I, 256–57).

Two further aspects of the collection are striking. While book learning and intellectual effort are scorned, presumably a residual consequence of his hated school days (Schnack even creates the verb 'sich zersinnen' to intimate that bookkeeper Daniel Kallischan died from excessive mental strain ('Todesanzeige', I, 269)), Schnack proves to be peculiarly sensitive to life's sadnesses, to what lies behind and lies beneath:

---

93   'Goldene Brosche verloren' (I, 242–44).
94   'Das Kinderfräulein' (I, 258–59).
95   In the poems 'Das Wiedersehen' (I, 251–52) and 'Venezianische Nacht' (I, 253–54).
96   'Die gewechselten Blicke' (I, 247–48).

Denn hinter der Tagesglätte
Blüh'n Sehnsucht und Liebestraum: [...]
('Die gewechselten Blicke', 1, 247)

[...] Wunderliche Wünsche unter Alltagsworten flehen,
Wünsche, heiß, erregend, toll. ('Das Wiedersehen', 1, 251)

He is aware that we can never really know what other people are thinking or feeling; there is a 'secret world' marked by intense feelings (see the poem 'Das Wiedersehen') and, to some extent at least, exposed by advertisements. He wonders about the faces behind the names, the people behind the faces ('Vermählungsanzeige', 1, 252), he reads that people go away, that their lives are ruled by chance, that feelings are too often suppressed, ironically often beneath the everyday events he is extolling, and that people are constantly seeking answers to what he calls 'Fragen des Daseins' (ibid., 1, 252). Such existential experiences can give rise to 'geheime Wunde[n]' (ibid.). These ruminations, often no more than asides or homilies, resonate with the kind of pathos which is missing in the relatively bloodless *Flaschenpost*. In the meantime, Robinson has been killed (see the poem 'Wer erteilt Unterricht?', 1, 239–40), but Grandmother Elise, bustling through her domestic routines ('Trinkt Kräutertee', 1, 261–62), comes alive more than any of the figures invoked in the 'Buch der Familienbilder' section of that volume. The wild sensuality of the three early Expressionist collections has given way to an impressive sensitivity. Retrenchment and cutting of losses (what Schnack in the poem 'Der Angler' (1, 267–68) calls 'Geduld und Weltbeschaulichkeit') are called for: men turn out to be too reserved to make physical advances and the 'ordtl. Mädchen' in 'Heiratsgesuch' learns the harsh lesson that passion, let alone love, withers (1, 248–49). Promising encounters will most likely end up in failure. Apart from brief references to, for example, black jazz pianists, to Gottfried Eis's advertising agency (even here the name Eis 'softens' any edge), to the excessive chopping down of forests (but children's cradles and coffins are still necessary ('Holzversteigerung', 1, 266)) and to one or two business transactions, the modern world of 'technological innovation [...] the robust physicality of popular entertainment [...] invasive "Americanism"'[97] is wholly ignored. Neither car nor train nor any other form of transport is mentioned, similarly with radio and even cinema. Schnack appears much more interested in those anxieties and problems which are the common currency of being human, and he deals with them with a mixture of good humour, gentle irony and considerable compassion.

The second noticeable feature of *Der Annoncenleser* is Schnack's astonishingly rich choice of vocabulary and rhyming words. We are used to the multiple variety of line lengths and his insistence upon rhyme. There is no diminution of his inventiveness here: if anything, he has excelled himself in this late collection. 'Pianisten-Tam-Tam'/'Klangprogramm', 'Verwirrnis'/'Wort-Firnis', 'Yes'/'oui'/'si', 'Foxtrott'/'Gott' (alongside near misses such as 'Renommée'/'Welttournee' and 'Qualsynkopen'/'hergeschoben') are a few among many examples: he is having fun and raising a smile. His tour de force emerges in the poem 'Das Kinderfräulein' (1, 258–59) where the last word of each stanza ends in an '-ören' sound,

---

97   Midgley, p. 22.

making seven rhymes in all. Then there are the ever more startling compound confections — 'aneinandergekutschelt', 'lebkuchengerüchig', 'verhandlungstüchtig' and 'zonenbegehrt'. The sonnets of *Tier rang* had already prepared us for such accumulations. As for the equally impressive range of vocabulary, it can be divided into three principal groupings. First there is the colloquial and dialectal: 'Pensionist', 'verdattert', 'schmoren', 'Gören', 'lappig' ('limp') rhyming amusingly with 'tappig' ('fumbly') in the poem 'Todesanzeige' (I, 269). Then he offers a host of unusual words often with heavy localized connotations: 'gewunken', 'geklaftert', 'die Lefze', 'die Raufe' and 'Nasenpobel'. Finally we have a series of specialist terms which serve to display Schnack's expert knowledge of particular subjects such as plants, the countryside, music, fishing and rural life: 'äsen', 'Lodenjoppen', 'Weitwurf-Spinngerte', 'gespließt' [should it not be 'gespleißt'?], 'der Blinker' and 'hinsintern'. A good deal of research has presumably enabled him not only to praise various types of herbal tea ('Trinkt Kräutertee', I, 261–62), but also to list all their ingredients, and the poem 'Holzversteigerung' (I, 265–66) is a paean to those who live and work in Franconia's forests. All these formal and linguistic features create a strong foundation for the unusually complex range and depth of emotion invoked in this collection and held together by the unifying device of advertisements.

The last line of the poem 'Immobilien' is a jokey prediction of what will appear on Anton Schnack's marble gravestone: 'Hier ruht † 1972 Herr Anton Schnack, Gemeinderat. Gott möge ihm gnädig sein!' (I, 267). Schnack was never to be a local councillor, but otherwise the prediction is not far out: he was to die in 1973. Just as accurate, it turns out, is a fortuitous summary of Schnack's achievement in *Der Annoncenleser*. 'Geschäftsempfehlung', the final poem in the collection, contains the stanza:

> Ingesamt ein ungeheurer Spiegel,
> Schillernd, farbenreich, ein Mosaik;
> Leben kochte mannigfaltig, wie in einem Tiegel,
> Glück und Trauer, Liebe, Mißgeschick. (I, 270)

It may not be 'ein ungeheurer Spiegel' or a seething 'Tiegel', but in an unpretentious way it *is* a 'Mosaik' of 'Glück und Trauer, Liebe, Mißgeschick': there is certainly more to it than emerges at an initial, superficial reading. Exploiting to the full the abbreviated concision of the advertisement and apparently unshackled by the form's intrinsic confines, it is a sensitive audit of the limitations (and limits) of human happiness and ambition.

★　★　★　★　★

Jene Dame, welche...', Schnack's final collection, is an 'extended, new version' of *Der Annoncenleser*.[98] It consists of only fifteen newly added poems (I, 275–96). Each poem again has an advertisement, either making an offer or seeking somebody or something, as a subheading. The same idiosyncratic pattern emerges in the shape of advertisements announcing, for example, a tango-band concert in Munich's 'Kolosseumstraße', the availability of fully equipped apartments, a special New

---

98   I, 433–34.

York hat, a compulsory auction, the death of Nikolaus Merkl in Laufen (Upper Bavaria) and the charms of two Dalmatian hotels. And again there are a few more bizarre instances: lawyer Alfred Schönwiese, for example, is pleased to announce his return from his travels 'so sehr mich auch Meere, Berge, und fremde Frauen freuten' ('Von der Reise zurück', 1, 287–89). The lyrical I, as usual, intrudes: in 'Verlobungsanzeige', for example, where the I reflects wistfully on the fact that Frieda Bickel has selected Johann Kobert, and not Anton Schnack, to be her fiancé (1, 280–81).

What *is* different from *Der Annoncenleser* is that three interlocking themes emerge in short order: all of them are familiar from Schnack's pre-1940 poetry, but tone and emphasis are different. *'Jene Dame, welche...'* circles gently round a concern with the contemporary quest for luxury and the superficial glamour of the modern world, especially when that glamour is represented by the upper classes: Dr Alfred Schönwiese, in his sudden lunge for freedom from his responsibilities as a respected lawyer, for instance, 'trug Knickerbocker zur Schau', and was summoned by a Venetian Duchess 'zu einer Gondelfahrt in den Mondschein [...] als sei er Lord oder gar ein Marchese' (1, 288). A sense of time passing, of illusions waning and of the folly of human ambition attaches to many of the poems. Thomas à Kempis's 'sic transit gloria mundi' comes to mind.

The first of the three principal themes is the reader's/writer's suspicion, even his disapproval, of the priorities and aspirations of the wealthy classes of his day. A socialist and traditionalist cast of mind is revealed here, but suspicion and disapproval never escalate into direct, let alone strident, repudiation. A discreet tone is maintained. We are introduced to a world of eloquent gentlemen (a young domestic female employee is looking for just such a person who will satisfy her 'Sehnsucht nach Schönheit und Pracht', 1, 276–77), and although there is certainly no overt criticism of the young woman's actions, we are left in no doubt that there are worthier ambitions and more immediately available natural sources of self-fulfilment:

> Denn Schönheit gäbe es überall. In meiner Mutter fränkischem Küchenleben
> Hätte es Herrlichkeit in Hülle und Fülle gegeben.

> Wieviel Schönheit könnte doch aus einem Korb voll jungem Gemüse strahlen
> Und wieviel Pracht würde aus dem Gefieder eines Bauernhahns prahlen!

> Und wieviel Sommerfreude frohlocke aus Äpfeln, Birnen und Trauben!
> Wie schön wären fliegende und wie schmackhaft gebratene Tauben!
>
> ('Sehnsucht', 1, 277)

We are also in a world of wealthy patrons ('Edeldenkender oder Edeldenkende') being sought for a young 'Heldentenor' ('Mäzen gesucht', 1, 275–76), of young men with cars advertising for a 'hübsches Mädchen für gemeinsame Fahrten' ('Freundin für Autofahrten', 1, 278–79), of high-class dance tuition for 'Damen u. Herren' offered by Fridolin Kurzelütje and daughter ('Einladung zum Tanzunterricht', 1, 279–80), of posh girls' boarding schools providing 'Klavier bis Konservatoriumsreife, Haushaltungsabteilg., Handelsfächer [...]' ('Töchterpensionate', 1, 282), of Grand Hotels (Hotel Therapia and Hotel Miramare) on the Dalmatian coast ('Dalmatinische

Hotelanzeigen', 1, 286–87) and of fashionable women's 'hunger for Paris' and for the latest styles (Dobbs Blazzer hats) at 205 West 39th Street, New York 18/NY. The Americanized language in this advertisement insinuates a degree of mild disapproval which becomes something much stronger by the end of the poem:

> Alles ist für Wirkung berechnet, raffiniert, erlesen und teuer:
> Handschuhe in Zebrastreifen, der Dinner dress, Hüte aus kostbarem Stroh,
> Unter hauchfeinen Dessous Haut wie Eis über Feuer,
> Und begierig nach Paris-Parties und Romanzen in Mexiko.
>
> Sind sie kühl, klug, dumm? Oder verlogen, gelangweilt, verwegen?
> Sind es Wesen mit Seele? Oder Vampire, die Qualen bereiten?
> ('Kauft Blazzers Hut', 1, 284)

Contempt for the vacuous lives led by a certain kind of aristocratic lady (are they symbols 'für Untergangs- oder Prosperity-Zeiten'? [ibid.]) and for the seductive charms of the '20 hinreißende Künstler, [...] Troubadoure der Massengefühle', of the Tangokapelle Juan Tarzana ('Konzertanzeige: Tangokapelle', 1, 289–90) is unmistakeable. Ironic use of current clichés ('Paris-Parties', 'Prosperity-Zeiten', 'kesse Taille') underlines this scornful attitude.

The second principal theme is the intrinsic emptiness and inevitable evanescence of this meretricious world. Merchant Richard Rotkraut, once upon a time 'Klasse', finds himself, 'wegen Nichtskönnens zu zahlen' ('Zwangsversteigerung', 1, 293), compelled to sell an array of his household possessions — ladies' and gentlemen's shoes, a fox fur, a dinner jacket, a silver cigarette case and eight volumes of Gerhart Hauptmann ('Gott sei Dank!', ibid., 1, 293), and, more painfully, less tangible belongings:

> Was einmal beseligte, geht hinweg und entfernt sich brutal.
> Geheimnisse entschwinden; Kinderlachen, Zank, Küsse und Qual. (1, 294)

The frivolous tone of the final couplet of the poem does not conceal the pain of the enforced losses even if now he proposes to raise himself above and beyond the disappointments of the physical world:

> Rotkrauts Leibwort ist seitdem: 'Alles ist eitel auf Erden!'
> Und er möchte am liebsten nun metaphysisch werden. (ibid.)

The availability of a flat on the market gives rise to a poignant litany of shattered hopes and dreams, of human loss and distress, of what-used-to-be. Each of its twenty-four lines begins 'Hier war einmal':

> Hier war einmal die Angst — Verzerrter Mund.
> Hier war einmal ein Lachen — Schlechter Witz.
> Hier war einmal ein Pfeifen — Ohne Grund.
> Hier war einmal der Zorn — Verkniff'ner Augenschlitz.
> ('Wohnungsmarkt', 1, 291)

And into this landscape of disillusionment and transience intrudes genuine human tragedy — the failed search for love ('Sehnsucht', 1, 276–77), a woman's destructive revenge ('Der Widerruf', 1, 284–85), the tarnishing of a gentleman's good name (ibid.) and the premature death of the thoroughly worthy 'Straßenwärter' Nikolaus Merkl ('Todesanzeige für einen Straßenwärter', I, 294–96).

The third theme is the clear preference, sometimes explicitly stated, for ordinary pleasures, plain comforts and, above all, for the natural world as a sanctuary of eternal values:

> In den Städten wuchsen Riesenhäuser, Kinos glühten, in den Sälen jubelten Konzerte,
> Polizisten standen winkend, junge Mädchen schrieben stundenlang Kuverte.
>
> Merkl sah die Regenbogen nach den Maigewittern siebenfarbig steigen,
> In den Schlehdornbüschen fand er Vogelnester, rastlos war das Grillengeigen.
>
> ('Todesanzeige für einen Straßenwärter', I, 295)

Modern youth, lured away to the cities by 'Tanznacht, Film, die Autobahn', no longer appreciates these values. The opposition new versus old is most clearly articulated in the configuration of the poem 'Freundin für Autofahrten' where the implicitly empty values by which the 'heutiger Jüngling' lives are confronted by the age-old consolations sought and found in nature by the 'vorgestriger Jüngling':

> Er streifte durch Wälder, um Gott zu lauschen,
> Dessen Zorn im Sausen der Wipfel sprach.
> Er träumte am Flußwehr, am Wasserrauschen,
> Woraus gewalttätige Lockung der Weltmeere brach.
> [...]
> Der Schwärmer von einst machte es romantischer, [...] (I, 278–79)

As always with Schnack, there is a strong autobiographical undertow of nostalgia, this time accompanied by a (usually) implicit critique of the modern world. We learn, for example, that before the glories of a particular Bavarian mansion began to fade and its occupants grew old, with only their memories to cherish, its rooms were filled with genuine country folk, now also gone:

> Bergsteiger, Jäger, braungebrannt im Gletschereise,
> Spielten auf Zithern alte Melodien
> Und sangen Jagdballaden, Jodler, Volksliedweise.
> Und wurden beim Gesang die rauhen Stimmen leise,
> Heulte der Nachtwind beklemmend im Kamin.
> ('Herrensitz zu verkaufen', I, 292–93)

In *Tier rang* the word 'Tand' was used to describe the futility of war and the detritus of the battlefield. Here, in 'Herrensitz zu verkaufen', the lord of the manor's noble possessions are now no more than 'Sand und Tand der Zeit — ein Hauch Erinnerung' (ibid.), the residue of a way of life now extinct.

It may be fashionable to book into smart Dalmatian hotels, but their decay is in-built, and so they will not be there forever, unlike the sea:

> In den Zimmern [of the hotels] ist Schlaf, das Graue des Staub's.
> Doch das Meer spricht wie je dieselbe Ewigkeitsmelodie
> Und schimmert zeitlos schön durch das Grün des Olivenlaub's.
> Es trauert nicht. Es ist groß wie noch nie.
> ('Dalmatinische Hotelanzeigen', I, 287)

The timelessness (repeated) of the sea stands in sharp contrast to the ephemerality of man's artificial creations. The old preferred to the new, the country to the city, the natural to the mechanical and the affected, the eternal to the ephemeral, the inconspicuous to the blatant, the humbly domestic to the gaudily exotic — none of this is original, but it is the nearest we get in Schnack's later work to any critique of materialist society. With the odd exception where an untypical bitterness intrudes (for example, in 'Wohnungsmarkt', I, 291) these oppositions are presented to us with a wry, self-knowing and sometimes humorous resignation. We are, as it were, invited to take the contemporary situation, or rather Schnack's depiction of it, seriously, but not too seriously, and in the process we note that the lyrical I quietly prides himself on *now* being able to see through and beyond that which used to 'betören' (another favourite word) when he and his contemporaries were just eighteen-year-olds (see the first stanza of 'Einladung zum Tanzunterricht', I, 279). All things, it is confirmed, will pass, but if there are echoes of Brecht's 'Vom armen B.B.' there is in Schnack's poetry little of that famous poem's generalized and explicit lament (or of its pessimism bordering on nihilism) about contemporary man's condition:

> Von diesen Städten wird bleiben: der durch sie hindurchging, der
> Wind!
> Fröhlich machet das Haus den Esser; er leert es.
> Wir wissen, daß wir Vorläufige sind,
> Und nach uns wird kommen: nichts Nennenswertes.[99]

The wind which blows through the last stanza of the final poem in *'Jene Dame, welche...'* has a happier purpose. The growth of modern traffic may well mean that a road will eventually be driven through the late 'Straßenwärter' Merkl's grave, but

> [...] als Säule Staub wird man den Straßenwärter Merkl himmelwärts
> aufsteigen sehen. ('Todesanzeige für einen Straßenwärter', I, 296)

---

99   Bertolt Brecht, *Gedichte* I: *Gedichte 1918–1929* (Suhrkamp, 1960), p. 149.

CONCLUSION

Any considered assessment of Anton Schnack's poetry should allow that the three early Expressionist volumes are powerful and significant documents of their time and that *Tier rang gewaltig mit Tier* is a wholly original (in form and content) account of the realities of frontline warfare. *Tier rang* and the Expressionist volumes were compiled together, as we have seen, over a period of four years, and their themes interlock. If *Strophen der Gier* and its accompanying collections are about man as sexual predator, apparently all powerful and sublimely confident, *Tier rang* depicts the lyrical I as a desperate, violent animal whose hold on life and sanity becomes ever feebler. Writing in a recent collection of essays about Ford Madox Ford's *Parade's End* (1924–28), Julian Barnes coincidentally points to a way in which Schnack's first four volumes of verse might be linked: 'War and sexual passion are not opposites: they are in the same business, two parts of the same pincer attack on the sanity of the individual.'[1] Schnack's presentation of the lyrical I enables us to trace the metamorphosis of an exaggeratedly self-assured hedonist into an increasingly embattled, and ultimately doomed, victim. *Tier rang* remains Schnack's abiding achievement and deserves far more than the cursory and superficial treatment it customarily receives, ostensibly dignified by obligatory comparisons with Wilfred Owen who, at all events, composed a very different kind of war poetry. In his wide-ranging history of the First World War Ian Beckett offers a typical example of an assessment which is barely more than a mixture of glib aside and unsubstantiated assertion. Even the poet's name is misspelled in the haste to move on:

> German modernist poets frequently supported the war at first, a number such as Hans Leybold and August Stramm, being killed. Others, however, became disillusioned though the German poetic tradition tended towards an idealism, abstraction and remoteness from reality which made it difficult to get to grips with the experience of war. Nonetheless, the best, like Georg Trakl and Anton Schnak [sic], are comparable to Wilfred Owen.[2]

Close analysis of several poems in *Tier rang* has revealed that there is nothing idealistic or abstract about the collection, whose intrinsic power is founded in its closeness to reality.

After 1920 Expressionism as an influential cultural movement had exhausted itself and Expressionist writers, those who survived the First World War, went their separate ways: 'Die Federhalter des Expressionismus haben sich sehr

---

1   Julian Barnes, *Through the Window* (Vintage, 2012), p. 70.
2   Beckett, p. 627.

verschiedenartig gemausert. Anton Schnack wählte die kleine Form, die Miniatur, einen Laute, Gerüche, Schreck, Verzauberung und inwendige Schaubilder sehr sinnlich malenden Impressionismus.'[3] Schnack did not stop writing, but over the course of more than twenty-five years he published only one collection of verse. It is interesting, perhaps even significant, that he chose to publish *Die Flaschenpost* in the mid-1930s, but the interest and significance are diluted, if not undermined, by the rather innocuous, studiedly uncontroversial nature of the volume. Praise for Schnack's post-1920 poetry on various commemorative occasions — on his seventy-fifth birthday, for example, and, of course, in his obituary — is fulsome, but it appears predominantly in local newspapers whose writers are always keen to claim him for their own:

> Freuen wir uns darum, daß wir Dichter haben wie Anton Schnack, die ganz in Franken aufgehen [...] Schließen wir mit einem für den Dichter typischen Stimmungsbild aus fränkisch atmender, pulsierender Nähe, die ihn zum bedeutendsten Vertreter der fränkisch-literarischen Atmosphäre stempelt [...]:
> > Wenn die Traube wird geschnitten,
> > Und die Kufen zu den Keltern schwanken,
> > Leuchten sie als letzte Frucht in Franken.[4]

Part of Schnack's local celebrity had indeed to do with his fondness for, and expert knowledge of, Franconian wine: in the publicity material prepared for the presentation of Manfred Frühwacht's *Wege zum Wein auf Frankens Urgestein* Schnack is proudly described as 'ein hervorragender Botschafter und Marketing-Profi für die Weine aus seinem geliebten Frankenland'.[5] Two streets are named after him in Kahl am Main and nearby Alzenau and he has a handsome memorial stone in the beautiful Kahl cemetery.[6] These very local tributes are a natural consequence of his resolve to stay within carefully demarcated limits, both creatively and in the living of his daily life. Another consequence is that commentators tend to see his later poetry and prose in terms of 'Kleine Glückseligkeiten, Bruchstücke aus einer paradiesischen Welt [...][7] Petitessen [...] Miniaturen [...][8] Liebevoll ausgefeiltes Detail',[9] and in the process the earlier volumes are pushed into the background.

Patrick Bridgwater has been a lone voice in drawing attention to the unique strengths of Schnack's war poetry. Indeed, it was precisely in the early volumes that Schnack came nearest to propounding and demonstrating an admittedly narrow kind of Expressionism and, much more important, to depicting the visceral

---

3   Signed simply C.G., 'Ein Glas "Harfe" für den Dichter', *Main-Post*, no. 163, 19 July 1967.
4   Maria Forster-Rettelbach, 'Sindbad, der Seefahrer von Franken: Anton Schnack und sein neuestes Werk', *Main-Echo*, no. 67, 2 June 1950.
5   The presentation was held in 19 September 2011 in the Gasthaus Alte Post in Alzenau. The relevant correspondence is held in the archive in Kahl's town-hall.
6   It was also proposed to erect a small 'Gedenkstein' in his former garden. His niece and a neighbour, Herr Karl Heinz Schmitt, invited me to the 'little ceremony' on 14 June 2013.
7   See the programme printed to commemorate the thirtieth anniversary of Schnack's death. Hartmut Vollmer delivered the celebratory lecture with these words as his title on 26 September 2003 in Kahl where copies of this programme can be found.
8   Essig, 'Blaue Beeren'.
9   H. L., 'Meister der kleinen Prosa', Anton Schnack 70 Jahre Alt', *Main-Post*, no. 166, 21 July 1962.

realities of the First World War. In his preface to *Menschheitsdämmerung* Kurt Pinthus asserts that the one characteristic binding together the whole spectrum of Expressionist poets and all the disparate elements of Expressionism was intensity.[10] The language and highly charged emotionality of Schnack's first four volumes qualify for this description, but for whatever reason, with whatever purpose, Schnack never achieved the same level again. It is possible to interpret this change as a positive retrenchment and economizing of ambition, as one of his obituarists argues: 'Der Auseinandersetzung mit dem Erlebnis des Ersten Weltkriegs war eine expressionistische Sturm-und-Drangperiode gefolgt [...] Später verloren die Titel ihre bissige Aggressivität. Sonne kam durch, der Alltag schimmerte im milden Licht.'[11] Subsequent huge global events — the rise and fall of the Weimar Republic, the hegemony of National Socialism, the Second World War and its aftermath in the 1940s and 1950s — are barely acknowledged in Schnack's poetry or prose. On the occasion of the commemoration of what would have been Schnack's hundredth birthday a radio broadcaster offers a measured assessment of Schnack's career:

> Die vor 1933 entstandenen Werke wurden rasch vergessen, Neuauflagen gab es nicht. Während der Zeit des Dritten Reiches blieb Anton Schnack merkwürdig still, beteiligte sich an keiner öffentlichen Literatur-Diskussion, schrieb kein Heldenepos und versuchte auch nicht mit Skizzen aus seinem fränkischen Tagebuch [...] an die Öffentlichkeit zu gehen [...] Die 'innere Emigration', in die er sich geflüchtet hatte, ermöglichte es ihm, kurz nach Kriegsende wieder Bücher schreiben und veröffentlichen zu können.[12]

It is, of course, impossible to gauge whether those collections published after the Second World War — *Mittagswein*, *Der Annoncenleser* and '*Jene Dame, welche ...*' — did indeed fulfil their proclaimed purpose beyond a local readership of raising the spirits of 'die große Masse des Volkes' who are 'seelisch zerstört, entwurzelt und deprimiert'.[13] What can be said is that the poems of these volumes are generally good-humoured, breezy, innocuous and resolutely low-key. A harsh critic might call them bland, frivolous, trivial and irrelevant. There is, as has been shown, perhaps more to them than to the poems in *Die Flaschenpost*, but, possibly, as a Swiss friend rather gloomily suggests in a letter written in 1955, Schnack would have to write in more 'epic' and 'dramatic' fashion if he wanted to find a wider readership. His work, it is implied, is too 'slight in scope' alongside 'weightier' volumes:

> Es zeigt sich auch hier einmal mehr, daß der Dichter heute nur durchdringen kann, wenn er entweder umfangreiche epische oder dramatische Werke zu schreiben gewillt ist. Alles an Umfang Geringe, wenn vielleicht oder doch oft gerade deswegen Überragende, ertrinkt in der Masse der Wälzer und äußerlich gewichtigeren Bücher.[14]

The rueful pessimism which informs these lines is pragmatic and seems to be kindly

---

10   Pinthus, p. 30.
11   Anonymous, *Main-Echo*, Aschaffenburg, 28 September 1973.
12   Regionalstudio Mainfranken transcript, pp. 13–14.
13   I, 461.
14   Letter from Ernst Otto Marti in Zürich dated 12 April 1955, Manuscript Department Marbach.

meant, but the challenge implicit in them is not one which Schnack ever looks like taking up. Between the first poem he published after the spring of 1920 when *Tier rang* appeared[15] and his last published poem ('Blanchefleur, die Weiße Blüte', 1, 418–19) there is, with the exception of the use of advertisements, virtually little change of form or style, no raising of voice or profile or temperature. Nothing is allowed to disturb his conviction that poems of a certain kind, the kind which we find in *Die Flaschenpost* and his post-war collections, will always survive and should always survive. For once, in the last poem of this 1936 volume, we have seen how he feels sufficiently emboldened to emerge from his self-imposed purdah to defend poetry and to praise it for its universal application:

> Sie [die Gedichte] sitzen zu Tausenden noch an den weißen Landstraßen,
> An den Brunnen, auf Steinen, im Schnee, am Rain,
> Im Lächeln der Kinder, in alten Vasen
> Leben sie fort mit Seelenschein:
> Wo ein Herz sich öffnet, wo ein Herz zerbricht,
> Blüht das Gedicht. ('Verteidigung der Gedichte', 1, 198)

---

15   From the timing, this is likely to be 'Fränkische Nacht' which was published in July 1920 in *Die Sichel*. See 1, 124.

BIBLIOGRAPHY

Primary Sources

Archival Material

For archival material I have depended on the archives in Marbach, Kahl am Main and Würzburg. The Deutsches Literaturarchiv Marbach holds, in addition to Schnack's entire published work, his Nachlass, comprising a considerable amount of unpublished material together with personal effects not appropriate for publication. The other personal items (letters, postcards, newspaper cuttings, notebooks, passes, etc.) in the Nachlass can be accessed in the Handschriftensammlung: for the most part these are not catalogued and often not dated. The archival material is divided into the following categories:

1. Magazine and newspaper sources by or about Schnack held in the library of the Deutsches Literaturarchiv, Marbach, abbreviated as DLA Marbach. This is by no means an exhaustive list: I have included only that material which is directly or indirectly relevant to this book.

2. Material from the Manuscript Department. I shall use the abbreviation for these sources: Schnack-Nachlass DLA, Marbach. I have selected material which is clearly relevant or of particular interest.

3. Selected material (articles, transcripts, newspaper cuttings, essays) held in the archive in the town hall of Schnack's hometown of Kahl am Main (Postfach 50 63792 Kahl am Main).

4. Selected material held in the City Archive (Neubaustraße, 12) in Würzburg, again mainly cuttings and reviews.

1. DLA Marbach

The archival material in each case is arranged in chronological order (wherever the date is known or shown) and includes articles and essays written by or about Anton Schnack.

'Anton Schnack über sich selbst', Darmstadt 1918

Anton Schnack, 'Nachruf auf Ernst Wilhelm Lotz', *Das literarische Echo*, 20, 11, March 1918

Anton Schnack reviewing Fritz Usinger's *Der ewige Kampf*, *Menschen* , 2.5, 1 March 1919

Anton Schnack, 'Ich', *Die Junge Kunst*, 1.8, 15 September 1919

Anton Schnack, 'Der Lyriker Hans Schiebelhuth', *Feuer*, 1 (1919/20), 829–31

Anton Schnack reviewing 'Die Gedichte Kasimir Edschmids', *Feuer*, 2 (1920/21), 314–15

Anton Schnack reviewing Rabindranath Tagore's novel *Das Heim und die Welt*, ibid., 244

Anton Schnack — photocopy (with critical blurb) of outside cover of *Tier rang gewaltig mit Tier* — *Börsenblatt für den deutschen Buchhandels*, 88 (1922)

R. C. Muschler, *Die Bergstadt*, no. 4, January 1921. Untitled essay on Schnack

Hanns Martin Elster, 'Neue Lyrik', *Die Flöte*, 3 (1920/21), 209–11 (including a review of *Tier rang*)

Anton Schnack reviewing Edschmid's collection 'Stehe von Lichtern gestreichelt', ibid., 138–42

Anton Schnack reviewing the poetry of Ludwig Thoma, *Das Tagebuch*, 4 (1923), 1331–32

Albert Morhof, 'Im Zeichen der Galeere', *Freude an Büchern*, 2 (1950–51), pp. 310–11

Anton Schnack, 'Literatur-Prognose 1953', *Freude an Büchern*, 4.1 (1953), 5–7

Walter Höllerer, 'Anton Schnack', *Weltstimmen: Weltbücher in Umrissen*, 22.3 (1953), 97–102

Karl Ude, 'Pastelle in Prosa, Anton Schnack zum 70. Geburtstag', *Welt und Wort*, 17 (1962), 267

Georg Schneider, 'Anton Schnack zum 75. am 21. Juli 1967', *Die Tat* (Zürich), no. 170, 21 July 1967

Edwin Kuntz, 'Epitaph für Anton Schnack', *Rhein-Neckar-Zeitung*, no. 224, 28 September 1973, p. 2

Dieter Hoffmann, Anton Schnack obituary in *Frankfurter Neue Presse*, 29 September 1973

E.J., Anton Schnack obituary, *Frankfurter Allgemeine Zeitung*, no. 237, 11 October 1973

Ralph Glöckler, 'Kleine Anton-Schnack-Chronik', *Main Echo*, no. 219, 23 September 1978

Rolf-Bernhard Essig, 'Blaue Beeren: Die Werke des fränkischen Schriftstellers Anton Schnack', *Süddeutsche Zeitung*, no. 97, 27 April 2004, p. 14

2. *Schnack-Nachlass DLA, Marbach*

Much of this is undated. There is a host of autobiographical snippets with titles like 'Anton Schnack Biographie', 'Biographisches', 'Lebenslauf Anton Schnack' (very difficult to decipher), 'Anton Schnack über sich selbst', individually not particularly useful, but adding up to an interesting picture of Schnack's personality.

There are two files of military and political information containing a record of his official travel abroad (no mention of an involvement in a First Word War Italian campaign), an army pass, notification of his conscription into the Landsturm, a letter (dated 25 February 1943) from the Reichsverband der deutschen Presse indicating that he has been accepted onto the *Neueste Zeitung* in Frankfurt am Main as 'Schriftsteller für Unterhaltung', a pass (Number 1813, dated 26 June 1934) from the Reichskulturkammer in Berlin and two questionnaires from the Military Government of Germany in 1946 enquiring about his political allegiances in the 1930s. Reference is made to many of these in Chapter 7.

A third large collection (available in the file 'Zeitungsausschnittsammlung der Mediendokumentation', but unsorted and largely undated) consists of Schnack's notebooks, which are of interest in demonstrating how their author's eye was caught by bizarre, unlikely or individually tragic events — London-style smog in Berlin, a butterfly caught at Christmas, a Freemason lodge dispersed in Berlin, eccentric weather-forecasts, a Gemsjäger killed on the Spitzenstein, etc. Such items confirm the picture of Anton Schnack that I have sought to invoke, as someone who based himself in domestic seclusion and took on the role of none too serious observer and collector of life's anomalies and human foibles.

The Nachlass also contains three significant letters to which reference is made in this book:

Willibald Omankowski writing to Schnack on 23 December 1937

Ossip Kalenter (President of the Pen-Centre of German Speaking Writers abroad) writing to Schnack on 14 December 1950

Ernst Otto Marti, letter to Anton Schnack, 12 April 1955

And an important article written by Julius Kühn, 'Die Brüder Schnack' (undated) referred to in Chapter 1

3. Kahl am Main Archive

The headlines of these usually anonymous articles are often very illuminating in themselves because of the way they reveal local perceptions of Schnack's work, character and literary stature. Again they have helped to create a cumulative effect:

Dekan Hufgard (Geistl. Rat), 'Eine schmachvolle Beleidigung der Aschaffenburger Mädchenwelt', *Beobachter am Main*, 9 July 1929

Anon., 'Die Heimat seines Herzens ist Franken', *Main-Echo*, 20 July 1967

Anon., 'Begegnungen mit dem Dichter Anton Schnack', *Spessart*, November 1976

Anon., 'Zwei Brüder aus Rieneck: Gleiche Herkunft, gleicher Beruf, verschiedene Lebenswege', *Main-Echo*, 13 April 1992

Anon., 'Dichter Anton Schnack: Ein Sucher nach den kleinen Dingen des Lebens', *Main-Post*, 19 July 1992

Anon., 'Wir freuen uns, daß Anton Schnack lange Zeit in Kahl unser Mitbürger war' (Mayor Helmut Röll), *Main-Echo*, 21 July 1992

Anon., 'Fränkischer Wein- und Frauenverehrer', ibid.

Anon., 'Anton Schnack Ausstellung überrascht mit einer Fülle schönster Raritäten' (Kahler Festhalle), *Main-Echo*, 2 July 2003

Luise Glaser-Lotz, 'Expressionistischer Dichter der Heimat und der Stille', *Frankfurter Allgemeine Zeitung*, 2 August 2003, p. 60

Luise Glaser-Lotz, ' "Glückserfüllte Wunderwelten." Festakt zu Ehren des expressionistischen Dichters Anton Schnack', *Frankfurter Allgemeine Zeitung*, 29 September 2003

Anon., 'Das Inferno "Verdun" und "Brevier der Zärtlichkeit"', *Main-Echo*, 6 December 2003

Anon., 'Der Ruch der treuen Gesellschaft. Literatur und NS-Regime: Schnack und Becker', *Main-Echo*, 22 August 2012

Two other important documents are available in the Kahl am Main archive:

A transcript entitled 'Mir ist in Franken vieles wert und teuer' of a discussion transmitted by the Regionalstudio Mainfranken in Würzburg on 19 July 1992 on the occasion of what would have been Schnack's 100th birthday: Author — Franz Schaub, Editor — Rainer Lindemann, Director — Ralf Sarrazin

An eight-page typescript of Frau Ursula Stickler's (Schnack's niece) evaluation of Schnack's work to mark the same day. It is entitled 'Lesung aus seinen Werken'.

4. Würzburg City Archive

Unsurprisingly, because of Friedrich Schnack's close links with Würzburg, most of the material is dedicated to him. I have listed just four such items together with a few interesting cuttings/essays about Anton: these again confirm a familiar picture. The material on Friedrich is gathered in a folder entitled 'Friedrich Schnack Schriftsteller und Kulturpreisträger der Stadt Würzburg'. See Chapter 1.

Anon., 'Dichter des Naturwunders', *Main-Echo*, 2 March 1963

Alois Keck, 'Friedrich Schnack 80 Jahre', *Fränkisches Volksblatt*, 2 March 1968

Stephan Linhardt, 'Einer der letzten Romantiker', *Main-Echo*, 5 March 1968

Otto Schmitt-Rosenberger, 'Das Poetische hat immer recht' (Friedrich's 100th birthday), *Fränkisches Volksblatt*, 4 March 1988

Maria Forster-Rettelbach, 'Sindbad, der Seefahrer von Franken Anton Schnack', *Main-Echo*, no. 67, 2 May 1950

Anon., [AS] 'Meister der kleinen Prosa', *Main-Post*, no. 166, 21 July 1962

Anon., 'Ein Glas "Harfe" für den Dichter Anton Schnack', *Main-Post*, no. 163, 19 July 1967

Works by Anton Schnack

Schnack, Anton, *Werke*, ed. by Hartmut Vollmer, 2 vols (Elfenbein, 2003), including the eight collections of poetry:

Der Abenteurer (Verlag Die Dachstube, 1919)

Strophen der Gier (Dresdner Verlag, 1919)

Die tausend Gelächter (Paul Steegemann, 1919)

Tier rang gewaltig mit Tier (Rowohlt, 1920)

Die Flaschenpost (Paul List, 1936)

Der Annoncenleser (Winkler, 1947)

Mittagswein (Hoffmann und Campe, 1948)

'Jene Dame, welche ...' Gedichte zu kleinen Anzeigen (Pohl, 1953)

Not included in the *Werke* is Schnack's short story *Der finstere Franz* (List, 1937), referred to in Chapter 7.

Works by Other Authors

ANDERSCH, ALFRED, *Die Kirschen der Freiheit* (Diogenes, 1968)

ANZ, THOMAS, and MICHAEL STARK (eds), *Manifeste und Dokumente zur deutschen Literatur 1910–1920* (Metzler, 1982)

ANZ, THOMAS, and JOSEPH VOGL (eds), *Die Dichter und der Krieg: Deutsche Lyrik 1914–1918* (Hanser, 1982)

BARNES, JULIAN, *A History of the World in 10½ Chapters* (Jonathan Cape, 1989)

—— *Through the Window* (Vintage, 2012)

BECHER, JOHANNES R., 'Philosophie des Sonetts oder Kleine Sonettlehre', in *Bemühungen II* (Aufbau, 1972)

—— *Becher und die Insel: Briefe und Dichtungen 1916–1954*, ed. by Rolf Harder and Ilse Siebert (Insel, 1981)

BECKETT, SAMUEL, 'Beckett by the Madeleine', in *Drama in the Modern World: Plays and Essays*, ed. by Samuel A. Weiss (Heath, 1974)

BENDER, HANS (ed.), *Mein Gedicht ist mein Messer: Lyriker zu ihren Gedichten* (List, 1961)

BENN, GOTTFRIED, *Gesammelte Werke*, ed. by Dieter Wellershoff, 4 vols (Limes, 1959)

—— *Dichter über ihre Dichtungen: Gottfried Benn*, ed. by Edgar Lohner (Heimeran, 1969)

—— *Sämtliche Werke*, VI: *Prosa 4*, ed. by Holger Hof (Klett-Cotta, 2001). 'Einleitung zu Lyrik des expressionistischen Jahrzehnts', pp. 208–20

BERGENGRUEN, WERNER, *Der ewige Kaiser* (Schmidt-Deyter, 1937)

—— *Schreibtischerinnerungen* (Nymphenburger, 1961)

—— *Dichtergehäuse* (Arche, 1966)

BLUNDEN, EDMUND, *Undertones of War* (Penguin, 1987; first published 1928)

BRECHT, BERTOLT, *Gedichte I: Gedichte 1918–1929* (Suhrkamp, 1960)

—— *Gedichte IV: Gedichte 1934–1941* (Suhrkamp, 1961)

—— *Gedichte VI: Gedichte im Exil* (Suhrkamp, 1964)

CAROSSA, HANS, *Briefe II 1919–1936*, ed. by Eva Campmann-Carossa (Insel, 1978)

CARY, JOYCE, *Marching Soldier* (Michael Joseph, 1945)

CELAN, PAUL, *Gesammelte Werke*, ed. by Beda Allemann and Stefan Reichert, 5 vols (Suhrkamp, 1983)

CONRADI, HERMANN, *Gesammelte Schriften*, 3 vols (Müller, 1911)

DEHMEL, RICHARD, *Gesammelte Werke*, 3 vols (Fischer, 1913)

DEPPE, WOLFGANG G., CHRISTOPHER MIDDLETON and HERBERT SCHÖNHERR (eds), *Ohne Hass und Fahne: Kriegsgedichte des zwanzigsten Jahrhunderts* (Rowohlt, 1959)

DÖBLIN, ALFRED, 'Von der Freiheit eines Dichtermenschen', *Die Neue Rundschau*, 29.2 (1918), pp. 843–50; repr. in Anz and Stark, *Manifeste*, pp. 69–74

——'Neue Zeitschriften', *Die Neue Rundschau*, 30 (1919), pp. 621–32

EDSCHMID, KASIMIR, 'Expressionismus in der Dichtung', *Die Neue Rundschau*, 29 (1918), I, pp. 359–74, repr. in Anz and Stark, *Manifeste*, pp. 42–55

——*Lebendiger Expressionismus* (Desch, 1961)

——*Frühe Schriften* (Luchterhand, 1970)

EHRENSTEIN, ALBERT, *Werke*, ed. by Hanni Mittelmann (Boer, 1997)

EICHENDORFF, JOSEPH VON, *Sämtliche Werke*, 18 vols, ed. by Harry Fröhlich and Ursula Regener (Kohlhammer, 1993)

ENGELKE, GERRIT, *Das Gesamtwerk*, ed. by Hermann Blome (List, 1960)

ENGELKE, GERRIT, HEINRICH LERSCH, and KARL ZIELKE, *Schulter an Schulter: Gedichte von drei Arbeitern* (B. Vopelius, 1916)

FORSTER, E. M., *Howard's End* (Vintage Books, 1921)

FREILIGRATH, FERDINAND, *Freiligraths Werke in einem Band*, selected and introduced by Werner Ilberg (Volksverlag, 1962)

GARDNER, BRIAN (ed.), *Up the Line to Death: The War Poets 1914–1918* (Methuen, 1964)

GEORGE, STEFAN, *Sämtliche Werke in 18 Bänden* (Klett-Cotta, 1982–2013)

GOETHE, JOHANN WOLFGANG, *Sämtliche Werke: Briefe, Tagebücher und Gespräche*, ed. by Friedmar Apel and others, Deutsche Klassiker-Ausgabe, 40 vols (Deutscher Klassiker Verlag, 1986–2000)

GOTTSCHED, JOHANN CHRISTOPH, *Versuch einer Critischen Dichtkunst: Ausgewählte Werke*, ed. by Joachim and Brigitte Birke (De Gruyter, 1971), vol. VI

GRAVES, ROBERT, *Over the Brazier* (The Poetry Workshop, 1916)

GUNDOLF, FRIEDRICH, 'Stefan George und der Expressionismus', *Die Flöte*, 3 (1920/21), pp. 217–23; repr. in Anz and Stark, *Manifeste*, pp. 92–97

HEISSENBÜTTEL, HELMUT, *Über Literatur* (Walter, 1966)

HEYM, GEORG, *Dichtungen und Schriften*, ed. by Karl Ludwig Schneider, 4 vols (Ellermann, 1964)

HEYNICKE, KURT, *Jeder Tag: Das lyrische Gesamtwerk* (Scheffler, 2000)

HOFMANNSTHAL, HUGO VON, *Sämtliche Werke*, XXXI: *Erfundene Gespräche und Briefe*, ed. by Ellen Ritter (Fischer, 1991)

HUCHEL, PETER, *Die Gedichte* (Suhrkamp, 1984)

JUNG, FRANZ, *Der Weg nach unten* (Luchterhand, 1961)

JÜNGER, ERNST, 'Kriegerische Mathematik', *Der Widerstand*, 5 (1930), p. 270

——*In Stahlgewittern* (Mittler, 1942)

KAISER, GEORG, *Werke*, IV, ed. by Walther Huder (Ullstein, 1971)

KASCHNITZ, MARIE LUISE, *Gesammelte Werke*, ed. by Christian Büttrich and Norbert Müller, 7 vols (Insel, 1981–89)

KINDERMANN, HEINZ (ed.), *Deutsche Literatur: Dem neuen Reich entgegen 1850–1871* (Reclam, 1920)

KÖRNER, THEODOR, *Körners Werke*, ed. by Hans Zimmer, 2 vols (Biographisches Institut, 1893)

LEVIN, PHILLIS (ed.), *The Penguin Book of the Sonnet* (Penguin, 2001)

LILIENCRON, DETLEV VON, *Gesammelte Werke: Gedichte II* (Deutsche Verlagsanstalt, 1923)

LINDEMANN, GISELA (ed.), *Deutsche Lyrik von den Anfängen bis zur Gegenwart*, 12 vols (Deutscher Taschenbuch Verlag, 2001)

LOERKE, OSKAR, *Die Gedichte*, ed. by Peter Suhrkamp (Suhrkamp, 1958)

LOEWENSON, ERWIN, 'Zur Schopenhauer-Psychologie: Der Masochismus des Unter-bewußtseins'. Lecture in Der Neue Club, 23 November 1910, unpublished. Quoted in Gunter Martens, *Vitalismus und Expressionismus* (Kohlhammer, 1971), p. 192

LOWELL, ROBERT, *Notebooks 1967–1968* (Farrar, Straus and Giroux, 1969)

MANN, THOMAS, *Betrachtungen einer Unpolitischen* (Fischer, 1918), pp. 563–83; repr. in Anz and Stark, *Manifeste*, pp. 90–92

MANN, THOMAS, 'Gladius Dei', in *Frühe Erzählungen 1893–1912*, ed. by Terence J. Reed and Malte Herwig (Fischer, 2004), pp. 222–42

MARC, FRANZ, in *Der Sturm* I (1916/17), H.1 (April 1916), S.2; repr. in Anz and Stark, *Manifeste*, pp. 303–05

MARCUSE, LUDWIG, *Mein zwanzigstes Jahrhundert* (List, 1960)

MUSIL, ROBERT, *Gesammelte Werke*, ed. by Adolf Frisé, 9 vols (Rowohlt, 1978)

NIETZSCHE, FRIEDRICH, *Werke Kritische Gesamtausgabe*, ed. by Giorgio Colli and Mazzina Montinari, III: *Die Geburt der Tragödie. Unzeitgemäße Betrachtungen I–III* (De Gruyter, 1972)

PANDER, OSWALD, 'Revolution der Sprache', *Das junge Deutschland*, 1.5 (1918), pp. 147–48; repr. in Anz and Stark, *Manifeste*, pp. 612–13

PINTHUS, KURT (ed.), *Menschheitsdämmerung* (Rowohlt, 1920)

RAABE, PAUL (ed.), *Expressionismus: Aufzeichnungen und Erinnerungen der Zeitgenossen* (Walter, 1965)

REILLY, CATHERINE (ed.), *Scars upon my Heart: Women's Poetry and Verse of the First World War* (Virago, 1981)

REMARQUE, ERICH MARIA, *Im Westen nichts Neues* (Propyläen, 1929)

RENN, LUDWIG, *Krieg* (Frankfurter Societäts-Weimar Druckerei, 1929)

RESO, MARTIN (ed.), *Expressionismus: Lyrik* (Aufbau, 1969)

RILKE, RAINER MARIA, *Briefe*, ed. by Horst Nalewski, 2 vols (Insel, 1991)

——*Werke: Kommentierte Ausgabe in vier Bänden*, ed. by Manfred Engel and Ulrich Fülleborn (Insel, 1996)

ROTH, PHILIP, 'The Art of Fiction', interview with Hermione Lee, *Paris Review*, 93 (1984)

——(ed.), *Kameraden der Menschheit* (1919) (Reclam, 1971)

RUBINER, LUDWIG, *Der Dichter greift in die Politik: Ausgewähltre Werke, 1908–19* (Philipp Reclam, 1976)

RÜCKERT, FRIEDRICH, *Gesammelte poetische Werke* (Sauerländer, 1882)

RÜHMKORF, PETER (ed.), *131 expressionistische Gedichte* (Wagenbach, 1976)

SASSOON, SIEGFRIED, *Collected Poems 1908–1956* (Faber & Faber, 1961)

——*Memoirs of an Infantry Officer* (Faber and Faber, 1930)

SCHLEGEL, AUGUST WILHELM, *Kritische Schriften und Briefe*, ed. by Edgar Lohner (Kohlhammer, 1965)

SCHREYER, LOTHAR, 'Expressionistische Dichtung', *Sturm-Bühne*, Folge 4/5 (1918/19), pp. 19–20, Folge 6 (1918/19), pp.[1–3]; repr. in Anz and Stark, *Manifeste*, pp. 623–29

SHAKESPEARE, WILLIAM, *The Sonnets*, ed. by Peter Jones (Palgrave, 1977)

SILKIN, JON, *The Penguin Book of First World War Poetry* (Penguin, 1996)

SPITTELER, CARL, *Kritische Schriften* (Artemis, 1965)

STADLER, ERNST, *Dichtungen, Schriften, Briefe: Kritische Ausgabe*, ed. by Klaus Hurlebusch and Karl Ludwig Schneider (Beck, 1983)

STIFTER, ADALBERT, *Briefe*, ed. by Friedrich Seebaß (Wunderlich, 1936)

SUSMAN, MARGARETE, *Das Wesen der modernen deutschen Lyrik* (Strecker & Schröder, 1910)

THOMAS, EDWARD, *Letters of Edward Thomas to Jesse Berridge*, ed. by Anthony Berridge (Enitharmon, 1983)

TUCHOLSKY, KURT, *Gedichte*, ed. by Mary Gerold-Tucholsky (Rowohlt, 1983)

WALTER, GEORGE (ed.), *The Penguin Book of First World War Poetry* (Penguin, 2006)

WEDEKIND, FRANK, *Werke*, ed. by Elke Austermühl, Rolf Kieser and Hartmut Vinçon, 8 vols (Häusser, 1996)

WEINHEBER, JOSEF, *Sämtliche Werke*, ed. by Josef Nadler and Hedwig Weinheber, 5 vols (Otto Müller, 1954)

WERFEL, FRANZ, *Das lyrische Werk*, ed. by Adolf D. Klarmann (Fischer, 1967)

WHITMAN, WALT, *Complete Poetry and Selected Prose and Letters*, ed. by Emory Holloway (The Nonesuch Press, 1964)

WORDSWORTH, WILLIAM, *Poetical Works*, ed. by E. de Selincourt and Helen Darbishire (Clarendon, 1947)

ZECH, PAUL, *Die eiserne Brücke* (Verlag der Weißen Blätter, 1914)

ZUCKMAYER, CARL, *Geheimreport*, ed. by Gunther Nickel and Johanna Schrön (Wallstein, 2002)

ZYCH, ADAM A. and MÜLLER-OTT, DOROTHEA, *Auschwitz Gedichte II* (Verlag Staatliches Museum Auschwitz-Birkenau Oświęcim, 2001)

Secondary Sources

ADAM, CHRISTIAN, *Lesen unter Hitler* (Galiani, 2010)

ADORNO, T. W., 'Die auferstandene Kultur' (1949), in *Gesammelte Schriften*, ed. by Rolf Tiedemann, 20 vols (Suhrkamp, 1986), XX/II, pp. 453–64

ALLEN, ROY F., *German Expressionist Poetry* (Twayne, 1979)

ANZ, THOMAS, *Literatur des Expressionismus* (Metzler, 2002)

ARNOLD, ARMIN, *Die Literatur des Expressionismus* (Kohlhammer, 1966)

——*Die Prosa des Expressionismus* (Kohlhammer, 1972)

BECKETT, IAN F. W., *The Great War 1914–1918* (Longman, 2007)

BELMORE, H. W., *Rilke's Craftmanship* (Blackwell, 1954)

BERMAN, SANDRA L., *The Sonnet over Time* (University of North Carolina Press, 1988)

BERTON, PIERRE, *Vimy* (Anchor Canada, 2001)

BOGNER, RALF GEORG, review of Anton Schnack, *Werke*, *Germanistik*, 45 (2004), p. 442

BONADEO, ALFREDO, *Mark of the Beast: Death and Degradation in the Literature of the Great War* (University Press of Kentucky, 1989)

BRIDGWATER, PATRICK, *The German Poets of the First World War* (Croom Helm, 1985)

BRINKMANN, RICHARD (ed.), *Expressionismus: Internationale Forschung zu einem internationalen Phänomen* (Metzler, 1980)

BRONNER, STEPHEN ERIC, and DOUGLAS KELLNER (eds), *Passion and Rebellion: The Expressionist Heritage* (Croom Helm, 1983)

DAHLKE, BIRGIT, *Jünglinge der Moderne: Jugendkult und Männlichkeit in der Literatur um 1900* (Böhlau, 2006)

DENKLER, HORST, and KARL PRÜMM (eds), *Die deutsche Literatur im Dritten Reich* (Reclam, 1976)

DÖBLIN, ALFRED, *Aufsätze zur Literatur* (Walter, 1963)

DONAHUE, NEIL H., and DORIS KIRCHNER (eds), *Flight of Fantasy: New Perspectives on Inner Emigration in German Literature 1933–1945* (Berghahn, 2003)

DONAHUE, NEIL H. (ed.), *A Companion to the Literature of German Expressionism* (Camden House, 2005)

EHRKE-ROTERMUND, HEIDRUN, and ERWIN ROTERMUND, *Zwischenreiche und Gegenwelten: Texte und Vorstudien zur 'Verdeckten Schreibweise' im 'Dritten Reich'* (Fink, 1999)

ELLIOTT, MARK CHRISTOPHER, 'German Poetry beyond the Boundaries of the Nazi Era: The Modernist Legacy' (unpublished doctoral thesis, University of Oxford, 2006)

ENGEN, ROB, 'Steel against Fire: The Bayonet in the First World War', *Journal of Military and Strategic Studies*, 8.3 (2006), pp. 1–21

FARWELL, BYRON, *Mr Kipling's Army: All the Queen's Men* (Norton, 1981)

FECHNER, JÜRG-ULRICH, *Das deutsche Sonett* (Fink, 1969)

FERGUSON, NIALL, *The Pity of War* (Basic Books, 1999)

FITCH, NOËL RILEY, *The Grand Literary Cafés of Europe* (New Holland, 2006)

FRÜHWACHT, MANFRED, and JOACHIM SCHULMERICH, *Wege zum Wein: Kulturgeschichtlicher Gang durch die Stadt Alzenau und benachbarte Weinorte* (CoCon, 2011)

FULLER, JOHN, *The Sonnet* (Methuen, 1972)

FUSSELL, PAUL, *The Great War and Modern Memory* (Oxford University Press, 1975/2000)

GERHARD, CORDULA, *Das Erbe der 'Grossen Form': Untersuchungen zur Zyklus-Bildung in der expressionistischen Lyrik* (Peter Lang, 1986)

GLÖCKLER, RALPH ROGER, 'Die frühen Gedichtbände von Anton Schnack und ihr literarischer Standort im expressionistischen Jahrzehnt' (unpublished master's thesis, University of Tübingen, 1976)

GODÉ, MAURICE, *L'Expressionisme* (Presses Universitaires de France, 1999)

HERRNSTEIN SMITH, BARBARA, *Poetic Closure: A Study of How Poems End* (University of Chicago Press, 1968)

HIBBERD, DOMINIC, *Wilfred Owen: A New Biography* (Weidenfeld & Nicholson, 2002)

HÖLLERER, WALTER, 'Anton Schnack', *Weltstimmen: Weltbücher in Umrissen*, 3 (1953), pp. 97–102.

HOLLIS, MATTHEW, *Now All Roads Lead to France: The Last Years of Edward Thomas* (Faber & Faber, 2011)

HOLMES, RICHARD, *Tommy: The British Soldier on the Western Front 1914–1918* (Harper Collins, 2004)

HUGELSHOFER, ANDREA, *Rückert-Studien VI. Jahrbuch der Rückert-Gesellschaft 1991–2* (Ergon, 1992)

JENS, INGE, *Dichter zwischen rechts und links* (Kiepenheuer, 1994)

JUNG, FRANZ, *Der Weg nach unten* (Luchterhand, 1961)

KAYSER, WOLFGANG, *Das sprachliche Kunstwerk: Eine Einführung in die Literaturwissenschaft* (Francke, 1976)

KEEGAN, JOHN, *The Face of Battle* (Viking, 1976; Pimlico, 2004)

KETELSEN, UWE-K., 'Nationalsozialismus und Drittes Reich', in *Geschichte der politischen Lyrik in Deutschland*, ed. by Walter Hinderer (Reclam, 1978), pp. 291–314

KIRCHER, HARTMUT (ed.), *Deutsche Sonette* (Reclam, 1979)

KOHL, KATRIN, 'Sprache als Metapher in der Lyrik des zwanzigsten Jahrhunderts', *German Life and Letters*, 60 (2007), pp. 329–47

KOLINSKY, EVA, *Engagierter Expressionismus* (Metzler, 1970)

KONRAD, RUPRECHT, 'Nationale und internationale Tendenzen im *Simplicissimus* 1896–1933' (unpublished doctoral thesis, Ludwig-Maximilians-Universität, 1975)

KORTE, HERMANN, 'Energie der Brüche: Ein diachroner Blick auf die Lyrik des 20. Jahrhunderts und ihre Zäsuren', in *Lyrik des 20. Jahrhunderts*, ed. by Heinz Ludwig Arnold (Text + Kritik, 1999)

——'Lyriker des Expressionismus', in *Deutschsprachige Lyriker des 20. Jahrhunderts*, ed. by Ursula Heukenkamp and Peter Geist (Erich Schmidt, 2007)

KRELL, MAX, 'Expressionismus — Glück und Ende', in *Expressionismus: Aufzeichnungen und Erinnerungen der Zeitgenossen*, ed. by Paul Raabe (Walter, 1965), pp. 306–08

KROLOW, KARL, 'Gedenkwort für Anton Schnack', in *Deutsche Akademie für Sprache und Dichtung*, 1973 (Lambert Schneider, 1974), pp. 231–33

LEEDER, KAREN (ed.), '*Flaschenpost*': German Poetry and the long Twentieth Century, special issue of *German Life and Letters*, 60 (2007), no. 3

LEEDER, KAREN, and ROBERT VILAIN (eds), *The Cambridge Companion to Rilke* (Cambridge University Press, 2010)

LEVER, J. W., *The Elizabethan Love Sonnet* (Barnes & Noble, 1968)

LÖSCHNIGG, MARTIN, *Der Erste Weltkrieg in deutscher und englischer Dichtung* (Winter, 1994)

LOUTH, CHARLIE, 'Enchantment and Loss in Ernst Stadler', *Oxford German Studies*, 41 (2012), pp. 310–26

MARTENS, GUNTER, *Vitalismus und Expressionismus* (Kohlhammer, 1971)

MAXSON, H. A., *On the Sonnets of Robert Frost: A Critical Examination of the 37 Poems* (McFarland, 2005)

MAYER, PAUL, *Ernst Rowohlt in Selbstzeugnissen und Bilddokumenten* (Rowohlt, 1967)

MAYNC, HARRY, *Detlev von Liliencron: Eine Charakteristik des Dichters und seiner Dichtungen* (Schuster & Loeffler, 1920)

McCOBB, EDWARD A., review of Patrick Bridgwater, *The German Poets of the First World War*, *Modern Language Review*, 81 (1986), pp. 1044–45

McGUINNESS, PATRICK, 'Altered States', *Daily Telegraph*, 31 December 2011

MICHEL, MARC, *Les Africains et la Grande Guerre: l'appel à l'Afrique* (Karthala, 2003)

MIDGLEY, DAVID, *Writing Weimar* (Oxford University Press, 2000)

MONAGHAN, JEROME, 'A Monumental Task', *Times Educational Supplement*, 30, 15 November 2002, p. 21

MÖNCH, WALTER, *Das Sonett: Gestalt und Geschichte* (Kerle, 1955)

MÜLLER, JOACHIM, 'Das zyklische Prinzip in der Lyrik', *Germanisch-Romanische Monatsschrift*, 20 (1932), pp. 1–20

MUSTARD, HELEN MEREDITH, *The Lyric Cycle in German Literature* (King's Crown Press, 1946)

NEWTON, ROBERT P., 'Some Aspects of Expressionist Form in the *Menschheitsdämmerung*' (unpublished doctoral dissertation, Johns Hopkins University, 1964)

PAPE, WALTER, 'Hurra Germania — mir graut vor dir', in *German Unification and the Change of Literary Discourse*, ed. by Walter Pape (De Gruyter, 1993), pp. 107–34

PARKER, STEPHEN, *Peter Huchel: A Literary Life in 20th Century Germany* (Peter Lang, 1998)

PAULSEN, WOLFGANG, *Expressionismus und Aktivismus* (Gotthelf, 1935)

RAABE, PAUL, *Die Zeitschriften und Sammlungen des literarischen Expressionismus: Repertorium der Zeitschriften, Jahrbücher, Anthologien, Sammelwerke, Schriftenreihen und Almanache 1910–1921* (Metzler, 1964)

RASCH, WOLFDIETRICH, *Zur deutschen Literatur der Jahrhundertwende* (Metzler, 1967)

RITCHIE, J. M., 'The Expressionist Revival', *Seminar*, 2 (1966), pp. 37–49

ROBERTSON, RITCHIE, 'Modernism and the Self 1890–1924', in *Philosophy and German Literature 1700–1990*, ed. by Nicholas Saul (Cambridge University Press, 2002), pp. 150–96

ROTH, PHILIP, 'The Art of Fiction', interview with Hermione Lee, *Paris Review*, (1984) [accessed 8 March 2025]

ROTHE, WOLFGANG (ed.), *Expressionismus als Literatur* (Francke, 1969)

RUPP, HEINZ, and CARL LUDWIG LANG (eds), *Deutsches Literatur-Lexikon* (Saur, 1993)

RYAN, JUDITH, *Rilke, Modernism and Poetic Tradition* (Cambridge University Press, 1999)

SCHLAWE, FRITZ, *Literarische Zeitschriften 1910–1933* (Metzler, 1962)

SCHLÜTTER, HANS-JÜRGEN, *Sonett* (Metzler, 1979)

SCHNELL, RALF, *Literarische innere Emigration 1933–1945* (Metzler, 1976)

——*Dichtung in finsteren Zeiten* (Rowohlt, 1998)

SHARP, FRANCIS MICHAEL, '*Menschheitsdämmerung*: The Aging of a Canon', in *A Companion to the Literature of German Expressionism*, ed. by Neil H. Donahue (Camden House, 2010), pp. 137–55

SHEPPARD, RICHARD (ed.), *Expressionism in Focus* (Goethe Institute, 1986)

SOKEL, WALTER H., *The Writer in Extremis* (Stanford University Press, 1959)

SPRENGEL, PETER, *Geschichte der deutschsprachigen Literatur 1900–1918* (Beck, 2004)

STAHL, ERNEST L., 'Rilke's Sonnets to Orpheus: Composition and Thematic Structure', *Oxford German Studies*, 9 (1978), pp. 119–38

STROTHMANN, DIETRICH, *Nationalsozialistische Literaturpolitik* (Bouvier, 1963)

THOMKE, HELMUT, *Hymnische Dichtung im Expressionismus* (Francke, 1972)

VOLLMER, HARTMUT, *Alfred Lichtenstein: Zerrissenes Ich und verfremdete Welt* (Alano, 1988)

WANDREY, UWE, *Das Motiv des Krieges in der expressionistischen Lyrik*, Geistes- und Sozialwissenschaftliche Dissertationen 23 (Lüdke, 1972)

WATANABE-O'KELLY, HELEN (ed.), *The Cambridge History of German Literature* (Cambridge University Press, 1997)

WATSON, PETER, *The German Genius* (Simon & Schuster, 2010)

WEBER, THOMAS, *Hitler's First War* (Oxford University Press, 2011)

WEINSTEIN, JOAN, *The End of Expressionism* (University of Chicago Press, 1990)

WILK, WERNER, *Werner Bergengruen* (Hess, 1968)

WINTER, JAY, *Sites of Memory, Sites of Mourning: The Great War in European Cultural History* (Cambridge University Press, 2010)

WINTRINGHAM, TOM, *Weapons and Tactics* (Faber & Faber, 1943)

WRIGHT, BARBARA D., 'Intimate Strangers: Women in German Expressionism', in *A Companion to the Literature of German Expressionism*, ed. by Neil H. Donahue, pp. 287–320

WULF, JOSEPH, *Literatur und Dichtung im Dritten Reich: Eine Dokumentation* (Mohn, 1963)

YATES, W. E., *Tradition in the German Sonnet* (Peter Lang, 1981)

ZELLER, BERNHARD (ed.), *Expressionismus: Literatur und Kunst 1910–1923*, eine Ausstellung des Deutschen Literaturarchivs im Schiller-Nationalmuseum 8 May 1960–31 October 1960 (Schiller-Nationalmuseum, 1960)

ZIMMERMANN, INGO, *Reinhold Schneider: Weg eines Schriftstellers* (Union, 1982)

INDEX